Communications
in Computer and Information Science   3007

Series Editors

Gang Li, *School of Information Technology, Deakin University, Burwood, VIC, Australia*
Joaquim Filipe, *Polytechnic Institute of Setúbal, Setúbal, Portugal*
Zhiwei Xu, *Chinese Academy of Sciences, Beijing, China*

Rationale

The CCIS series is devoted to the publication of proceedings of computer science conferences. Its aim is to efficiently disseminate original research results in informatics in printed and electronic form. While the focus is on publication of peer-reviewed full papers presenting mature work, inclusion of reviewed short papers reporting on work in progress is welcome, too. Besides globally relevant meetings with internationally representative program committees guaranteeing a strict peer-reviewing and paper selection process, conferences run by societies or of high regional or national relevance are also considered for publication.

Topics

The topical scope of CCIS spans the entire spectrum of informatics ranging from foundational topics in the theory of computing to information and communications science and technology and a broad variety of interdisciplinary application fields.

Information for Volume Editors and Authors

Publication in CCIS is free of charge. No royalties are paid, however, we offer registered conference participants temporary free access to the online version of the conference proceedings on SpringerLink (http://link.springer.com) by means of an http referrer from the conference website and/or a number of complimentary printed copies, as specified in the official acceptance email of the event.

CCIS proceedings can be published in time for distribution at conferences or as post-proceedings, and delivered in the form of printed books and/or electronically as USBs and/or e-content licenses for accessing proceedings at SpringerLink. Furthermore, CCIS proceedings are included in the CCIS electronic book series hosted in the SpringerLink digital library at http://link.springer.com/bookseries/7899. Conferences publishing in CCIS are allowed to use our online conference service (Meteor) for managing the whole proceedings lifecycle (from submission and reviewing to preparing for publication) free of charge.

Publication process

The language of publication is exclusively English. Authors publishing in CCIS have to sign the Springer CCIS copyright transfer form, however, they are free to use their material published in CCIS for substantially changed, more elaborate subsequent publications elsewhere. For the preparation of the camera-ready papers/files, authors have to strictly adhere to the Springer CCIS Authors' Instructions and are strongly encouraged to use the CCIS LaTeX style files or templates.

Abstracting/Indexing

CCIS is abstracted/indexed in DBLP, Google Scholar, EI-Compendex, Mathematical Reviews, SCImago, Scopus. CCIS volumes are also submitted for the inclusion in ISI Proceedings.

How to start

To start the evaluation of your proposal for inclusion in the CCIS series, please send an e-mail to ccis@springer.com

Kathrin Kirchner · Jussi Mikkonen ·
Gerald Eichler · Christian Erfurth ·
Günter Fahrnberger

Editors

Innovations for Community Services

26th International Conference, I4CS 2026
Copenhagen, Denmark, June 15–17, 2026
Proceedings

 Springer

Editors
Kathrin Kirchner ⓘD
Technical University of Denmark
Kongens Lyngby, Denmark

Jussi Mikkonen ⓘD
Technical University of Denmark
Kongens Lyngby, Denmark

Gerald Eichler ⓘD
Deutsche Telekom Technology
and Innovation
Darmstadt, Hessen, Germany

Christian Erfurth ⓘD
University of Applied Sciences Jena
Jena, Germany

Günter Fahrnberger ⓘD
University of Hagen
Hagen, Germany

ISSN 1865-0929   ISSN 1865-0937 (electronic)
Communications in Computer and Information Science
ISBN 978-3-032-27095-5   ISBN 978-3-032-27096-2 (eBook)
https://doi.org/10.1007/978-3-032-27096-2

This Springer imprint is published by the registered company Springer Nature Switzerland AG
The registered company address is: Gewerbestrasse 11, 6330 Cham, Switzerland

If disposing of this product, please recycle the paper.

Foreword

In 2026, the International Conference on Innovations for Community Services (I4CS), now in its 26th edition, visited Denmark for the first time. Nordic culture aligns perfectly with the modern community approach.

25 years ago, at the Technical University of Ilmenau, Germany, Herwig Unger and Thomas Böhme launched the Workshop on Innovative Internet Community Systems (IICS) as a platform for publishing project results. The event continued its success story under the revised name I2CS and, since 2014, under the name I4CS. The conference published its first proceedings in Springer's Lecture Notes in Computer Science (LNCS) series until 2005, followed by publication with Gesellschaft für Informatik e. V. (GI) in Köllen Verlag and with Verein Deutscher Ingenieure (VDI) in 2013. I4CS also started a collaboration with the Institute of Electrical and Electronics Engineers (IEEE) before returning to Springer's Communications in Computer and Information Science (CCIS) series in 2016 and establishing a permanent partnership in 2018. This unique combination of printed proceedings and the SpringerLink online edition attracts remarkable interest from external readers. With about 12,000 web accesses last year at https://link.springer.com/conference/i4cs, the conference again surpassed its previous annual figure.

The selection of conference locations reflects the conference concept: members of the Program Committee (PC) propose suitable venues where our scientific community can share and deepen its common passion. For 2026, the I4CS Steering Committee proudly entrusted the organizational responsibility to Kathrin Kirchner and Jussi Mikkonen at DTU Copenhagen, Ballerup campus, Denmark. Near the national capital of a country ranking third in the World Happiness Report 2025, after Finland and Iceland, the campus offered a natural setting. This year's motto, "People Empower Technology," highlighted the leading role of human beings in a world of emerging AI.

Interdisciplinary thinking remains a key success factor for any community. Accordingly, the conference addressed three sets of five updated scientific, academic, social, and industrial topics, grouped into our three long-established key areas: Technology, Applications, and Socialization.

Technology: Distributed Architectures and Frameworks

- Smart architectures and enablers for data sharing,
- Cryptography and cryptology,
- 5G/6G technologies and ad hoc wireless networks,
- Data models, analytics, and big data management,
- Quantum and cloud computing.

Applications: Communities on the Move

- Social networks, open data, and distributed coworking,
- Barrier-free collaboration, publishing, and eLearning,

- Recommender solutions and chat-bots,
- Virtual & augmented reality, robotics, and mobile e-sports,
- Intelligent traffic, logistics, and connected cars.

Socialization: Ambient Work and Living

- Distributed work challenges and eHealth-assisted living,
- Machine Learning, human-centered AI, and governance,
- Smart home, energy control, and public infrastructure,
- Internet of things and dynamic sensor networks,
- Cyber- and information security.

Many thanks go to the 34 active members of the Program Committee for 2026, representing 14 countries worldwide, for their 192 valuable reviews. Special thanks also go to conference chair Christian Erfurth, this year's program chairs Kathrin Kirchner and Jussi Mikkonen, and our publication chair, Günter Fahrnberger, who facilitated successful cooperation with the Springer publishing board and helped maintain the high reputation of I4CS, currently rated at CORE C level.

Following the alternation rule, the 27th edition of I4CS will take place at a German university around June 2027. Please check our permanent conference URL regularly at http://www.i4cs-conference.org/ for upcoming details.

We warmly welcome proposals on new and emerging topics, as well as applications from prospective Program Committee members and potential conference hosts and venues, at info@i4cs-conference.org.

Kind regards on behalf of the entire Steering Committee and the Editors' Board.

June 2026
Gerald Eichler
I4CS Steering Chair

Preface

It gives us great pleasure to welcome you to the 26th International Conference on Innovations for Community Services (I4CS) in Copenhagen, Denmark, from June 15 to 17, 2026. Under the motto "People Empower Technology," we reaffirmed a principle that has always stood at the heart of I4CS: the conviction that the most meaningful technological advances grow from human needs, draw on human creativity, and gain value through their impact on human lives. Perhaps no place in the world reflects this philosophy more naturally than Denmark. Danish society has long embraced a model in which technology serves to strengthen communities and improve quality of life. From digital public services to a culture of trust and collaboration, Denmark offers a living example of what "people empowering technology" can mean in practice and therefore provided an ideal host nation for this conference in 2026.

Copenhagen itself inspires. Cycling along its canals, wandering through Nyhavn's colorful harborside, or experiencing the Danish concept of *hygge* (that sense of warmth, togetherness, and well-being) quickly helps every visitor understand why this city consistently ranks among the happiest and most livable in the world. We warmly encourage all participants to spend time beyond the conference hall exploring Copenhagen and experiencing firsthand the blend of openness, creativity, and civic pride that characterizes this city.

The conference convened at DTU Engineering Technology at the Technical University of Denmark, one of Europe's leading technical universities. DTU Engineering Technology pursues research on technology implementation and engineering education and develops tools and methods for the successful implementation of technology across technical, organizational, and business dimensions. This emphasis on connecting rigorous research with real-world impact strongly aligns with the applied, community-oriented spirit of I4CS. As program chairs, we thank our colleagues at DTU for their hospitality and for creating such a stimulating intellectual environment for our discussions.

The 2026 program brought together contributions across three interconnected pillars. The Technology pillar addressed resilient and secure digital infrastructures, data architectures, and emerging AI-enabled methods, with topics including denial-of-service detection in information-centric networking, fountain code resilience, fog computing for agricultural monitoring, data catalogs in data mesh and data space implementations, contextual metadata generation with GenAI, and AI-assisted software development. The Applications pillar highlighted intelligent systems in practice, covering decision support for hiring, industrial procurement, healthcare analytics and disease progression modeling, smart neighborhoods, multi-sensor monitoring, urban micromobility infrastructure, and priority-aware traffic management, alongside new approaches to negotiation and maturity assessment. The Socialization pillar foregrounded the institutional, organizational, and human dimensions of digital transformation, with contributions on identity management, blockchain governance, municipal data exchange, cyber incident response, cybersecurity training, human-machine collaboration in critical environments, and technology-supported living and aging in place.

I4CS 2026 proudly offered a strong selection of scientific presentations, along with a keynote, two invited talks, and an excellent social program to strengthen a sense of cultural community. The I4CS 2026 proceedings contain seven chapters covering 15 full papers and four short papers, selected from 48 submissions by 100 authors from 13 countries through four single-blind reviews per submission. The I4CS 2026 proceedings again appear through Springer in the *Communications in Computer and Information Science* (CCIS) series, with submission planned for indexing in DBLP and Scopus. We gratefully acknowledge our hosts at DTU Engineering Technology and Ernst-Abbe-Hochschule Jena for their longstanding organizational support, as well as Deutsche Telekom for continued sponsorship.

We extend our sincere thanks to the authors for their contributions, to the members of the program committee for their careful reviews, and to the local organizing team for making this conference possible in one of Europe's most vibrant and forward-thinking capitals.

As program chairs, we genuinely enjoyed to meeting you, whether you have accompanied the I4CS community for many years or joined us for the first time. We hope Copenhagen, with all its charm, offered not only stimulating discussions and new ideas, but also moments of inspiration, connection, and Danish *hygge* along the way.

June 2026

Kathrin Kirchner
Jussi Mikkonen
Gerald Eichler
Christian Erfurth
Günter Fahrnberger

Organization

Program Committee

Sebastian Apel	Technical University of Applied Sciences Ingolstadt, Germany
Christof Brandauer	Salzburg Research, Austria
Udo Bub	Eötvös Loránd University, Hungary
Boris Delibašić	University of Belgrade, Serbia
Gerald Eichler	Deutsche Telekom Darmstadt, Germany
Christian Erfurth	University of Applied Sciences Jena, Germany
Günter Fahrnberger	University of Hagen, Germany
Sebastian Feld	Delft University of Technology, The Netherlands
Andreas Fink	Helmut Schmidt University of the Federal Armed Forces Hamburg, Germany
Hacène Fouchal	University of Reims Champagne-Ardenne, France
Hanno Friedrich	Kühne Logistics University Hamburg, Germany
Sapna Ponaraseri Gopinathan	i.k.val Softwares LLP Coimbatore, India
Maximilian Greiner	Infodas Munich, Germany
Michal Hodoň	University of Žilina, Slovakia
Christoph Jungbauer	University of Vienna, Austria
Kathrin Kirchner	Technical University of Denmark, Denmark
Udo Krieger	University of Bamberg, Germany
Peter Kropf	University of Neuchâtel, Switzerland
Ulrike Lechner	University of the Bundeswehr Munich, Germany
Andreas Lommatzsch	Technical University of Berlin, Germany
Karl-Heinz Lüke	Ostfalia University of Applied Sciences, Wolfsburg, Germany
Jussi Mikkonen	Technical University of Denmark, Denmark
Raja Natarajan	Tata Institute of Fundamental Research, India
Deveeshree Nayak	University of Washington Tacoma, USA
Dana Petcu	West University of Timisoara, Romania
Frank Phillipson	Netherlands Organisation for Applied Scientific Research, The Netherlands
Jörg Roth	Nuremberg Institute of Technology, Germany
Amardeo Sarma	Society for the Scientific Investigation of Parasciences, Germany
Lucie Schmidt	University of Applied Sciences Jena, Germany
Karl Seidenfad	Siemens Erlangen, Germany

Pranav Kumar Singh	Indian Institute of Technology Guwahati and Central Institute of Technology Kokrajhar, India
Julian Szymanski	Gdańsk University of Technology, Poland
Leendert W. M. Wienhofen	SINTEF Digital, Norway
Sebastian Zielinski	SAP Munich, Germany

Additional Reviewers

Francis, Deena
Palovuori, Karri

Tracking Minds and Movements: Adaptive Reading Systems and Eye Tracking in Natural Settings: Leveraging Gaze, Cognition, and Real-world Data to Build the Next Generation of Human-aware Technologies

Per Bækgaard

Technical University of Denmark, Lyngby, Denmark
pgba@dtu.dk

Abstract. For more than a century, eye tracking has offered a window into users' attention. In the 1960s, Kahneman and Beatty pioneered the use of pupil dilation as a physiological marker of cognitive load, laying the groundwork for cognitive-state inference in modern gaze-based systems. Recent advances in affordable, portable eye-tracking hardware, together with progress in machine learning and neural networks, now position eye tracking as a powerful tool for studying human cognition across diverse real-world contexts. One emerging application involves cognitively adaptive reading systems that dynamically adjust typography, layout, and content presentation in response to indicators of reading strategy, cognitive load, intent, and fatigue. Such systems demonstrate how gaze can function as a continuous, unobtrusive source of information about mental states, opening the door to interfaces that respond intelligently and empathetically to readers' needs. This keynote also examines eye-tracking technology in the wild, with an emphasis on applications in which gaze behavior and pupillary measures provide insights beyond traditional Human–Computer Interaction (HCI). Examples include systems that support immediate and longitudinal diagnostic assessment outside clinical settings, such as tools that capture nystagmus during vertigo attacks despite limited precision. Together, these examples illustrate a broader shift toward eye tracking as a versatile, everyday method for understanding human behavior, whether supporting learning, improving accessibility, or documenting perceptual events in natural environments. By linking adaptive cognitive interfaces with real-world gaze sensing, this keynote advances a unified vision of gaze-driven technologies that honor the richness of human perception and support a wide range of community-facing applications, from enriched HCI through shared attention in collaboration to remote diagnostic support in eHealth. The keynote outlines emerging opportunities and challenges while also offering design principles for systems that respect user agency, promote empowerment, and unlock deeper, more actionable insights.

Keywords: Adaptive cognitive interfaces · Cognitive-state inference · Eye tracking

From Cells to Systems: A Cross Disciplinary Perspective on the Potential and Challenges of Digital Twins

Martin Wolfgang Lauer-Schmaltz 🆔

Liquid Wind, Hørsholm, Denmark
`martin.lauer-schmaltz@liquidwind.com`

Abstract. Digital Twins now reshape both personalized healthcare and large-scale industrial systems. While all Digital Twins share the same underlying core concept—a continuously updated virtual representation of a physical system—their goals, data landscapes, and development pathways may differ profoundly. Drawing on experience with Human Digital Twins and Digital Twins for eFuel production facilities, this talk highlights how virtual models can unlock new insights, improve decision-making, and drive operational excellence across disciplines. It outlines where development steps align and where each application introduces its own distinct challenges, shaped by the nature of the system under study. Together, these contrasts illustrate how a single foundational idea can evolve into markedly different Digital Twin architectures, each tailored to its specific domain.

Keywords: Digital twins · eFuel production facilities · Personalized healthcare

Contents

Artificial Intelligence for Work Processes

Artificial Intelligence for Decision Support

Smart Urban Infrastructure

Distributed Systems

People Empower Technology, When They Can
Evidence-Based Perspectives on Generative AI Adoption in Software Engineering

Daniel Russo$^{(\boxtimes)}$

Department of Computer Science, Aalborg University, Copenhagen, Denmark
`daniel.russo@cs.aau.dk`

Abstract. Generative AI tools are changing how software gets built, but we still have a limited grasp of what determines whether practitioners adopt these tools on their own terms. This paper pulls together findings from a program of empirical research on GenAI adoption in software engineering, built around the Human-AI Collaboration and Adaptation Framework (HACAF). Across convergent mixed-methods evidence from 283 software engineers, companion studies on cultural values and task-specific adoption, and a community-driven research agenda on creativity, the paper makes a simple argument: workflow compatibility, not perceived usefulness, is what actually drives adoption. It then presents the Copenhagen Manifesto, a normative framework written by 35 researchers, organized around four principles for human-centered AI in software engineering: responsibility, transparency, inclusivity, and sustainability. The paper closes with implications for communities deploying AI-powered services, connecting the empirical findings to the I4CS 2026 conference theme "People Empower Technology".

Keywords: Copenhagen Manifesto · Generative AI · Human-centered AI · Software engineering · Technology adoption

1 Introduction

Large language models now touch nearly every phase of software development: code generation, automated testing, documentation, requirements analysis. The productivity gains are real. But whether practitioners adopt these tools effectively, and on terms that preserve their own agency, is a question the field has barely begun to answer [8].

K. Kirchner et al. (Eds.): I4CS 2026, CCIS 3007, pp. 1–6, 2026.
https://doi.org/10.1007/978-3-032-27096-2_1

This matters for the I4CS community in particular. The 2026 conference motto, "People Empower Technology," assumes that human communities can still direct how technology gets adopted. The evidence in this paper both supports and complicates that assumption. Software engineers do shape GenAI adoption, but through mechanisms that look quite different from what conventional technology acceptance theories would predict.

This paper brings together: (1) a convergent mixed-methods study that produced the HACAF framework, validated through PLS-SEM with 283 software engineers [8]; (2) companion studies on cultural values [5] and task-specific adoption patterns [6]; (3) a community-driven research agenda on creativity and GenAI [4]; and (4) the Copenhagen Manifesto, a normative framework for human-centered GenAI in software engineering, written by 35 researchers [10].

2   Adoption Dynamics: The HACAF Model

The foundational study used a convergent mixed-methods approach across three levels of analysis: individual, technological, and social [8]. The research moved in three phases. First, a questionnaire survey with 100 software engineers, grounded in the Technology Acceptance Model [2], Diffusion of Innovation Theory [7], and Social Cognitive Theory [1], established baseline adoption patterns. Second, qualitative analysis following the Gioia methodology [3] produced the HACAF model. Third, PLS-SEM validation with an independent sample of 183 software engineers confirmed the framework's structural relationships.

The central finding cuts against a core assumption in the technology acceptance literature: at this stage of AI integration, compatibility with existing development workflows, not perceived usefulness, is what drives adoption. The practical implication is blunt. A tool that fits how engineers already work will get adopted regardless of how sophisticated it is; one that disrupts established routines will be resisted, no matter how capable.

Self-efficacy and prior experience with AI tools matter more at the individual level than general enthusiasm about AI's potential. At the social level, peer usage and community norms do influence willingness to engage, but the relationship is more complicated than earlier theory predicted. Social influence by itself does not sustain adoption over time. The study has accumulated substantial citation impact since its publication, and a Replicated Computational Results report with a full replication package is available on Zenodo [9].

3 Beyond Adoption: Culture, Tasks, and Creativity

3.1 Cultural Values

Even when adoption is strong, the question remains whether cultural context shapes the process. Lambiase et al. [5] investigated this by testing whether Hofstede's cultural dimensions moderate the UTAUT2 adoption relationships among 188 software engineers. The empirical result was clear: habit and performance expectancy emerged as the primary drivers of LLM adoption, while cultural values did not significantly moderate the process. In practical terms, this means that organizations can encourage LLM use by demonstrating performance benefits and supporting habitual integration, regardless of cultural differences.

However, the absence of statistically significant moderation effects does not mean culture is irrelevant to governance. For a community like I4CS, with participants drawn from institutions across Europe and beyond, the normative argument still holds: governance frameworks should not assume that adoption dynamics are culturally uniform, even if the quantitative moderating effects measured in one study were not significant. The study's value lies precisely in having tested the assumption rather than taking it for granted.

3.2 Task-Specific Adoption

Engineers do not adopt GenAI uniformly across all their work. Lambiase et al. [6] surveyed 188 software engineers and found that task-specific adoption is influenced by distinct factors, some of which negatively impact adoption when considered in isolation. Blanket adoption mandates, whether organizational or policy-driven, are likely to backfire. Effective deployment requires knowing which tasks engineers actually trust AI with.

3.3 Creativity Under Pressure

As routine coding gets increasingly automated, human creativity becomes the differentiating factor. Jackson et al. [4] structured a research agenda around the 4P framework of creativity: Person (how does AI reliance change creative self-efficacy?), Product (does AI expand or narrow the solution space?), Process (does AI accelerate or replace brainstorming and exploration?), and Press (how do team norms around AI affect creative freedom?). Any community that depends on innovative software should care about the answers.

4   The Copenhagen Manifesto

The empirical findings above describe what is happening. The Copenhagen Manifesto [10] addresses what should be done about it. Written by 35 researchers from institutions worldwide, the manifesto grew out of the Copenhagen Symposium on Human-Centered Software Engineering AI, held at Aalborg University in Copenhagen in November 2023, with support from the Alfred P. Sloan Foundation and the Carlsberg Foundation.

Four principles organize the manifesto. Responsibility: AI should support human dignity and agency, with clear lines of accountability when AI-powered services affect communities. Transparency: decision-making processes involving AI must be open and explainable, especially when citizens interact with AI-enhanced services. Inclusivity: diverse perspectives must be built into AI adoption processes, or we risk a two-tier system where resource-rich communities benefit while others fall behind. Sustainability: AI practices should support long-term well-being rather than short-term productivity gains that erode developer skill and community capacity.

These principles are informed by, though not strictly deducible from, the empirical evidence. If compatibility drives adoption, responsible deployment must respect existing workflows. If habit proves a stronger predictor than cultural moderation, governance still ought to be inclusive, precisely because the empirical picture is incomplete and the stakes of getting it wrong are high. If automation threatens creativity, practices have to be sustainable enough to preserve human capacity. The manifesto represents a normative synthesis of what the evidence suggests, not a deductive conclusion from it.

5   Implications for Community Services

Software engineering sits upstream of the digital services communities depend on. When engineers adopt AI poorly, without assessing compatibility, without inclusive design, without governance, the consequences flow downstream into every service built on that software.

Service designers should evaluate GenAI tools through workflow compatibility, not feature lists. A tool that fits existing practices will be adopted; one that demands fundamental process change will be abandoned. Managers and team leads should encourage diverse mental models of AI within teams; training that frames AI as filling multiple roles (assistant, advisor, reference) works better than positioning it as a single-purpose productivity booster. Policymakers can use the Copenhagen Manifesto's four principles as a starting template for governance wherever AI is deployed in community-facing services. And for educators, the shift from coding proficiency to judgment and oversight capacity calls for curricular rethinking, a concern that applies directly to the eLearning and education topics within I4CS.

6 Conclusion

"People Empower Technology" captures an aspiration that the evidence both supports and qualifies. People do shape GenAI adoption, but primarily through workflow compatibility, modulated by habit, performance expectancy, and individual characteristics, with real consequences for the creative capacity of software teams. The Copenhagen Manifesto provides a principled framework for preserving that capacity as AI becomes embedded in the software underlying community services.

The question left for the I4CS community is practical: as your communities adopt AI-powered services, what governance structures will make sure people continue to direct the technology, rather than the other way around?

Acknowledgment. The Copenhagen Symposium on Human-Centered Software Engineering AI was supported by the Alfred P. Sloan Foundation (Grant G-2023-21020) and the Carlsberg Foundation (Grant CF23-0208). The author thanks the 35 co-authors of the Copenhagen Manifesto and the organizers of I4CS 2026 for the invitation to present this work.

References

1. Bandura, A.: Social Foundations of Thought and Action: A Social Cognitive Theory. Prentice-Hall, Englewood Cliffs (1986)
2. Davis, F.D.: Perceived usefulness, perceived ease of use, and user acceptance of information technology. MIS Q. **13**(3), 319–340 (1989). https://doi.org/10.2307/249008
3. Gioia, D.A., Corley, K.G., Hamilton, A.L.: Seeking qualitative rigor in inductive research: notes on the Gioia methodology. Organ. Res. Methods **16**(1), 15–31 (2013). https://doi.org/10.1177/1094428112452151
4. Jackson, V., et al.: The impact of generative AI on creativity in software development: a research agenda. ACM Trans. Softw. Eng. Methodol. **34**(5), 1–28 (2025). https://doi.org/10.1145/3708523
5. Lambiase, S., Catolino, G., Palomba, F., Ferrucci, F., Russo, D.: Investigating the role of cultural values in adopting large language models for software engineering. ACM Trans. Softw. Eng. Methodol. **35**(1), 1–43 (2026). https://doi.org/10.1145/3725529
6. Lambiase, S., Catolino, G., Palomba, F., Ferrucci, F., Russo, D.: Exploring individual factors in the adoption of LLMs for specific software engineering tasks. arXiv preprint arXiv:2504.02553 (2025)
7. Rogers, E.M.: Diffusion of Innovations, 5th edn. Free Press, New York (2003)
8. Russo, D.: Navigating the complexity of generative AI adoption in software engineering. ACM Trans. Softw. Eng. Methodol. **33**(5), 1–49 (2024). https://doi.org/10.1145/3652154

9. Russo, D.: Navigating the complexity of generative AI adoption in software engineering: RCR report. ACM Trans. Softw. Eng. Methodol. **33**(8), 1–5 (2024). https://doi.org/10.1145/3680471
10. Russo, D., et al.: Generative AI in software engineering must be human-centered: the Copenhagen Manifesto. J. Syst. Softw. **216**, 112115 (2024). https://doi.org/10.1016/j.jss.2024.112115

Authentication and Resilience

Multi-Factor Authentication (MFA) for Secure Shell (SSH) Guards Linux Fleets Against Intrusion and Lateral Movement

Günter Fahrnberger(✉)(iD)

University of Hagen, Hagen, North Rhine-Westphalia, Germany
`guenter.fahrnberger@studium.fernuni-hagen.de`

Abstract. Cyberattacks that exploit weak or reused authentication credentials introduce persistent risks to Linux fleets, especially when intruders leverage Secure Shell (SSH) for unauthorized access and lateral movement among fleet members. This disquisition presents an innovative Identity and Access Management (IAM) approach enforcing centralized Multi-Factor Authentication (MFA) for SSH with up to four independent factors. Unlike conventional host-based setups, the proposed design utilizes a centralized OpenLDAP instance, removes local storage of secrets, mitigates password reuse, and minimizes opportunities for attackers to extract sensitive material from compromised nodes. The implementation accommodates regular, emergency, and Machine-to-Machine (M2M) authentication workflows while maintaining usability across operational environments. A subsequent security evaluation shows resilience against Brute Force Attacks (BFAs), buffer overflows, and exposure of authentication assets, yet acknowledges the continuing challenge of complete compromise, which demands behavioral monitoring and anomaly detection. This IAM approach enhances defenses against intrusion and lateral movement in large-scale Linux fleets and lays groundwork for integration with orchestration tools and zero-trust architectures.

Keywords: Access Control · Authentication · Authenticity · Four-Factor Authentication (4FA) · Identity and Authentication Management (IAM) · Information Security · Multi-Factor Authentication (MFA) · One-Time Password (OTP) · Pluggable Authentication Modules (PAM) · Random One-Time Password (ROTP) · Secure Shell (SSH) · Three-Factor Authentication (3FA) · Two-Factor Authentication (2FA)

1 Introduction

A glimpse of contemporary information security reports, such as Europol's Internet Organised Crime Threat Assessment (IOCTA) 2025, provides clear evidence that cybercrime incidents continue rising rapidly worldwide [6]. The level of

K. Kirchner et al. (Eds.): I4CS 2026, CCIS 3007, pp. 9–38, 2026.
https://doi.org/10.1007/978-3-032-27096-2_2

security precautions adopted by an entity tends to correlate positively with its perceived or actual asset value, suggesting that high-value targets typically implement more sophisticated defense mechanisms. Conversely, empirical studies indicate a proportional relationship between adversarial resource investment and anticipated payoff, implying that increased attacker effort often corresponds to higher potential gains from compromise or exploitation. Such efforts range from financial expenditures, like purchasing valid credentials on the dark web, through organizational means, such as workforce parallelization by establishing criminal hierarchies, to technical measures, e.g., development of red-team skills. Cyber-adversaries demonstrably leverage publicly accessible educational and training platforms such as Hack The Box[1], Hack This Site[2], ImmersiveLabs[3], and Try-HackMe[4] to enhance technical proficiency, emulate legitimate learning scenarios, and refine offensive capabilities [20]. These learning platforms primarily serve ethical information security practitioners but cannot fully prevent misuse. Educational hubs typically maintain students' motivation by allowing them to solve manageable problems with clearly defined objectives and validate their progress through the submission of strings, also known as flags. Consequently, Capture The Flag (CTF) functions as a widespread denomination for this game type. The aforementioned platforms organize problems into so-called rooms or networks, each containing one or several virtual machines. TryHackMe further divides every room into one or more tasks. Walkthrough rooms supply CTF players with ample information, hints, and tutorials, whereas challenge rooms leave participants to rely solely on their own skills. Users who need help and encounter obstacles often turn to Discord[5] for support or consult publicly available write-ups for suggested solutions.

Overcoming Identity and Authentication Management (IAM) mechanisms plays a crucial role in CTF games, penetration tests (pentests), and malicious incursions. If no vulnerabilities apply to such a mechanism, attackers must resort to the electronic crowbar, a Brute Force Attack (BFA) that iteratively attempts all relevant items from dictionaries or combinations of character sets until cancelation, exhaustion, or success. For instance, Hydra stands out as a prominent tool enabling Brute Force Attacks (BFAs). It supports a multitude of well-known protocols, including the Secure Shell (SSH) [24, 36–39]. While CTF games rarely permit successful BFAs on SSH Daemons (SSHDs), weak credentials on business or private hosts provide an opportunity.

The implementation of robust password composition and renewal policies represents an incremental advancement in organizational authentication resilience and contributes to measurable improvements in access control security. Unfortunately, many people develop habitual patterns and frequently recycle their

---

[1] https://www.hackthebox.com/.

[2] https://hackthissite.org/.

[3] https://www.immersivelabs.com/.

[4] https://tryhackme.com/.

[5] https://discord.com/.

credentials. Independent IAM systems lack the capability to detect previously used passwords, which undermines even the strongest security measures.

One remedy involves employing web services like *Have I Been Pwned*[6], which aggregate data breaches that IAM platforms can query to prevent the reuse of compromised passwords [17]. Unfortunately, not all IAM solutions leverage these data sources. In addition, a password may start out securely but later may encounter exposure during its lifecycle. However, relying on One-Factor Authentication (1FA), also known as Single-Factor Authentication (SFA), with passwords alone no longer provides adequate protection for IAMs against BFAs.

A well-known implementation of Two-Factor Authentication (2FA) for SSH employs Time-based One-Time Passwords (TOTPs) based on Google Authenticator and limits credential-reuse risks by demanding a volatile secret paired with a typically longer-lasting password [2]. This method can secure an individual SSH Daemon (SSHD) effectively, yet it fails to protect a Linux fleet once a host becomes malicious after compromise. A Linux fleet consists of several Linux-based systems managed collectively within an organization or infrastructure. The issue intensifies when every host across that fleet holds identical local credentials such as usernames and password hashes in */etc/shadow* and Time-based One-Time Password (TOTP) seeds in *.google_ authenticator* files within user home directories. An attacker with access to both files can move laterally across peer nodes after cracking a hash from */etc/shadow*.

Compared with TOTPs, e-mail-distributed Random One-Time Passwords (ROTPs) offer greater resistance to predictable generation attacks because their architecture avoids seed dependence, thus reducing risks linked to seed compromise [21]. However, ROTPs lose robustness when delivered to e-mail accounts also used for password recovery [11]. Optimal protection arises when the IAM system transmits ROTPs only to secondary e-mail addresses dedicated exclusively to authentication rather than sending them independently from each host.

This paper presents a novel IAM solution that manages centralized Four-Factor Authentication (4FA) for standard logins. It then examines how the IAM can mitigate post-compromise credential reuse within Linux fleets. For this purpose, the IAM employs an asymmetric key pair for public key authentication, a password, a TOTP, and an e-mail-based Random One-Time Password (ROTP). The IAM relies exclusively on the Lightweight Directory Access Protocol (LDAP) in its third version (LDAPv3 [16, 22, 23, 30, 31, 33, 34, 40–56]) and SSH for communication, removing the need for additional protocols commonly used to authenticate network devices such as Terminal Access Controller Access Control System (TACACS) [12], Remote Authentication Dial-In User Service (RADIUS) [28], or related successors. Through this design, the IAM upholds the information security objective of authenticity and delivers effective safeguards against subtechniques of technique T1110 (Brute Force) under tactic TA0006 (Credential Access) from the Massachusetts Institute of Technology

---

[6] https://haveibeenpwned.com/.

Research and Engineering (MITRE) Adversarial Tactics, Techniques, and Common Knowledge (ATT&CK) Framework [35].

Beyond intrusion prevention, this method delivers substantial protection when an attacker gains control of a Linux host and obtains root privileges. Even after such a compromise, the IAM blocks intruders on the affected node from reaching legitimate users' authentication factors, thereby hindering lateral movement via subtechnique T1021.004 (SSH) of technique T1021 (Remote Services) under tactic TA0008 (Lateral Movement) from the MITRE ATT&CK Framework to additional fleet hosts. Although experts generally agree that public key authentication offers robust security, legitimate users may still store their private keys on Linux hosts to simplify lateral movement, a practice that attackers could exploit after compromise. By incorporating additional authentication factors, the IAM system withstands such incidents more effectively.

Moreover, the concept covers two administrative scenarios without compromising security. The first scenario permits access to every host during critical situations when the IAM experiences a failure or loses connectivity with one or multiple nodes, for example, during network issues or Mail Transmission Agent (MTA) outages. The second scenario facilitates integration with orchestration tools, such as Ansible or Puppet, which do not support complex Multi-Factor Authentication (MFA) workflows [27].

A brief look at the MITRE Detection, Denial, and Disruption Framework Empowering Network Defense (D3FEND) [18], serving as the counterpart to the MITRE ATT&CK Framework [35], reveals coverage of four out of five subtechniques under D3-AA (Agent Authentication). These include D3-CBAN (Certificate-based Authentication) as the initial factor, D3-PWA (Password Authentication) as the second, D3-TBA (Token-based Authentication) as both third and fourth, and D3-MFA (Multi-factor Authentication) representing the integration of all methods.

In keeping with standard practices in scientific publications, Sect. 2 presents a thorough survey of academic literature for two reasons. Firstly, valuable related work may exist that could be extended to implement the suggested IAM. Secondly, ensuring novelty requires verifying that no prior work has already established the recommended IAM. Section 3 delivers sufficient technical details to enable reproduction of the IAM for interested readers. To demonstrate its security, Sect. 4 evaluates the IAM's threat model and the mitigations applied to the detected threats. Section 5 concludes this publication and suggests worthwhile directions for future work.

2   Related Work

This section presents an almost chronological overview of relevant literature that explores similar challenges and outlines approaches adoptable, adaptable to, or incompatible with implementing MFA for SSH, aiming to safeguard Linux fleets from intrusion and lateral movement. Although numerous solutions support SSH MFA, this section acknowledges them but deliberately concentrates on LDAPv3 as the communication protocol, since the proposed IAM framework maintains all four authentication factors through LDAP. LDAP enables access and management of organizational information across a network. In this context, the service functions as a specialized database optimized for read-intensive operations and hierarchical data structures such as records on users, computers, groups, and permissions.

Binnie outlines methods for securing SSH access on Linux systems through Pluggable Authentication Modules (PAM) and Google Authenticator [2]. He highlights foundational hardening techniques such as changing default ports, enforcing user-specific access controls, and configuring Transmission Control Protocol (TCP) wrappers for Internet Protocol (IP)-based restrictions. The core enhancement implements TOTP authentication using Google Authenticator, which adds a verification layer beyond password-based SSH logins. The setup supports Android and other devices, provides emergency access codes, and manages time-skew issues with some resilience. Despite these strengths, the method permits lateral movement within a compromised network environment, since each host in the Linux fleet keeps its own TOTP seed locally.

Several feasible options support implementation of the IAM in question. PAM, the default authentication framework for UNIX derivatives, offers one such approach. Lucas published a comprehensive reference book titled *PAM Mastery*, which explores the complexities of PAM, a topic many developers and system administrators consider challenging [25]. They often avoid modifications due to fear of misconfiguration. Within the context of the IAM described in this document, one must choose between creating a single pluggable authentication module that supports centralized TOTP and e-mail-based ROTP, or separate modules for each factor. Alternatively, the *pam_ exec* module enables delegation of TOTP and e-mail-based ROTP generation and prompting to external programs or scripts.

A robust Information Technology (IT) security framework for military online collaboration platforms addresses the rising need for secure coordination among reservist forces in Europe [7]. It outlines five essential security goals: authenticity, integrity, nonrepudiation, privacy, and resilience. To meet these, the author introduces a multi-layered security architecture that employs continuous Three-Factor Authentication (3FA) through password credentials, ElectroCardioGram (ECG) biometric verification, and a wearable multi-parameter medical monitoring and alert system known as AMON. The ECG signal, which reflects a physiological trait with high distinctiveness and permanence, undergoes encryption and transmits via Bluetooth and Transport Layer Security (TLS). This system mitigates threats such as impersonation, session hijacking, and data tampering through a blend of platform-level security policies, cryptographic protocols, and comprehensive user activity logging. A prototype simulation demonstrates acceptable performance, even under constrained mobile network conditions. However, despite its innovative design and strong theoretical basis, the dependence on the AMON device (originally developed for medical applications) makes the solution cumbersome and excludes it from consideration as a practical, topical IAM implementation.

Simmel and Filus outline an approach that integrates MFA into SSH login through PAM by selectively applying Duo Security's MFA service according to group membership or user-specific lists [32]. This enforcement operates by patching the *pam_duo* module while configuring SSH and PAM to prompt MFA only for designated users with access to sensitive information. However, the design depends on validating user identity using a password or federated login, then invoking Duo as a second factor. As a result, the approach does not allow more than two consecutive authentication methods.

Lucas, author of the already known *PAM Mastery*, also provides a detailed practitioner-oriented description *SSH Mastery: OpenSSH, PuTTY, Tunnels, and Keys* to help developers and system administrators advance from mere familiarity toward confident command of SSH's diverse capabilities [26]. His book demystifies SSH through detailed practical applications such as eliminating password-based logins, managing access controls, securely transferring files, forwarding graphical interfaces, and establishing secure tunnels and Virtual Private Networks (VPNs). It further explores advanced topics like key distribution, configuration management, and the creation of Certificate Authorities (CAs) for large-scale deployments. By focusing on real-world scenarios and delivering clear explanations, Lucas empowers concerned parties with tools necessary to enhance security and efficiency in remote system management.

Another approach treats real-time risk assessment based on monitoring SSH login attempts as a more meaningful strategy for authentication schemes than any anti-hammering technique [8]. It highlights shortcomings in existing literature, which detect BFAs without addressing the varying risks posed by each attempt, and introduces a lightweight system that modifies SSHD to extract username-password pattern data, generate metrics, and report real-time risk using the third and final version of the Simple Network Management Protocol (SNMP), also known as SNMPv3, for integration with Condition Monitoring Systems (CMSs) such as Checkmk[7] or Nagios[8]. This methodology advances simple BFA detection by quantifying the probability of successful intrusions based on observed attack patterns, offering a practical and scalable tool that supports proactive security monitoring instead of authentication enhancement. Rather than focusing on IAM, this work concentrates on analyzing attempted password patterns and comparing them against existing credentials to evaluate threat levels dynamically.

A subsequent disquisition refines the original monitoring approach by improving the accuracy of risk assessment for SSH BFAs through a novel Bloom Filter (BF) technique [9]. It introduces enhanced similarity metrics that compare incorrect login attempts with legitimate credentials more precisely, offering a significant advancement over pattern-based monitoring. By using multiple Bloom Filters (BFs) with different bit lengths, the system evaluates the risk of each

---

[7] https://checkmk.com/.
[8] https://www.nagios.org/.

failed attempt in realtime and integrates with CMSs via SNMPv3. Through experiments and metrics analysis, this treatise demonstrates improved detection precision without compromising system performance, contributing further to proactive risk management. Like its predecessor, this contribution avoids focus on IAM, instead advancing information security monitoring by providing early warnings when BFAs resemble legitimate login patterns too closely.

A third and final study completes a trilogy and advances realtime risk monitoring of SSH BFAs by refining similarity assessments through original and adapted BFs of varying sizes [10]. Building on its predecessors, it systematically compares login attempts with legitimate credentials by generating twelve independent similarity metrics, each representing different BF configurations. The prototype integrates these metrics with CMSs via SNMPv3 for dynamic threshold evaluation and anomaly detection. Experimental results, leveraging a deliberately weak root password, show that larger BFs reduce False Positives (FPs), while adapted BFs produce more reliable similarity scores. Despite significant improvements in threat sensitivity and detection stability, the contribution still omits IAM, focusing instead on proactive intrusion risk analysis through refined password similarity monitoring.

Ge and Zhu introduce an architecture called GAme-Theoretic ZEro-Trust Authentication (GAZETA), that mitigates lateral movement in 5G-enabled IoT environments [13]. Their approach models access control as a dynamic Markov game with one-sided incomplete information, allowing defenders to adapt authentication strategies based on Bayesian trust updates from multi-source evidence. By employing moving-horizon computation, GAZETA adapts in realtime to adversarial behavior and promotes resilience without substantially degrading system performance. A tactical 5G network case study shows that GAZETA significantly delays attacker lateral movement while maintaining high efficiency for legitimate users. However, GAZETA focuses exclusively on trust management and access control policies rather than on MFA, which limits its applicability to the current work.

Kraft evaluates MFA solutions for Västerås Stad, a Swedish municipality facing increased cybersecurity risks due to digitalization and hybrid cloud adoption [21]. Using the Analytical Hierarchy Process (AHP), the study defines five key selection criteria: cost, compatibility, user acceptance, management, and conditional access. Surveys and interviews with municipal employees reveal that cost and compatibility hold the highest importance, with cost outweighing other factors by 143% on average. Among six evaluated MFA solutions, Microsoft Entra ID ranked highest overall, with IBM Security Verify and OneLogin following closely. Microsoft Entra ID's strengths included strong user experience and administrative features, while Cisco Duo led in compatibility. The study underscores the importance of integrating cost-effective, compatible MFA systems into municipal infrastructures, particularly under constrained budgets. Despite a methodical evaluation process, the solution space remains bounded by the municipality's specific context and needs.

Fahrnberger provides direction for MFA in the current scholarly piece through a pluggable authentication module that integrates e-mail as a second factor for secure 2FA on Linux systems [11]. To counter limitations of anti-hammering mechanisms against BFAs and Denial-of-Service (DoS) attacks, the module sends a cryptographically secure ROTP to a secondary e-mail address after primary password verification via LDAP. The work highlights the lack of prior PAM solutions supporting secondary e-mails and discusses implementation details, including SSHD integration. A comprehensive threat model outlines nine categories of potential vulnerabilities, including Man-in-the-Middle (MitM) attacks, social engineering, and BFAs. Experimental development demonstrates resilience against buffer overflow exploits. Although the solution strengthens authentication without reliance on expensive hardware tokens, the work acknowledges inherent risks tied to MFA methods and proposes areas for future refinement toward market-ready deployment.

Kim introduces an Out-of-Band (OOB) One-Time-Password (OTP) architecture for Linux-based control and automation systems, emphasizing centralized OTP generation, multi-layer authentication, and transmission through a distinct encrypted channel to strengthen defenses against BFAs and credential-stuffing attacks [19]. The model demonstrates strong security performance, preventing all simulated intrusions while adding only minimal authentication delay. However, dependence on a mobile push service for OOB OTP delivery increases operational complexity through continuous synchronization, app management, and reliance on mobile network availability. A simpler alternative employs ROTPs via End-to-End (E2E) encrypted e-mail channels, eliminating the need for device-specific push infrastructure. ROTPs delivered through encrypted e-mails ensure equivalent confidentiality and message integrity with broader interoperability, offering a more practical and standards-aligned approach than custom push-service OTP distribution.

Table 1 provides an overview of this section at a glance.

Table 1. Summary of related work

Year	Authors	Title	Objective
2006	Sermersheim	Lightweight Directory Access Protocol (LDAP): The Protocol [31]	LDAP details as component of MFA
2016	Binnie	Securing SSH with PAM [2]	2FA
2016	Lucas	PAM Mastery [25]	PAM details as component of MFA
2017	Fahrnberger	Contemporary IT Security for Military Online Collaboration Platforms [7]	3FA
2017	Simmel and Filus	Flexible Enforcement of Multi-factor Authentication with SSH via Linux-PAM for Federated Identity Users [32]	2FA

(continued)

Table 1. (*continued*)

Year	Authors	Title	Objective
2018	Lucas	SSH Mastery: OpenSSH, PuTTY, Tunnels, and Keys [26]	SSH details as component of MFA
2022	Fahrnberger	Realtime Risk Monitoring of SSH Brute Force Attacks [8]	Risk monitoring
2023	Fahrnberger	Bloom Filter-Based Realtime Risk Monitoring of SSH Brute Force Attacks [9]	Risk monitoring
2024	Fahrnberger	Pattern- and Similarity-Based Realtime Risk Monitoring of SSH Brute Force Attacks with Bloom Filters [10]	Risk monitoring
2024	Ge and Zhu	GAZETA: GAme-Theoretic ZEro-Trust Authentication for Defense Against Lateral Movement in 5G IoT Networks [13]	Game theory
2024	Kraft	Municipal Cybersecurity Enhancement [21]	MFA
2025	Fahrnberger	A Pluggable Authentication Module for E-Mail as a Secure Additional Authentication Factor [11]	2FA
2025	Kim	Out-of-band OTP-based 2FA Architecture for Secure Linux Platforms in Control and Automation Systems [19]	2FA

3 Implementation

Before discussing implementation details, Fig. 1 presents a scenario in which an attacker gains control over a Linux fleet member with user accounts federated through OpenLDAP. The IAM described in this section offers no defense if an intruder acquires root privileges on the affected node by exploiting a vulnerability in a protocol, service, or software component unrelated to SSH. Other Linux fleet members with comparable weaknesses remain exposed to risks from external attackers or propagation via an already compromised host. However, the proposed IAM restricts lateral movement over SSH, preventing the intruder from collecting authentication factors from the breached node for further access.

Both component types in Fig. 1 require changes to support 4FA. OpenLDAP functions as the authentication backend, while each Linux fleet member acts as a corresponding client. Accordingly, Subsect. 3.1 explores the necessary extensions for each authentication factor within an OpenLDAP instance. The discussion then shifts to client-side modifications for each authentication factor in Subsect. 3.2 covering all Linux nodes. Subsequently, Subsect. 3.3 details the exact interplay between a Linux node and OpenLDAP by outlining the resulting authentication flow.

All authentication factors use mechanisms that ensure the OpenLDAP server retains only verifiable derivatives, never the raw secrets transmitted by a Linux client. Although not all methods qualify as formal zero-knowledge proofs, they follow the principle that client-conveyed inputs differ from server-resident data.

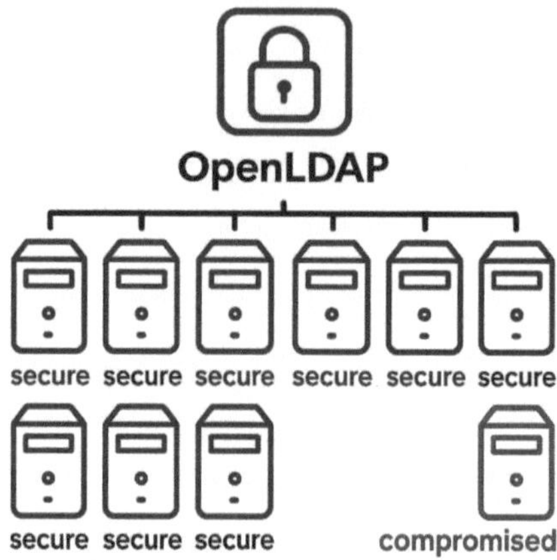

Fig. 1. Single compromised member in an OpenLDAP-federated Linux fleet

3.1   OpenLDAP

Storing all required authentication settings together within each OpenLDAP user object offers a clear organizational advantage. To the author's best knowledge, no existing LDAP objectClass natively supports all four authentication factors outlined below. Fortunately, LDAP schemas allow straightforward extension through additional objectClasses and/or custom attributes. One such example involves a schema based on the common objectClass *inetOrgPerson*, extended by inheriting *shadowAccount* to include attributes for password aging.

A less-than-ideal option involves misusing existing, unused LDAP attributes, using them to store authentication settings for which they never served as intended containers. If all other approaches fail, third-party data sources, such as databases or repositories, may supply the missing LDAP attributes.

The following subsubsections present design details showing how OpenLDAP enables all four authentication factors for its connected Linux nodes.

Asymmetrical Key Pair (1. Authentication Factor). Since their length defies memorization, keys belong to possession factors. Among authentication methods, they offer the strongest and most effective defense against BFAs, so systems give them priority. The term *pair* indicates an asymmetric combination, comprised of private and public elements. OpenLDAP may distribute the latter to Linux nodes for authentication, but neither OpenLDAP nor any system entity accesses confidential key material stored on user devices. Even outside the scenario illustrated in Fig. 1, always protect private credentials at rest using strong passphrases. Every operation involving such authentication secrets requires the corresponding passphrase.

Unlike the native attribute *userCertificate* in Active Directory (AD), the prevalent objectClass *inetOrgPerson* lacks *userCertificate* by default [50]. To inherit this attribute, one can extend *inetOrgPerson* with the objectClass *pkiUser*. Alternatively, rather than adding *pkiUser*, one may choose to assign only the attribute *userCertificate* directly to *inetOrgPerson*. Because an asymmetric cryptosystem ensures that no one can derive a private from a public key, OpenLDAP can allow all Linux fleet members to access all stored public keys without authentication.

Adopters of the presented IAM might lack permission or capability to modify OpenLDAP. In such cases, a centralized orchestration tool like Ansible or Puppet enables distribution of legitimate users' public keys throughout the entire Linux fleet. The orchestration service logs into each system using the Machine-to-Machine (M2M) authentication flow outlined in Subsect. 3.3, transfers each public key to the correct ~/.ssh/authorized_keys file, then adjusts ownership and access permissions for that file and its enclosing folder ~/.ssh/ according to the least-privilege principle. After the initial process, any alteration of public key material should trigger the described dissemination mechanism.

Password (2. Authentication Factor). Unlike an asymmetric key pair, passwords, which represent the oldest and most widely used authentication factor, function as knowledge factors. Replacement frequency differs between these mechanisms. While users typically rotate asymmetric key pairs infrequently, OpenLDAP configuration can enforce password changes at regular intervals. Users may create passwords that nobody can memorize and must store them in a password manager. Alternatively, they may choose passwords suitable for memorization (although nothing prevents storage in a password manager).

Virtually all OpenLDAP objectClasses handle password security natively using the *userPassword* attribute, which relies on a range of hashing algorithms. This native support eliminates any need to consider alternatives to OpenLDAP. For password hashes, only the respective user can view their own, while administrators obtain access to all attributes, including password hashes.

TOTP (3. Authentication Factor). After using a relatively long-lived asymmetric key pair and a periodically renewed password, volatile TOTPs serve as the third authentication element. Systems frequently select a configuration with six digits, which change every 30 s and rely on an initial string known as the seed, combined with the current timestamp through hashing. Possession of the correct seed enables calculation of TOTPs without difficulty. Such capability places this method into the possession-based category. Therefore, users must handle a seed that they cannot memorize and must safeguard diligently. Devices or applications, such as authenticator apps or hardware tokens, typically compute the current valid TOTP when supplied with the seed. Members of the Linux fleet must refrain from accessing any reusable seed, as such exposure allows offenders to derive TOTPs and obtain unauthorized access to other hosts.

For that reason, OpenLDAP requires two adaptations. Firstly, each user profile must inherit the objectClass *oathTOTPToken* or at least receive the attribute *oathSecret* in addition to the well-known *inetOrgPerson*. Secondly, OpenLDAP must guarantee appropriate Access Control Lists (ACLs) that only service accounts and administrators can retrieve or set any *oathSecret* attribute. This restriction extends even to entry owners in order to prevent exposure of seeds.

If a third-party tool, for example a relational database, should retain the TOTP seeds rather than OpenLDAP, protective ACLs must follow the approach in the preceding paragraph.

E-Mail-Based ROTP (4. Authentication Factor). Regarding ephemerality, e-mail-based ROTPs function as the fourth and final authentication factor, exhibiting greater volatility compared with the three preceding factors, since each serves only a single use. Because an ROTP reaches only the corresponding e-mail address, ROTPs fall within possession factors.

For example, the attribute *mail* often serves as the main choice to store an e-mail address within a user profile built upon the objectClass *inetOrgPerson*. If that e-mail address also enables password recovery, receiving temporary Uniform Resource Locators (URLs) for password resets, a separate attribute holding a distinct e-mail address must handle this role [11]. Extension of *inetOrgPerson* by a new attribute, such as one named *rotpMail*, may address this requirement. Alternatively, one might reuse an existing but redundant attribute from *inetOrgPerson*, such as *labeledURI*, which typically stores a user's web address.

Some administrators might consider a third-party tool to supply an additional e-mail address, yet such a solution usually introduces unnecessary complexity compared with OpenLDAP.

OpenLDAP-Side Algorithm. While OpenLDAP allows sharing public keys and passwords with Linux fleet members via LDAP during authentication attempts, it must conceal reusable TOTP seeds and secondary e-mail addresses from interconnected Linux nodes. Disclosing this information could permit attackers lateral movement and facilitate compromise of additional Linux hosts. Equivalent secrecy must apply when a third-party service supplies any authentication factor instead of OpenLDAP. The LDAP standard lacks mechanisms that properly conceal TOTP seeds and secondary e-mail addresses. Therefore, OpenLDAP requires an additional, dedicated interface that securely prompts for

TOTPs and ROTPs without leaking TOTP seeds or secondary e-mail addresses. Algorithm 1 outlines simplified server-side pseudocode for such an interface.

Algorithm 1. OpenLDAP-side

1: Ignore all *SIGINT* signals during input from client (Linux fleet member)
2: Generate *rotp* as random 6-digit string
3: Set *totp_passed* to *false*
4: Prompt client (Linux fleet member) for input with *Question:*
5: Set *username_totp_entered* to client input
6: **if** *username_totp_entered* contains character # **then**
7:     Split *username_totp_entered* into *username* and *totp_entered*
8:     Query third-party source or OpenLDAP for TOTP seed (attribute *oathSecret*) of *username*
9:     **if** TOTP seed of *username* found and currently valid TOTP equals *totp_entered* **then**
10:         Query OpenLDAP for secondary e-mail address of *username*
11:         **if** secondary e-mail address of *username* found **then**
12:             Send *rotp* to secondary e-mail address
13:             Set *totp_passed* to *true*
14:         **end if**
15:     **end if**
16: **end if**
17: Wait a random period up to one second
18: Prompt client (Linux fleet member) for input with *Answer:*
19: Set *rotp_entered* to client input
20: **if** *totp_passed* equals *true* and *rotp* equals *rotp_entered* **then return** *true*
21: **else return** *false*
22: **end if**

Early deactivation of all *SIGINT* signals for user input in line 1 plays a crucial role in thwarting offenders who attempt illegal circumvention of the third and fourth authentication factor using malicious key combinations. The command in line 2 instructs a Real Random Number Generator (RRNG) to generate an ROTP, not a Pseudo Random Number Generator (PRNG) with weaker randomness. The variable *totp_passed* in line 3 receives the Boolean value *false* during initialization and changes to *true* in line 13 only if both TOTP authentication and ROTP generation succeed. Upon connection, a client (Linux fleet member) encounters a simple prompt, *Question:* (see line 4), then must transmit a concatenated string, *username_totp_entered*, which combines *username*, the delimiter symbol #, and the currently valid TOTP (line 5). After checking in line 6 that *username_totp_entered* includes the expected separator #, line 7 splits *username_totp_entered* into the variables *username* and *totp_entered*. The code in line 8 attempts to retrieve a TOTP seed for *username* from OpenLDAP or another third-party source. When retrieval succeeds and the currently valid TOTP based on this seed matches *totp_entered* in line 9, line 10 requests the secondary e-mail address attribute for *username* from OpenLDAP. Success at this step fulfills the condition in line 11, triggering transmission of *rotp* to the fetched secondary e-mail address in line 12 and switching *totp_passed* to *true* in line 13. Clients receive no indication regarding the outcome of TOTP authentication at this stage of the algorithm. In addition, a random sleep period of up to one second in line 17 helps prevent time-based attacks through statistical analysis, ensuring an arbitrary algorithm runtime. Afterward, according to line 18, the interface displays a minimalist *Answer:* prompt and requests the transmitted *rotp*. Line 19 stores the client's response in the variable *rotp_entered*. In line 20, the code verifies that the client has correctly supplied the currently valid TOTP (*totp_passed* equals *true*) and the proper ROTP (*rotp* matches *rotp_entered*). When both conditions hold, the function returns *true* to signal positive authentication. Otherwise, line 21 returns *false* to indicate negative authentication.

Subsection 3.3 showcases the protocol making the interface characterized in Algorithm 1 accessible for clients (Linux fleet members). Earlier, Subsect. 3.2 illuminates the client side.

3.2   Linux Fleet

In addition to preventing successful malign initial access targeting Linux fleet members, the second directive focuses on averting lateral attacks originating from compromised peers. Accordingly, administrators should refrain from storing authentication material locally whenever feasible, thus reducing the attack surface in line with least-privilege principles. Since network or service outages and M2M communications demand special handling, authentication material stored locally for these scenarios qualifies as an exception.

Following the style of the previous subsection, the next subsubsections outline the configuration requirements for all four authentication factors on the client side, along with corresponding code that interacts through the interface defined in Algorithm 1.

Asymmetrical Key Pair (1. Authentication Factor). When a user with credentials stored in OpenLDAP logs in to any Linux host shown in Fig. 1, use of the correct private key grants access through the initial authentication barrier. The Linux node attempts to decrypt messages, encrypted with this private key, by using the corresponding public key, which it retrieves dynamically from OpenLDAP. Administrators should include two configuration directives in the */etc/ssh/sshd_config* file to define how the system obtains the user's public key from the directory. The directive

– AuthorizedKeysCommand /usr/bin/sss_ssh_authorizedkeys

instructs SSHD to execute the specified command, a part of the System Security Services Daemon (SSSD), to retrieve an authorized public key from external sources such as OpenLDAP or AD. The second directive

– AuthorizedKeysCommandUser nobody

executes the preceding instruction as the unprivileged *nobody* user, minimizing security risks associated with running external commands under elevated privileges.

The first subsubsection of Subsect. 3.1 already hints at an alternative scenario involving the dissemination of public keys by Ansible or Puppet if OpenLDAP cannot or should not handle this task. Tools such as these orchestration solutions can distribute each user's public key to the $\sim$/.ssh/authorized_keys file on Linux hosts with configuration management scripts or manifests that copy authorized public key material from a central repository or variable into each target user's home directory. These tools push public key data during scheduled runs or on-demand deployments. Updates or removals of keys occur only when a new configuration applies, not in realtime as with dynamic public key retrieval from systems such as AD or OpenLDAP. To ensure seamless key-based authentication, the tools must explicitly create a user's home directory and the subordinate *.ssh* folder within it with correct permissions prior to populating the *authorized_keys* file, particularly if the user account remains new and has not logged in yet.

Password (2. Authentication Factor). Classic password authentication for accounts federated through OpenLDAP requires SSSD installation on Linux fleet members. This configuration supports integration with AD or OpenLDAP. During user login on a system running SSSD, the service intercepts the password and issues an LDAP bind operation using the submitted credentials. If validation succeeds, SSSD provides access. If authentication fails, the system rejects the login attempt. Administrators may configure SSSD to cache accepted credentials locally for a limited time. This cached information offers offline authentication. However, the method described in this document intentionally disables credential caching because the additional three authentication factors cannot undergo storage for offline use.

TOTP (3. Authentication Factor). Deploying TOTP seeds, for example by placing *.google_authenticator* files in user home directories as described by Binnie [2], across an entire Linux fleet enables automation and consistency using tools such as Ansible or Puppet, much like the previously explained alternative process for distributing public keys. However, adversaries may extract TOTP seeds during a system compromise and then generate valid TOTPs to facilitate lateral movement within the environment, so local verification of TOTPs on each host introduces security risks. Instead, each Linux host should forward user-entered TOTPs to a central validation service co-hosted on OpenLDAP. This method supports uniform enforcement of authentication policies, helps detect anomalous activity across the environment, and prevents attackers from exploiting individual systems following a compromise.

E-Mail-Based ROTP (4. Authentication Factor). Initiating e-mail-based ROTPs from such a central validation service rather than relying on each individual Linux host further improves security and consistency. Centralized delivery strengthens control over ROTP generation and dispatch, reduces risks posed by inconsistent configurations, and simplifies auditing. Administrators gain a unified vantage point for monitoring ROTP activity and enforcing security policy updates. Users experience reliable and uniform notification outcomes, regardless of which Linux host receives their authentication request. With this architecture, attackers encounter fewer opportunities to exploit local weaknesses or avoid detection, since all e-mail-based ROTPs originate from a trusted, centrally managed platform rather than potentially misconfigured or vulnerable hosts scattered throughout the fleet.

Client-Side Algorithm. Following the outlined requirement for concealing all TOTP seeds and secondary e-mail addresses from every OpenLDAP-connected Linux fleet member, such systems receive exclusively ephemeral TOTPs and ROTPs. In summary, Linux nodes prompt users for TOTPs and ROTPs, then forward these values to OpenLDAP, which handles generation and verification with Algorithm 1. The corresponding workflow on the Linux platforms appears in Algorithm 2.

Algorithm 2. Linux-side

 1: Ignore all *SIGINT* signals during input from client (user)
 2: Set *username* to executor of this algorithm
 3: Connect securely to OpenLDAP and wait for prompt with *Question:*, timeout after 10 seconds
 4: Prompt client (user) for input with *TOTP:*
 5: Set *totp_entered* to client input
 6: Send *username#totp_entered* to OpenLDAP
 7: Wait for prompt with *Answer:*, timeout after 10 seconds
 8: Prompt client (user) for input with *ROTP:*
 9: Set *rotp_entered* to client input
10: Send *rotp_entered* to OpenLDAP
11: Wait for answer from OpenLDAP, timeout after 10 seconds
12: Set *answer* to answer from OpenLDAP
13: **if** *answer* equals *true* **then**
14:     Regard all *SIGINT* signals during input from client (user)
15:     Replace current process with Linux shell
16: **else return** *Permission denied, please try again.*
17: **end if**

Line 1 of Algorithm 2 matches 1 in function as it instructs Linux to block all *SIGINT* signals from the user during authentication. This procedure sanitizes user input and prevents bypass attempts. Line 2 acquires the authenticating user's name and assigns it to the variable *username*. Line 3 initiates a second secure connection to OpenLDAP, adding it to the earlier LDAP link. Progress depends on OpenLDAP presenting Linux with the prompt *Question:* within ten seconds. Exceeding this time forces Algorithm 2 to exit. With a successful prompt, Linux requests the current TOTP in line 4 using the prompt *TOTP:*. Line 5 records this entry as the variable *totp_entered*, and Linux forwards this string, together with *username* (separated by #), to OpenLDAP in line 6. The sequence resumes for ROTP in the fourth verification step. Linux waits up to ten seconds for OpenLDAP to show *Answer:* (line 7). Passing this time frame also triggers Algorithm 2 to terminate. When OpenLDAP replies promptly, Linux prompts for the correct ROTP in line 8, records it in the variable *rotp_entered* in line 9, and sends it to OpenLDAP in line 10. Line 11 consists of waiting up to ten seconds for OpenLDAP's verdict. If delayed, Algorithm 2 ends. With a timely result, line 12 stores it in the variable *answer*. A positive verdict in line 13 causes Linux to unblock all *SIGINT* signals for the verified user (line 14) and replaces the current process with a shell in line 15. A negative outcome in line 16 prompts Linux to display a notification about failed verification.

3.3 Authentication Flows

The two preceding subsections describe Algorithms 1 and 2. The first targets OpenLDAP, while the second runs on Linux clients. Their joint operation enables secure verification of TOTP as a third authentication factor and ROTP as a fourth. However, neither subsection outlines a secure protocol governing message exchanges between these components, nor do they detail complete flows with all authentication factors. This subsection fills those gaps by introducing three comprehensive authentication flows.

The first outlined mechanism enables standard authentication under typical conditions. This subsection regards it as the initial scenario, with an assumption that OpenLDAP or its connectivity might suffer failures impacting Linux fleet members. In the event of such disruptions, robust emergency authentication, described as the second workflow, ensures access regardless of outages. When administrators manage subordinate Linux systems through Ansible or Puppet, for example by distributing Algorithm 2 along with required information for fallback authentication, an independent third process for M2M purposes supports this functionality.

Regular Authentication. Each user who attempts to log in to a Linux fleet member triggers this regular authentication flow.

For the first authentication factor, the SSHD on a Linux node checks whether a user utilizes the correct private key by fetching the matching public counterpart from OpenLDAP via LDAP. This process requires insertion of two directives

– AuthorizedKeysCommand /usr/bin/sss_ssh_authorizedkeys

and

– AuthorizedKeysCommandUser nobody

into the SSHD configuration file */etc/ssh/sshd_config*, as delineated in Subsect. 3.2.

SSHD employs the default frameworks PAM and SSSD for password verification as the second authentication factor. The commented list below presents the required configuration files with sample content that supports this setup [11]. */etc/ssh/sshd_config # SSHD configuration file*

- UsePAM yes # Invocation of PAM

/et./pam.d/sshd # PAM configuration file of SSHD

- @include common-auth # Invocation of the main PAM authentication stack of Debian-based Operating Systems (OSs)
- auth substack password-auth # Invocation of the PAM password authentication stack of Red Hat-based OSs

/etc/pam.d/common-auth PAM authentication configuration file of Debian-based OSs , /etc/pam.d/password-auth PAM password authentication configuration file of Red Hat-based OSs

- auth sufficient pam_sss.so use_first_pass # Invocation of the PAM SSSD stack

/etc/sssd/sssd.conf # SSSD configuration file

- [domain/default]
- auth_provider = ldap
- autofs_provider = ldap
- cache_credentials = True
- chpass_provider = ldap
- id_provider = ldap
- ldap_id_use_start_tls = True
- ldap_search_base = ou=users,dc=example,dc=org
- ldap_tls_cacert = /usr/local/share/ca-certificates/example.org.crt
- ldap_tls_cacertdir = /usr/local/share/ca-certificates
- ldap_tls_reqcert = hard
- ldap_uri = ldaps://ldap.example.org/
- [nss]
- homedir_substring = /home
- [sssd]
- domains = default

For verification of TOTPs as the third and ROTPs as the fourth authentication factor, Algorithm 1 resides in a file within the home directory of a designated service account on OpenLDAP. Each Linux fleet member receives Algorithm 2 through an orchestration tool such as Ansible or Puppet. Every deployed instance of Algorithm 2, implemented either as a pluggable authentication module or another binary, holds a unique private key. Generation and assignment of each key pair occur individually for every Linux fleet member, ensuring distinct authentication credentials across the fleet. The system collects and aggregates the corresponding public keys for all members in the *.ssh/authorized_keys* file located in the service account's home directory on OpenLDAP. Centralized key management enables rapid credential revocation when needed. Network-level controls further strengthen SSH access for this dedicated user. SSHD on the OpenLDAP server permits connections only from specific source IP addresses or subnets within the fleet and relies exclusively on public key authentication. The configuration snippet of */etc/ssh/sshd_config* below reduces the attack surface and ensures access only for approved systems.

- Match User <service account name> Address <source IP address range>
- AuthenticationMethods publickey
- PubkeyAuthentication yes

Beyond maintaining a whitelist of source IP addresses or subnets, limiting active SSH sessions per source IP address helps thwart BFAs on valid TOTPs and blocks DoS attempts against uninfected nodes, with both attack types originating from compromised Linux hosts. iptables controls session counts using the persistent rule listed below.

- -A INPUT -p tcp –dport 22 -m connlimit –connlimit-above <session limit value> –connlimit-mask 32 -j REJECT

A corresponding iptables rule on each Linux fleet member in turn prevents BFAs and DoS attempts against its SSHD.

After completing a secure configuration for SSH sessions among Linux fleet members and OpenLDAP to verify TOTPs and ROTPs, the deployed pluggable authentication module or binary on a Linux fleet member initiates an SSH connection via Algorithm 2 to the service account on OpenLDAP, using its unique private key for authentication. Once authenticated, SSHD on OpenLDAP forcefully launches Algorithm 1 by setting it as the user shell in */etc/passwd*. Regardless of any client input, the session calls only Algorithm 1 and blocks access to any shell or alternative command invocation. This protocol permits Algorithm 1 to run exclusively for authenticated and authorized Linux fleet members, while centralizing key management, logging, traceability, and access revocation through network-based ACLs.

Emergency Authentication. In contrast to regular authentication, emergency cases require all credentials to rely on local rather than network-based information, triggering the alternative scenarios described in the last two subsections.

For public key authentication as the first factor, Ansible or Puppet, as the chosen orchestration utility, must distribute an emergency user's public key across the entire Linux fleet. This requires logging into each system via M2M authentication to check for the presence, correct ownership, and permissions of the emergency user's home directory, its subordinate *.ssh* folder, and the *authorized_keys* file within. These elements must follow the least-privilege principle for ownership and permissions. Furthermore, the public key has to appear in ~/.ssh/authorized_keys. As with ordinary users, any change to the emergency user's key pair triggers this distribution process again.

Each Linux node includes an emergency user, set up as a local account. Its password hash, which serves as the second authentication factor, resides in the /etc/shadow file. If a hacker acquires this hash from a compromised machine, tools such as *Hashcat, John the Ripper*, or rainbow tables enable attempts to crack it. To mitigate such risks, Ansible or Puppet should assign a distinct password to the emergency login on every Linux fleet node.

The emergency user's TOTP seed for the third factor should reside locally in the file ~/.google_authenticator, just as with the first and second authentication factors. This setup allows comparison of generated TOTPs without reliance on network-based sources like OpenLDAP. If an attacker obtains this local seed from a compromised Linux host, the breach grants no opportunity for lateral movement to additional Linux fleet members. Therefore, Ansible or Puppet should configure the emergency account on each Linux node using a unique TOTP seed.

Secondary e-mail addresses, intended for receiving ROTPs as a fourth authentication factor, should remain undisclosed to Linux nodes. Therefore, emergency authentication replaces ROTPs with access restrictions to specific source IP addresses or subnets. This approach prevents disclosure of any secondary e-mail addresses to Linux hosts and eliminates any possibility for directly delivering ROTPs to users from those systems.

Machine-to-Machine (M2M) Authentication. This authentication method relies exclusively on nonvolatile factors, since orchestration frameworks such as Ansible or Puppet have not yet incorporated support for ephemeral alternatives. Although each framework permits either public key or password authentication independently, a configuration that combines both factors necessitates a workaround, for example delegating connection establishment to *sshpass* on the orchestration host. M2M authentication typically either leverages a centralized IAM that enforces access control in parallel with standard mechanisms or employs node-local credentials analogous to those reserved for emergency procedures. The centralized model introduces vulnerability to IAM outages or communication failures that interrupt connectivity. With locally stored secrets, every Linux system requires administration of an additional password. During initial provisioning, administrators configure M2M authentication manually through SSHD and SSSD directives or by defining static credentials.

For public key authentication as the first factor, this approach provides flexibility. Administrators can either insert the two previously mentioned directives into the SSHD configuration file /etc/ssh/sshd_config while configuring SSSD, or distribute the M2M user's public key to every Linux node as practiced with the emergency account.

A similar principle applies when password authentication functions as the second factor. All Linux nodes share the same password if a centralized IAM manages authentication through SSHD and SSSD. In contrast, local M2M credentials require unique passwords on every Linux fleet member.

The integration of TOTP as a third authentication factor in Ansible or Puppet sounds promising for future work, but no one has implemented it so far. Using ROTP as a fourth authentication factor seems even more challenging. Hence, the block below in the SSHD configuration file *of /etc/ssh/sshd_config* enforces only 2FA for M2M authentication at first glance. To completely prevent exploitation of the M2M account, the IP filter in the first line restricts its use to the source IP addresses of the permitted orchestration nodes.

- Match User <M2M account name> Address <source IP address(es) of orchestration hosts>
- AuthenticationMethods publickey,keyboard-interactive
- PubkeyAuthentication yes

4   Security Scrutiny

To ensure the market viability of a defensive appliance such as the instituted IAM, its robustness requires validation against all recognized offensive techniques. For this purpose, Fahrnberger [11] analyzes the nine plausible attack vectors listed below, which target his pluggable authentication module for e-mail verification, and reference Roger Grimes's article *The Many Ways to Hack 2FA* [14] along with his comprehensive monograph *Hacking Multifactor Authentication* [15]. The latter offers a systematic synthesis of more than two dozen attack methodologies documented across decades of MFA compromise research and industry case studies. Drawing on literature, breach investigations, and first-hand penetration testing experiences, Grimes integrates diverse findings from the broader cybersecurity corpus, covering endpoint compromises, interception, impersonation, and manipulation of MFA flows, to develop a structured taxonomy of attack strategies and countermeasures. Consequently, the referenced attacks represent a vetted and aggregated understanding of MFA vulnerabilities widely acknowledged within the applied security community and furnish an empirically grounded framework for evaluating IAM robustness.

- Man-In-The-Middle (MITM) Attacks
- Social Engineering Attacks
- Programming Attacks against Server Infrastructure
- Programming Attacks against Client Infrastructure
- Recovery Attacks
- Brute Force Attacks (BFAs)
- Buffer Overflow Attacks
- Side-Channel Attacks
- Physical Attacks

The same set of attacks targets the newly designed IAM. Its prototype underwent thorough testing for susceptibility to buffer overflow attacks and withstood all trials thanks to automatic memory management and rigorous bounds checking. The remaining eight attack vectors still pose risks if left unmitigated, as the cited writ supports.

This section examines susceptibility of the first authentication factor to mathematical attacks and the other three factors to BFAs, referring to subtechniques of technique T1110 (Brute Force) under tactic TA0006 (Credential Access) from the MITRE ATT&CK Framework. It also evaluates consequences after a credential leak or successful guess, focusing on lateral movement from an affected Linux host to an uncompromised host via subtechnique T1021.004 (SSH) within technique T1021 (Remote Services) under tactic TA0008 (Lateral Movement). The assessment adopts the perspective of an attacker, in sequence with the four authentication factors.

Whitelisting source IP addresses or subnets limits potential attack vectors. This restriction constitutes a fundamental requirement for M2M authentication, enabling automated entities to verify identity reliably without manual intervention. It provides an effective control mechanism and a practical alternative to TOTP or ROTP in non-interactive systems. During emergency authentication, enforcing IP whitelisting offers a safer approach than storing secondary e-mail information on Linux hosts, which introduces significant security risks. For regular authentication workflows, adopting source IP address or subnet whitelisting remains optional yet beneficial when applying least-privilege access controls and confining SSHD connections wherever possible. When Linux fleet members operate independently, they have to omit mutual whitelisting to reduce lateral movement across distributed environments.

4.1 Asymmetrical Key Pair (1. Authentication Factor)

With a permitted source IP address, the private key of an asymmetric cryptosystem PK functions as the first barrier to access and demands guessing during all authentication flows. Attackers might attempt to guess PK in the same manner as the secret key of a symmetric cryptosystem SK. However, PK does not cover every value because of numeric constraints. Consequently, the National Institute of Standards and Technology (NIST) defines comparable strengths between private keys of asymmetric algorithms and secret keys of symmetric block ciphers [1]. Subsequent calculations rely on the length of an SK that yields strength comparable to PK. The probability P_{SK} that an attacker correctly guesses an SK on a single attempt depends on the total number of possible combinations. Let k_{SK} denote the bit length of SK. Each bit offers two choices, expressed as $C_{SK} = 2$. Choosing one option per bit across k_{SK} positions produces $N_{SK} = C_{SK}{}^{k_{SK}} = 2^{k_{SK}}$ possible values. The reciprocal of N_{SK} yields the probability $P_{SK} = \frac{1}{N_{SK}} = \frac{1}{2^{k_{SK}}}$, which measures the likelihood that a single guess matches the correct value.

Table 2 lists five representative comparisons between the strengths of secret keys of symmetric block ciphers and private keys of asymmetric algorithms. For example, a contemporarily recommended minimum private key size of $k_{\text{PK}} = 3{,}072$ bits for the widely adopted asymmetric cryptosystem of Rivest, Shamir, and Adleman (RSA) [29] equals $k_{\text{SK}} = 128$ bits of the Advanced Encryption Standard (AES) [4,5]. The number of possible secret keys for AES-128 reaches $N_{\text{SK}} = 2^{128} \approx 3.40 \times 10^{38}$. A single guess results in probability $P_{\text{SK}} = \frac{1}{2^{128}} \approx \frac{1}{3.40 \times 10^{38}} \approx 2.94 \times 10^{-39}$, a value small enough to render attacks infeasible with current computational resources. Even coordinated efforts by large attacker networks hardly improve the likelihood of success, illustrating the practical security level achieved at such key lengths.

Table 2. Comparable security strengths of symmetric block cipher and asymmetric-key algorithms [1]

Security Strength	Symmetric Key Algorithms	Finite-Field Cryptography (Digital Signature Algorithm, Diffie-Hellman, Menezes-Qu-Vanstone)	Integer Factorization Cryptography (RSA)	Elliptic Curve Cryptography (Elliptic Curve Digital Signature Algorithm, Edwards-Curve Digital Signature Algorithm, Diffie-Hellman, Menezes-Qu-Vanstone)
≤ 80	Two-key Triple Data Encryption Algorithm	$k_{\text{PK}} = 160$	$k_{\text{PK}} = 1{,}024$	$k_{\text{PK}} = 160 - 223$
112	Three-key Triple Data Encryption Algorithm	$k_{\text{PK}} = 224$	$k_{\text{PK}} = 2{,}048$	$k_{\text{PK}} = 224 - 255$
128	AES-128	$k_{\text{PK}} = 256$	$k_{\text{PK}} = 3{,}072$	$k_{\text{PK}} = 256 - 383$
192	AES-192	$k_{\text{PK}} = 384$	$k_{\text{PK}} = 7{,}680$	$k_{\text{PK}} = 384 - 511$
256	AES-256	$k_{\text{PK}} = 512$	$k_{\text{PK}} = 15{,}360$	$k_{\text{PK}} \geq 512$

However, leakage of *PK* grants access across all Linux fleet members and allows reuse in all authentication flows, thereby facilitating lateral movement.

4.2 Password (2. Authentication Factor)

An attacker who acquires a private key for regular, emergency, or M2M login can initiate a BFA against the corresponding password as the second authentication factor. Let C_{PWD} indicate the set of available characters for each position and k_{PWD} denote the maximum length. Password creation requires selection of one character for every position up to k_{PWD}, resulting in $N_{\text{PWD}} = \sum_{k=1}^{k_{\text{PWD}}} C_{\text{PWD}}^{k} = \frac{C_{\text{PWD}}^{k_{\text{PWD}}+1} - C_{\text{PWD}}}{C_{\text{PWD}} - 1}$ possible combinations. Each attempt offers a probability of $P_{\text{PWD}} = \frac{1}{N_{\text{PWD}}} = \frac{1}{\sum_{k=1}^{k_{\text{PWD}}} C_{\text{PWD}}^{k}} = \frac{C_{\text{PWD}} - 1}{C_{\text{PWD}}^{k_{\text{PWD}}+1} - C_{\text{PWD}}}$.

For instance, consider $C_{\text{PWD}} = 94$ for all human-readable characters and $k_{\text{PWD}} = 16$ as the upper password length limit. Selection of a distinct character per position produces $N_{\text{PWD}} = \sum_{k=1}^{16} 94^{k} = \frac{94^{17} - 94}{93} \approx 3.76 \times 10^{31}$ unique combinations. Therefore, the likelihood that a solitary random guess results in a valid password equals $P_{\mathrm{PWD}} = \frac{1}{\sum_{k=1}^{16} 94^k} = \frac{93}{94^{17}-94} \approx 2.66 \times 10^{-32}$, which illustrates the strength provided by long and varied passwords.

A compromised IAM-federated password from a standard account enables immediate use as a second authentication factor, facilitating lateral movement among other Linux fleet members. Emergency users remain unaffected because each Linux system relies on an individual local password. M2M credentials act as either local, distinct values or function through IAM-federated, shared secrets. Since passwords undergo periodic changes, Chiasson and van Oorschot quantify the security advantage of a password expiration policy, concluding that the improvement offers only minimal benefit and raises doubts when considering overall cost [3].

4.3   TOTP (3. Authentication Factor)

After successful acquisition of a private key and password, an offender proceeds with TOTP as the third factor for regular or emergency authentication. If a TOTP contains k_{TOTP} characters from a set C_{TOTP}, then $N_{\mathrm{TOTP}} = C_{\mathrm{TOTP}}^{k_{\mathrm{TOTP}}}$. The probability for guessing a correct TOTP in one attempt equals $P_{\mathrm{TOTP}} = \frac{1}{N_{\mathrm{TOTP}}} = \frac{1}{C_{\mathrm{TOTP}}^{k_{\mathrm{TOTP}}}}$. Each TOTP remains valid for T_{valid} seconds, then rotates to a fresh value. The IAM delivers a success or failure response exactly T_{resp} seconds after each submission. When a maximum of n authentication requests undergo processing at any given time, no more than n attempts enter evaluation concurrently. The formula for guesses per validity period reads $N_{\mathrm{TOTP},T_{\mathrm{resp}},T_{\mathrm{valid}},n} = \left\lfloor \frac{T_{\mathrm{valid}}}{T_{\mathrm{resp}}} \right\rfloor \times n$, and the chance of obtaining at least one valid TOTP within that window uses $P_{\mathrm{TOTP},T_{\mathrm{resp}},T_{\mathrm{valid}},n} = 1 - (1 - P_{\mathrm{TOTP}})^{N_{\mathrm{TOTP},T_{\mathrm{resp}},T_{\mathrm{valid}},n}}$, a calculation derived from Jacob Bernoulli.

Applying representative values for the IAM prototype with a six-digit TOTP ($k_{\mathrm{TOTP}} = 6$), sourced from ten digits ($C_{\mathrm{TOTP}} = 10$), yields $P_{\mathrm{TOTP}} = \frac{1}{10^6} = 10^{-6}$. If TOTPs expire after $T_{\mathrm{valid}} = 30$ and responses require $T_{\mathrm{resp}} = 5$ seconds, while $n = 2$ parallel requests gain permission, the maximum number of guesses per interval computes as $N_{\mathrm{TOTP},5,30,2} = \left\lfloor \frac{30}{5} \right\rfloor \times 2 = 6 \times 2 = 12$. The likelihood of at least one successful guess per validity window evaluates to $P_{\mathrm{TOTP},5,30,2} = 1 - (1 - 10^{-6})^{12} \approx 1.2 \times 10^{-5}$. This combination of short lifespan, enforced response delay, and strict limit on guesses per slot considerably reduces the practicality of BFAs.

A leaked or guessed TOTP assigned to a regular user allows exploitation through lateral movement within its limited lifetime. Obtaining the underlying TOTP seed creates a much higher risk, since an attacker creates future valid TOTPs and gains opportunities for extended lateral movement. Knowledge or guessing of a TOTP for an emergency account allows reuse on the same host during the short configured window, as each Linux server uses a different seed for this special login. Discovery of such a seed permits the prediction of subsequent emergency TOTPs on the same endpoint, but does not allow movement between different servers.

4.4 E-Mail-Based ROTP (4. Authentication Factor)

After overcoming the first three of four credentials for a typical IAM-federated account, an attacker faces the challenge of executing a BFA on ROTP via e-mail during the final authentication stage. Entering the correct TOTP as the third factor prompts the IAM system to transmit the ROTP to the user's secondary e-mail address, granting access only to the legitimate account holder. Algorithm 1 specifies the ROTP as a six-digit value, matching the TOTP format for user convenience. Greater ROTP complexity significantly increases the difficulty of BFAs. Algorithms 1 and 2 allow only one attempt for each ROTP entry. An incorrect ROTP forces an attacker to restart the authentication process and guess a newly generated ROTP. The probability P_{ROTP} of guessing the correct ROTP with a single attempt depends on the total number of possible permutations. For an ROTP containing k_{ROTP} characters, each drawn independently from a human-readable set of size C_{ROTP}, the formula $N_{\mathrm{ROTP}} = C_{\mathrm{ROTP}}^{k_{\mathrm{ROTP}}}$ calculates the number of available options, meaning $P_{\mathrm{ROTP}} = \frac{1}{C_{\mathrm{ROTP}}^{k_{\mathrm{ROTP}}}}$.

For example, each position allows any of $C_{\mathrm{ROTP}} = 94$ printable characters (uppercase, lowercase, digits, and symbols) when the ROTP contains $k_{\mathrm{ROTP}} = 6$ places. This arrangement yields $P_{\mathrm{ROTP}} = \frac{1}{94^6} \approx 1.45 \times 10^{-12}$, offering strong resistance against guessing. If a system sets the ROTP as six digits (0–9), the character set shrinks to $C_{\mathrm{ROTP}} = 10$, so $N_{\mathrm{ROTP}} = 10^6 = 1{,}000{,}000$, producing $P_{\mathrm{ROTP}} = \frac{1}{10^6} = 10^{-6}$.

The latter setup yields lower entropy than a ROTP that uses arbitrary human-readable characters, yet it still limits BFA opportunities, especially when expiration after failed attempts prevents repeated guessing and lateral movement. This highlights the importance of reducing attempts and selecting longer or more complex ROTPs in high-security environments.

Table 3 summarizes all aforementioned exemplary guessing probabilities and lateral movement opportunities, focusing on attacks originating from whitelisted source IP addresses or subnets. Note that BFAs targeting only TOTP or ROTP do not create significant impact, since the IAM system does not disclose which authentication factor fails. Therefore, the combined likelihood of successfully guessing TOTP and ROTP, $P_{\mathrm{TOTP},T_{\mathrm{resp}},T_{\mathrm{valid}},n \cap \mathrm{ROTP}} = P_{\mathrm{TOTP},T_{\mathrm{resp}},T_{\mathrm{valid}},n} \times P_{\mathrm{ROTP}}$, provides more relevant information than each individual probability. With the introduced exemplary values, the calculation $P_{\mathrm{TOTP},5,30,2 \cap \mathrm{ROTP}} = P_{\mathrm{TOTP},5,30,2} \times P_{\mathrm{ROTP}}$ yields 10^{-12} per attempt or approximately 1.2×10^{-11} per TOTP.

Despite the robustness of the presented IAM, analysis must address a catastrophic scenario involving an attacker who acquires every item of a user's authentication material. With these assets, the intruder impersonates the genuine user flawlessly, navigating all authentication layers while executing actions as the legitimate account holder. At this point, traditional access controls and credential checks deliver no meaningful protection.

Such a breach produces severe consequences. Attackers move laterally across the Linux fleet, escalate rights, and establish persistent footholds. Standard logs

Table 3. Summary of likelihoods related to guessing unknown authentication credentials and evaluating sharing status across Linux fleet

Unknown Authentication Credential	Guessing Probability	Regular Authentication	Emergency Authentication	M2M Authentication
1. Private Key	$\approx 2.94 \times 10^{-39}$ per attempt	shared	shared	shared
2. Password	$\approx 2.66 \times 10^{-32}$ per attempt	shared	distinct	distinct or shared
3. TOTP	10^{-6} per attempt $\approx 1.2 \times 10^{-5}$ per TOTP	shared	distinct	not applicable
4. ROTP	10^{-6} per attempt	shared	not applicable	not applicable

record valid authentication events, which obscures the line between malicious and benign activity.

Detection at this stage demands mechanisms that extend beyond authentication. Integrating behavioral and contextual anomaly detection into security monitoring frameworks yields high-fidelity indicators of compromise, enhancing the precision of threat identification and the effectiveness of response within dynamic environments. For example, logins from unexpected locations or during unusual hours often indicate intrusion. Access patterns that deviate from a user's routine, such as interaction with rarely used systems or execution of uncommon commands, suggest compromise. Device fingerprinting, network path analysis, and rate-of-access monitoring strengthen defenses, especially when integrated with Security Information and Event Management (SIEM) or anomaly-detection platforms.

An IAM platform that supports MFA cannot distinguish an intruder wielding fully compromised credentials from a legitimate user. In this worst-case scenario, defenders must shift focus away from credential verification and concentrate on continuous observation of behavior, environmental context, and deviations from established baselines. Only such strategies deliver reliable protection against adversaries who evade every authentication measure.

5   Conclusion

The literature survey in Sect. 2 shows that no current IAM proposal dedicates itself to preventing both intrusion and lateral movement within Linux fleets via SSH.

Section 3 presents an IAM with MFA for SSH, filling a critical security gap. The IAM introduces a novel design that combines four independent authentication factors across three login scenarios, strengthening defenses against BFAs, credential reuse, and other common attack vectors. Unlike conventional setups that store secrets separately on each host, OpenLDAP-based centralized authentication prevents easy extraction of factors for lateral movement even after attackers compromise a single node.

The security evaluation in Sect. 4 explores resilience against varied attacks, such as BFAs, buffer overflows, and credential leaks. However, the evaluation identifies a single limitation. When adversaries collect all authentication factors, the IAM cannot distinguish legitimate activity from malicious incidents. Organizations, therefore, must adopt continuous monitoring and advanced detection strategies for behavior, anomalies, and baselines in such extreme cases.

In practice, the work offers robust protection for organizations that deploy large-scale Linux environments. Future research should enhance orchestration platforms to support TOTP as a third authentication factor and ROTP as a fourth, while simplifying integration within modern Linux distributions. Moreover, further scrutiny of the order of the four authentication factors merits attention. Ultimately, a successor to this treatise should position itself more clearly with respect to existing SSH access management solutions and modern identity architectures. Progress along these lines will strengthen readiness for emerging threats while maintaining rigorous security across increasingly targeted infrastructures.

Acknowledgement. Many thanks to Bettina Baumgartner from the University of Vienna for proofreading this paper!

References

1. Barker, E.: Recommendation for Key Management: Part 1 – General. National Institute of Standards and Technology (NIST) (2020). https://doi.org/10.6028/NIST.SP.800-57pt1r5
2. Binnie, C.: Securing SSH with PAM. In: Practical Linux Topics, pp. 51–59. Apress, Berkeley, CA (2016). https://doi.org/10.1007/978-1-4842-1772-6_6
3. Chiasson, S., van Oorschot, P.C.: Quantifying the security advantage of password expiration policies. Des. Codes Cryptograph. **77**(2), 401–408 (2015). https://doi.org/10.1007/s10623-015-0071-9
4. Daemen, J., Rijmen, V.: The Design of Rijndael: AES – The Advanced Encryption Standard. Information Security and Cryptography, Springer, Heidelberg, 1st edn. (2001). https://doi.org/10.1007/978-3-540-42580-9
5. Daemen, J., Rijmen, V.: The Design of Rijndael: The Advanced Encryption Standard (AES). Information Security and Cryptography, Springer, Heidelberg, 2nd edn. (2019). https://doi.org/10.1007/978-3-662-60769-5
6. Europol: Internet Organised Crime Threat Assessment (IOCTA) 2025. Europol (2025). https://doi.org/10.2813/4926508
7. Fahrnberger, G.: Contemporary IT security for military online collaboration platforms. In: Proceedings of the 18th International Conference on Distributed Computing and Networking. ICDCN 2017, pp. 33:1–33:10. Association for Computing Machinery, New York (2017). https://doi.org/10.1145/3007748.3007754

8. Fahrnberger, G.: Realtime risk monitoring of SSH brute force attacks. In: Phillipson, F., Eichler, G., Erfurth, C., Fahrnberger, G. (eds.) Innovations for Community Services, pp. 75–95. Communications in Computer and Information Science, Springer Cham (2022). https://doi.org/10.1007/978-3-031-06668-9_8

9. Fahrnberger, G.: Bloom filter-based realtime risk monitoring of SSH brute force attacks. In: Krieger, U.R., Eichler, G., Erfurth, C., Fahrnberger, G. (eds.) Innovations for Community Services, pp. 48–67. CCIS, Springer, Cham (2023). https://doi.org/10.1007/978-3-031-40852-6_3

10. Fahrnberger, G.: Pattern-and similarity-based realtime risk monitoring of SSH brute force attacks with bloom filters. In: 2024 36th Conference of Open Innovations Association (FRUCT), vol. 36, pp. 133–144. IEEE (2024). https://doi.org/10.23919/FRUCT64283.2024.10749895

11. Fahrnberger, G.: A pluggable authentication module for E-Mail as a secure additional authentication factor. In: Zielinski, S., Eichler, G., Erfurth, C., Fahrnberger, G. (eds.) Innovations for Community Services, pp. 23–35. Communications in Computer and Information Science, Springer, Cham (2025). https://doi.org/10.1007/978-3-031-94263-1_2

12. Finseth, C.A.: An Access Control Protocol, Sometimes Called TACACS. RFC 1492 (Informational) (1993). https://doi.org/10.17487/RFC1492

13. Ge, Y., Zhu, Q.: GAZETA: GAme-Theoretic ZEro-trust authentication for defense against lateral movement in 5G IoT networks. IEEE Trans. Inf. Forensics Secur. **19**, 540–554 (2024). https://doi.org/10.1109/TIFS.2023.3326975

14. Grimes, R.A.: The many ways to Hack 2FA. Netw. Secur. **2019**(9), 8–13 (2019). https://doi.org/10.1016/S1353-4858(19)30107-2

15. Grimes, R.A.: Hacking Multifactor Authentication. Wiley (2020). https://doi.org/10.1002/9781119672357

16. Harrison, R.: Lightweight Directory Access Protocol (LDAP): Authentication Methods and Security Mechanisms. RFC 4513 (Proposed Standard) (2006). https://doi.org/10.17487/RFC4513

17. Hien, T.N.T., Sangsongfa, A., Amm-Dee, N.: Discovering personal data security issues: insights from "Have I Been Pwned". In: Singh, M., Tyagi, V., Gupta, P.K., Flusser, J., Ören, T., Cherif, A.R., Tomar, R. (eds.) Advances in Computing and Data Sciences, pp. 259–269. Springer, Cham, Switzerland (2024). https://doi.org/10.1007/978-3-031-70906-7_22

18. Kaloroumakis, P.E., Smith, M.J.: Toward a Knowledge Graph of Cybersecurity Countermeasures. Technical report, Massachusetts Institute of Technology Research and Engineering (MITRE) Corporation (2021). https://d3fend.mitre.org/resources/D3FEND.pdf

19. Kim, I.: Out-of-band OTP-based 2FA architecture for secure linux platforms in control and automation systems. Int. J. Control, Autom. Syst. **23**(9), 2611–2619 (2025). https://doi.org/10.1007/s12555-025-0225-0

20. Kjorveziroski, V., Mishev, A., Filiposka, S.: Cybersecurity Training Platforms Assessment. In: Dimitrova, V., Dimitrovski, I. (eds.) ICT Innovations 2020. Machine Learning and Applications, pp. 174–188. Springer, Cham (2020). https://doi.org/10.1007/978-3-030-62098-1_15

21. Kraft, A.: Municipal Cybersecurity Enhancement (2024). https://www.diva-portal.org/smash/record.jsf?dswid=-8666

22. Legg, S.: Lightweight Directory Access Protocol (LDAP): Syntaxes and Matching Rules. RFC 4517 (Proposed Standard) (2006). https://doi.org/10.17487/RFC4517

23. Legg, S.: Lightweight Directory Access Protocol (LDAP): The Binary Encoding Option. RFC 4522 (Proposed Standard) (2006). https://doi.org/10.17487/RFC4522

24. Lehtinen, S., Lonvick, C.: The Secure Shell (SSH) Protocol Assigned Numbers. RFC 4250 (Proposed Standard) (2006). https://doi.org/10.17487/RFC4250
25. Lucas, M.W.: PAM Mastery. Tilted Windmill Press, 1st edn. (2016)
26. Lucas, M.W.: SSH Mastery: OpenSSH, PuTTY, Tunnels, and Keys. Tilted Windmill Press, 2nd edn. (2018)
27. Qiao, L., Bo, J., Guo, L., Hu, F., Hu, N., Ran, R.: Tools of centralized management platform based on puppet and ansible. In: IOP Conference Series: Materials Science and Engineering, vol. 750, no. 1, pp. 1–6 (2020). https://doi.org/10.1088/1757-899X/750/1/012226
28. Rigney, C., Rubens, A.C., Simpson, W.A., Willens, S.: Remote Authentication Dial In User Service (RADIUS). RFC 2865 (Draft Standard) (2000). https://doi.org/10.17487/RFC2865
29. Rivest, R.L., Shamir, A., Adleman, L.: A method for obtaining digital signatures and public-key cryptosystems. Commun. ACM **21**(2), 120–126 (1978). https://doi.org/10.1145/359340.359342
30. Sciberras, A.: Lightweight Directory Access Protocol (LDAP): Schema for User Applications. RFC 4519 (Proposed Standard) (2006). https://doi.org/10.17487/RFC4519
31. Sermersheim, J.: Lightweight Directory Access Protocol (LDAP): The Protocol. RFC 4511 (Proposed Standard) (2006). https://doi.org/10.17487/RFC4511
32. Simmel, D., Filus, S.: Flexible enforcement of multi-factor authentication with SSH via linux-PAM for federated identity users. In: Practice and Experience in Advanced Research Computing 2017: Sustainability, Success and Impact PEARC 2017, pp. 1–9. Association for Computing Machinery, New York (2017). https://doi.org/10.1145/3093338.3093392
33. Smith, M., Howes, T.: Lightweight Directory Access Protocol (LDAP): String Representation of Search Filters. RFC 4515 (Proposed Standard) (2006). https://doi.org/10.17487/RFC4515
34. Smith, M., Howes, T.: Lightweight Directory Access Protocol (LDAP): Uniform Resource Locator. RFC 4516 (Proposed Standard) (2006). https://doi.org/10.17487/RFC4516
35. Strom, B.E., et al.: Finding Cyber Threats with ATT&CK^{TM}-Based Analytics. Technical report, Massachusetts Institute of Technology Research and Engineering (MITRE) Corporation (2017). https://apps.dtic.mil/sti/trecms/pdf/AD1107945.pdf
36. Ylönen, T., Lonvick, C.: The Secure Shell (SSH) Authentication Protocol. RFC 4252 (Proposed Standard) (2006). https://doi.org/10.17487/RFC4252
37. Ylönen, T., Lonvick, C.: The Secure Shell (SSH) Connection Protocol. RFC 4254 (Proposed Standard) (2006). https://doi.org/10.17487/RFC4254
38. Ylönen, T., Lonvick, C.: The Secure Shell (SSH) Protocol Architecture. RFC 4251 (Proposed Standard) (2006). https://doi.org/10.17487/RFC4251
39. Ylönen, T., Lonvick, C.: The Secure Shell (SSH) Transport Layer Protocol. RFC 4253 (Proposed Standard) (2006). https://doi.org/10.17487/RFC4253
40. Zeilenga, K.D.: Considerations for Lightweight Directory Access Protocol (LDAP) Extensions. RFC 4521 (Best Current Practice) (2006). https://doi.org/10.17487/RFC4521
41. Zeilenga, K.D.: COSINE LDAP/X.500 Schema. RFC 4524 (Proposed Standard) (2006). https://doi.org/10.17487/RFC4524
42. Zeilenga, K.D.: Internet Assigned Numbers Authority (IANA) Considerations for the Lightweight Directory Access Protocol (LDAP). RFC 4520 (Best Current Practice) (2006). https://doi.org/10.17487/RFC4520

43. Zeilenga, K.D.: Lightweight Directory Access Protocol (LDAP) Absolute True and False Filters. RFC 4526 (Proposed Standard) (2006). https://doi.org/10.17487/RFC4526
44. Zeilenga, K.D.: Lightweight Directory Access Protocol (LDAP) Assertion Control. RFC 4528 (Proposed Standard) (2006). https://doi.org/10.17487/RFC4528
45. Zeilenga, K.D.: Lightweight Directory Access Protocol (LDAP): Directory Information Models. RFC 4512 (Proposed Standard) (2006). https://doi.org/10.17487/RFC4512
46. Zeilenga, K.D.: Lightweight Directory Access Protocol (LDAP) entryUUID Operational Attribute. RFC 4530 (Proposed Standard) (2006). https://doi.org/10.17487/RFC4530
47. Zeilenga, K.D.: Lightweight Directory Access Protocol (LDAP): Internationalized String Preparation. RFC 4518 (Proposed Standard) (2006). https://doi.org/10.17487/RFC4518
48. Zeilenga, K.D.: Lightweight Directory Access Protocol (LDAP) Modify-Increment Extension. RFC 4525 (Informational) (2006). https://doi.org/10.17487/RFC4525
49. Zeilenga, K.D.: Lightweight Directory Access Protocol (LDAP) Read Entry Controls. RFC 4527 (Proposed Standard) (2006). https://doi.org/10.17487/RFC4527
50. Zeilenga, K.D.: Lightweight Directory Access Protocol (LDAP): Schema Definitions for X.509 Certificates. RFC 4523 (Proposed Standard) (2006). https://doi.org/10.17487/RFC4523
51. Zeilenga, K.D.: Lightweight Directory Access Protocol (LDAP): String Representation of Distinguished Names. RFC 4514 (Proposed Standard) (2006). https://doi.org/10.17487/RFC4514
52. Zeilenga, K.D.: Lightweight Directory Access Protocol (LDAP): Technical Specification Road Map. RFC 4510 (Proposed Standard) (2006). https://doi.org/10.17487/RFC4510
53. Zeilenga, K.D.: Lightweight Directory Access Protocol (LDAP) Turn Operation. RFC 4531 (Experimental) (2006). https://doi.org/10.17487/RFC4531
54. Zeilenga, K.D.: Lightweight Directory Access Protocol (LDAP) "Who am I?" Operation. RFC 4532 (Proposed Standard) (2006). https://doi.org/10.17487/RFC4532
55. Zeilenga, K.D.: Requesting Attributes by Object Class in the Lightweight Directory Access Protocol (LDAP). RFC 4529 (Informational) (2006). https://doi.org/10.17487/RFC4529
56. Zeilenga, K.D., Choi, J.H.: The Lightweight Directory Access Protocol (LDAP) Content Synchronization Operation. RFC 4533 (Experimental) (2006). https://doi.org/10.17487/RFC4533

Individual Trust and Preferences for Identity Management in Private, Professional, and Community Service Contexts

Michael Hofmeier[(✉)][ID], Isabelle Haunschild[ID], and Wolfgang Hommel[ID]

University of the Bundeswehr Munich, Neubiberg, Germany
`{michael.hofmeier,isabelle.haunschild,wolfgang.hommel}@unibw.de`

Abstract. Digital identity management systems constitute a fundamental building block of modern digital services. While federated identity management is widely deployed due to its usability and administrative efficiency, self-sovereign identity (SSI) has emerged as a privacy-preserving, user-centric alternative. However, the suitability of these paradigms depends strongly on the context in which digital identities operate. In this paper, we investigate users' trust and preferences regarding identity management approaches across private, professional, and community service contexts. We report on the results of an online survey with 876 valid participants conducted in Germany. The study examines technology commitment, preferences for personal data control, and context-dependent trust in self-managed wallets, internal organizational identity providers, and external federated providers. Our results indicate a general tendency toward SSI for personal data control, which correlates with higher technology commitment and age. At the same time, trust assessments clearly differ by context: while SSI is preferred in private and community settings, internal organizational identity management systems are perceived as most trustworthy in professional environments. These findings underline the importance of context-aware identity management designs and suggest that hybrid approaches combining centralized and self-sovereign elements may best align with user expectations.

Keywords: Digital sovereignty · Identity management · System trust

1 Introduction

Digital identity management systems (IDMS) are the central building block for digitized processes [12]. Federated identity management in particular, i.e., authentication via central platforms using single sign-on (SSO) protocols, is now a well-standardized and widely used procedure. Due to data protection concerns, approaches such as self-sovereign identity management (SSI) have been developed, whereby users store their data and verification material in a self-managed digital wallet, usually on their smartphone [2]. Since this gain in data protection

© The Author(s), under exclusive license to Springer Nature Switzerland AG 2026
K. Kirchner et al. (Eds.): I4CS 2026, CCIS 3007, pp. 39–54, 2026.
https://doi.org/10.1007/978-3-032-27096-2_3

and sovereignty also brings additional responsibility in terms of data protection and security, it is necessary to examine which systems make sense from the user's point of view, and in which contexts. It is also important to consider where and by whom a central service is hosted. For example, it can be assumed that a system managed by the organization is acceptable in the context of professional identity, but this needs to be verified. This study was conducted using a questionnaire with 876 valid participants.

1.1 Motivation

In our previous work [11], we surveyed users' ratings of the usability of electronic signature systems. We found correlations between usability ratings and individual technology commitment. In order to further investigate how digitization can be designed to take users into account, we now want to determine users' preferences for identity management. We differentiate between the contexts in which identity management systems are used. An individual may have a private identity, a professional identity, and also a community service identity.

While both federated identity management and self-sovereign identity have been extensively discussed from architectural, cryptographic, and governance perspectives, little is known about how end users perceive and trust these approaches in different identity contexts [14]. Existing work often treats digital identity as a uniform concept, despite the fact that individuals routinely separate their private, professional, and community-related roles and apply different expectations regarding control, responsibility, and trust accordingly [17]. Moreover, the shift toward self-sovereign identity entails not only increased autonomy but also a transfer of responsibility to end users, which may affect acceptance and trust depending on individual characteristics such as technology commitment and perceived self-efficacy [3].

Against this background, this paper investigates how users evaluate and trust different identity management approaches across distinct identity contexts. In particular, we address the following research questions: (1) How does user trust in federated identity management and self-sovereign identity differ between private, professional, and community service contexts? (2) How are preferences for personal data control related to individual factors such as age, gender, and technology commitment? (3) Which identity management approaches are perceived as appropriate for professional use from the user's perspective?

To answer these questions, we present the results of a large-scale empirical study with 876 participants. The contribution of this work is threefold: first, we provide a quantitative analysis of context-dependent trust in identity management systems; second, we identify correlations between technology commitment and preferences for self-sovereign versus federated identity approaches; and third, we derive implications for the design of context-aware and hybrid identity management architectures that better align with users' expectations regarding trust, responsibility, and digital sovereignty.

1.2 Content

This work is structured as follows. Section 2 explains federated and self-sovereign identity management. Section 3 discusses the methodology and structure of the underlying questionnaire. Section 4 analyzes and interprets the results, and Sect. 5 discusses the results as a whole. Finally, Sect. 6 provides a conclusion and Sect. 7 presents the future outlook.

2 Federated and Self-Sovereign Identity

Digital identity systems can be distinguished by who controls identity data and how authentication and attribute assertions are exchanged between parties. Two prominent paradigms are *Federated Identity*, which is widely deployed in contemporary web and enterprise environments, and *Self-Sovereign Identity (SSI)*, which proposes a user-centric alternative emphasizing autonomy and data minimization [4,6].

2.1 Federated Identity

Federated Identity refers to an architectural model in which authentication and identity management are delegated to a trusted *Identity Provider (IdP)*, which vouches for a user toward one or more *Service Providers (SPs)*. Trust relationships are established at the organizational level, enabling users to access multiple services using a single digital identity [4].

Federated identity systems are commonly implemented using standardized protocols such as SAML, OAuth 2.0, or OpenID Connect [8]. They are prevalent in both private and professional contexts. In private usage, federated identity is often realized through social login mechanisms, where users authenticate to third-party services using existing accounts. In professional environments, federated identity forms the foundation of enterprise *Single Sign-On (SSO)* infrastructures, allowing employees to access internal systems and cloud services with centrally managed credentials.

From a community or public-service perspective, federated identity is widely adopted in e-government platforms, academic identity federations, and inter-organizational collaborations. While this model offers high usability and administrative efficiency, it introduces central points of control and observability, as identity providers may gain insight into users' authentication behavior across services. Furthermore, attribute disclosure is typically coarse-grained, and continued access depends on the availability and trustworthiness of the identity provider [4].

2.2 Self-sovereign Identity

Self-Sovereign Identity (SSI) represents a paradigm shift toward user-controlled digital identities, where individuals manage their own identifiers and credentials without relying on a central identity provider [18]. SSI systems are commonly based on *Decentralized Identifiers (DIDs)* and *Verifiable Credentials*, which can be cryptographically issued by trusted authorities and selectively presented by users [6].

In contrast to federated identity, SSI decouples authentication from identity data storage. Credentials are typically stored locally by the user, for example in digital wallets, and only the minimum required information is disclosed to a service provider. This enables fine-grained selective disclosure, supports privacy by design, and reduces linkability between interactions [15].

SSI is particularly relevant in private usage scenarios that require increased autonomy and privacy, such as age verification or membership proofs without persistent user accounts. In professional contexts, SSI has been proposed for representing qualifications, certifications, and employment credentials across organizational boundaries, reducing reliance on centralized identity infrastructures while preserving verifiability [6].

For community and civic services, SSI enables novel participation models, including community-issued credentials, volunteer attestations, or access to local services without long-term identity registration. However, SSI also introduces challenges related to key management responsibility for end users, ecosystem bootstrapping, governance, and interoperability across issuers and verifiers [15].

2.3   Comparison and Implications

In summary, federated identity prioritizes organizational trust, centralized administration, and usability, making it well suited for controlled environments such as enterprises, academic institutions, and government services [4]. SSI, by contrast, emphasizes user sovereignty, decentralization, and privacy, offering advantages in scenarios that require selective disclosure and cross-domain interoperability [6,18]. The choice between these paradigms involves trade-offs between usability, governance, scalability, and user empowerment, which are particularly relevant when designing identity solutions spanning private, professional, and community-based domains.

3   Method

The data in this study were collected through an online survey using a suitable and common web application [13] hosted on a server of our organization. The participants in the study were acquired by an external provider and the participants received financial compensation for their participation. For this reason, an attention check was implemented and quotas for age (18–34, 35–51, 52–66) and gender (male, female) were specified in order to achieve an appropriate spread. After completion, the data sets were analyzed and any invalid entries were eliminated. Before taking part, the participants were informed about the study procedure and data privacy. Participants then had to confirm that they were at least 18 years old and give their consent to take part in the study by ticking a box. Participation was voluntary. This study was approved by the ethics committee of the University of the Bundeswehr Munich (file reference number: EK UniBw M 25–48).

3.1 Structure of the Questionnaire

The questionnaire was structured as follows: First, demographic data was collected. After that, among other aspects, participants had to rate statements to determine their technology commitment. This was followed by questions on their preference for personal data control, questions on their trust on identity management approaches depending on the identity context (private, professional, community services), and a rating of statements on trust.

3.2 Technology Commitment

For each participant, we computed a Technology Commitment Score (TCS) [16]. The TCS comprises three subscales with four items each, capturing attitudes toward technology (*technology acceptance*), as well as *technology competence convictions* and *technology control convictions* [9]. Participants responded to twelve statements by indicating their level of agreement on a five-point Likert scale ranging from *not true at all* to *completely true*. The resulting score, $s_{TC} \in [1, 5]$, was calculated as the mean across all items. Since some statements (marked with *) were phrased negatively, their ratings had to be inverted. The twelve statements (items), translated from German, are listed below.

- **TB02-01**: I am very curious about new technical developments.
- **TB02-02**: I quickly take a liking to new technical developments.
- **TB02-03**: I am always interested in using the newest technical devices.
- **TB02-04**: If I had the opportunity, I would use technical products much more often than I currently do.
- **TB02-05***: I'm often afraid of failing when dealing with modern technology.
- **TB02-06***: For me, dealing with technical innovations is usually too much of a challenge.
- **TB02-07***: I'm afraid of breaking technical innovations rather than using them properly.
- **TB02-08***: I find dealing with technology difficult – I just can't handle it in most cases.
- **TB02-09**: Whether I am successful in using modern technology essentially depends on me.
- **TB02-10**: It is up to me whether I succeed in using new technical developments – it has little to do with chance or luck.
- **TB02-11**: If I have difficulties with technology, it is ultimately up to me to solve them.
- **TB02-12**: What happens when I deal with new technical developments is entirely under my control.

Subsequently, we categorized the participants' scores into three groups based on percentile cut-off values: *low* (below the 33rd percentile), *medium* (between the 33rd and 66th percentiles), and *high* (above the 66th percentile). Cronbach's alpha (α) was calculated in order to test the reliability of the scales.

3.3 Personal Data Control

In order to determine whether participants prefer self-managed wallets in the sense of SSI or a federated identity provider, twelve statements (items) were drafted, six of which were phrased positively (federated tendency) and six negatively (SSI tendency). Participants were asked to rate these statements on a five-point scale, with the negative statements (marked with *) being inverted for the overall score. This allows a score ($s_{PDC} \in [1,5]$) to be calculated, which indicates the preferred approach. A score of $s_{PDC} = 3$ indicates that none of the approaches is preferred, $s_{PDC} = 1$ represents SSI, and $s_{PDC} = 5$ represents federated identity management. The resulting ratings do not differ the different identity contexts and thus represent the general preference. Here also Cronbach's alpha (α) was calculated in order to test the reliability of this scale. ChatGPT (GPT-5.1, December 2025) was used to formulate and optimize the statements:

- **ID02-01**: I feel more comfortable when my important data is managed by a professional provider.
- **ID02-02**: I'm worried that I'll do something wrong with my own digital wallet and lose data.
- **ID02-03**: I trust that large providers or authorities can protect my data better than I can myself.
- **ID02-04**: I want to worry as little as possible about data security and backups in my everyday life.
- **ID02-05***: I want to have control over who can see and use my personal data.
- **ID02-06***: It is important to me that my data is not permanently stored on servers belonging to companies or other third parties.
- **ID02-07***: I trust myself to use an app on my smartphone responsibly when it comes to my personal data.
- **ID02-08***: I prefer to take responsibility for my digital data myself rather than relying on others.
- **ID02-09***: I'm more worried about a major provider being hacked than about me losing my smartphone.
- **ID02-10**: When in doubt, convenience is more important to me than maximum control over my data.
- **ID02-11***: I think it's okay that I am responsible for backups when I have my own digital wallet.
- **ID02-12**: The risk of irretrievably losing my digital IDs would be a deal-breaker for me when it comes to having my own digital wallet.

There was no single input that led to this item set. Rather, it was a lengthy discussion with the chatbot that allowed us to gradually refine and optimize the set.

3.4   Trust Rating by Identity Type

To determine the contexts in which participants trust different types of identity management more or less, they were asked to rate their trust in self-managed wallets, internal identity providers, and external identity providers on a five-point scale (*not at all, rather not, partly, rather yes, completely*). For private identity, only a rating for external providers and the self-managed wallet is possible.

3.5   Statements on Trust

In order to further interpret and confirm the results of the previous questions, participants were asked to rate on a five-point scale. The four statements to be evaluated are listed below:

- **ID07-01**: I want my work data to be managed by my employer. I don't want to store and control it myself in my own digital wallet.
- **ID07-02**: I trust my community organization to handle my data appropriately.
- **ID07-03**: I do not think that a self-managed digital wallet is useful for work.
- **ID07-04**: However, for my identity in the association or other communities, I would like to have a digital wallet that is under my control.

These items cannot be used to calculate a score, but they provide insight into the participants' views and may help to support or explain the results of the other questions.

4   Results and Findings

After the online survey was successfully completed, 876 valid data sets were available for evaluation. Figure 1 shows the demographic distribution of the participants and the distribution of their education. School education was the decisive factor for education.

4.1   Technology Commitment

Cronbach's alpha was calculated for technology commitment and for its subscales. technology commitment as a whole has an $\alpha = .84$, *technology acceptance* has an $\alpha = .89$, *technology competence convictions* have an $\alpha = .89$, and *technology control convictions* has an $\alpha = .82$ for $N = 876$. The TCS results in $s_{TC} = 3.35$ ($M = 3.35$, $SD = .676$). As mentioned in Subsect. 3.2 the participants have been categorized into three groups by the 33rd and 66th percentile.

The observed distribution of technology commitment provides an important lens for interpreting subsequent findings. The relatively balanced spread across low, medium, and high commitment groups ($N_{low} = 301, N_{med} = 303, N_{high} = 272$) allows evaluations of the other results by group with solid counts. High internal consistency values across all subscales suggest that technology acceptance,

Fig. 1. Demographic distribution of the participants and their education

competence convictions, and control convictions form a coherent construct, in line with prior validation studies [9, 16]. This supports the use of technology commitment as an explanatory variable for identity management preferences, as it reflects not only openness toward technology but also perceived self-efficacy and control, which have been shown to influence trust in complex digital systems [3].

4.2   Personal Data Control

Figure 2 shows the occurrences per statement (item) and rating as a relative bar chart. A rating of 1 is classified as favoring SSI, 2 as tending toward SSI, 3 as neutral, 4 as tending toward federated, and 5 as favoring federated. Items marked with an asterisk (*), which were qualitatively inverse, have been reversed accordingly. Cronbach's alpha for this item set results in $\alpha = .67$.

These results reveal a general trend toward SSI, as can be seen in Fig. 3. However, this overview does not provide information about which variants are preferred by different social groups across contexts.

Breaking down these ratings into groups provides a clearer picture. Figure 4 shows the ratings as a relative bar chart, grouped according to the three groups of technology commitment. Here, it can be observed that greater technology commitment is accompanied by a greater tendency toward SSI. The number of undecided ratings also increases with increasing technology commitment. However, it should be noted that this is still a context-independent rating.

Figure 5 shows the ratings as a relative bar chart, grouped by age and gender. It can be observed that there is nearly no difference between gender, but a higher age is combined with a higher tendency to SSI, or in other words, a lower readiness for federated approaches. Table 1 shows the correlation values for personal data control in combination with gender, age, technology commitment,

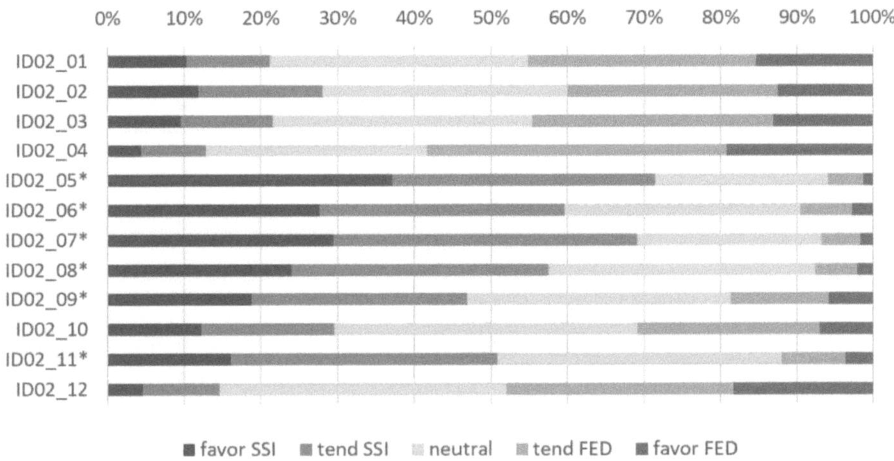

Fig. 2. Personal data control rating per item

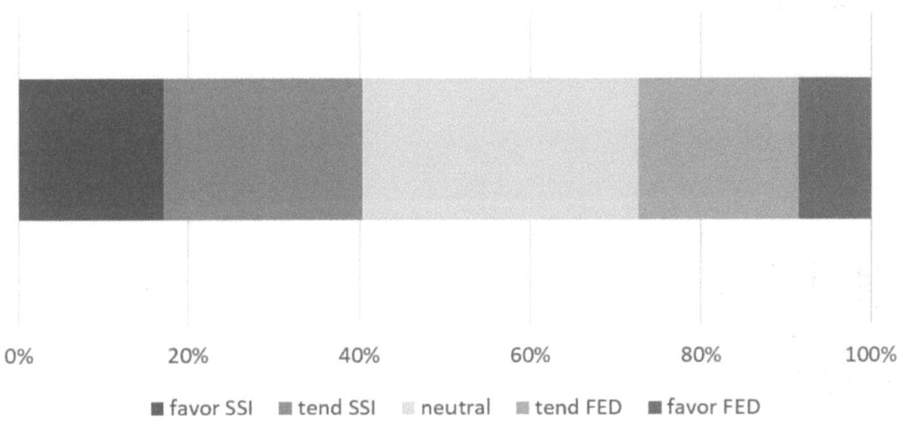

Fig. 3. General personal data control rating

and the technology commitment subscales in detail. Age, technology commitment, and *technology control convictions*, each show a weak negative correlation. *Technology competence convictions* shows a moderate negative correlation. All correlations, except with gender and technology acceptance, are significant.

Interpretation. The general tendency toward self-sovereign identity in terms of personal data control reflects a normative preference for autonomy and informational self-determination. However, the correlation analysis reveals that this tendency is not uniform across all participants. In particular, the moderate negative correlation with technology competence convictions suggests that users who

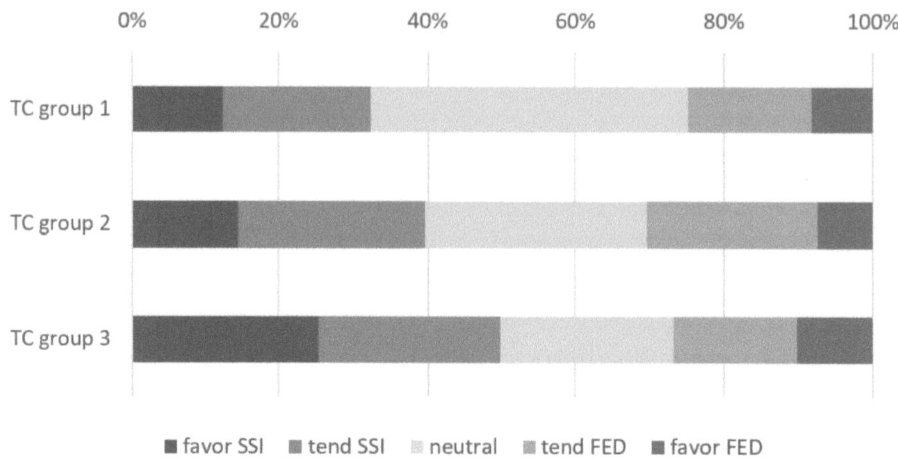

Fig. 4. Personal data control rating per technology commitment group

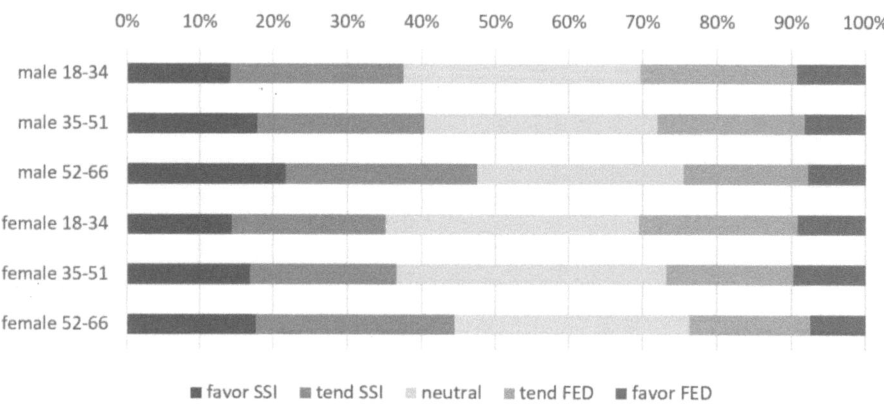

Fig. 5. Personal data control rating per age and gender

perceive themselves as technically capable are more willing to assume responsibility for managing their own digital identities. This finding aligns with research on self-efficacy in security and privacy contexts, which shows that perceived competence strongly affects users' willingness to engage with user-controlled security mechanisms [3]. At the same time, the substantial proportion of neutral responses indicates uncertainty rather than clear rejection of either approach, highlighting the importance of usability, recovery concepts, and support mechanisms in SSI designs.

Table 1. Correlations for personal data control

	gender	age	TC	TC_{acc}	TC_{cmp}	TC_{ctr}
Pearson corr.	.05	$-.20$**	$-.27$**	$-.05$	$-.34$**	$-.18$**
Sig. (2-tailed)	.164	$<.001$	$<.001$	.115	$<.001$	$<.001$

$N = 876$, ** The correlation is significant at the 0.01 level (two-tailed).

4.3   Trust by Context

Figure 6 shows the assessment of trust in internal organizational federated systems, external federated providers, and SSI wallets, separated by context. Trust in SSI is higher in the private context than in external providers. In the professional context, on the other hand, trust in internal federated systems is highest, while trust in external providers is lowest. In the context of community services, however, SSI is again in the lead, closely followed by internal systems, placing it between the private and professional contexts in terms of results. The results suggest that, also from the user's perspective, an internal organizational system for identity management is the most suitable choice in a professional context.

Interpretation. The context-dependent trust ratings clearly demonstrate that users apply different trust heuristics depending on the identity domain. In professional environments, trust is strongly associated with organizational responsibility and established accountability structures, which explains the preference for internally managed federated identity systems. This finding is consistent with the concept of contextual integrity, according to which privacy and trust expectations depend on social roles and norms rather than abstract technical properties [17]. In contrast, private and community contexts emphasize autonomy and limited disclosure, making SSI-based solutions more attractive. The community service context occupies an intermediate position, suggesting that users value both organizational trust and personal control, depending on the nature and perceived sensitivity of the interaction.

4.4   Statements on Trust

The interpretation that an internal organizational system is the better choice in the professional sphere, even from the user's point of view, is also supported by the evaluation of the statements shown in Fig. 7. The majority agrees that professional identity data should be managed by the employer. A majority also considers SSI wallets to be of little use in the professional sphere. In the context of community services, however, SSI wallets are preferred by a slight majority. Nevertheless, trust in internal data management is still relatively high.

Interpretation. The evaluation of the trust-related statements further substantiates the quantitative trust ratings. The strong agreement that employers

Fig. 6. System trust rating per context and approach

should manage professional identity data reflects a clear delegation of responsibility, indicating that users do not perceive self-sovereign identity as desirable in environments characterized by formal obligations and hierarchical structures. Conversely, the preference for self-managed wallets in community contexts points toward a desire for participation without long-term institutional dependency. Together, these findings reinforce the interpretation that trust in identity management systems is shaped less by technical decentralization alone and more by perceived responsibility, governance, and contextual expectations.

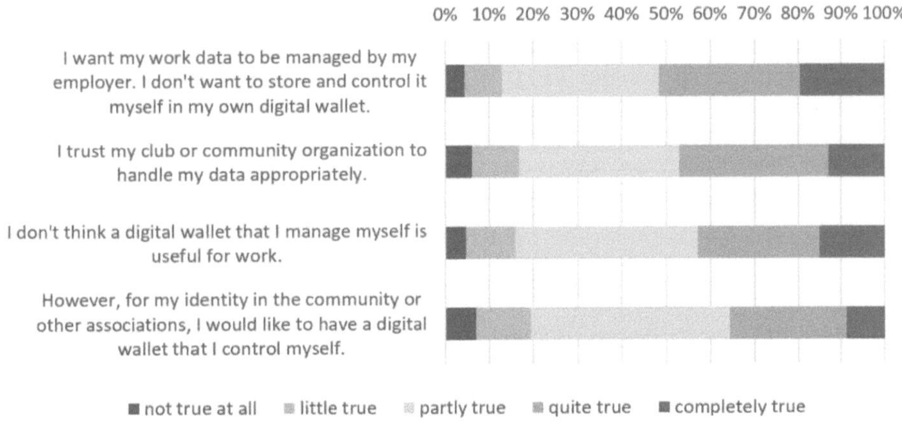

Fig. 7. Trust statement rating per item

5   Discussion

The results of this study highlight the contextual nature of trust and preferences in digital identity management. While self-sovereign identity is often promoted as a universally superior solution due to its privacy-preserving and user-centric properties, our findings suggest that its perceived suitability strongly depends on the identity context. Users differentiate between private, professional, and community-related identities and apply expectations regarding control, responsibility, and trust in each case.

In private contexts, SSI aligns well with users' mental models and normative expectations of digital sovereignty. In professional environments, however, users may prefer to delegate identity management responsibilities to their employer, valuing reliability, accountability, and organizational support over personal control. This delegation could indicate a rational response to the increased cognitive and operational burden associated with self-managed identity systems, which has been identified as a key barrier to adoption in prior security research [7, 10].

The community service context illustrates a hybrid trust model, combining elements of organizational trust with a desire for personal control. This intermediate position suggests that neither fully centralized nor fully self-sovereign approaches optimally address all user expectations. Instead, the findings point toward the potential of hybrid identity management architectures that integrate self-sovereign credentials into organizational frameworks, allowing users to retain control over attributes while benefiting from institutional trust anchors.

From a broader perspective, the results underline that digital sovereignty should not be interpreted solely as maximal technical decentralization. Rather, sovereignty from the user's perspective appears to include the freedom to delegate responsibility when appropriate. Designing identity management systems that respect this nuance requires a shift from purely technical decisions toward user-centric, context-aware approaches that explicitly consider trust, responsibility, and usability as design goals.

Several limitations of this study must be acknowledged. First, the results are based on self-reported attitudes and stated preferences, which may differ from actual behavior in real-world identity management scenarios, particularly in security- and privacy-related domains where intention-behavior gaps are well documented [1]. Second, the survey evaluates hypothetical trust in identity management approaches rather than hands-on experience with concrete SSI wallets or federated systems.

Third, the study was conducted exclusively in Germany, a context characterized by comparatively high institutional trust and a strong regulatory framework for data protection, most notably the General Data Protection Regulation (GDPR). Cultural, legal, and organizational differences may therefore limit the transferability of the findings to other regions [5]. Finally, the personal data control scale is acceptable due to the corresponding Cronbach's alpha.

6   Conclusion

This paper presented an empirical study on users' trust and preferences regarding identity management approaches across different identity contexts. Based on data from 876 participants, we analyzed how technology commitment, demographic factors, and contextual usage are associated with attitudes toward federated identity management and self-sovereign identity. The results show that, on an abstract level, many users express a preference for greater personal control over their data, which is associated with a tendency toward SSI-based solutions. This tendency increases with higher technology commitment and age, while gender shows no significant influence. However, in professional environments, participants prefer internal organizational identity providers and largely reject the idea of managing work-related identities in self-sovereign wallets. In contrast, SSI is perceived as more trustworthy for private identities and slightly preferred in community service contexts, where both self-managed wallets and internal organizational solutions receive comparatively high trust ratings.

These findings highlight that user trust in identity management is context-dependent and cannot be captured by a one-size-fits-all approach. While SSI aligns well with expectations of autonomy and privacy in private and civic scenarios, centralized and employer-managed identity systems remain the preferred solution for professional use cases. From a user perspective, this supports the continued relevance of federated identity management in organizational settings while simultaneously motivating the integration of SSI concepts where user sovereignty and selective disclosure are paramount.

7   Future Work

Future research should extend this work in several directions. First, longitudinal studies could investigate how trust and preferences evolve over time as users gain more hands-on experience with SSI wallets and decentralized identity ecosystems. Second, qualitative methods such as interviews or focus groups could provide deeper insights into the underlying mental models, concerns, and expectations that shape users' trust judgments in different contexts. Furthermore, replicating the study in other regions would help assess the generalizability of the findings beyond Germany. From a design perspective, future work should explore hybrid identity management architectures that combine organizational control with self-sovereign mechanisms, for example by integrating SSI-based credentials into enterprise identity infrastructures.

Acknowledgement. This work originates from the LIONS research project. LIONS is funded by dtec.bw—Digitalization and Technology Research Center of the Bundeswehr, which we gratefully acknowledge. dtec.bw is funded by the European Union—NextGenerationEU.

References

1. Acquisti, A., Brandimarte, L., Loewenstein, G.: Privacy and human behavior in the age of information. Science **347**(6221), 509–514 (2015)
2. Babel, M., et al.: Self-sovereign identity and digital wallets. Electron. Mark. **35**(1), 1–14 (2025)
3. Bandura, A.: Self-Efficacy: The Exercise of Control. Macmillan (1997)
4. Cameron, K.: The laws of identity. Microsoft Corp **12**, 8–11 (2005)
5. Dinev, T., Hart, P., Mullen, M.R.: Internet privacy concerns and beliefs about government surveillance-an empirical investigation. J. Strateg. Inf. Syst. **17**(3), 214–233 (2008)
6. Ferdous, M.S., Chowdhury, F., Alassafi, M.O.: In search of self-sovereign identity leveraging blockchain technology. IEEE Access **7**, 103059–103079 (2019)
7. Gaw, S., Felten, E.W., Fernandez-Kelly, P.: Secrecy, flagging, and paranoia: adoption criteria in encrypted email. In: Proceedings of the SIGCHI Conference on Human Factors in Computing Systems, pp. 591–600 (2006)
8. Hardt, D.: The OAuth 2.0 authorization framework. Tech. rep. (2012)
9. Haunschild, I., Leipold, B.: The relevance of the facets of technology commitment for dealing with digital media and security precautions. In: Sovereign by Design - The LIONSApproach to Digital Sovereignty, pp. 199–210 (2024)
10. Herley, C.: So long, and no thanks for the externalities: the rational rejection of security advice by users. In: Proceedings of the 2009 Workshop on New Security Paradigms Workshop, pp. 133–144 (2009)
11. Hofmeier, M., Haunschild, I., Hofmeier, M., Hommel, W.: Individual technology commitment and the rating of usability and trustworthiness of electronic signature systems. In: International Conference on Human-Computer Interaction, pp. 42–55. Springer (2025)
12. ISO/IEC: ISO/IEC 24760-1: 2019 it security and privacy—a framework for identity management—part 1: terminology and concepts (2021)
13. Leiner, D.: SoSci survey [computer software] (2019). Accessed May 9 2024
14. Martin, N., Metzger, F.M.: The chimera of control: self-sovereign identity, data control, and user perceptions. Hum. Technol. **20**(2), 183–223 (2024)

15. Naik, N., Jenkins, P.: Self-sovereign identity specifications: govern your identity through your digital wallet using blockchain technology. In: 2020 8th IEEE International Conference on Mobile Cloud Computing, Services, and Engineering (Mobile-Cloud), pp. 90–95. IEEE (2020)
16. Neyer, F.J., Felber, J., Gebhardt, C.: Entwicklung und Validierung einer Kurzskala zur Erfassung von Technikbereitschaft. Diagnostica (2012)
17. Nissenbaum, H.: Privacy in context: technology, policy, and the integrity of social life. In: Privacy in Context. Stanford University Press (2009)
18. Tobin, A., Reed, D.: The inevitable rise of self-sovereign identity. Sovrin Found. **29**(2016), 18 (2016)

Re-Visited: Fountain Code Implementation with Resilience Measurement

Dirk Westhoff[✉]

Offenburg University of Applied Sciences, Offenburg, Germany
`dirk.weshoff@hs-offenbug.de`

Abstract. We examine fountain codes (LT-codes) and their suitable parameterization based on our own PoC implementation with regard to their resilience. We use benchmark values from Hyytiä and co-authors for comparison. We achieve i) partially better results and, as a new aspect, also offer ii) detailed evaluations for noise and different jamming types. Moreover, our work addresses iii) previously unaddressed aspects which need to be considered for a performant implementation of on-the-fly decoding and how this impacts jamming. We remark that RaptorQ originate from LT-codes with its inner encoding derived from it.

Keywords: Fountain codes · Jamming · LT codes · Noise · PoC implementation

1 Introduction

Resilient digital systems require fault-tolerant communication that is robust to a certain extent against external interference. For multicast/broadcast communication, methods belonging to the class of forward error correction methods are to be evaluated. The appeal of forward error correction methods lies in the fact that, in the event of errors in the form of undelivered data units due to noise on the transmission path, no feedback in the form of negative acknowledgments (NACKs) is required on the sender side. This feature is becoming increasingly relevant with a growing number of addressed recipients, as it can lead to many NACKs being sent due to lost payload data. This can result in further reductions in the payload data actually to be transmitted and, in the worst case, complete congestion of the transmission channel. The aim of this work is to gain a better understanding of fountain codes respectively LT-codes and to examine different parameterizations in more detail. One focus is on the investigation of its inherent resilience with respect to interferences such as noise, but also jamming and selective jamming on the transmission path. We aim to propose suitable parameterizations and validate it with our own PoC-implementation[1].

We started by reading Michel Luby's landmark work on LT codes [2]. Then we tried to understand individual mathematical formulas with the aim of developing pseudo code

---

[1] We could have used available implementations, or, to ease the implementation process, apply AI for code generation. However, both approaches would not have revealed the results we present in this work.

K. Kirchner et al. (Eds.): I4CS 2026, CCIS 3007, pp. 55–69, 2026.
https://doi.org/10.1007/978-3-032-27096-2_4

from them. This serves as the basis for implementing a transmitter process and a receiver process to be executed later. In doing so, one inevitably has to go through different phases of technical penetration. At each of these levels, there are "manual manufacturing tolerances" wherever the descriptions in the publication are too vague, or because (un)conscious decisions during the implementation of algorithms and data structures have led to further dependencies or constraints (see Fig. 1). In Michel Luby's landmark work, as well as in subsequent work, researchers have devoted themselves intensively to an essential parameter of this type of coding, known as degree distribution. Different degree distributions have been presented and discussed and analyzed mathematically in terms of their advantages and disadvantages. It is undisputed that the choice of a suitable degree distribution is very decisive for the functioning of codes of this type in terms of their robustness against interference, but also in terms of their fundamental ability to successfully complete the decoding process on the receiver side. Certainly, we are not going to reinvent degree distributions here and will use existing, well-researched degree distributions [1–3]. However, other parameters whose effects on the decoding result are not such influential at first glance have so far been completely omitted from the discussion and analysis. But it is precisely these parameters that require decisions to be made when moving from thinking to doing, i.e., implementing. Decisions whose effects on the overall result are often rather subtle. For example, implementing fountain codes also requires the implementation of "randomness" at one point or another. How should this be converted into rigid program code, and does the randomness implemented in this way still have the desired properties? What is advantageous and even essential for a high-performance implementation of fountain codes has to be considered. These and other design decisions, which are often underestimated, provide the value of this work.

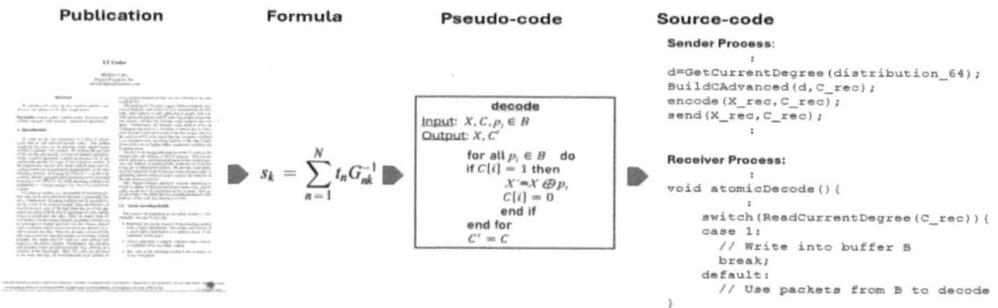

$$s_k = \sum_{n=1}^{N} t_n G_{nk}^{-1}$$

Fig. 1. "Manual manufacturing tolerances" at each level of the development process

The rest of the paper is structured as follows: In Sect. 2 we discuss related work, whereas in Sect. 3 we briefly introduce LT-Codes. Before discussing implementation aspects in Sect. 5 in Sect. 4 we identify relevant parameters. Sections 6, 7, and 8 evaluate our PoC-implementation with respect to noise, different jamming types and pollution. Section 9 concludes and denotes open issues.

2 Related Work

Michael Luby [2] and co-authors [4] have described a coding method that can be used to transmit data robustly over a noisy medium. LT codes or fountain codes in general are designed to be resilient to interference caused by noise on the transmission path by using redundancy in the data to enable the receiver to calculate the originally transmitted data despite individual losses. Such coding not only detects errors, but is also able to correct errors in the data on the receiver side. This means that such codes can be classified as forward error correction methods, in contrast to backward error correction methods, where the receiver can only detect whether a transmission error has occurred, but cannot correct it independently. Backward error correction methods/protocols always require the sender to be asked to resend the incorrectly received data in order to correct an error. This is not necessary with these codes. After receiving a certain number of data units, the receiver is able to independently deduce the correct data without requesting the sender to resend the incorrectly received data. In general, it can be said that receiver-side error correction methods require significantly more redundancy in the data than error detection methods. One could thus argue that it is always better to use a backward error correction method, as this reduces the amount of data required in addition to the user data. However, this argument does not take into account the fact that, especially if we assume there are many receivers, the higher the noise level, the more requests the receivers will send to the sender to resend the data[2]. At worst the system can become blocked. This cannot happen with fountain codes. The codes are therefore characterized by their robustness against noisy transmission. This is formally discussed in [2, 4], where mathematical suggestions are made regarding degree distribution. Later, in [1], based on [2, 4], degree distributions were examined using simulation series, and recommendations were made for smaller data volumes. RaptorQ Codes [5] offer a more powerful realization with an enhanced degree distribution. However, LT-codes can be considered as their predecessor. Finally, even though fountain codes were originally intended for robust multicast data transmission over a noisy medium, other applications are also conceivable: [6] examines their suitability for designing a covert channel. However, this is not the focus here.

3 How Do Fountain Codes Work?

Fountain codes work as follows at the sender and at the receiver(s) sides:

On the sender side: If the sender wants to send the data stream D, it divides it into n equal blocks $D := p_1,\ldots, p_n$. However, it is not the plaintext blocks themselves that are sent, but rather coded blocks/packets of the type $X := \oplus \sum_{i=1}^{d} p_i$ and an associated coefficient C. Many pairs X_j, C_j are sent, where X is an encoded packet that has the same length as a plaintext packet p, and C is a coefficient that enables the receiver to recognize the specific variations of p that make up X. [2] provides hints as to how exactly the composition is communicated to the recipient. However, precise details are lacking[3].

---

[2] Our simulations have shown that even for small groups (> 10) and 1% noise, yet the break-even point is reached in favor of fountain codes.

[3] Michael Luby: „*There are a variety of ways to associate a degree on a set of neighbors with an encoding symbol depending on the application, and **these implementation details are beyond the scope of this paper.**"*

We decide to do this here by means of a coefficient C. . The decisions that the sender has to make during encoding are, on the one hand, i) how many, and on the other hand, ii) which specific plaintext packets p an encoded packet X should be composed of. For i), Luby introduced the so-called degree distribution D (), from which this can be derived.

At the receiver: The receiver(s) continuously receive pairs of type X_j, C_j. In order to create the original data D from the received data, it checks the respective composition of an encoded packet X by looking at the coefficient C. It is possible to collect incoming pairs X, C until the recipient is able to solve a linear equation system from it[4]. However, in our implementation we use an "on-the-fly" approach. Here, the receiver attempts to decode incoming pairs X, C directly upon receipt, or at least to decode them partially. How well this succeeds in individual cases depends on how much of the previously incoming data it has already been able to decode successfully, i.e., which packets p are already available to the receiver as plaintext packets. If the receiver was able to decode the packet p_i in advance upon receiving X, C, it checks whether a 1 is entered in the C at the i-th position. If this is the case, the receiver can calculate $X\prime = X \oplus p_i$. For $X\prime$, this means that, in contrast to X, this data no longer contains any portion of p_i, because in general, $X = (X \oplus Y) \oplus Y$. If the receiver still has additional plaintext packets p_j, it now checks the j-th position of the coefficient vector C: if it is 0, it cannot continue decoding $X\prime$ and must therefore cache $X\prime$. However, if the j-th position in C is 1, it can continue decoding and calculate $X\prime \oplus p_j$. On the receiver side, according to [6] and derived from [2], two buffers are required:

Buffer A: This contains all the pairs $X\prime$, $C\prime$ that could only be partially decoded so far or could not be decoded at all at the time of their reception.

Buffer B: All already decoded plaintext packets are entered into this buffer. It has a length of n and initially contains no entries. If an $X\prime$ could be decoded to such an extent that its $C\prime$ only contains a 1 at exactly one position, then $X\prime$ is a plaintext packet and is stored in buffer B at position i if $C\prime$ at position i has the value 1.

The entire decoding process on the receiver side is successfully completed when buffer B contains entries at all n positions. In [7], a pseudo code notation is presented based on [2] (see Fig. 2). Appendix A (see Fig. 7) shows an exemplary snapshot with three receivers each having currently stored different data in buffer B due to in the most general case different noise characteristics on each transmission path.

---

[4] The decoding approach in [5] solves a sparse system of linear equations based on Gaussian elimination.

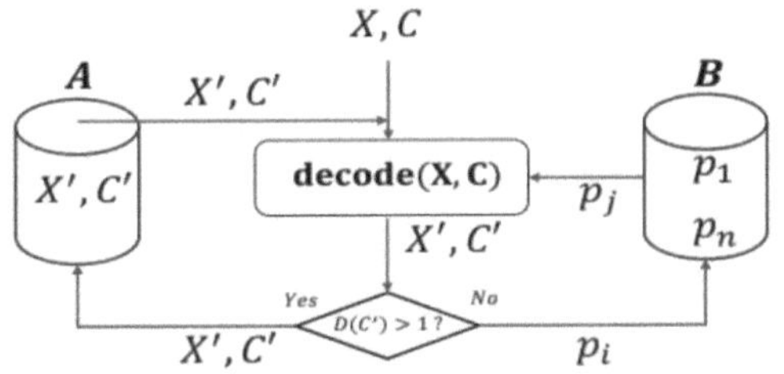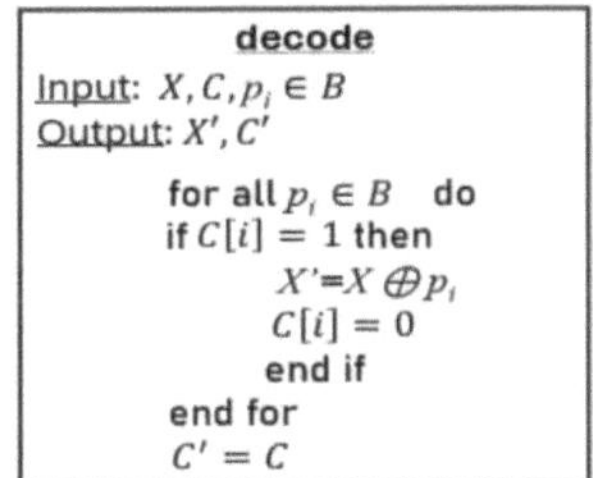

Fig. 2. Illustration of receiver-side decoding of incoming X,C with buffer A and buffer B according to [7]

4 Relevant Parameters

The parameters that have a particular influence on successful decoding are now presented. While the discussion and analysis of the degree distribution has been addressed in the early design of fountain codes from the beginning, a number of other relevant parameters were not addressed at all in the work of Luby and his co-authors.

4.1 Degree Distribution

Hyytiä and co-authors [1] have identified key characteristics for the degree distribution $D()$ based on their simulation results and suggested their use: i) Use small d most frequently, ii) $d = 2$ should occur most frequently, and iii) $d = 1$ should occur less frequently (less than $d = 2$), and iv) very few very large d values significantly improve performance. Specifically, the degree distributions *(ideal) soliton distribution, robust soliton distribution, robust soliton distribution with spike*, and *ISG* were analyzed. However, the authors received their simulation results purely under an ideal channel in which, by definition, there is no data loss on the transmission path. In [1] it has been shown that the best measured degree distribution can be achieved using Robust Soliton distribution with Spike. For the predominant metric *"number of sent packets"* they measured mean values 43.6 (StdDv 6.8) and 81.9 (StdDv 7.7) for $n = 32$ and $n = 64$. Noteworthy: RaptorQ apply other degree distributions designed for larger source code sizes.

4.2 Additional Parameters

Luby [2] describes his method quite precisely on a mathematical level and, in parts, on a pseudo code level. Nevertheless, the question arises: Where are the degrees of freedom in his notation when it comes to its translation into program code? In other words, parameters that have not been addressed, but whose effects can be considerable. The following, we believe, are worth mentioning here:

Size of buffer A - While the size of buffer B is predetermined (it is always n), the choice of the size of buffer A is a degree of freedom. Intuitively, one would also set A to n, but under certain circumstances it may make sense for the decoding process to set the value to greater than n. On the other hand, full utilization of the entries in a buffer A of size n would mean that the required data overhead would be at least 100%.

Return of a packet from A - For an on-the-fly solution, it must be determined at what intervals entries $X\prime$ that have only been partially decoded should be attempted to be decoded again. An argument in favor of prompt subsequent decoding is that only a few additional pairs X, C need to be sent. On the other hand, a longer waiting time until a new decoding attempt is made is justified by the fact that further plain texts have arrived in B in the meantime, which favor successful complete decoding.

When and how many in each case? - Furthermore, with regard to a return of entries $X\prime$, it must be decided whether only one entry or all entries currently contained in buffer A or a subset thereof are to be processed. It is also important to determine which event triggers the return of one or more entries. For example, a return can always occur after a certain number of additional entries in buffer A, or always when another plaintext packet p is stored in buffer B.

Storage selection in A - Another consideration concerns the question of whether all packets are written to buffer A or only a selection, e.g., those with a relatively small residual degree. This would potentially increase their future chances of successful decoding, but would actually be an implicit "readjustment" of the originally selected degree distribution.

Selection of d packets - The degree distribution is the parameter that has the greatest impact on performance (and robustness). However, a $D()$ resulting in, for example, $d = 4$ does not yet indicate which specific d packets are included in the current coding.

5   Implementation Aspects

5.1   Degree Distribution

For the degree distribution, we followed the recommendations from [1], especially for small n, specifically $n = 32$ and $n = 64$. [2] did not consider such small n. The theoretically determined recommendations for degree distributions are based on significantly larger n. Within our PoC implementation, our GetCurrentDegree() function randomly returns a degree d based on a specific degree distribution. For the degree distribution specified in [1] for $n = 64$, this means, for example, that d can take the values 1, 2, 4, 8, 16, or 32, where $Pr[d = 1] = 9\%$, $Pr[d = 2] = 49\%$, $Pr[d = 4] = 20\%$, $Pr[d = 8] = 13\%$, $Pr[d = 16] = 2\%$ and $Pr[d = 32] = 7\%$.

5.2   Buffer A

The following aspects have proven to be advantageous in the design of Buffer A. It should always be significantly larger than Buffer B (with $n = 64$, min. Size 100). Always write all packets to Buffer A, regardless of the remaining degree, otherwise this could damage the original degree distribution. Always read all entries from A whenever a new entry is added to Buffer B.

5.3   Selection of Packets – What Kind of Randomness?

In addition to the degree distribution, the appropriate implementation of 'randomness' turned out to be another predominant parameter. Contrary to other requirements, such as those necessary for the implementation of a random function for cryptographic primitives with regard to security, the requirements for a random function in the context of fountain codes are not that challenging at first glance. However, it has been shown that the influence on the data surplus incurred during transmission is considerable. Our implementation measurements have shown this. On the sender side, according to [2], 'randomness' is needed for choosing the current d and subsequently for building a suited C based on this d. In our implementation we achieve this with the following functions:

int **GetCurrentDegree**(int degree_distribution[])
Based on a predefined degree distribution, the degree d is assigned to each packet to be encoded. This value must be weighted taking into account the frequency with which a degree occurs within the degree distribution according to [1].

void **BuildC**(int degree)
Based on the current degree d from the above function, d coefficients of the vector C are now randomly set to '1'. The remaining values remain at '0'.

Every coefficient vector C created in this way is used to XOR the packets p addressed in this way to form an encoded packet X. The respective pair X, C is then transmitted.

Contrary to their use for cryptographic primitives, purely sender-side use of the deterministic C random functions rand()/srand() appears to be possible in principle for the robustness sought in fountain codes. However, there are a few things to consider here as well. The implementation with the original BuildC routine based on rand() for $n = 32$ packets showed that after a certain amount of time, the receiver-side decoding process actually decoded the packets X, C to the original data stream $D := p_1, ..., p_n$ but this was always associated with an unacceptably high data surplus on the transmission link. In short: Although this version of our own implementation was able to decode the data (a real interim success!), the resulting data surplus was absolutely not competitive with the reference values from [1]. For example, with $n = 32$, significantly more than 10^2 packets were always sent, compared to a mean number of 43.6 listed in [1].

For this reason, we tested an ideal channel (absolutely error-free transmission) and a degree distribution in which a degree of $d = 1$ is always taken for the purpose of error localization. GetCurrentDegree() therefore always returns the value 1, and a plaintext packet p_i is always sent as X. Which one is chosen then depends only on the implementation of randomness in the BuildC function. It turned out that for $n = 32$, with a constant $d = 1$ and 50 calls to BuildC, only 20 of the 32 possible positions were selected. Even after 100 calls to BuildC, only about 25 of the total 32 possibilities had been selected by BuildC. This effect corresponds to that of the classic Coupon collector's problem [8]: The expected value $E(Y_i)$ for the next candidate not yet received is $E(Y_i) = E(Y_i) = \frac{n}{n-i+1}$. Thus, $\sum_{i=1}^{n} E(Y_i)$ indicates how often draws are made until all n candidates are present. This means for our problem, ignoring the variance for small n, approximately 130 pairs X, C must be sent for $n = 32$ in order to have received every plaintext packet at least once in an X on the receiver side for the first time. For a larger number of plaintext packets, e.g., $n = 64$, this effect is even worse, and approximately 304 packets are necessary before the receiver is able to decode the entire data stream for the first time. Recall that with an ideal channel, only 32 or 64 plaintext packets would need to be received. It should be noted that 130 or 303 pairs X, C received is an estimate for a lower limit for the first possibility of successful decoding. However, a few more pairs X, C may be needed to actually decode completely. These considerations led to the above function being replaced by a function BuildCAdvanced(), which takes the coupon collector's problem into account and gives chance a little help. With such 'guided' chance, the effect of the collection problem on the fountain codes becomes manageable because BuildCAdvanced() stores which of the possible positions are already occupied with each call to rand(). If the result of rand() is a value i that has not occurred before, then i is also the return value of BuildCAdvanced. Otherwise, rand() is called multiple times until a value is thrown that has not been selected before. Only when all positions have been considered at least once in this way multiple assignments become possible. This is because it is only possible to successfully decode the entire data stream if all packets are present at least once in an X.

This adjustment means that for $n = 32$, an ideal channel, and a $D()$ with $Pr(d = 1)$ $= 100\%$, only 32 pairs X, C actually need to be sent. After this adjustment, confidence increased regarding the data surplus of the implementation on the transmission path. The next step was to use the degree distributions from [1]. However, it quickly became apparent that the above-mentioned adjustment alone would not be sufficient to achieve an acceptable overhead (for an ideal channel). Still more than 60 packets (with $n = 32$) were certainly not very competitive.

5.4 BuildCAdvanced – C with Adaptable Freshness

We have therefore expanded BuildC() on the receiver side with additional adjustment that influences the composition of current plaintext packets for an X to a certain extent in terms of their 'freshness'. This requires:

1. *chosen[]*: the sender's memory – it records whether a plaintext has ever been used in any previous X
2. Variable *proportion*: value between 0 and n-1

   For every $d \geq 2$:

1. if there are more than *proportion* 1s in *chosen[]*, then fill d/x positions in the current C to be created with 1s that were already occupied in previous C s.
2. All remaining $d - d/x$ 1s are placed in the current C in positions that have not yet been placed in any previous process.
3. Reset: If *chosen[]* is full of 1s, then set all 1s to 0.

From well over a thousand preliminary test runs with a wide variety of parameter assignments for x and *proportion*, two favorites emerged: K1 (*proportion* $= 0$, $x = 2$) and K2 (*proportion*$=\frac{3}{4}$ n, $x = 4$). The results for both candidates are listed in more detail in Sects. 6 and 7 and by again applying the recommended degree distributions from [1]. For simplicity K1 could be described as the best candidate from "*some old ones, many fresh ones*" and K2 as the best representative from "*hardly any old, almost only fresh.*"

What is also noteworthy: Variants with 100% *"fresh"* were indeed worse than candidates K1 or K2.

6   Evaluation Under Noise and Naïve Jamming

After preliminary selection for K1 and K2, a total of 5K additional runs were performed (100 runs per parameterization) under different settings. The following are examined: i) an ideal channel, ii) noise (1% and 10%) with random packet loss, and iii) naive jamming (20% and 50%) with random packet loss, but in the two latter cases with significantly more packet loss. The results are shown in Table 1.

Table 1. Number of sent packets [mean value and StdDev.] and overhead [%][5]

		Ideal	*Noise*		*Naive Jamming*	
		0%	*1%*	*10%*	*20%*	*50%*
$n = 32$	K1	44,38 (7,6) **38.6%**	44,01(5,7) **37,5%**	50,67 (7,80) **58,3%**	61,26 (11,30) **91,4%**	101,8 (12,7) **218%**
	K2	41,2 (3,9) **28.7%**	42,6 (5,1) **33,1%**	47,39 (4,78) **48%**	55,3 (6,0) **72,8%**	105,24 (14,4) **228%**
$n = 64$	K1	81,9 (7,4) **28%**	85,07 (7,1) **32,9%**	95,4 (8,79) **49%**	112 (13,2) **75%**	199 (21,5) **210%**
	K2	81,5 (7,3) **27%**	85,5 (7,3) **33,5%**	94,3 (7,63) **47%**	109,5 (9,99) **71%**	193 (13,0) **201%**
$n = 96$	K1	121 (10,3) **26%**	123,8 (9,6) **28,9%**	139,5 (13,2) **45,3%**	147,54 (17,3) **53,6%**	292,8 (31,5) **205%**
	K2	120 (9,6) **25%**	120,6 (7,3) **25,6%**	138,6 (10,8) **44,3%**	163,28 (13,3) **70%**	288,2 (19,9) **200%**
$n = 128$	K1	163 (17,9) **27,3%**	160 (12,78) **25%**	183(11,5) **42,9%**	214(19,3) **67,2%**	400,6(63,2) **212%**
	K2	157 (11,64) **22,6%**	159 (9,77) **24,2%**	175(9) **36,7%**	210(11,64) **64%**	371,5 (20,8) **190,2%**

It is very encouraging that the parametrization of candidate K2 for $n = 32$ performs better than the benchmark value of 43.6 (std. Dev. 6.8) [1] with a mean value of 41.2 and a standard deviation of 3.91. Even for $n = 64$, K2 is minimally better with 81.5 (7.3) ([81.9 (7.7) in [1]). These measurements reinforce confidence in the performance of our implementation. The mean values for $n = 96$ and $n = 128$ are all respectable with varying noise levels and are better in percentage terms than for smaller n. No comparative measurements from other studies are available here. Overall, it is noticeable that candidate K2 always performs better than K1, except for two measurement series ($n = 32$, 50%) ($n = 96$, 20%). The enormous fluctuations in the (StdDev) are a general characteristic of fountain codes, which can have serious implications when aiming at a guaranteed transmission. Figures 3 and 4 provide examples of this for K2 (*ideal*, $n = 32$)

and (10%, $n = 96$). This shows that in order to decode successfully with 90% statistical certainty, 46 packets would have to be sent in example 1, and 156.2 packets would have to be sent in example 2 with 83% statistical certainty.

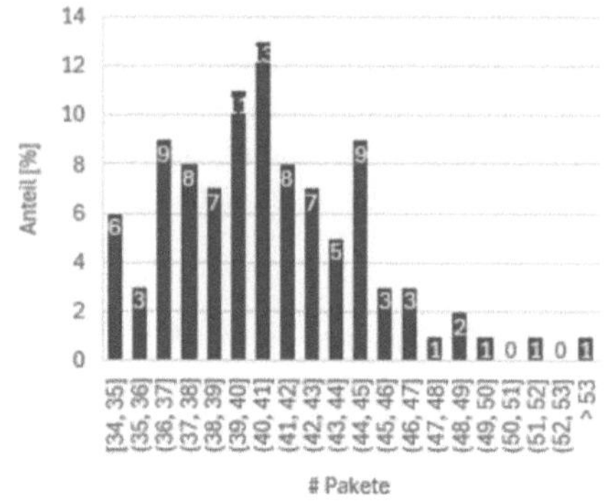

Fig. 3. *(n = 32, proportion = 0, x = 2, NO_NOISE)*: Required packets for successful decoding with 102 simulations both for K2

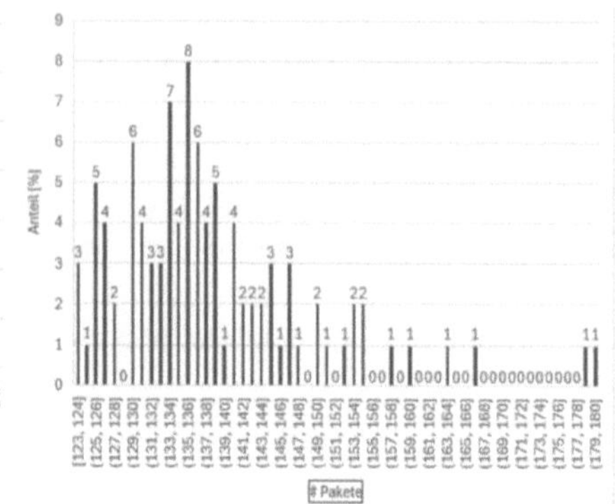

Fig. 4. *(n = 96, proportion = 0, x = 2, noise = 10%)*: Required packets for successful decoding with 10^2 simulations both for K2

This is probably the biggest weakness of fountain codes: there is always a degree of uncertainty as to whether all data could actually be successfully decoded. For practical application, it is therefore probably unavoidable to send at least one ACK from the receiver to the sender after having successful decoded.

Figures 5 and 6 show an aggregated representation of the above measurement series for candidates K1 and K2. The respective *y*-axis is shown in logarithmic representation with the overhead [%]. The *x*-axis denotes the number of successfully transmitted packets with *n*. It is clear to see that for all measurement series, the overhead decreases as *n* increases. Overall, the differences are very significant for small $n = 32$ with 50% noise (228% average overhead) compared to large $n = 192$ with an ideal channel (only 19% average overhead). One open question is the lower limit for overhead as *n* continues to increase: At what *n* does the percentage data overhead stop decreasing and tends to approach a certain value?

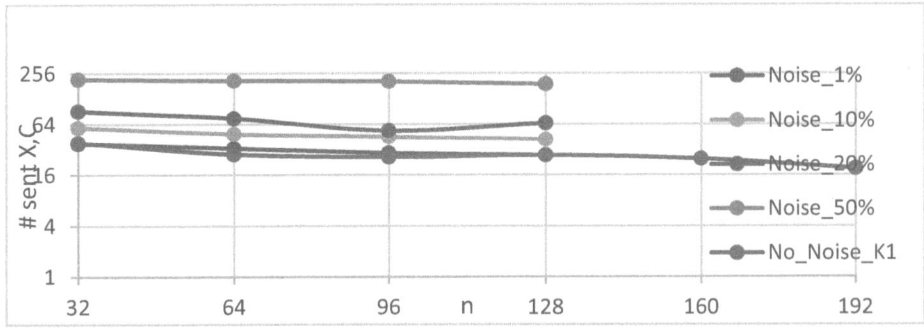

Fig. 5. Mean data overhead for K1 for different n and different transmission conditions

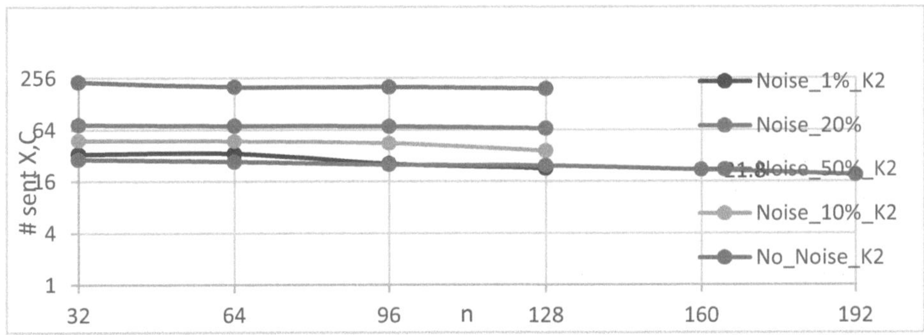

Fig. 6. Mean data overhead for K2 for different n and different transmission conditions

7 Evaluation Under Selective Jamming

Selective jamming refers to the targeted "shooting" of individual packets on the (preferably wireless) transmission path. If a jammer were able to always hit all pairs X, C in which the same p occurs, the decoding process could never be completed. The jamming would therefore be maximally successful in the sense of a DoS attack, and an endless number of pairs X, C would be transmitted. The fewer packets that need to be jammed for this, the better the selective jamming, because then it is less likely that this jamming will be detected. There are (at least) two approaches to this: i) without or ii) with real-time analysis of, for example, all C on the transmission path. In both cases, we assume that the seed of the random function is only known to the sender and that its period length is greater than the number of packets X, C to be transmitted. Otherwise, the order of the currently used grades d could be deduced in advance.

Selective jamming type 1 - Regarding i), in order to optimize the data volumes of fountain codes, we have addressed the coupon collector's problem by ensuring that all n different packets p are included at least once in an X after n transmissions before further 'purely random' X s are generated. A jammer that certainly knows n and $D()$ can therefore act as follows: It can use $D()$ to calculate the expected value $\mu = E(Y)$, i.e., $E(Y) = \sum_{i=1}^{n} Pr(Y = i)d_i$. For $D_{Hyyti\ddot{a}}(n = 64)$ it is $\mu = 5{,}47$. An attacker could now block the $\lfloor n/\mu \rfloor$-th packet X, C and its direct successor, as these are highly likely to contain the missing p. For $D_{Hyyti\ddot{a}}(n = 64)$, $\lfloor n/\mu \rfloor = 11$, so X_{11}, C_{11} and X_{12}, C_{12} and their multiples would have to be blocked. Please note that the attacker does not need to know which specific packets p are still missing. With our simple selective jammer, we replicated this for $n = 64$ and $n = 96$ and *tested various other variants of the above strategy*. In particular, we also tested those based on an expected value in which only the number of fresh d, depending on the parameterization of the candidates K1 resp. K2, is included in the calculation of μ. On average, however, it was never possible to generate more traffic than would be possible with naive noise with the same percentage of blocked packets – let alone achieve a complete blocking of the service. This simple form of selective jamming confirms the inherent robustness of fountain codes against type 1 selective jamming: the decoding process still works even when individual packets are blocked in such a smart way.

Selective jamming type 2 - Regarding ii): However, if the attacker succeeds in using real-time analysis based on all previously intercepted X, C to log which of the packets p are still missing, they can specifically block X, C that have a 1 entry in C, which indicates that such a p was used in the creation of X. Compared to i), this requires significantly more equipment for the attacker, as packets must not only be blocked, but also analyzed on the fly in advance in order to be able to analyze <u>and</u> block them in real time. We have replicated the capability of this jammer in our implementation by discarding all packets X, C with $C[10] == 1$ on the sender side, for example. For example, for $n = 32$ and NO_NOISE, we obtained a mean value of 1239 transmitted packets with a standard deviation of 1351 in 50 runs until the process aborted and output the data stream. Of course, this always results in a decoding error at position 10. The mean value of jammed packets was 155 with a standard deviation of 220.54. This corresponds to an average of 9.19% of all transmitted packets X, C. Unlike selective jamming type 1, selective jamming type 2 therefore has a much more serious potential for DoS attacks if the attacker is able to analyze and block in real time on the transmission path. As a reminder: with $n = 32$ and an ideal channel, an average of approximately 42.3 packets needs to be sent.

The measured proportion of packets contributing to selective jamming appears plausible (albeit a little too high). It can be explained by the proportion of a specific packet p in a packet X, C: According to $D_{Hyyti\ddot{a}}(n = 32)$, the following applies: $(1x12 + 2x51 + 4x28 + 9x16)/100 = 3.7$. For $n = 32$, $32/3.7 = 8.64$. On average, therefore, one packet with the same p proportion is sent in every 8.64 packets X, C.

We assume that the value is slightly smaller than the one measured with our PoC implementation, since according to $D_{Hyyti\ddot{a}}(n = 32)$, a very high degree 16 occurs in only 9% of cases and, although it occurs rarely in percentage terms, it accounts for 26% of the summand.

Even though successfully implementing selective jamming type 2 is significantly more challenging (at least on the wireless transmission link), it is worth considering hardening against this type of jamming. One option would be encryption such as $Enc(X_i, C_i)$. The challenge here is certainly key management. A second option could be encoding with a 3rd receiver-side buffer put in front. Instead of the sequence $X_i, C_i \dots X_{i+1}, C_{i+1}$ it would be conceivable to send a sequence of packets of the type $X_i, C_{i-1} \dots X_{i+1}, C_i$ and start decoding only if both parts of the X_i, C_i tuple are available. However, this variant also has some obvious disadvantages which, due to space limitations, we do not address in the work at hand.

8 Pollution

If the attacker succeeds in injecting a packet (*pollution*), this will result in parts of the data being contaminated. It is therefore essential to always provide fountain codes with mechanisms for authenticating the data and the sender like e.g. TESLA [8] as proposed in [4]. If this is not done, the effects mentioned above will occur, which we analyzed in more detail for $n = 32$ and an ideal channel. We proceeded as follows: We start test series by replacing one packet with a polluted packet. In the polluted packet, $C[1] = 1$ and the remaining values 0. The corresponding X can be freely selected. To do this, we inject the packet as the 1st, 8th, 16th, and 31st packet to be received, with the respective test series. In the same way, test series follow for $C[10] = 1$, $C[20] = 1$, and $C[30] = 1$. The results obtained in this way can be found in Table 2 in each case.

Table 2. Number of polluted packets #e [mean value and StdAbw.] and number of overall sent packets #p (mean) when infiltrating a single polluted packet with $n = 32$

Paket i		1	8	16	24	31
$C[1]$	#e	**12,5(8,1)**	**11,8(6,14)**	**14,2(5,3)**	**13,9(7,42)**	**12,6(6,22)**
	#p	131,9	40,8	89,2	78,6	100,3
$C[10]$	#e	**11,6(5,63)**	**14,2(7,79)**	**11,8(7,63)**	**15,8(6,85)**	**13,0(6,48)**
	#p	49,5	83,2	67,4	80,0	88,0
$C[20]$	#e	**14,2(7,33)**	**14,23 (7,3)**	**12,8(6,45)**	**12,2(6,07)**	**13,7(5,22)**
	#p	87,7	65,5	51,4	47,1	77,7
$C[30]$	#e	**12,7(9,34)**	**12,6(8,83)**	**12,1(7,77)**	**14,8 (8)**	**14,1(7,08)**
	#p	88,9	76,19	76	45	51,66

It can be seen that even a single corrupted packet usually has a major impact on many other data items in the data stream. For $n = 32$, an average of 41.25% of the data is corrupted. Based on these initial test series, this appears to be completely independent of both the time of injection and the occupancy position in the coefficient vector. However, we also observed one case with 0 errors and four cases with 32 errors in the measurement series. This shows the breadth of the spectrum.

Contrary to the diffusion properties sought in e.g. hash functions, where changing one input bit mandatorily shall change at least 50% of all output bits, this guarantee of diffusion is not given in the case of pollution by a single packet. At first glance, at least on the basis of this limited series of measurements, no pattern, rule, or quantity can be identified with regard to diffusion across the data stream. Since it is always necessary (see above) to use mechanisms for authenticating the data and the sender, we have refrained from further considerations, for example for varying n.

9   Conclusion and Discussion

One aim of the work at hand was to draw attention to 'manual manufacturing tolerances' in the implementation of fountain codes. It is apparently not enough to simply 'code down' the description from [2] in order to obtain results that fall within the range of the benchmark values from [1]. The line between a competitive on-the-fly solution and a 'completely useless' one is very narrow. For a competitive solution it is of predominant relevance to address the coupon collector's problem in the implementation like we did. With respect to the encoding strategy considering adaptable freshness under a given degree distribution [1] our results show that candidate K2 "*hardly any old, almost only fresh*" performs better in 17 from 20 of our settings. Overall, the current implementation has confirmed and quantified the inherent suitability of fountain LT-codes for resilient data transmission in the presence of *noise* and *naive jamming*. This is especially true for larger n, because here it can be seen that, especially in the presence of only low to moderate noise, the data overhead can be reduced to close to 20%. However, our research has also shown that a high-performance implementation of fountain codes is vulnerable to *type 2 selective jamming*. Preventing this is still an open research question, although we sketched two options to address this issue. Finally, authentication of data and originator is a must, otherwise even a single infiltrated data unit would destroy major portions of the data stream at the receiver side. RaptorQ originate from LT-Codes and thus future work could be testing if they behave similarly with respect to jamming. They are mainly designed for first collecting data and subsequently solving a linear equation system, whereas we chose a realization allowing on-the-fly decoding.

Appendix A – Example with Multiple Receivers.

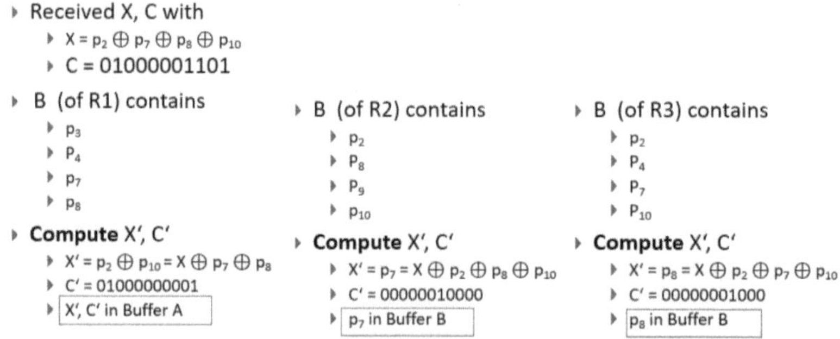

Fig. 7. Computation of X', C' if receivers *R1, R2, R3* could yet successfully partially decode

References

1. Hyytiä, E.; Tirronen, T.;Virtamo, J.: Optimizing the degree distribution of LT codes with an importance sampling approach. In: 6th RESIM 2006, Bamberg, Germany (2006)

2. Luby, M.: LT codes. In: 43rd IEEE Symposium on Foundations of Computer Science (2002)
3. Hyytiä E., Tirronen T, Virtamo J.: Optimal degree distribution for LT codes with small message length. In: IEEE INFOCOM 2007 - 26th IEEE International Conference on Computer Communications, Anchorage, AK, USA, pp. 2576–2580 (2007)
4. Byers, J.W., Luby, M., Mitzenmacher, M.: A digital fountain approach to asynchronous reliable multicast. IEEE J. Sel. Areas Commun. **20**(8), 1528–1540 (2002)
5. Luby, M, Shokrollahi, A, Watson, M, Stockhammer M., Minder L.: Forward error correction scheme for object delivery. IETF, RFC 6330 (2011)
6. Keller, J., Marciniszyn, E.: Improved concept and implementation of a fountain code covert channel. J. Wirel. Mob. Netw. Ubiq. Comput. Dependable Appl. (2022)
7. Bohli, J.M., Hessler, A., Ugus, O., Westhoff, D.: Security enhanced multi-hop over the air reprogramming with Fountain Codes. In: LCN 2009 (2009)
8. Perrig, A., Tygar, J.D.: TESLA broadcast authentication, secure broadcast communication. In: Wired and Wireless Networks, pp. 29–53 (2003)
9. Motwani, R., Raghavan, P.: 3.6. The coupon collector's problem. In: Randomized Algorithms, pp. 57–63. Cambridge University Press, Cambridge (1995). ISBN 9780521474658, MR 1344451

Cybersecurity

Aligning Governance and Value Exchange in Permissioned Blockchain Consortia: A Model-Based Study in a Regulated Milk Supply Chain

Jan Biermann[(✉)], Maximilian Greiner, Karl Seidenfad, Benedikt Roosen, and Ulrike Lechner

University of the Bundeswehr Munich, Neubiberg, Germany
`{jan.biermann,maximilian.greiner,karl.seidenfad,benedikt.roosen,`
`ulrike.lechner}@unibw.de`

Abstract. The digital transformation of supply chains challenges traditional governance structures in decentralized, multi-stakeholder environments. While blockchain technology enables transparent and tamper-resistant coordination, the design of governance mechanisms that support sustainable economic value exchange in consortium blockchains remains insufficiently understood. This paper examines how governance structures in blockchain-based consortia must be designed to enable viable value exchange and long-term cooperation. Using a Design Science Research approach, governance and value models are developed for a permissioned blockchain consortium in the drinking milk supply chain. The study integrates a systematic literature review, expert interviews, and model-based analysis. Governance structures are modeled using the DECENT ontology, while economic value exchanges are analyzed through the E^3 value method. The results show that viable blockchain consortia require a tight alignment between formalized governance mechanisms, incentive structures, and value flows. The paper provides design-oriented insights for researchers and practitioners developing sustainable blockchain-based consortia in regulated supply chain contexts.

Keywords: Blockchain · Consortium · Governance · Supply chain · Value exchange

1 Introduction

Digital transformation pushes supply chains toward shared data, cross-company processes, and platform-based coordination [29]. Many supply chains are decentralized: firms remain independent, processes span multiple organizations, and no single actor can mandate standards or compliance [31]. This creates governance challenges. Partners must agree on data definitions, access rights, responsibilities, cost sharing, and procedures for exceptions and disputes [28]. They also

K. Kirchner et al. (Eds.): I4CS 2026, CCIS 3007, pp. 73–95, 2026.
https://doi.org/10.1007/978-3-032-27096-2_5

face limited trust and conflicting incentives. As a result, coordination often fails even when suitable technology exists [20].

Blockchain has been proposed to support inter-organizational coordination in such settings [27]. A permissioned blockchain can provide a shared ledger, traceable transactions, and auditable process histories [32]. It can also support identity management, access control, and automated execution of agreed rules (e.g., via smart contracts [22]). These features are relevant for supply-chain use cases such as provenance, certification, reconciliation, and dispute handling. Consortium blockchains therefore appear as a practical option for shared infrastructure across firms.

Yet governance and incentive alignment remain unresolved in consortium blockchains [19]. Many projects stall because participants do not agree on decision rights, onboarding rules, operating costs, benefit allocation, enforcement, or change management [35]. Blockchain reduces the need for a central intermediary, but it does not remove governance. Governance shifts to the consortium: members must define roles, rules, and mechanisms that make participation worthwhile and rule enforcement credible.

Existing research discusses blockchain governance concepts and design principles, but offers limited guidance on how to operationalize governance design while explicitly linking it to economic value exchange [35]. There is a lack of operationalizable models that connect governance structures to who provides what, who receives what, and under which enforceable rules.

This paper asks: How must governance structures in blockchain-based consortia be designed to enable sustainable economic value exchange and incentives?

The paper makes three contributions to blockchain governance's body of knowledge: (1) A governance–value framework that links governance elements (actors, roles, rules, enforcement, incentives) to value exchange. (2) A model-based analysis that operationalizes this framework using the DECENT framework for governance specification [15] and the E^3 value-model for value modeling [6]. (3) An empirically grounded case in the drinking-milk supply chain, treated as a critical-infrastructure context to test and illustrate the approach.

2   Theoretical Background

2.1   Types of Blockchains

Blockchains can be classified along two main dimensions (see Fig. 1): (i) access to the network and data (who may read and submit transactions) and (ii) participation in consensus (who may validate transactions and append blocks). Based on these dimensions, a common distinction is between permissionless and permissioned systems, and between the types public, private, consortium, and hybrid [32].

Permissionless (Public) Blockchains. These blockchains form open networks in which participants can join without prior authorization and can take part in transaction validation and data processing. They are often implemented as open-source systems and frequently use native tokens (e.g., Bitcoin [21]). This openness supports broad participation and transparency, but it can entail trade-offs. Reported limitations include high resource consumption (notably in Proof-of-Work settings), lower throughput and scalability when many nodes participate, and privacy concerns because transaction data and identifiers can become widely visible [26].

Permissioned Blockchains. Restricting participation in validation to an identified set of participants characterizes this type of blockchain. Using Hyperledger Foundation's definition, permissioned networks limit validators to a set group and thereby reduce anonymity; transparency and access can be configured to match organizational objectives [32]. A smaller, known validator set can improve performance (faster validation, fewer nodes) and supports role-based access control for data visibility. At the same time, restricting validation reduces decentralization and may introduce governance risks if control over validation and rule changes concentrates in a small group [20].

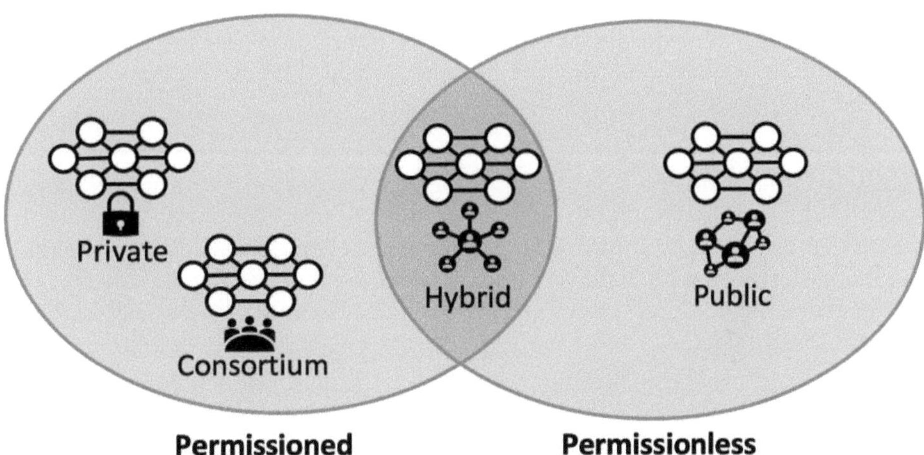

Fig. 1. Types of blockchains [24]

Within permissioned systems, three types are relevant:

Private Blockchains. Private blockchains are typically operated under the control of a single organization (or a tightly controlled owner structure). They can achieve high transaction speed and controlled scaling, but the limited validator set can increase manipulation risk and can reduce trust if the operator's incentives diverge from other stakeholders [7].

Consortium Blockchains. In a consortium blockchain, management and validation is distributed across multiple organizations. Access remains restricted, but authority is shared among consortium members. This setup can increase efficiency (limited participants) while improving security compared to a single-operator design by spreading control across organizations. Remaining risks include collusion among members and attacks on key nodes [33].

Hybrid Blockchains. A hybrid blockchain combines private and public elements (also discussed in the context of sidechains/cross-chains). Selected information or processes can be kept within a restricted domain while other parts are made public. This can reduce incentives to tamper compared to fully private setups, but increases design complexity and can reduce transparency if information is selectively withheld [18].

For regulated supply chain scenarios, permissioned consortium designs are often the practical focus because they support identified membership, configurable transparency, and shared control among stakeholders [32].

2.2   Blockchain Consortium Archetypes

To capture different coordination logics and governance challenges, the three consortium archetypes according to Seidenfad et al. [25] are distinguished and modeled comparatively.

Vertical Consortium. A vertical consortium integrates actors from different stages of the supply chain [29], such as producers, processors, and retailers. Its primary objective is to improve traceability, reduce information asymmetries, and increase transparency across organizational boundaries. Governance in this configuration must address asymmetric power relations and heterogeneous incentive structures [25].

Horizontal Consortium. A horizontal consortium comprises actors operating at the same level of the supply chain [25], for example multiple producers or processors. The main motivation lies in sharing infrastructure costs, standardizing processes, and increasing collective bargaining power. Governance challenges in horizontal consortia primarily concern fair cost allocation, equal decision rights, and prevention of free-riding behavior [9,23].

Ecosystem Consortium. An ecosystem consortium extends beyond core supply chain actors to include service providers, auditors, and regulatory stakeholders. This configuration enables broader value creation, such as compliance verification or data-driven services, but also introduces increased complexity in governance and coordination. Decision-making structures must accommodate diverse objectives while maintaining enforceability [25].

These archetypes provide a structured basis for comparative modeling, allowing the analysis of how different consortium compositions affect governance requirements, incentive structures, and economic viability.

2.3 Governing the Commons

We treat a consortium blockchain as a digital commons [10]: a shared resource system (e.g., a data platform and related governance mechanisms) used by several actors, where use by one actor can reduce the value or availability for others, and where excluding non-members is costly or difficult. In such settings, governance must address contribution, monitoring, rule changes, and responses to non-compliance [13].

For this purpose, we use the eight commons design principles authored by Elinor Ostrom [23] (see Table 1). We do not introduce new principles; we apply Ostrom's principles as a lens to analyze and design governance for permissioned blockchain consortia.

Table 1. Ostrom's design principles

#	Principle	Description
1	Boundaries	Define the resource scope and membership/roles.
2	Congruence	Align rules with local conditions and balance costs and benefits.
3	Collective Choice	Allow affected members to participate in rule making and modification.
4	Monitoring	Monitor users and the resource through accountable roles or members.
5	Graduated Sanctions	Apply proportional penalties for rule violations.
6	Conflict Resolution	Provide accessible and low-cost dispute resolution mechanisms.
7	Recognition	Ensure external authorities recognize the consortium's right to self-organize.
8	Nested Enterprises	Establish multiple governance layers for complex ecosystems.

In the remainder of the paper, these Ostrom principles guide the derivation of governance requirements and their operationalization in formal governance and value-exchange models.

2.4 Modeling Frameworks

DECENT and E^3 value were selected to address the objective of this study, which is to design governance structures and to assess economic value exchange in a blockchain-based consortium [6,15]. While DECENT provides an experimental framework for modeling decentralized governance, E^3 value represents a proven value-modeling framework that enables the systematic analysis of value flows and incentive structures.

DECENT Ontology for Governance Design. The DECENT ontology provides a structured framework for modeling governance mechanisms in decentralized and multi-actor ecosystems [14]. It is specifically designed to capture governance decisions in environments where authority, rule enforcement, and accountability are distributed across independent actors. In contrast to traditional governance frameworks, DECENT enables an explicit representation of decentralized decision rights and incentive mechanisms, making it particularly suitable for blockchain-based consortia. DECENT models governance through a set of interrelated constructs, including actors, groups, roles, goals, rules, policies, mechanisms, and incentives. These constructs allow governance structures to be expressed independently of specific technical implementations while maintaining a clear link to operational enforcement mechanisms [15]. By distinguishing between goals, objectives, and mechanisms, the ontology supports a systematic decomposition of high-level governance intentions into implementable governance components. In the context of permissioned blockchain consortia, DECENT enables the formalization of governance rules that can later be operationalized through smart contracts and organizational procedures. Its ontological structure facilitates transparency, consistency, and traceability of governance decisions, which are critical requirements in regulated and inter-organizational environments [16].

E^3 Value for Economic Value Exchange. The E^3 value framework is a value-oriented modeling approach designed to analyze how economically independent actors create, exchange, and capture value within a networked system [6]. Rather than focusing on process execution or technical workflows, E^3 value places economic value flows at the center of analysis, making it well suited for evaluating incentive structures in consortium-based ecosystems [30]. E^3 value represents actors, value objects, value activities, and value exchanges in a formal and visual manner. It enables the identification of reciprocal dependencies between actors and supports the assessment of economic sustainability by ensuring that each participant receives sufficient value to justify continued participation. This perspective is particularly relevant for blockchain-based consortia, where participation is voluntary and long-term viability depends on balanced incentive structures [3]. In this study, E^3 value is used to model value exchanges across different consortium configurations. The framework allows for the explicit representation of costs, benefits, and non-monetary value objects, such as data access or compliance assurance. By abstracting from technical implementation details, E^3 value provides a clear analytical lens for comparing alternative consortium designs and their economic implications.

2.5   Integration of Governance and Value Models

While governance and economic value exchange are often analyzed separately, blockchain-based consortia require an integrated perspective in which governance mechanisms directly influence value flows [34]. To address this interdependency, the DECENT ontology and the E^3 value framework are combined into a unified modeling approach. The integration is based on a conceptual mapping between governance constructs and value modeling elements. Actors and groups defined in DECENT correspond to actors or market segments in E^3 value, while governance goals and objectives are reflected as customer needs driving value exchanges. Governance mechanisms, such as policies and rules, are translated into value activities and dependency paths that condition economic interactions. Incentives, rewards, and sanctions are represented as value transfers or value objects that directly affect the economic position of consortium participants. This integrated modeling approach enables a systematic analysis of how governance design choices shape economic incentives and, conversely, how value dependencies constrain feasible governance structures. By linking governance rules to economic consequences, the combined framework supports the design of governance mechanisms that are both enforceable and economically viable. This alignment is essential for the long-term sustainability of blockchain-based consortia in regulated supply chain environments [33].

3   Research Design

This study follows a Design Science Research (DSR) approach. DSR develops and evaluates technical and organizational artifacts to address relevant problems in practice. Artifact construction draws on an existing knowledge base and on insights from an application environment; evaluation produces findings that can be fed back into the knowledge base. In information systems research, DSR places the utility of the artifact in the foreground and treats usefulness as a central evaluation criterion.

DSR is used here as an overarching research logic (following Hevner et al. [11]) and is operationalized with the iterative process model by Kuechler and Vaishnavi [17] (see Fig. 2). They extend the original DSR framing by adding a theory-building perspective and by specifying DSR as an iterative research strategy in which knowledge is generated in cycles. The model structures the project into five recurring phases: problem awareness, suggestion, development, evaluation, and conclusion. In this project, problem awareness is the observation that consortium blockchain initiatives in regulated supply chains often fail due to misalignment between governance rules, enforcement arrangements, and incentive structures. The suggestion phase formulates an integrated modeling approach that links governance design to economic value exchange. Development constructs and refines the conceptual artifacts (governance and value models plus their mapping logic). Evaluation uses empirical input to test consistency, comprehensibility, and practical plausibility of the artifacts. The conclusion phase consolidates the resulting design knowledge in the form of refined constructs, mapping logic, and implications for governance design in consortium settings.

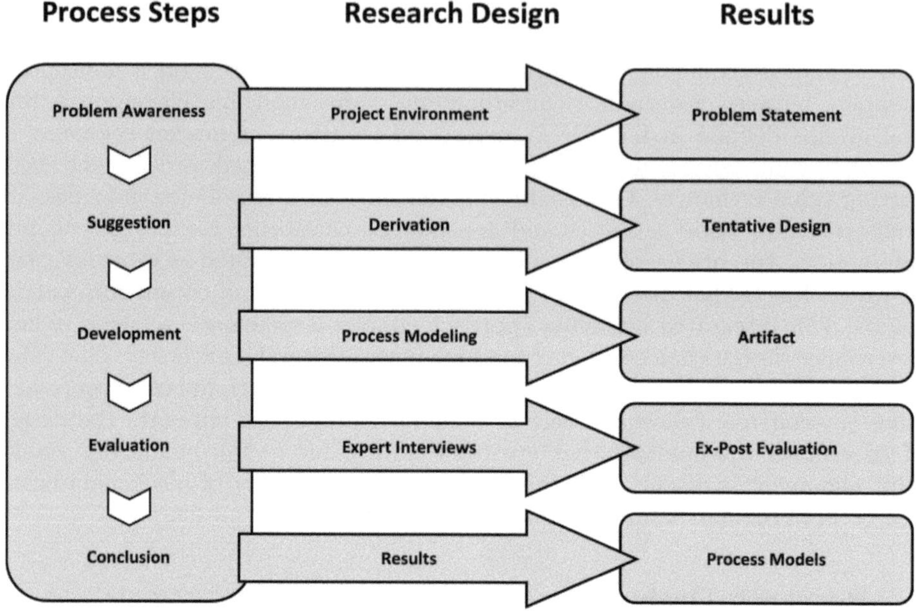

Fig. 2. Research design [17]

Within this DSR process, the project produces two complementary artifact types. First, an integrated modeling approach is constructed that explicitly links governance design to economic value exchange. Governance is specified using the DECENT ontology to represent actors, roles, rules, mechanisms, and incentives; economic value exchanges are modeled using E^3 value to represent reciprocal value dependencies and the distribution of costs and benefits. This provides an explicit bridge between governance choices and incentive effects in consortium participation. Second, the artifacts are instantiated in a case-driven comparative analysis of consortium archetypes in the drinking milk supply chain. The instantiations are used to derive governance requirements, translate governance choices into enforceable on-chain and off-chain mechanisms, and assess whether modeled value flows provide sufficient incentives for sustained participation across archetypes.

Data collection supports both artifact construction and evaluation and combines three sources. First, a systematic literature review is used to build the knowledge base for governance mechanisms, incentive alignment, and design principles. The selection and screening are documented using a PRISMA-style flow logic to ensure traceability of inclusion/exclusion decisions and reduce selection bias. Second, qualitative expert interviews are used to evaluate the artifacts.

Expert interviews are treated as a qualitative method that prioritizes depth of statements over quantitative representativeness and is suited to elicit specialized knowledge through an open and flexible conversation guided by an interview protocol [2,5]. Third, domain and system documentation from the case context (e.g., process descriptions, role definitions, data exchanges, and compliance constraints) is used to parameterize the scenario and to check whether the modeled governance and value exchanges match the assumptions of a regulated supply chain environment. Insights from these sources are used iteratively to revise constructs, adjust mappings between governance and value elements, and strengthen the empirical plausibility of the resulting design knowledge in the sense of the evaluation and conclusion phases of the adopted DSR process model.

4   The Blockchain-Based Milk Supply Chain

4.1   Case Context

The drinking milk supply chain represents a highly regulated and economically constrained segment of the food industry. Continuous availability, product safety, and regulatory compliance are essential, as disruptions can have immediate societal and economic consequences. At the same time, the sector is characterized by low profit margins, high cost pressure, and a fragmented actor landscape consisting largely of small and medium-sized enterprises. The supply chain involves multiple independent stakeholders, including dairy farms, logistics providers, processing facilities, retailers, certification bodies, and regulatory authorities. These actors operate under asymmetric information conditions and pursue heterogeneous economic objectives, which complicates coordination and trust-based collaboration. Increasing regulatory requirements regarding food safety, traceability, and sustainability further intensify the need for reliable cross-organizational information sharing. Against this background, blockchain-based coordination mechanisms offer potential benefits by enabling tamper-resistant data sharing, increased transparency, and automated rule enforcement. The drinking milk supply chain therefore provides a suitable empirical context for analyzing governance and value exchange in blockchain-based consortia operating under regulatory and economic constraints.

4.2   Organizational and Technical Setting

The following two sections specify the application context and its technical instantiation used in this study. The organizational perspective defines the actors, process stages, and critical process risks of the drinking-milk supply chain setting, including the roles of certification and public oversight. The technical perspective then maps this setting to a permissioned consortium blockchain design, specifying the participating organizations, access rights, and rule enforcement via smart contracts.

Organizational Setting. The study uses a drinking-milk supply chain as the application context because it provides a clear sequence of actors and standardized processes (see Fig. 3). The chain is represented as five sequential stages: production, transport, processing, distribution, and retail. To keep the scenario tractable, a milk collection point and direct farm-gate sales are not included. The resulting setting focuses on the stepwise product handover between five core actors until the product reaches consumers.

In addition, two oversight actors are included. A certifier verifies product and process data recorded by supply chain participants to support trustworthy claims and compliance evidence. State institutions act as the external authority that defines requirements, accredits certification, and oversees compliance, thereby protecting end consumers. Verified information contributes to consumer trust by providing evidence-backed product and process statements.

The scenario also highlights operational vulnerabilities that can impact product quality and availability. Three critical process areas are emphasized: maintaining the cold chain, handling disposal of raw milk when transport fails or quality problems occur, and ensuring timely delivery of packaging material. Transport disruptions (e.g., congestion, road closures, vehicle defects) can delay deliveries and compromise freshness or deadlines. Limited on-farm storage increases the risk that missed pickup requires disposal. Packaging is treated as a production constraint because just-in-time replenishment and low stock levels can lead to shortages that halt processing.

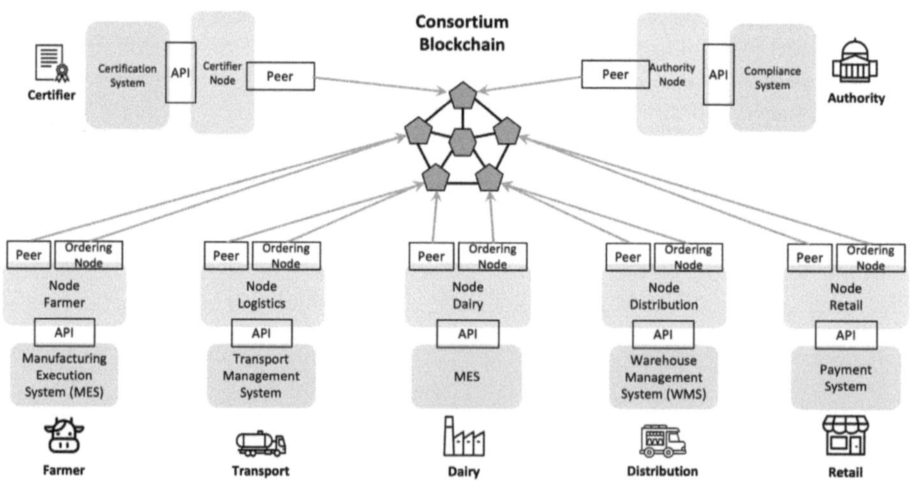

Fig. 3. Information systems view of the actors

Technical Setting. The technical realization is modeled as a permissioned consortium network implemented with Hyperledger Fabric. The network instantiates the organizational setting as seven organizations (R0–R6) (see Fig. 4): five supply chain actors plus a certifier and state institutions. Responsibilities for recording events follow the process stages: the farmer records production and initial product data; transport records shipment; the dairy records processing steps (e.g., pasteurization, homogenization, filling); distribution records storage and delivery to retail; and the retailer records the sale and potential complaints. The certifier and state institutions access recorded data to certify stakeholder data and to assess compliance with legal requirements. Consumers are not represented as peers because they have no direct read/write access; verified information can be provided through an external interface such as an app.

Each organization operates a peer (P0–P6) to access the ledger and smart contracts and uses at least one application (A0–A6) that represents its internal information system. Applications connect to peers via an API and can initiate read/write operations through the Fabric Gateway Service on the peer. The certifier and state institutions are modeled as read-only participants: they do not write data and do not operate ordering or endorsing peers, preserving neutrality and keeping operational data control with supply chain actors. All participants authenticate through certificate authorities (CA0–CA6) to establish identity within the network.

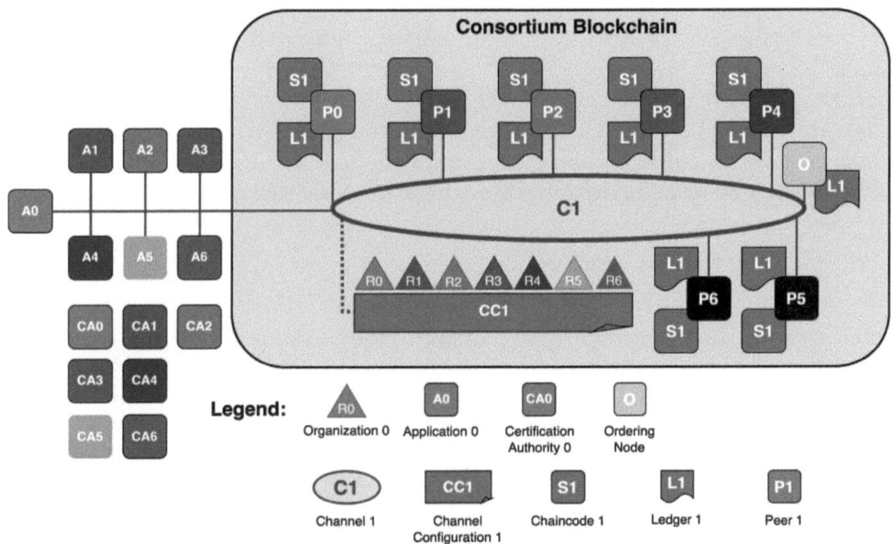

Fig. 4. Network design using the notation from the Hyperledger Fabric docs [12]

All peers are connected through a shared channel (C1), while the channel configuration (CC1) defines access policies and role allocations. Business logic is implemented as chaincode (S1) that enforces transaction rules before committing them to the ledger (L1). For example, a rule can ensure that a transport order is triggered only if temperature measurements remain within the specified range throughout transport.

4.3 Mapping of Use Cases and Blockchain Consortium Archetypes

In the milk supply chain scenario, use cases are not independent of consortium structure. They depend on (i) which actors must share data, (ii) whether a product is handed over between actors, and (iii) whether shared services beyond the supply chain should participate. The scenario distinguishes three consortium archetypes—vertical, horizontal, and ecosystem—and uses them as design alternatives for governance and value modeling.

Vertical Consortium: Cross-Tier Handover and Traceability. A vertical consortium connects actors across sequential stages of the supply chain (milk farmer, logistics/transport, dairy processor, distribution, retail). The core use cases focus on product handover, shared records, and verifiable compliance:

- **Traceability across Handovers:** Product-related data (e.g., quality, storage conditions, transport routes) is recorded on the shared ledger to improve traceability and support compliance with regulatory requirements.
- **Rule Enforcement at Process Boundaries:** Smart contracts can enforce acceptance criteria at handover points. For example, a transport order to the dairy is only triggered if the measured temperature remained within the required range during transport; otherwise the delivery is marked as non-processable and not accepted. The ledger is updated only when the rule is met.
- **Shared Audit Trail:** Because the main actors participate in the same channel and follow shared transaction rules, audits can rely on a consistent process history (who recorded what, when, under which rule).
- **Fit:** Vertical consortia are suitable when the use case requires data continuity across handovers and when compliance depends on process evidence that spans organizational boundaries.

Horizontal Consortium: Shared Obligations Among Peers. A horizontal consortium groups actors from the same business field (e.g., multiple milk farmers). In this archetype, there is no product handover between members; actors operate in parallel. Use cases therefore center on shared processes and shared costs rather than end-to-end product tracing:

- **Shared Documentation, Monitoring, and Reporting:** Members can exchange and standardize documentation, monitoring, and reporting processes within the consortium. This allows reuse of process artifacts and reduces duplicated effort.
- **Cost Sharing for Compliance Work:** By pooling efforts, members can lower costs and implement legal requirements more consistently because obligations can be handled collectively (e.g., shared templates, shared reporting workflows, shared monitoring routines).
- **Fit:** Horizontal consortia are suitable when the main problem is not handover transparency, but repeated compliance work across many similar organizations, and when benefits come from standardization and scale effects.

Ecosystem Consortium: Hybrid Structure and Supportive Services.
The ecosystem consortium is described as a hybrid that often grows from a vertical integration. It does not assume a fixed chain structure; instead it forms a network in which a supportive service is attached and creates additional utility beyond the existing consortium. This archetype supports use cases that go beyond vertical supply-chain links and beyond peer coordination:

- **Integration of Services that Extend the Core Network:** The ecosystem includes relationships that exceed pure supply-chain handovers or peer collaboration. In the milk scenario, this can include service providers and certification bodies.
- **Separation of Interest Groups:** Actors may share the same physical infrastructure but remain logically separated. Hyperledger Fabric can implement this separation via distinct channels, enabling strict partitioning of data access and governance scope by stakeholder group.
- **Shared Regulatory Intelligence as a Service:** A use case highlighted is the coordinated exchange of regulatory changes and legal requirements, creating a knowledge advantage that can translate into lower costs or faster action.
- **Fit:** Ecosystem consortia are suitable when additional stakeholders (e.g., certifiers, insurers, auditors, IT/analytics providers) should contribute services, and when governance must support multiple, partly overlapping communities with different information needs.

The mapping is grounded on the following selection rules. A **vertical consortium** is appropriate when the use case depends on shared evidence across supply chain handovers, such as traceability records, process status updates, and rule enforcement at transfer points. A **horizontal consortium** is appropriate when the use case targets coordination among peers without product handovers between members, in particular shared documentation, monitoring, reporting, and cost sharing for recurring compliance tasks. An **ecosystem consortium** is appropriate when the use case requires participation of additional service actors beyond the core chain or peer group, while still needing controlled information sharing and separation of stakeholder interests, for example through channel-based partitioning and governance that supports multiple communities.

5 Results

5.1 Governance Requirements

The eight design principles for governing commons by Ostrom [23] have already been applied to blockchain-based consortia in prior research. Jain et al. [13] analyze their application in clusters of small and medium-sized enterprises, while Greiner et al. [8] develop a practical governance model for blockchain-based consortia. Building on these interpretations, the principles are transferred to the drinking milk consortium scenario as follows:

1. **Boundaries:** Relevant data on origin, quality, and transport conditions must be clearly defined and accessible to consortium members. All participants should benefit equally from shared resources.
2. **Congruence:** The pricing of raw milk should reflect actual costs. In practice, benefits are often unevenly distributed, to the disadvantage of farmers [1]. Governance rules must therefore promote fair value distribution.
3. **Collective Choice:** All consortium members should participate in governance decisions, including the design of smart contracts and off-chain agreements.
4. **Monitoring:** Hyperledger Fabric enables technical monitoring and logging. In addition, governance rules must define how data is processed and supervised within the consortium.
5. **Graduated Sanctions:** To ensure compliance, proportional sanctions and incentives are required. Since farmers and dairies have different interests, sanctions must reflect these differences.
6. **Conflict Resolution:** The consortium must establish procedures to resolve disputes and align individual objectives with collective goals.
7. **Recognition:** As the scenario is located in Germany, contractual cooperation is legally recognized under the German Civil Code (§§311 ff.) [4]. Membership implies acceptance of consortium rules.
8. **Nested Enterprises:** This principle is not explicitly considered, as the analysis focuses on a clearly defined consortium and its internal value exchange.

Except for recognition and nested enterprises, the design principles are integrated into the DECENT governance modeling and the E^3 value analysis. Recognition is assumed, while nested governance levels are outside the scope of this study.

5.2   Governance Modeling (DECENT)

In the following, the meta-perspective of the initial scenario from a governance standpoint uses the DECENT framework. The modeling integrates Ostrom's [23] design principles to ensure a fair governance structure (see Table 2). To maintain conceptual clarity, the model focuses solely on the fundamental supply chain scenario, as a functioning blockchain-based consortium requires a fair and coherent governance foundation. The validity of the DECENT ontology is supported by prior applications in the EU Green Deal [14] and Fractional Reserve Banking [15], where it enabled structured modeling of governance mechanisms at a consistent level of abstraction. Nevertheless, further research is required to strengthen external validity across additional sectors and governance contexts. The drinking milk supply chain scenario comprises eight actors grouped into Operators, Consumers, and Regulators. This classification follows a governance-oriented perspective rather than the operational sequence of the value chain. It clarifies the distribution of roles within the consortium and enables a structured analysis of incentives, responsibilities, and objectives. The milk farmer keeps dairy cows and produces raw milk, acting as a primary data provider by documenting information related to origin, husbandry conditions, and the production process. The transport actor collects the raw milk and delivers it to the dairy, assuming transport-related risks and providing logistics data, such as temperature and delivery conditions, to the consortium. The dairy processes the raw milk into drinking milk and generates data on raw milk quality, processing parameters, and final product quality. Subsequently, the distribution actor delivers the finished product to retail outlets. Similar to transport, distribution assumes logistical risk and contributes relevant transport and storage data. The retail actor sells the drinking milk to the end customer. In addition to its commercial function, retail serves as an important data interface by collecting customer feedback, reporting quality issues, and coordinating product recalls in cases where batches fail to meet statutory food safety requirements. The goals of the actors can be derived from their membership in the respective groups, as these groups can be understood as communities of shared interests [14]. The group of Operators pursues shared objectives, most notably selling the final product at a fair price. Achieving this requires cost-efficient cooperation within the consortium, which can only be realized collectively. Operators must also comply with statutory requirements imposed by public authorities and meet certification criteria. In addition to these common goals, individual actors pursue specific objectives, such as improving processing methods and operational efficiency. For the milk farmer in particular, this includes enhancing the husbandry conditions of dairy cows. The group of Regulators follows more abstract, oversight-oriented objectives. Public authorities monitor compliance with legal requirements along the supply chain and ensure food safety in the interest of consumer protection. They also verify adherence to husbandry standards and sustainability criteria. The certifier aims to enhance food safety and strengthen consumer protection through independent verification, thereby increasing trust in the product. The group of Consumers does not actively shape governance rules but derives its interests from the objectives of the other groups. Consumers seek to purchase a safe product at a fair price and to access transparent product information provided by the consortium. From the goals, objectives can subsequently be derived. These serve to operationalize the housing conditions of dairy cows, for example by ensuring compliance with a minimum space requirement of $5\,m^2$ per animal (lying and walking area) and increasing it to $6\,m^2$ per animal (lying and walking area) . The DECENT framework can also be used to model rule sets that are essential for effective decentralized governance. In order to achieve the goals described above, a coherent set of rules is required [14]. The first set of rules applies to the group of Operators. (1) All actors must be enabled—both organizationally and technically—to operate their own network node in order to ensure direct access to the ledger. (2) All operators are granted equal access rights to consortium product information, including data classified as business-critical. This does not imply a loss of data sovereignty. (3) Ownership of all shared data remains with the respective originators. (4) Prior to publication or disclosure to external stakeholders, data must be verified by an independent certifier. (5) The introduction of new rules or modification of existing ones requires consensus-based decision-making within the consortium. This includes participation rights in decisions regarding the admission of new members or the exit of existing ones. (6) Given the differing interests of actors in production, processing, and distribution, governance mechanisms must ensure fair cooperation by aligning company-specific objectives with overarching consortium goals. The second set of rules concerns the group of Regulators, and partly Consumers. Consumers do not have a separate rule framework but are addressed through access-related provisions. (7) Publicly accessible data must exclude business-critical or sensitive information, except where necessary for the verification of product information, sustainability standards, and husbandry conditions. (8) Authorized consortium data must be reviewable by certifiers and public authorities. Once certified, relevant process and product data may be accessed by regulators and end customers. (9) Reporting deadlines are defined by public authorities. (10) In addition to data verification, the actors themselves must undergo audits conducted by independent certifiers.

The first action plan, Access Authorization and Data Sovereignty, defines who is allowed to access the consortium's data and the publicly available blockchain information. The second measure, Rule Conformity, aims to ensure that the consortium's rules are adapted to specific needs and contextual conditions. These requirements may, for example, be articulated by governmental authorities, certification bodies, or customers. The third action plan, Participatory Decision-Making, ensures that stakeholders affected by the resource system are able to participate in decision-making processes. The objective is to reach consensus in order to prevent the disadvantage of individual actors. Through Auditing, companies are monitored with regard to their compliance with sustainability standards and supervisory obligations. Audits must be conducted by external and independent certification bodies. The fifth action plan, Conflict and Sanction Mechanisms, aims to individually sanction unfair and opportunistic behavior. In addition, mechanisms for conflict resolution should be provided, for example through mediation by an independent mediator. The DECENT ontology provides a structured approach to incentive design. An incentive is intended to support the achievement of predefined objectives and, consequently, overarching goals [14]. Conceptually, incentives generalize the components of reward and penalty. In the drinking milk consortium, goal fulfillment may generate several benefits for participating actors. Compliance with sustainability standards and improved husbandry conditions can increase consumer trust and enhance market competitiveness. An independently certified end product may attract a broader customer base. Moreover, the immutability and transparency of blockchain-based product data allow consumers to trace the entire production process—going beyond traditional quality labels that provide only limited information. Additionally, a sales price that adjusts to rising production costs may serve as a financial reward for achieving defined sustainability and quality targets. Conversely, failure to meet agreed objectives or violations of consortium rules may trigger sanctions. Suitable measures include restricting read access to

Table 2. Mapping of Ostrom's design principles to action plans, rules, and mechanisms

Principle	Action Plan	Rule	Mechanism
1	Access Authorization & Data	(1)	Enable actors to operate the technical infrastructure
		(2,4)	Assign read/write permissions to consortium members and certifiers
		(3)	Data sovereignty remains with the originator
		(4)	Public read access after prior certification
		(7)	Verification of data intended for public access
2	Rule Compliance	(8)	Awareness of compliance with husbandry conditions and product quality
		(8)	Auditable data access by authorized entities
		(9)	Compliance with reporting, documentation, control, and labeling
3	Participatory Decision-Making	(5)	Equal and transparent rule introduction and modification
		(1)	Enable technical and knowledge prerequisites for participation
4	Auditing	(10)	Audits by independent certifiers
		(8)	Public authority access for sustainability monitoring
5,6	Conflict & Sanction Mechanisms	(6)	Company- and interest-specific incentives and sanctions
		(6)	Dispute resolution services and independent mediators

product data, imposing monetary compensation payments to the consortium, or, in severe cases, excluding actors from the network. Transparent communication of the incentive structure is essential to ensure that all members understand both the benefits of compliance and the consequences of rule violations.

5.3 Value Exchange Modeling (E^3 Value)

Building on the DECENT meta-perspective, this section examines the analysis results of economic value exchange across the three consortium archetypes (vertical, horizontal, and ecosystem) using the e^3 value framework. The objective is to examine how different structural configurations affect value distribution, incentive alignment, and long-term viability. For illustration purposes, the e^3 value model of the horizontal consortium is shown as an example to visualize the modeling logic (see Fig. 5). However, the following analysis gives equal consideration to all three archetypes.

In the **vertical consortium**, actors operate at different stages of the supply chain, such as production, processing, distribution, and retail. Value exchange follows the sequence of product flows and associated information flows. Upstream actors primarily contribute production and quality data, while downstream actors benefit from enhanced traceability, certification support, and increased consumer trust.

The analysis of the E^3 value model shows that value creation is interdependent but asymmetrically distributed. Actors at later stages may capture higher financial margins, while upstream actors often bear significant operational and compliance costs. Without governance mechanisms that ensure fair compensation or additional incentives, economically weaker actors may have limited motivation to participate. The sustainability of the vertical consortium therefore depends on balancing value capture across supply chain levels and aligning incentives with actual contributions.

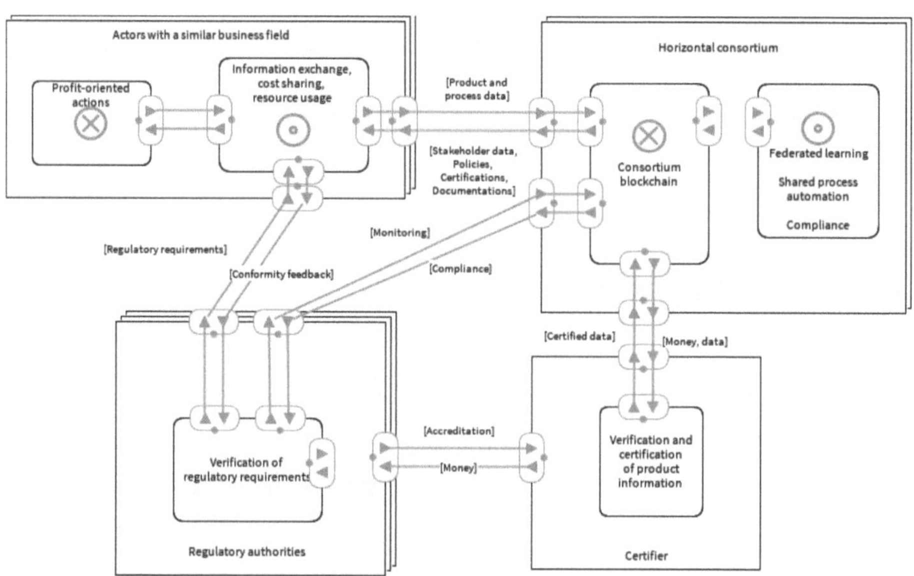

Fig. 5. Implementation example E^3 value model: Horizontal consortium

In the **horizontal consortium**, actors operate at the same level of the supply chain. The main economic rationale lies in shared infrastructure, standardization, and collective transparency. Each actor contributes operational data and financial resources to maintain the blockchain network. In return, they receive efficiency gains, reduced documentation effort, compliance support, and reputational benefits.

Because actors occupy a similar economic position, value flows are structurally symmetric. However, this configuration introduces the risk of free-riding. Participants may attempt to minimize their own contributions while benefiting from shared transparency and cost reductions. The modeling highlights that horizontal consortia require clear cost allocation rules, collective decision-making structures, and enforceable contribution mechanisms to remain viable.

The **ecosystem consortium** extends beyond core supply chain actors by including additional stakeholders such as certifiers or regulatory bodies. In this configuration, value exchange becomes multi-directional and includes both monetary and non-monetary value objects, such as certification, compliance validation, and enhanced credibility.

While the inclusion of external stakeholders can increase overall system trust and create new value propositions, it also increases governance complexity and coordination effort. Actors depend not only on each other's operational data but also on validation and oversight functions. The analysis shows that sustainability in ecosystem consortia depends strongly on clearly defined roles, responsibilities, and incentive mechanisms that compensate additional coordination costs.

Across all three archetypes, the modeling shows that economic viability depends on a clear alignment between value contribution and value appropriation. However, the dominant incentive risks differ structurally: vertical consortia face asymmetric value capture across supply chain levels, horizontal consortia are vulnerable to free-riding among equal actors, and ecosystem consortia struggle with governance complexity and increased coordination costs. Despite these differences, one common insight emerges: blockchain technology alone does not ensure sustainable value exchange. Long-term viability requires governance mechanisms that transparently define contributions, allocate costs fairly, and guarantee that each participant receives sufficient economic or strategic benefit. This confirms that consortium architecture and governance design must be closely aligned to establish stable incentive structures in blockchain-based supply chains.

6   Discussion

The central research question examined how sustainable governance structures can be designed for blockchain-based consortia in regulated supply chains and the results show that governance cannot be reduced to a purely technical design problem. Instead, sustainable consortium governance requires the alignment of economic value exchange, incentive structures, and institutional rules. The comparative modeling of vertical, horizontal, and ecosystem consortia demonstrates that different architectural configurations generate different incentive risks and coordination challenges.

The integration of Ostrom's design principles provided a normative framework to derive governance requirements. These principles helped to structure boundaries, participation rights, monitoring mechanisms, sanctions, and conflict resolution procedures. By modeling governance with the DECENT ontology, these principles were translated into formal governance components such as actors, roles, rules, and incentives. The E^3 value models then enabled the analysis of whether the resulting governance structures generate sufficient economic incentives for sustained participation.

Overall, the research question allows for the following answer: sustainable blockchain consortia require coherent alignment among governance rules, economic value flows, and incentive mechanisms. Without such alignment, structural weaknesses such as power imbalances, free-riding, or coordination overload can undermine long-term viability.

The results provide both theoretical and practical implications for the design of governance structures in blockchain-based consortia.

From a theoretical perspective, the study contributes to the further development of blockchain governance concepts. By combining Ostrom's design principles [23] with the DECENT ontology and the E^3 value framework, the research demonstrates how classical governance theory can be transferred into digital and decentralized environments. The DECENT-based modeling enables a standardized description of governance structures, allowing systematic comparison across different consortium types. The development of abstract E^3 value models for vertical, horizontal, and ecosystem architectures shows how economic value exchange can be explicitly linked to governance design.

The integrated modeling approach highlights that blockchain governance must be understood as a socio-technical system. In addition to technical rules and smart contracts, organizational measures, institutional embedding, and legal frameworks are necessary. This supports an interdisciplinary perspective on digital governance and underlines the relevance of Ostrom's principles for technological infrastructures.

From a practical perspective, the results provide concrete guidance for designing viable and fair governance structures in supply chain consortia. The differentiation between three architecture types helps practitioners select a suitable structural configuration depending on strategic objectives and stakeholder constellations. The structured modeling approach allows organizations to systematically derive governance rules, define responsibilities, and translate them into operational processes and enforceable mechanisms within a blockchain-based consortium.

7   Conclusion

This paper examines how governance structures in a blockchain-based food supply chain consortium can be designed to support economic value exchange and sustainable incentive systems. By integrating Ostrom's design principles, the DECENT framework, and the E^3 value approach, an integrated model was developed to capture institutional, organizational, and economic dimensions of governance. The findings indicate that consortium viability increases when multiple use cases are bundled within a shared infrastructure, enabling cost distribution and shared value creation. A key insight is that effective governance requires a holistic approach combining technical, normative, and organizational mechanisms. Ostrom's principles highlight the importance of clearly defined boundaries, participatory decision-making, monitoring, and graduated sanctions for stable cooperation. The E^3 value models make economic incentives transparent and demonstrate the need for differentiated incentive structures along the value chain. Hyperledger Fabric proved to be a suitable technological foundation due to its modular architecture and fine-grained access control mechanisms. Overall, the developed methodology contributes to the systematic design of fair and resilient governance structures in digital consortia. Future research should further investigate regulatory interfaces, public authority integration, and the practical implementation of effective incentive systems.

References

1. agrarheute: Preiskampf trinkmilch (2022). https://www.agrarheute.com/management/preiskampf-aldi-co-pressen-bauern-industrie-589219, Accessed 14 Mar 2025
2. Bogner, A., Littig, B., Menz, W.: Das Experteninterview. Springer (2005)
3. Curty, S., Fill, H.G.: A domain-specific e3value extension for analyzing blockchain-based value networks. In: Almeida, J.P.A., Kaczmarek-Heß, M., Koschmider, A., Proper, H.A. (eds.) IFIP Working Conference on The Practice of Enterprise Modeling, pp. 74–90. Springer, Cham (2023). https://doi.org/10.1007/978-3-031-48583-1_5
4. Deutschland, B.: Rechtsgeschäftliche und rechtsgeschäftsähnliche schuldverhältnisse (2002), https://dejure.org/gesetze/BGB/311.html, Accessed 14 May 2025
5. Gläser, J., Laudel, G.: Experteninterviews und qualitative Inhaltsanalyse. Springer-Verlag (2010)
6. Gordijn, J., Akkermans, J.: Value-based requirements engineering: exploring innovative e-commerce ideas. Requirements Eng. **8**, 114–134 (2003)
7. Gramoli, V.: On the danger of private blockchains. In: Workshop on Distributed Cryptocurrencies and Consensus Ledgers (DCCL'16), pp. 1–4 (2016), https://allquantor.at/blockchainbib/pdf/gramoli2016danger.pdf
8. Greiner, M., Zeiss, C., Neis, N., Seidenfad, K., Lechner, U., Winkelmann, A.: Designing a governance model for blockchain-based traceability systems in supply chain consortia (2025)
9. Hardin, G.: The Tragedy of the Commons. Science **162**(3859), 1243–1248 (1968). http://www.jstor.org/stable/1724745
10. Hess, C., Ostrom, E. (eds.): Understanding Knowledge as a Commons. The MIT Press (2006). https://doi.org/10.7551/mitpress/6980.001.0001
11. Hevner, A.R., March, S.T., Park, J., Ram, S.: Design science in information systems research. MIS Q. 75–105 (2004)
12. Hyperledger Foundation: Hypereldger Fabric - Security Model (2024). https://hyperledger-fabric.readthedocs.io/en/release-2.5/security_model.html
13. Jain, G., Shrivastava, A., Paul, J., Batra, R.: Blockchain for SME clusters: An ideation using the framework of ostrom commons governance. Inf. Syst. Front. **24**(4), 1125–1143 (2022)
14. Kaya, F., Gordijn, J.: Decent: An ontology for decentralized governance in the renewable energy sector. In: 2021 IEEE 23rd Conference on Business Informatics (CBI), vol. 1, pp. 11–20. IEEE (2021)

15. Kaya, F., Perez, F., Dekker, J., Gordijn, J.: Decent: A domain specific language to design governance decisions. In: Nurcan, S., Opdahl, A.L., Mouratidis, H., Tsohou, A. (eds.) International Conference on Research Challenges in Information Science, pp. 603–610. Springer, Cham (2023). https://doi.org/10.1007/978-3-031-33080-3_43

16. Kaya, F., Wang, Y., Heringa, J., Gordijn, J.: The decent software modeling toolkit to design decentralized governance models. In: Boucher, X., Buchmann, R.A., Fill, HG., Kyritsis, D., Utz, W. (eds.) Domain-Specific Conceptual Modeling: The OMiLAB Community of Practice, pp. 3–22. Springer (2025). https://doi.org/10.1007/978-3-031-98660-4_1

17. Kuechler, B., Vaishnavi, V.: On theory development in design science research: anatomy of a research project. Eur. J. Inf. Syst. 17(5), 489–504 (2008)

18. Li, L., Wu, J., Cui, W.: A review of blockchain cross-chain technology. IET Blockchain 3(3), 149–158 (2023). https://doi.org/10.1049/blc2.12032

19. Liu, Y., Lu, Q., Zhu, L., Paik, H.Y., Staples, M.: A systematic literature review on blockchain governance. J. Syst. Softw. 197, 111576 (2023)

20. Lumineau, F., Wang, W., Schilke, O.: Blockchain governance–a new way of organizing collaborations? Organ. Sci. 32(2), 500–521 (2021)

21. Nakamoto, S.: Bitcoin: A peer-to-peer electronic cash system (2008)

22. Nick, S.: Smart contracts: building blocks for digital markets. EXTROPY J. Transhumanist Thought 16(18), 1–14 (1996). https://www.fon.hum.uva.nl/rob/Courses/InformationInSpeech/CDROM/Literature/LOTwinterschool2006/szabo.best.vwh.net/smart_contracts_2.html

23. Ostrom, E.: Governing the Commons: The Evolution of Institutions for Collective Action. Political Economy of Institutions and Decisions, Cambridge University Press (1990). https://doi.org/10.1017/CBO9780511807763

24. Seidenfad, K.: Collaborative Blockchain-based Information Systems on the Network Edge : Designs to Tackle Collective Problems. Ph.D. thesis, Universität der Bundeswehr München (2025). https://athene-forschung.unibw.de/85257?show_id=152416

25. Seidenfad, K., Wagner, T., Hrestic, R., Lechner, U.: Demonstrating feasibility of blockchain-driven carbon accounting–a design study and demonstrator. In: Phillipson, F., Eichler, G., Erfurth, C., Fahrnberger, G. (eds.) International Conference on Innovations for Community Services, pp. 28–46. Springer, Cham (2022). https://doi.org/10.1007/978-3-031-06668-9_5

26. Stoll, C., Klaaßen, L., Gallersdörfer, U.: The carbon footprint of Bitcoin. Joule 3(7), 1647–1661 (2019). https://doi.org/10.1016/j.joule.2019.05.012

27. Sunyaev, A.: Distributed Ledger Technology. In: Internet Computing, pp. 265–299. Springer, Cham (2020). https://doi.org/10.1007/978-3-030-34957-8_9

28. Symons, C.: It governance framework. Forrester Research (2005)

29. Tapscott, D., Ticoll, D., Lowy, A.: Digital capital: harnessing the power of business webs. Ubiquity 2000(May) (2000). https://doi.org/10.1145/341836.336231

30. Weigand, H., Johannesson, P., Andersson, B.: An Ontology of IS Design Science Research Artefacts. In: Dalpiaz, F., Zdravkovic, J., Loucopoulos, P. (eds.) RCIS 2020. LNBIP, vol. 385, pp. 129–144. Springer, Cham (2020). https://doi.org/10.1007/978-3-030-50316-1_8

31. Weill, P.: Don't just lead, govern: how top-perfoming firms govern IT. MIS Q. Executive 3(1), 18 (2004)

32. Yaga, D., Mell, P., Roby, N., Scarfone, K.: Blockchain technology overview. Tech. rep., National Institute of Standards and Technology, Gaithersburg, MD (2018). https://doi.org/10.6028/NIST.IR.8202

33. Yue, K.b., Kallempudi, P., Sha, K., Wei, W., Liu, X.: Governance attributes of consortium blockchain applications. In: 27th Americas Conference on Information Systems. Montreal (2021). https://aisel.aisnet.org/amcis2021/strategic_is/strategic_is/4/
34. Zavolokina, L., Ziolkowski, R., Bauer, I., Schwabe, G.: Management, governance and value creation in a blockchain consortium. MIS Q. Executive **19**(1) (2020). https://doi.org/10.17705/2msqe.00022
35. Ziolkowski, R., Miscione, G., Schwabe, G.: Decision problems in blockchain governance: old wine in new bottles or walking in someone else's shoes? J. Manag. Inf. Syst. **37**(2), 316–348 (2020). https://doi.org/10.1080/07421222.2020.1759974

WYSIWYHD: Collaborative Action Between Humans and Machines in Critical Safety and Security Environments

Mandy Balthasar$^{(\boxtimes)}$ [ID], Stefan Fleischmann [ID], and Ulrike Lechner [ID]

Institute for Protection and Dependability, University of the Bundeswehr Munich,
Neubiberg, Germany
`{mandy.balthasar,stefan.fleischmann,ulrike.lechner}@unibw.de`

Abstract. Effective human-computer collaboration (HCT) in collaborative intrusion detection systems (CIDS) presents challenges related to perception and evaluation in time-critical decision-making under uncertainty. The keys to this are situational awareness and a seamless and reliable connection between the hybrid actors. The effectiveness of these fundamentals depends on whether the human factors influencing the analysis of data and information are adequately taken into account. This raises the question of how facts can be visualized in an optimal CIDS. Within the framework of a user-centered design approach, design elements for a dashboard were identified and developed. The result is a portfolio of design objects that can be used in the development and redesign of human-in-the-loop systems (HITL) in CIDS, particularly in critical security environments. After all, WYSIWYHD applies: What you see is what you have to decide.

Keywords: Collaborative intrusion detection systems · Collective intelligence · Human in the loop · Human-computer interaction · Joint human-machine intelligence

1 Introduction

Based on the concept of human-in-the-loop (HITL), humans and machines work together toward a common, overarching goal. Coordinated by specific task assignments, the greatest challenge of HITL approaches in collaborative intrusion detection systems (CIDS) lies in striking a balance between human knowledge on a cognitive and affective level, and data-based algorithms on the part of the artificial actor. At the same time, such an approach takes place in an environment that is characterized by complexity and multi-optionality, forcing decisions to be made under uncertainty and time pressure, before cyberattacks can paralyze entire systems within a very short time. One possible approach may lie in the optimal distribution of tasks and roles in order to best balance the opposing strengths and weaknesses of the actors [2,3,27]. The goal is to increase the precision with which complex attacks and threats are identified

© The Author(s), under exclusive license to Springer Nature Switzerland AG 2026
K. Kirchner et al. (Eds.): I4CS 2026, CCIS 3007, pp. 96–118, 2026.
https://doi.org/10.1007/978-3-032-27096-2_6

and evaluated in terms of their potential and risks. A hybrid approach combining humans and machines also offers the possibility of a resilient security architecture that continues to evolve through continuous mutual feedback. As in other contexts, CIDS can also benefit from HITL [9,17,22,28]. If only automated intrusion detection activities are used, a data-driven approach is pursued, which is impressive because of its speed. If humans are integrated through HITL, a process-driven procedure is added at the same time, which consists of intuition, experience, and an understanding of causalities, among other things [24,49]. However, combining these different approaches requires optimal communication between the individual actors. Visualization as a means of conveying information content is a key factor here [33]. Visual stimuli must be used in a targeted manner in order to serve human factors. The human capacity for visual analysis must be taken into account, as well as the concepts behind cognitive heuristics and biases. The goal is to enable CIDS to detect attacks more efficiently and accurately and to respond effectively to incidents as they occur. This must be accompanied by evidence-based communication on a common analytical basis. To this end, this work compiles a portfolio of concepts for the design and implementation of HITL in CIDS, in order to optimally connect the various actors on the basis of a visual interface. The central design principles for this are: a clear distribution of tasks and roles, the facilitation of effective communication, and a strategic and recipient-centered visualization that takes into account human perception and potential cognitive distortions. The aim is to create a resilient security architecture that detects complex cyberattacks more accurately under time pressure and enables informed decisions. As a conceptual design framework for HITL CIDS, this work focuses on visualization and interaction principles. The contribution lies in structuring the design space, incorporating insights from HCT, and proposing a set of transferable design artifacts for an optimal human-machine visual interface and the resulting best possible decision under conditions of uncertainty and time constraints.

1.1   Background

Communication, as an exchange of information, is the fundamental process for a collaborative system such as CIDS [6,11,14,21]. In a hybrid environment consisting of numerous natural and artificial actors, visualization is the fundamental channel for a pronounced exchange (see the communication model according to [40]). If joint decisions on a current attack and threat situation are to be made based on visual communication, the following applies: what you see is what you have to decide (WYSIWYHD) (compare: WYSIWYG [32]). To this end, all aspects, background information, and options must be collected, analyzed, and clearly illustrated. This involves the presentation of both data and processes that must be adequately prepared. At the same time, the degree of networking between actors is evolving from a user-centered decision support system (DSS) to an HITL approach, as collaborative human-computer teaming (HCT) [35], with a focus on the distribution of tasks based on the respective strengths and weaknesses of the actors (see Fig. 1 based on [4]).

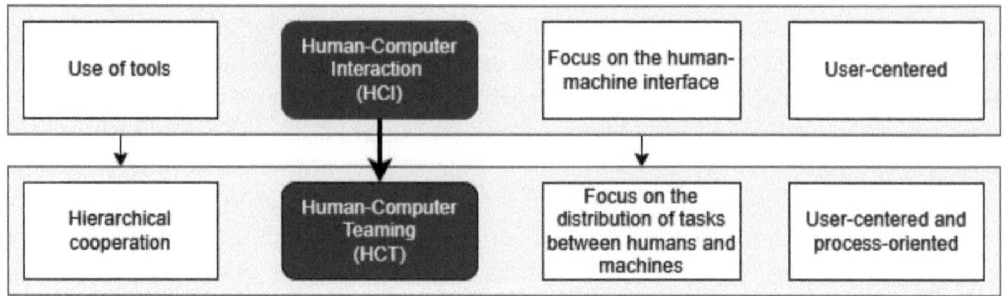

Fig. 1. Differentiation between Human-Computer Interaction (HCI) and Human-Computer Teaming (HCT)

The goal of HITL in CIDS is to enable cooperative action from human-computer interaction (HCI) to more closely integrate HCT, which supports both data-driven and process-driven cooperation (see also Fig. 1). The background to this is the effective use of the opposing strengths and weaknesses of the actors in favor of early detection of anomalies and security incidents. Although automated algorithms can efficiently process and communicate enormous amounts of data, human experts identify false alarms and evaluate attack patterns using their knowledge of causality and context. This cooperative approach can increase the detection rate, reduce false alarms, and highlight developments, but it also affects the initial response time, which is extended. To limit response time, data and processes must be displayed effectively so that information can be communicated quickly and efficiently within the available attention span. Due to the increasing cognitive load on human actors, such as analysts, as well as the growing quantity and complexity of data in CIDS [38], it is important to optimize communication exchange and thus minimize the response time of the system.

1.2 Challenges and Potential

For effective visualization in CIDS, it is essential to convey information quickly. Transparency must be created, context provided, and an overview conveyed, in order to correctly validate events and respond effectively and immediately to an overarching threat situation. At the same time, it must be taken into account that human attention is limited and that a large amount of diverse information already had to be processed. In addition, uncertainties influence visualization of analysis results and assessments at the human microlevel. Blind spots can arise, as can irresolvable contradictions. Nevertheless, assumptions must be made and probabilities calculated in order to bridge blind spots, revise misjudgments, and thus minimize uncertainties. In design, a distinction must therefore be made between the message and the information content. The visual message (VM) must be consistent with the information contained and highlight it in the best possible way. In order to detect anomalies and security incidents in networks at an early stage, data, information, indicators, and suspicious processes are communicated to each other in CIDS. This offers the following advantages and challenges for virtual messages:

- Increased detection quality through aggregated data, more context, and greater security
  VM: More context behind visual messages
- Shorter response times through joint alerts and coordinated measures
  VM: Uniform visual messages for all stakeholders
- Increased precision through correlations from multiple sources
  VM: Increased information content in a single visual message
- Optimization of scalability through distributed monitoring without central bottlenecks
  VM: Scaling of clear transparency of the visual message
- Ability to analyze long-term trends through continuous collection of data for attack forensics and pattern recognition
  VM: Visual message indicating direction

Even with a thorough representation of the threat infrastructure through optimal VM, attributing cyberattacks remains nontrivial. Various concealment tactics introduce uncertainty into visualization, creating additional complexity and further expanding the already existing range of options, which in turn inhibits decision-making under time pressure or stress [19]. The challenge in designing an effective VM with uncertain information content is to ensure that transparency can exist without over-complexity, clarity without under-complexity, and contextuality without incomprehensibility. In order to exploit the potential of visual communication, it is essential to transfer knowledge about the effects of visualization to design. Design, here, refers to the systematic config-uration of elements to create a targeted composition. In contrast, visualization is a form of representing a design that is intended to support people in performing their tasks [34]. The concept of visualization design study was applied as part of a user-centered design (UCD) approach. This involved analyzing the challenges facing people who are faced with the requirements of CIDS. A visualization design was created that meets the needs and abilities of users [39], while also taking into account the critical time context of a CIDS, which is characterized by uncertainty and complexity. Speed is crucial when responding to attacks in this environment. This pressure must be countered by an approach that effectively balances the analysis speed of artificial actors with human intuition and judg-ment [38]. In order to cooperatively combine technological precision and human judgment, numerous characteristics and abilities of individual actors must mesh precisely. For this optimal integration, the contextuality and focus of all actors on the task were evaluated. Since federated systems, in particular, optimize the processes necessary to coordinate numerous actors toward a common goal [26], the core of the numerous tasks in CIDS was carefully examined. The aspect of communication that connects to the reproduction of messages [40], such as attack data, analysis results, or options of action, forms the basis of HITL in CIDS. This is why an in-depth examination of information flows was carried out, from the development of diagrams and storylines to vignettes and use cases. A dashboard optimized for communication processes can be used to identify attacks more accurately, differentiate between attacks based on the existing context, and increase the speed of decision-making. Machine detection can increase the detection rate of IDS and, at the same time, improve the quality of attack assessment using HITL, which drives targeted learning processes for both humans and technical systems. CIDS with HITL respond more slowly to new types of attacks than purely technical systems would. However, the gain in accuracy in the evaluation and the associated reduction in false positives or false negatives means that the aspect of precision can outweigh that of speed, and the best possible communication through effective visualization can prove its added value.

2   Interface Design

In order to make optimal use of the sometimes conflicting strengths and weaknesses of numerous actors within a common CIDS, a visualization design that can serve as many characteristics of the actors as possible is required. To achieve this, it is essential to be able to effectively communicate the current situation, with existing uncertainties and potential risks, taking into account individual perceptions. In order to create a user-friendly design, existing needs must be understood and the respective tasks, their context, and the desired goals must be known. This requires a detailed survey of requirements using numerous complementary methods from user research and context analysis, as well as participatory development. This results in numerous insights from scenarios, sketches, vignettes, use cases, mock-ups, and prototypes in relation to visual communication, perception, and limitations, which must be taken into account, especially in the context of complex systems under uncertainty and time pressure, such as CIDS. To enable identification, analysis, and discussion of the HITL approach in CIDS, a dashboard interface was developed as part of this study. The presented dashboard should be understood as a conceptual artifact rather than a production-ready system. It serves as a design probe to explore how humanâĂŞmachine collaboration, uncertainty visualization, and decision-making processes can be structured in CIDS.

2.1   Design Objectives

The primary design goal is to promote shared situational awareness among distributed actors. In an CIDS, effective collaboration is based on actors developing a common understanding of the current threat situation. Consequently, the dashboard aims to provide a unified view by integrating heterogeneous status information into a common situational context. Another goal is to enable responsible decision-making under uncertain and time-critical conditions. Decisions about the detection of intruders are rarely based on complete or unambiguous information. Instead, analysts must act under uncertainty, balancing speed and accuracy. Mosqueira-Rey et al. emphasize that, in HITL systems, interface design and interaction paradigms are crucial to supporting human judgment in the best possible way [31]. The dashboard therefore aims to enable human actors to make informed decisions, while maintaining control and being able to take responsibility at all times. A third design goal is to reduce cognitive overload for users and mitigate frequent decision-making biases. Previous studies have shown that excessive information density and uncritical trust in automated recommendations can have a negative impact on human judgment, especially in high-stress environments [45]. The visual interface is therefore designed to reinforce the strengths of users, who can thus focus on relevant information while creating space for reflective thinking. Fundamentally, visualization aims to create a platform for continuous feedback and organizational learning. Human assessments and decisions, for example, are valuable sources of experiential knowledge. Integrating this resource as a core component of the system enables the iterative refinement of technical assessments and collaborative practices [31]. To ensure transparency between conceptual design goals and their implementation in the user interface, the main design goals are explicitly assigned to the corresponding visual and interactive elements of the dashboard (see Table 1).

Table 1. Traceability between design objectives and interface elements

Design Objective	Interface Element
Shared situational awareness	Map-based visualization and common operational picture
Trust calibration	Confidence gauge and uncertainty indicators
Evidence transparency	Evidence and provenance panel
Human oversight/control	Action (human approval) buttons (approve, reject, modify)
Collaborative coordination	Standardized reporting scheme and shared communication interface
Cognitive support	Cognitive guardrails and contextual prompts

2.2 Maps as an Effective Tool of HITL in CIDS

The context of the developed prototype describes a conceptual CIDS environment in which several national reporting centers from different European countries exchange status information about their operational capabilities, their own IT infrastructure, and the status of their country's critical national infrastructures (CNI), while also considering possible impacts. The respective impact of an attack depends on numerous factors: Does the incident have the potential to spread further (e.g., malware), how long could the infection of other systems take, have any related anomalies already occurred, what risks arise, and how high is the level of danger? However, none of these factors are completely predictable, which is why they cannot be visualized in advance. A shared overview of the situation can be provided, for example, using a map-based visualization, as shown in Fig. 2 as an example scenario, which can combine the incoming data sets into a shared picture of the situation. This creates a basis on which forecasts can be statistically calculated, visualized, and then intuitively evaluated, as more information is constantly added. As a visualization tool, maps also correspond to the human cognitive system, which can quickly perceive and process large amounts of information, especially when it can be absorbed in the form of a visualization [5,15,48]. To illustrate how the proposed interface supports decision-making, consider a simplified scenario: A reporting center, responsible for CNIs within its national jurisdiction, detects anomalous activity in one of them and informs the consortium. The map-based visualization automatically updates the status of both the reporting center and the affected CNI, notifies other actors, and highlights an increased risk level with reduced telemetry coverage and moderate confidence. The analyst reviews the evidence panel, identifies missing data sources (e.g. proxy telemetry) marked as blind spots, and—considering uncertainty indicators and potential propagation to interconnected entities—decides to escalate and initiate coordinated response actions. This scenario demonstrates how risk visualization, uncertainty representation, and evidence transparency support informed decision-making under time pressure. However, map-based visualizations are not universally suitable. Non-spatial incidents, such as logical dependencies or network-based attack propagation, may be better represented through graph-based or temporal views. Additionally, map-based representations can create a false sense of precision, which can lead users to overestimate the spatial accuracy of the data.

A map also enables human actors to efficiently interpret the state of the system and emerging threats, using the structured communication elements and context-related overlays provided. At the same time, this, in turn, enables a probabilistic assessment of the manner in which intervention can take place. This creates a visual dialog between humans and machines through the input of data, its statistical processing and visualization, the subsequent intuitive evaluation of the situation presented, and an assessment and output of possible forecasts based on probability calculations, which can ultimately lead to a decision on intervention. This combines the strengths and weaknesses of machine calculation and visualization with intuitive evaluation and cognitive and affective decision-making skills [3]. On a machine-based level, it is helpful to develop a mathematical model that includes key factors of critical infrastructure. The equations embedded in this model summarize the given elements and factors, which make attack processes, threats, and risks understandable, and thus can also resolve uncertainties. On a smaller scale, the creation of such a digital twin also enables predictions to be made about the potential effects of different tactics. The challenge in visualizing such an overview is to equip it with a calculable complexity that also accurately reflects the current situation. To increase the concreteness of the proposed system, the underlying dynamics of the CIDS can be described through a simplified conceptual model. Let $E = \{e_1, e_2, ..., e_n\}$ denote the set of entities, such as reporting centers and its related CNI.

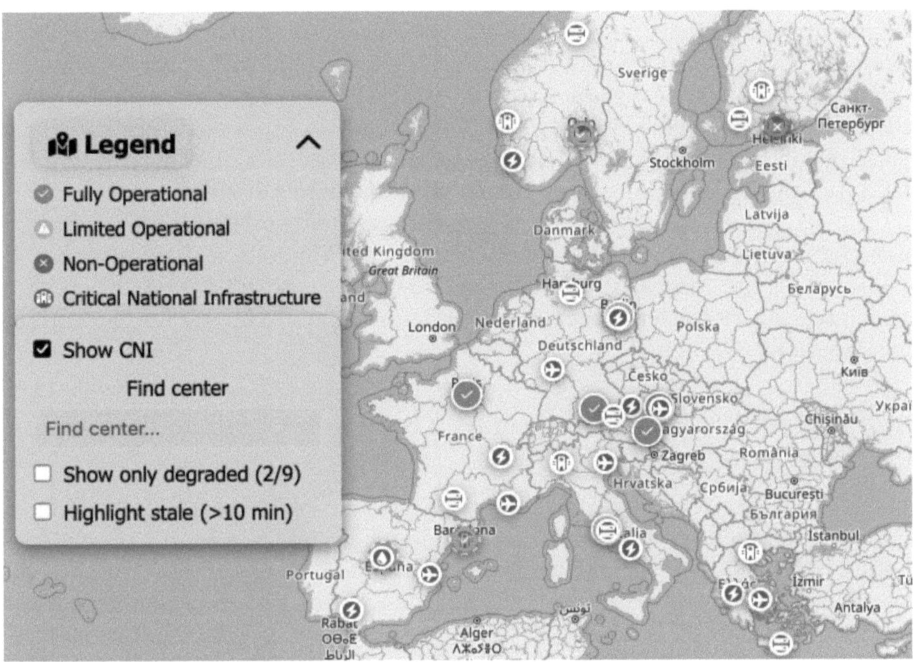

Fig. 2. Operational picture for a fictional example of situational awareness through status visualization by HITL in CIDS

Each entity $e \in E$ is characterized by a set of attributes derived from heterogeneous data sources:

- telemetry T_e (e.g., observed anomalies, alerts, logs),
- confidence C_e (reliability of the assessment),
- timeliness τ_e (freshness of available data).

Based on these inputs, the local risk level of an entity can be expressed as a function:

$$R_e = f(T_e, C_e, \tau_e)$$

where R_e represents the estimated risk associated with entity e.

In addition, dependencies between entities can be modeled to capture the potential propagation of incidents across the system. The probability of propagation from the entity e_i to e_j can be described as:

$$P_{i \to j} = g(R_{e_i}, d_{ij})$$

where d_{ij} represents the degree of interdependency or connectivity between entities.

This simplified model does not aim to provide a fully specified analytical formulation, but rather serves as a conceptual abstraction that links data input, uncertainty dimensions, and visualized system states. Provides a formal foundation for the visual representations used in the dashboard, such as risk indicators and propagation overlays. In the interface, these model components are reflected through visual elements, such as risk indicators, gauge-based confidence visualization, and propagation links between entities. The designed dashboard facilitates the exploration of mechanisms at the interface level, which enables HITL, even under time pressure and uncertainty. It emphasizes transparency, explainability, and coordinated interaction between human and machine actors. In this sense, the dashboard functions as a boundary object that connects technical intrusion detection processes with human cognitive, and organizational considerations.

2.3   Shared Situational Awareness Through a Common Operational Picture

Shared situational awareness is essential for effective collaboration. In distributed and federated security environments, individual actors often have a limited view of their micro level compared to a complex macro-level threat situation. If a shared view of the current situation is not guaranteed, coordination across organizational and technical boundaries becomes fragmented, which limits or delays the likelihood of identifying risks, and also increases the occurrence of uncoordinated, and thus mostly uncollaborative, responses. A dashboard addresses these challenges with a shared visualization of threats that combines status information from multiple national reporting centers and critical national infrastructures. Such a unified situation picture, as shown in Fig. 2, can, for example, draw on the visual structure of a map (see Subsect. 2.2). By displaying the current status of each reporting center within a jurisdiction, the interface helps to raise and maintain awareness among all stakeholders. Furthermore, a shared view enables stakeholders, such as analysts and decision-makers, to interpret individual incidents not in isolation, but in the context of the overall state of the system and the activities of other participants. The design thus reflects the federal nature of collaborative systems. Without a central control unit, the dashboard is populated with distributed reporting points. The heterogeneous data sources are subject to different organizational, technical, or contextual conditions, as well as possible manual input and processing. Each point provides standardized status information that is then integrated into the common interface without having to relinquish responsibility or decision-making authority at the micro level. This approach supports coordinated measures while respecting the decentralized structure characteristic of CIDS operations in the real world. To deal with complex long-term attacks in the real world that pursue both political and economic goals, efficient and smooth decision-making is necessary. At the same time, protection in cyberspace is usually preventive in nature. This makes up-to-date and high-quality data, human intuition, and immediate, targeted action all the more crucial in order to actively prevent, mitigate, limit, or even stop attacks.

The heterogeneous data from the individual reporting centers must be structured and transformed into a common, homogeneous situation overview before visualization, in order to be consistent, and thus comparable and efficiently presentable. For effective selection of the techniques for analyzing and visualizing the data sets, these are classified according to their structure into different data types. Descriptive statistics and visualization forms are defined for each type [1, 44].

Table 2. Data type-specific visualization

Data type	Property	Statement	Visualization example
Interval data	Measurable distances, without an absolute zero point	Distance from an randomly chosen "origin", and intervals	Annual temperatures
Categorical/ nominal data	Qualitative characteristics without natural ranking, numerical information	Category to which it belongs	Categories of simulations
Ordinal data	Logical order, without measurable distances, information about relative sizes	Relative order or ranking within a data set, for characteristics that are difficult to quantify (e.g., personal preferences)	Risk matrices, Likert scales
Ratio data	Measurable distances with an absolute zero point, with intrinsic origin	Ratio of size to unit of measurement	Costs, quantity of causalities

For visual communication within a CIDS, incoming data must be optimally processed. In addition to the data types that influence visualization by the technical transmitter, (see Table 2, the ability of the human receiver to perceive the data must also be taken into account when developing an effective visual interface. Human vision uses characteristics in the recognition of objects that, in the case of so-called preattentive attributes, take effect even before the cognitive system. Preattentive perception occurs involuntarily, without focusing or cognitive penetration of what is seen, in less than 0.2 s [29]. In contrast, humans need more time to process elements with non-preattentive attributes. This also applies to a combination of preattentive attributes in a representation [48]. Sorting the incoming data by type is also helpful in selecting a suitable preattentive attribute. For example, some attributes are suitable for certain data types. Based on visualization categories, such as movement, color, shape, frequency, and spatiality, a usefulness can be assigned to preattentive attributes. It can be assumed that categorical/nominal data types are particularly suitable for representation using preattentive attributes, such as movement, shape, and frequency, which accelerate the differentiation between displayed objects. For example, in the visualized interface of the CIDS (see Fig. 2), the critical infrastructure facilities are each displayed uniformly by means of a circle. In contrast, spatiality, i.e. positioning, is particularly effective for numerical data. Taking aspects of human cognition into account in visualization helps avoid misinterpretations, especially in time-critical contexts. In addition, the update of elements must be accompanied by smooth transitions from one status to the next. If a change in visualization is brought about by a brief interruption, change blindness occurs, which is the inability of human perception to recognize a correction. In addition to displaying existing facilities and internal system statuses, the CIDS visualization interface contextualizes the threat situation by integrating external factors. Visualizes dependencies on critical national infrastructures, such as energy supply, healthcare, aviation, and data centers, as well as reporting agencies, thus providing a situational context that goes beyond purely technical intrusion indicators. By incorporating these external elements, the dashboard enables users to assess the potential interaction between cyber incidents or national disasters and broader socio-technical dependencies, and to set priorities for response accordingly. Due to the large number of actors involved, other characteristics of vision must also be taken into account, which are not the same for all actors. These include, for example, the perception of colors. For example, 9% of the male population and $< 1\%$ of the female population are affected by red-green color blindness [42]. This is why the green and red marks on the CIDS dashboard are also visualized by a symbol (see Fig. 2). The focus of optimal visualization is particularly on supporting actors in communication and coordination. Due to complexity, uncertainty, and time pressure, human working memory is used to its full capacity. To also support this cognitive resource in the processing of data, the graphic design of a CIDS is constructed in such a way that the cognitive load is reduced.

2.4 Standardized Communication and Collaborative Coordination

Structured communication processes enable individual actors to coordinate their respective assumptions, assessments, and micro-decisions, and to jointly coordinate the resulting actions. Previous studies have shown that shared situational awareness does not arise exclusively and automatically from data availability, but is shaped by the way information is communicated, interpreted, and discussed between actors [36,41]. Depending on their individual experiences and preferences, actors focus on different aspects of their environment, thereby sharpening their existing, specific technical knowledge at the micro level. Communication and coordination give rise to collaborative processes and an awareness of the system or the prevailing situation at the macro level. At the same time, partial role-specific perspectives emerge, which combine to form a coherent understanding of the overall situation. These transformation processes of situational awareness through communication occur particularly in contexts characterized by an amount of information that cannot be managed individually and by uncertainty [41].

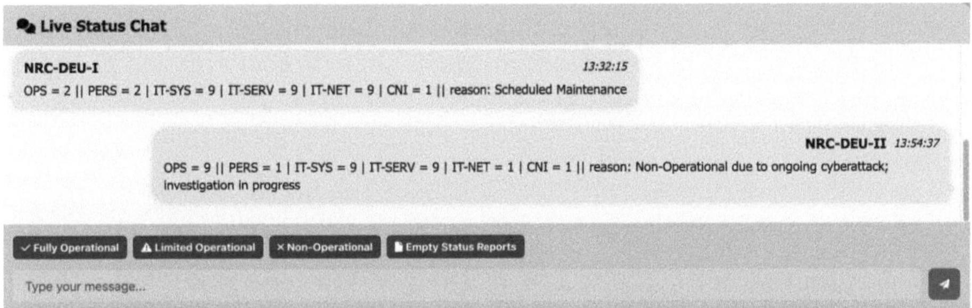

Fig. 3. Live status chat with reporting scheme from artifact

A communication scheme can promote the processes of exchange between actors and can also form a coordinating element. This could be achieved, for example, by means of a standardized cross-border chat function that is available to all actors and connects them (shown in Fig. 3). A uniform reporting scheme in terms of semantics and taxonomy creates a common basis on which data and information about people, technical systems and services, social and technical networks, and critical national infrastructures can be shared in real time. This gives every actor the opportunity to communicate the current state of their environment and event-related observations in a consistent, unambiguous format. At the same time, the accuracy of an interpretation of what is seen also depends on whether the respective actor takes into account the relative uncertainty of a source and thus adjusts the weighting proportionally. The "Bayesian brain" [23] of a human actor uses its experience to anticipate the existing situation. The more unknown the situation, or the greater its uncertainty, the greater the resource expenditure [16]. The rationale behind the use of a standard for the visual interface of CIDS is to create transparency by eliminating ambiguities and to reduce the cognitive effort required for interpretation that would otherwise be necessary [7,47]. Coordinated communication is therefore a key factor in complex, time-critical, socio-technical systems under uncertainty [36].

2.5 Visualizing Uncertainty, Evidence, and Trust Calibration

Uncertainty is defined here as the state of an actor that is formed from cognitive and affective signals and serves as a yardstick for hesitation in accepting what is perceived. Hesitation is usually caused by a lack of information or background knowledge and is related to events, their consequences, or their probability. This is followed by risks as a consequence of uncertainty about the objectives [18]. Especially in time-critical environments, such as CIDS, hesitation is an effect that should be avoided. Effective collaboration between actors in CIDS, therefore, requires explicit handling of uncertainties. This also applies to the design process of these visual interfaces. Uncertainties that arise must be recognized, accepted, and managed in order to achieve a robust result. To this end, needs must be identified in iterations together with users and stakeholders, and changes and potential risks must be optimally channeled [10]. Uncertainties in the perception and assessment of attacks can arise throughout the entire information processing process and can also be divided into different categories (see Table 3).

Table 3. Meaning of uncertainty categories in visualization [8, 46]

Category	Meaning
Timeliness	Time span between event and visualization
Accuracy	Difference between visualization and reality
Credibility	Reliability of the information and its source
Consistency	Consistency of individual pieces of information
Precision	Quality of measurement or estimation
Subjectivity	Degree of influence of the sender on the information
Completeness	Scope of the information passed on
Interdependence	Dependence of information on other pieces of information

Safety-related decisions are rarely based on complete, timely, or fully consistent data. This already affects 37.5% of the categories that cause uncertainty. In addition, other categories of uncertainty are often present in multitasking environments [16]. The visual interface of the CIDS makes these uncertainties visible and interpretable, allowing human actors to take into account both what is known and what is missing. As shown in Fig. 4, the dashboard displays uncertainties along three complementary dimensions: data timeliness, reliability, and telemetry coverage. Together, these indicators already provide an effective context for making informed decisions without delays due to uncertainties. The timeliness of the data indicates the length of time between the last report and its visualization. This shows both the elapsed time and any potentially outdated reporting. This prevents the use of outdated information and ensures certainty in terms of timeliness.

Data freshness indicates how reliable the underlying information is over time. The time since the last report is displayed and highlighted visually when the data becomes stale. This prevents outdated information from being treated as current by default and helps ensure that decisions are made with an appropriate sense of time. Confidence represents the system's assessment of the reliability of the current status assessment. Rather than presenting confidence as a binary value, it

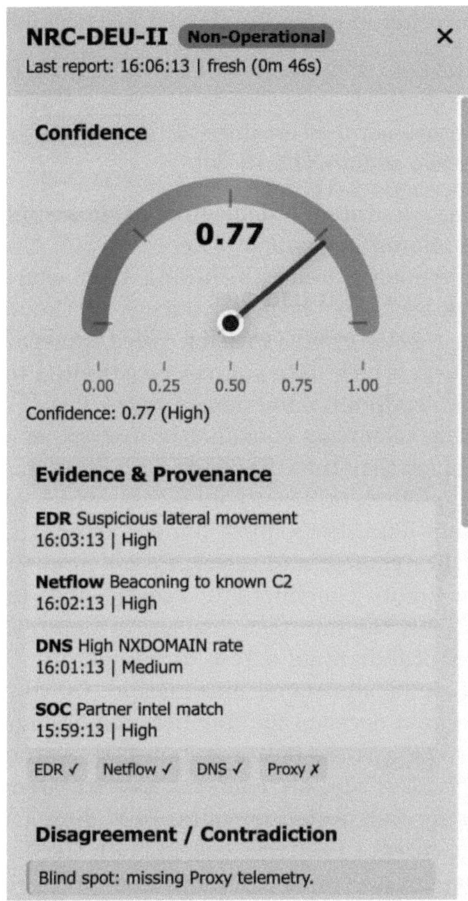

Fig. 4. Categories of uncertainty in visualization

is shown as a continuous score with an interpretable qualitative label (e.g., low, medium, or high). In the interface, confidence is visualized using a gauge-based representation, which maps continuous values onto a familiar circular scale. This design leverages intuitive metaphors (similar to a speedometer), enabling rapid interpretation under time pressure while preserving the underlying quantitative nuance. In addition to color encoding, the segmented structure of the gauge supports interpretation even in cases of limited color perception. Reyes et al. (2025) suggest in their research on trusting AI that visualizing uncertainty using continuous formats can improve decision-making confidence and trust in automated systems compared to binary output alone, particularly when users must integrate machine suggestions with their own judgment [37]. This is because such representations positively influence the calibration of trust and the perceived reliability, depending on the chosen visual encoding.

The visualization techniques can be divided into the following.

– Intrinsic representations: Uncertainties are integrated through variations in shape, color, or brightness;
– Extrinsic representations: Uncertainty is described by adding geometric shapes such as arrows or bars [12,13,20].

The dashboard also features a dedicated evidence and provenance panel that details how automated assessments were derived. Each status evaluation is related to specific evidence items, including their source, time stamp, and severity. This enables users to trace the output of the system to observable signals. Furthermore, telemetry coverage provides transparency over the available data. Figure 4 shows which data sources contributed to the assessment and which are missing (e.g., endpoint detection, network flow, DNS, and proxy logs). As an example, missing telemetry is explicitly marked as a blind spot, making data limitations visible rather than implicit. This level of transparency is consistent with previous research on trust calibration, which highlights that visible uncertainty and system limitations allow human actors to adapt their reliance on CIDS consciously in dynamic and uncertain environments, where the trustworthiness of system inputs can fluctuate rapidly [30]. Instead of just giving general recommendations, the interface displays evidence to reduce automation bias, i.e. the tendency of individual actors to rely on automated prompts while neglecting contradictory or additional information. In contrast, HITL in CIDS should be viewed as a joint decision-making between human and machine, which maximizes the effectiveness of the entire system [24]. Automation bias is a well-documented risk in decision support contexts, particularly when operators lack insight into the basis for automated outputs. Providing access to evidence and provenance encourages users to actively engage with the data, promoting reflective reasoning over passive acceptance. Disagreements between human judgment and machine assessment are explicitly highlighted. For example, conflicts arising from missing telemetry or differing risk evaluations are displayed as warnings. This turns disagreement into an opportunity for further analysis, discussion, or escalation. The combination of uncertainty visualization, evidence transparency, and traceability builds calibrated trust between actors. Rather than assumption or enforcement, trust is dynamically shaped through explainable and visible system behavior and informed human oversight. This type of trust calibration in hybrid teams is becoming increasingly recognized as human actors must align their level of confidence with the system's reliability. To facilitate this alignment in dynamic decision-making situations, the visual interface has proposed tools such as uncertainty indicators and explainable outputs.

2.6 Human Oversight, Responsible Action, and Cognitive Guardrails

Unlike traditional DSS, where automated outputs are primarily advisory, the proposed visual interface incorporates explicit human approval stages for critical actions, as illustrated in Fig. 5 . Machine-generated response options, such as"isolating affected hosts", "blocking indicators of compromise across the consortium", and "requesting partner support", are presented as actionable proposals that require human confirmation.

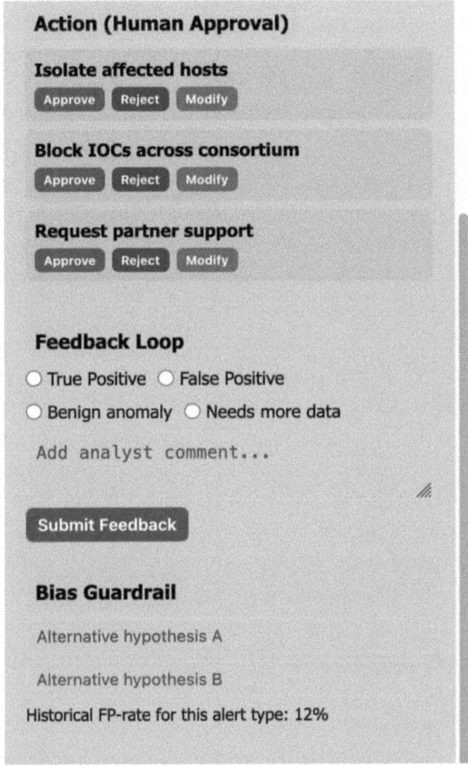

Fig. 5. Actionable response options, feedback mechanisms, and cognitive guardrails supporting responsible decision-making

As an analyst, the human actor can approve, reject, or modify each proposed action. This interaction design ensures that the responsibility for high-impact measures remains with the human decision-maker while also leveraging the speed and analytical capacity of machines. Approval gates such as these are a key design principle for maintaining meaningful CIDS systems, especially when automated actions could have cascading or irreversible consequences [31]. The three colors, green for approval, red for rejection, and yellow for modification, support the visual aspect of the interaction design. The application of a color system for visualization uses a familiar and easily understandable color scheme to conserve the cognitive resources of the actors in an efficient manner. Human decisions and assessments are valuable contributions to a continuous feedback loop. The dashboard enables analysts to categorize system detections (e.g., true positive, false positive, benign anomaly, or needs more data) and provide additional contextual information, as shown in Fig. 5. This feedback is recorded and linked to the relevant evidence and actions. Such mechanisms align with established approaches in HITL-ML, where iterative and structured human input is used to incrementally refine models and adapt them to changing environments. Previous work shows that models that incorporate human expertise through interactive and incremental feedback are less prone to performance degradation and are better able to cope with evolving contexts than static, one-off trained systems [31]. By embedding the feedback directly into the interface, the dashboard supports organizational learning. Human expertise becomes part of the socio-technical memory of the system, contributing to improved future assessments and reducing repeated misclassifications. Due to the susceptibility of decision-making environments to cognitive biases, such as confirmation bias, automation bias, or base rate neglect [45], the dashboard features cognitive guardrails that encourage reflection to minimize risks. These guardrails include prompts to consider alternative hypotheses, provide explicit base-rate information (e.g., historical false-positive rates for a given alert type), and highlight conflicts between human assessments and machine recommendations or gaps in telemetry coverage. Such design elements are consistent with research that indicates that subtle cognitive nudges can enhance the quality of decisions without compromising user autonomy [45]. Importantly, these mechanisms do not prescribe a "correct" decision. Instead, they encourage cognitive balance by prompting analysts to consider competing explanations, contextual probabilities, and uncertainty before committing to an action. This approach reflects recent findings of human-AI teaming research that emphasize the importance of supporting both intuitive and analytical reasoning processes for effective collaboration [25]. The historical false positive rate provides contextual base-rate information derived from previous human feedback. This information helps analysts counteract base-rate neglect while allowing them to make their own decisions. To promote transparent and accountable collaboration, the dashboard features a task queue that clearly organizes ongoing activities performed by humans and machines. The tasks generated by the system are displayed alongside the human-assigned actions, including information on priority, ownership, and time constraints. This representation of tasks serves multiple purposes. Firstly, it makes the distribution of responsibilities between human and machine actors visible, thereby reinforcing the HITL principle that critical judgment and escalation decisions remain under human control. Secondly, it facilitates coordination under time pressure by offering a shared operational overview of pending and completed actions.

By distinguishing between human and machine tasks, as shown in Fig. 6, the task queue also contributes to transparency with respect to system autonomy. Machine-generated tasks are clearly marked as such, while human decisions are recorded as deliberate actions rather than implicit system behavior. This distinction could help prevent unintended automation drift and supports the development of calibrated trust in hybrid teams. In addition to the task queue, the dashboard maintains a persistent audit log, as shown in Fig. 7, which records

Fig. 6. Task queue of human and machine tasks

relevant system events, decisions, and human interventions. Each entry captures the action performed, the responsible party, the outcome of the decision (e.g. approval, rejection, or modification), and the associated timestamp. Together, these entries provide a chronological record of how situations evolve and decisions are made.

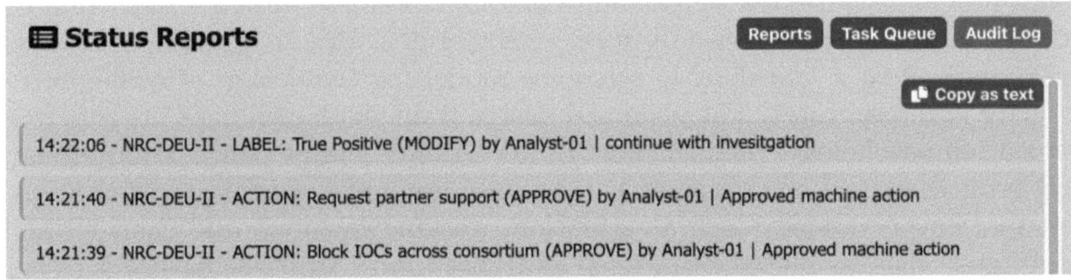

Fig. 7. Audit log

This level of auditability is essential for accountability and the ability to make revisions in environments critical to safety and security. Audit logs enable organizations to reconstruct decision paths following an incident, evaluate the appropriateness of actions taken, and identify procedural or technical vulnerabilities. Beyond compliance and accountability, the audit log provides a valuable foundation for post-incident analysis and organizational learning. By linking decisions to contextual evidence and results, analysts can retrospectively evaluate which indicators were informative, identify instances of misjudged uncertainty, and determine how human–machine interaction could be improved. Importantly, the audit log is designed to support transparency without overburdening users during live operations. Although detailed records are maintained in the background, interaction with the log is optional and usually deferred until the post-incident review phase. This separation enables the system to remain usable under time pressure, while ensuring full traceability when required.

3   Conclusion

3.1   Final Consideration

The article emphasizes that sustainable cybersecurity can only be achieved through consciously designed, transparent, and responsible human-machine collaboration, and presents a systematic collection of concepts for the design and implementation of HITL approaches in security-critical cyber systems like CIDS. It shows that their effectiveness depends primarily on the design of the visual interface and structured human-machine collaboration âĂŞ not on the isolated performance of individual actors or algorithms. According to the "WYSIWYHD" principle, visualization is an integral part of the decision-making architecture: What is displayed determines what can be decided. Particularly noteworthy is the consistent focus on shared situational awareness, federated coordination, and the reduction of cognitive biases through cognitive guardrails as a socio-technical surplus. Theoretically, the work extends existing concepts of human-computer interaction to human-computer teaming in safety-critical contexts. Methodologically, it demonstrates the applicability of a user-centered design approach to the development of complex visualization architectures. Practically, the conceptual dashboard offers a transferable reference model for the design of collaborative security infrastructures. The proposed design framework combines insights from perception psychology, the principles of uncertainty and evidence, transparency, and explicit control mechanisms. It takes into account key limitations of human information processing (such as attention, working memory, and change blindness), and relies on shared situational awareness and cognitive guardrails to promote precision, accountability, and appropriate trust calibration. This contribution can therefore be understood as a conceptual reference model for the design of resilient, transparent, and responsible human-machine collaboration in critical infrastructures. At the same time, the challenge remains to adequately consider the limits of human attention, the dynamics of uncertainty, and the increasing relevance of cognitive attacks. Future research should therefore increasingly integrate interdisciplinary perspectives from psychology, communication science, and security research to strengthen resilience, trust, and decision-making quality in hybrid systems.

3.2   Limitations and Next Steps

Despite taking into account numerous limitations in terms of actors, communication processes, and visualization, it was not possible to overcome all obstacles. For example, visualization has limitations at the boundaries of the human processing system's attention span. An actor's ability to consciously view the representations in their field of vision by focusing their cognitive system on them is limited. At the same time, attention is essential for the effectiveness of a visualization. In order to conserve this limited resource, the visual interface was designed in such a way that the elements and contexts can be perceived and evaluated as intuitively as possible by the actor. Nevertheless, there remains a limitation in the absorption capacity of the human actor. Another challenge concerns the possibilities for visualizing cognitive warfare, which will require numerous studies in the future. For example, there are currently no signals that can be visualized to detect cognitive attacks. At the same time, the entire ecosystem must be considered in these multidomain situations, which also poses some challenges to the representability of the relationships. The task of science in developing effective CIDS must therefore be to conduct more interdisciplinary research in psychology, sociology, communication studies, and behavioral research. In addition, it must be possible to visualize the validity of the data, including the presentation of data from social networks and synthetic media. However, this is not just about finding the tool for an attack, such as lies, disinformation, or fake news, but about the feeling it triggers. If the recipient, whether a person or society, is resilient and speaks with confidence, as a prerequisite for resilience, a cognitive attack will not work. This promotes low dissemination, which in turn minimizes the risk areas to be visualized, as well as the probability of security-critical consequences. This aspect of the measurability and visualizability of awareness, resilience, and trust is becoming increasingly important, as these cognitive attacks occur faster and more frequently thanks to generative artificial intelligence. The challenge therefore remains to adequately address the limits of human attention, the dynamics of uncertainty, and the increasing relevance of cognitive attacks. Future research should therefore integrate interdisciplinary perspectives from psychology, communication science, and security research more strongly in order to further strengthen resilience, trust, and decision-making quality in hybrid systems. In general, the article emphasizes that sustainable cybersecurity in critical infrastructures can only be achieved through consciously designed, transparent, and responsible human-machine collaboration. The contribution is intentionally conceptual and design-oriented with the objective of structuring the problem space and proposing interface mechanisms rather than evaluating them quantitatively. Future work should therefore include controlled user studies and real-world deployments to assess the effectiveness of the proposed design elements.

Acknowledgment. Funded by the European Union under the European Defence Fund (GA no. 101121403 - NEWSROOM). Views and opinions expressed are however those of the author(s) only and do not necessarily reflect those of the European Union or the European Commission. Neither the European Union nor the granting authority can be held responsible for them.

References

1. Andrienko, N., Andrienko, G.: Exploratory Analysis of Spatial and Temporal Data: A Systematic Approach. Springer, Heidelberg (2006). https://doi.org/10.1007/3-540-31190-4
2. Balthasar, M.: Balancing strengths and weaknesses in human-machine decision making. In: Froehlich, P., Cobus V. (Eds.) Mensch und Computer 2023, Work-

shop on User-Centered Artificial Intelligence, MCI-WS16 - UCAI 2023. Rapperswil (SG), CH (2023). https://doi.org/10.18420/muc2023-mci-ws16-388

3. Balthasar, M.: Aspects of decision-making in human–machine teaming. In: Elsenbroich C., Verhagen, H. (Eds.), Advances in Social Simulation, Proceedings of the 18th Social Simulation Conference, Glasgow, UK, pp. 561–573. Springer, Heidelberg (2024). https://doi.org/10.1007/978-3-031-57785-7_43

4. Balthasar, M.: Social Anthropology 4.0. i-com **23**(2), 273–292 (2024b). https://doi.org/10.1515/icom-2024-0016

5. Bertin, J.: La Graphique et le Traitement Graphique de l'Information. [Graphics and the Visual Presentation of Information] Zones sensibles, Brussels (2017)

6. Borghoff, U.M., Schlichter, J.H. (Eds.): Computer-Supported Cooperative Work. Springer, Heidelberg (2000). https://doi.org/10.1007/978-3-662-04232-8

7. Card, S.K., Mackinlay, J.D., Shneiderman, B.: Readings in Information Visualization: Using Vision to Think. The Morgan Kaufmann series in interactive technologies. Morgan Kaufmann Publishers, San Francisco (1999). https://doi.org/10.5555/300679.

8. Chung, J., Wark, S.: Visualising Uncertainty for Decision Support. Joint and Operations Analysis Division - Defence Science and Technology Group (DST-Group-TR-3325), Victoria, Australia (2016)

9. Daly, M.: Decision support: a matter of information supply and demand. J. Decis. Syst. **25**(sup1), 216–227 (2016). https://doi.org/10.1080/12460125.2016.1187423

10. Elliott, C., Deasley, P.: Creating Systems That Work: Principles of Engineering Systems for the 21st Century. The Royal Academy of Engineering, London (2007)

11. Fan, X., Yen, J.: Modeling and simulating human teamwork behaviors using intelligent agents. Phys. Life Rev. **1**(3), 173–201 (2004). https://doi.org/10.1016/j.plrev.2004.10.001

12. Gershon, N. D.: Visualization of fuzzy data using generalized animation. In: Proceedings Visualization '92, Boston, MA, USA, pp. 268–273 (1992). https://doi.org/10.1109/VISUAL.1992.235199

13. Gershon, N.: Visualization of an imperfect world. IEEE Comput. Graphics Appl. **18**(4), 43–45 (1998). https://doi.org/10.1109/38.689662

14. Grosz, B.J.: Collaborative systems. AI Mag. **17**(2), 67–85 (1996). https://doi.org/10.1609/aimag.v17i2.1223

15. Healey, C.G., Enns, J.T.: Attention and visual memory in visualization and computer graphics. IEEE Trans. Visual Comput. Graphics **18**(7), 1170–1188 (2012). https://doi.org/10.1109/TVCG.2011.127

16. Hornbæk, K., Kristensson, P. O., and Oulasvirta, A. Introduction to Human-Computer Interaction. Oxford University Press, Oxford (2025). https://doi.org/10.1093/oso/9780192864543.001.0001

17. Huegle, T.: Learning from chess engines: how reinforcement learning could redefine clinical decision-making in rheumatology. Ann. Rheum. Dis. **81**(8), 1072–1075 (2022). https://doi.org/10.1136/annrheumdis-2022-222141

18. ISO/Guide 73:2009. Risk management: Vocabulary. International Standards Organization, Vernier, CH (2009)

19. Iyengar, S.S., Lepper, M.R.: When choice is demotivating: can one desire too much of a good thing? J. Pers. Soc. Psychol. **79**(6), 995–1006 (2000). https://doi.org/10.1037/0022-3514.79.6.995

20. Jena, A., Engelke, U., Dwyer, T., Raiamanickam, V., Paris, C.: Uncertainty visualisation: an interactive visual survey. In: IEEE Pacific Visualization Symposium (PacificVis), Tianjin, China, pp. 201–205 (2020). https://doi.org/10.1109/PacificVis48177.2020.1014

21. Jennings, N.: Cooperation in Industrial Multi-Agent Systems. World Scientific series in computer science, vol. 43. World Scientific, Singapore (1994)
22. Kapetanios, E.: Quo Vadis computer science: from turing to personal computer, personal content and collective intelligence. Data Knowl. Eng. **67**(2), 286–292 (2008). https://doi.org/10.1016/j.datak.2008.05.003
23. Knill, D.C., Pouget, A.: The bayesian brain: the role of uncertainty in neural coding and computation. Trends Neurosci. **27**(12), 712–719 (2004). https://doi.org/10.1016/j.tins.2004.10.007
24. Kurvers, R.H.J.M., Nuzzolese, A.G., Russo, A., Barabucci, G., Herzog, S.M., Trianni, V.: Automating hybrid collective intelligence in open-ended medical diagnostics. Proc. Natl. Acad. Sci. U.S.A. **120**(34), e2221473120 (2023). https://doi.org/10.1073/pnas.2221473120
25. Lai, Y., Kankanhalli, A., Ong, D.C.: Human-AI collaboration in healthcare: a review and research agenda. In: Proceedings of the 54th Hawaii International Conference on System Sciences (HICSS 2021), pp. 1–10 (2021). https://doi.org/10.24251/HICSS.2021.046
26. Lee, C.-C., Comes, T., Finn, M., Mostafavi, A.: Roadmap Towards Responsible AI in Crisis Resilience Management, Advance online publication (2022). https://doi.org/10.48550/arXiv.2207.09648
27. Licklider, J.C.R.: Man-computer symbiosis. IRE Trans. Human Fact. Electron. **HFE-1**(1), 4–11 (1960). https://doi.org/10.1109/THFE2.1960.4503259
28. Lykourentzou, I., Vergados, D.J., Loumos, V.: Collective intelligence system engineering. In: Spyratos, N. (Eds.) MEDES '09: The International Conference on Management of Emergent Digital EcoSystems, Article 20, pp. 134–140. ACM (2009). https://doi.org/10.1145/1643823.1643848
29. Mallot, H.-P.: Visuelle Wahrnehmung. [Visual Perception] In: Funke J., Frensch, P. (eds.) Handbuch der Allgemeinen Psychologie - Kognition, pp. 127–137. Hogrefe, Goettingen (2006)
30. Marusich, L.R., Files, B.T., Bancilhon, M., Rawal, J.C., Raglin, A.: Trust calibration for joint human/AI decision-making in dynamic and uncertain contexts. In: Degen, H., Ntoa, S. (eds.) Artificial Intelligence in HCI. HCII 2025. Lecture Notes in Computer Science, vol. 15819. Springer, Cham (2025). https://doi.org/10.1007/978-3-031-93412-4_6
31. Mosqueira-Rey, J.L., Cuff, J., Gutierrez, M., Fuertes, J.M.: Human-in-the-loop machine learning: state of the art, challenges, and opportunities. Artif. Intell. Rev. **55**, 3101–3149 (2022). https://doi.org/10.1007/s10462-022-10246-w
32. Myers, B.A.: A brief history of human computer interaction technology. ACM Interact. **5**(2), 44–54 (1998)
33. Moon, A.: Negotiating With Robots: Meshing Plans and Resolving Conflicts in Human-Robot Collaboration. University of British Columbia, Vancouver (2017). https://doi.org/10.14288/1.0348225
34. Munzner, T.: Visualization Analysis and Design. A.K. Peters visualization series, CRC Press Taylor + Francis Group, New York (2015)
35. Pacaux, M.-P., Godin, S.D., Rajaonah, B., Anceaux, F., Vanderhaegen, F.: Levels of automation and human-machine cooperation: application to human-robot interaction. IFAC Proc. Vol. **44**(1), 6484–6492 (2011). https://doi.org/10.3182/20110828-6-IT-1002.00312
36. Rajivan, P., and Cooke, N. J.: Impact of team collaboration on cybersecurity situational awareness. In: Theory and Models for Cyber Situation Awareness. Lecture Notes in Computer Science, vol. 10030, pp. 203–226. Springer, Cham (2017). https://doi.org/10.1007/978-3-319-61152-5_8

37. Reyes, J., Batmaz, A.U., Kersten-Oertel, M.: Trusting AI: does uncertainty visualization affect decision-making? Front. Comput. Sci. **7**, 1464348 (2025). https://doi.org/10.3389/fcomp.2025.1464348
38. Roponena, E., Kampars, J., Grabis, J., Gailītis, A.: Towards a human-in-the-loop intelligent intrusion detection system. In: Baltic DB+IS Doctoral Consortium and Forum, Riga, Latvia, 03–06 July 2027 (2022)
39. Sedlmair, M., Meyer, M., Munzner, T.: Design study methodology: reflections from the trenches and the stacks. IEEE Trans. Visual Comput. Graphics **18**(12), 2431–2440 (2012). https://doi.org/10.1109/TVCG.2012.213
40. Shannon, C.E., Weaver, W.: The Mathematical Theory of Communication. The University of Illinois Press, Champaign (1964)
41. She, M., Li, Z.: Team situation awareness: a review of definitions and conceptual models. In: Harris, D. (ed.) Engineering Psychology and Cognitive Ergonomics: Performance, Emotion and Situation Awareness. EPCE 2017. Lecture Notes in Computer Science, vol. 10275, pp. 406–415. Springer, Cham (2017). https://doi.org/10.1007/978-3-319-58472-0_31
42. Simunovic, M.P.: Colour vision deficiency. Eye **24**(5), 747–755 (2010). https://doi.org/10.1038/eye.2009.251
43. Stewart, I.: Do Dice Play God? The Mathematics of Uncertainty. Profile Books Ltd., London (2019)
44. Stevens, S. S.: On the theory of scales of measurement. Science **103**(2684), 677–680 (1946). https://doi.org/10.1126/science.103.2684.677
45. Suresh, H., Guttag, J.V.: A Framework for understanding sources of harm throughout the machine learning life cycle. In: Proceedings of the 2021 ACM Conference on Fairness, Accountability, and Transparency. FAccT'21, pp. 319–328 (2021). https://doi.org/10.1145/3465416.3483305
46. Thomson, J., Hetzler, E., MacEachren, A., Gahegan, M., Pavel, M.: A typology for visualizing uncertainty. In: Proceedings SPIE, Visualization and Data Analysis, Electronic Imaging, San Jose, California, vol. 5669, p. 146 (2005). https://doi.org/10.1117/12.587254
47. Tory, M., Möller, T.: Human factors in visualization research. IEEE Trans. Visual Comput. Graphics **10**(1), 72–84 (2004). https://doi.org/10.1109/TVCG.2004.1260759
48. Ware, C.: Information Visualization: Perception for Design Morgan Kaufmann an imprint of Elsevier, Cambridge (2021)
49. Zoeller, N., et al.: Human-AI collectives most accurately diagnose clinical vignettes. Proc. Natl. Acad. Sci. U.S.A. **122**(24), e2426153122 (2025). https://doi.org/10.1073/pnas.2426153122

Count2zero, a Serious Escape Room Challenge for Cybersecurity Training

Markus Rebhan[1,2,3(✉)], Jens Holtmannspötter[1,2], and Ulrike Lechner[3]

[1] Bundeswehr Research Institute for Materials, Fuels and Lubricants, Erding,
Germany
`jensholtmannspoetter@bundeswehr.org`
[2] Bundeswehr Innovation Center, Erding, Germany
`markusrebhan@bundeswehr.org`
[3] University of the Bundeswehr Munich, Neubiberg, Germany
`ulrike.lechner@unibw.de`

Abstract. The digitization of military missions and the networking of critical infrastructures lead to threat situations in cyberspace. Situation reports document that both the number and complexity of attacks on information networks are increasing, along with the pivotal role of the human factor. We propose a serious game to raise awareness of cybersecurity in critical infrastructure and military missions. The serious game "Count2zero" is an escape game; as an escape game, it is particularly immersive and combines puzzles, teamwork, and time pressure. This article presents the serious escape game Count2zero, its design process, and selected challenges of the escape game. The escape room is located in an air-raid bunker and replicates a realistic cyber-physical environment in which IT infrastructure, IoT components, and networked end devices are combined. The article describes the background and related work, the didactic and technical concepts of Count2zero, and five exemplary modules, which are called a PC with login data, NFC interactions, a laptop with an HID attack mouse, a bedroom scenario with an emergency email, and a locker with adhesive tape, and discusses them with regard to security-relevant behavior. Finally, initial evaluation results are presented, and implications for research and practice of security awareness programs are derived.

Keywords: Cyber-physical systems · Design science · Escape room ·
IT security · Security awareness · Serious games

1 Introduction

The security of information and communication technology in armed forces, critical infrastructures, and government organizations is an important topic. Situation reports and studies show that the number of cyberattacks is increasing, that cyberattacks are becoming more professional, and that the potential impact of a cyberthreat is increasing. User misconduct or carelessness [22, 23] may result in

K. Kirchner et al. (Eds.): I4CS 2026, CCIS 3007, pp. 119–133, 2026.
https://doi.org/10.1007/978-3-032-27096-2_7

security policy non-compliance, which may, in turn, lead to incidents. The German Federal Ministry of Defense addresses cybersecurity as part of the digital transformation and emphasizes the importance of cybersecurity for leadership capabilities and operational readiness [24].

Traditional cybersecurity awareness measures, such as lectures, e-learning courses, or mandatory training, convey knowledge but only partially capture the complex interactions between motivation, workload, perceived benefits, and actual behavior. Models for specifying IT security awareness also emphasize that awareness must not be limited to knowledge but must also encompass perception, protection strategies, and behavior [11]. Most awareness measures address security topics in a typical office context. We address cybersecurity in the IoT domain in this article. In addition, the game is situated in a military setting, thereby reflecting an application context in which security-related decisions are particularly critical and operational conditions are more demanding than in conventional office environments.

Serious games offer an alternative approach to cybersecurity training, and they often attempt to address cognitive, emotional, and behavioral dimensions of learning. Early work and current reviews indicate that well-designed serious games can significantly increase willingness to learn, motivation, and transferability [32]. Escape games have established themselves as a game format in their own right, combining puzzle-oriented cooperation, time pressure, and immersion. They are being used in schools, universities, and continuing education [6]. In the field of cybersecurity, escape room approaches and other serious games are used to strengthen security awareness and promote security-compliant behavior in protected environments [8]. In our work, we design an escape room game named Count2zero as a measure to raise awareness of information security policies in a scenario that resembles a military context, incorporating office technology and military IoT devices. Our research question is "How to design a realistic, gamified environment in which participants can experience safety-critical situations, make decisions under stress, and reflect on their behavior afterwards?". Figure 1 provides insight into the bunker during a game run.

This article is structured as follows: first, it presents the relevant theoretical and technical background; second, it describes the concept and the five modules of Count2zero; third, it discusses the evaluation results. The article builds on previous research on the initial design of the escape room game and its first evaluations [8].

2   Background and Related Work

2.1   Serious Games and Escape Rooms

Serious games are generally understood to be games that pursue explicit learning or training goals in addition to entertainment. Abt coined the term back in the 1970s [1], while later works increasingly systematized serious games and distinguished them from other game-based formats. A systematic review by Connolly et al. [2] argue that serious games have advantages over traditional teaching

Fig. 1. Bunker view during the game play

formats, especially when it comes to complex cognitive learning goals. Ravyse et al. identify success factors such as clear learning goals, balanced difficulty, appropriate feedback, and coherent game design [3]. Escape rooms originated in the leisure sector, but were quickly adopted as a teaching tool [4]. Penttilä outlines the historical development and educational integration of escape games [35]. Studies from schools and universities show that escape rooms can promote motivation, teamwork, and problem-solving skills [5]. Makri et al. present a systematic literature review on digital escape rooms [6], while Botturi and Babazadeh propose the Star Model, a design reference model for educational escape rooms [36]. Sanchez and Plumettaz-Sieber emphasize the central role of debriefing for knowledge transfer [33].

2.2 Security Awareness, Serious Games, and Compliance

Awareness measures in the field of IT security aim to influence knowledge, attitudes, and behavior in such a way that security guidelines are understood and followed. In their model, Hansch and Benenson distinguish between perception, protection strategies, and behavior, and provide a formal specification of IT security awareness [34]. Sykosch develops a user behavior-based approach to measuring IT security awareness [11]. Reviews of security awareness approaches with a focus on gamification show that playful formats are particularly suitable for increasing motivation and supporting sustainable learning. A relevant example is the cybersecurity serious game Operation Digital Chameleon, in which red and blue teams develop attack and defense strategies to explore security-related aspects of critical infrastructures [30, 31].

Moody et al. propose a Unified Model of Information Security Policy Compliance, which brings together various theories on rule compliance in an integrated model [13]. D'Arcy et al. show how security-related stress caused by complex or burdensome security requirements can lead to avoidance strategies and non-compliance [14]. Vance and Siponen investigate the causes of policy violations and emphasize the role of attitudes, norms, and situational factors [15]. These works underscore that awareness must address not only knowledge transfer but also the motivational-psychological determinants of behavior.

Serious games have been used in various security-related domains: Cyber-CIEGE serves as a learning environment for information security, and playful approaches are used to defend against social engineering attacks. Board games and digital serious games for cloud security, such as Riskio and the board game proposed by Zhao et al., show that playful approaches can also be effective in technically demanding contexts [9, 10].

3   Research Design

The development of Count2zero follows a design science paradigm according to Hevner [16]. In Design Science, artifacts are designed as purpose-oriented solutions to practical problems and are subject to scientific reflection. Hevner et al. formulate guidelines for design science research in information systems [16].

The Escape Room Game Count2zero has been designed using an iterative approach with a refinement of the number of escape room puzzles and adventures. The version that we present here is the result of 2 years of refinement and experimentation. The current version consists of 10 escape room puzzles and is located in a World War II bunker on a military premises. Concerns in the iterative design process included balancing more serious and more playful puzzles, as well as the relevance of the puzzles. Concerns in the design process also included the instruments for collecting data on the game and the design of a setting that is secure enough for players in the bunker. Note that the setting meets work safety, fire protection regulations and has obtained the ethics committee approval.

4   The Serious Game Count2zero

This section provides information on Count2zero and its design rationale.

4.1   Objective and Target Group

Count2zero is developed to make security-critical situations in the use of networked systems, IoT devices, mobile devices, and classic IT infrastructure tangible and to promote security-compliant behavior in realistic scenarios. Unlike abstract simulations or purely digital serious games, participants interact with real system components whose incorrect operation has immediate and visible consequences. Count2zero thus builds on approaches used in security-related serious games and escape rooms, but goes one step further by strongly integrating a physical environment and real infrastructure [7–9].

The target group includes soldiers and civilian employees in security-critical areas who work with sensitive information, critical systems, or vulnerable infrastructure. The design is such that no specific IT expertise is required and heterogeneous teams can participate. In this way, a realistic picture of cooperation in operational and staff structures is created, as emphasized in current security policy strategies [24].

4.2   Game Area and Technical Setting

The escape room is installed in an air-raid shelter, whose structural features (sealed-off rooms, limited communication channels, physical security barriers) are deliberately used to create an immersive atmosphere. The technical infrastructure includes a local network with switches, access points, and structured cabling; IoT components for controlling lights, doors, and sensors; a camera system for monitoring the game; and various digital end devices. This is supplemented by components such as those found in industrial IoT environments or modern production facilities [25].

The combination of these elements creates a cyber-physical environment that reflects typical constellations from military command and control systems, control rooms, or industrial control systems. Technical authenticity is deliberately kept high in order to enable the greatest possible transferability of the gaming experience to everyday working life. The didactic design follows a design science approach in which artifact- and theory-related objectives are interlinked [16–18]. Figure 2 shows a schematic representation of the playing field with room designations (R1-4) and outlines the sequence of the individual sub-games (p 1–10).

4.3   Game Structure and Process

The game is structured into three phases: a briefing, a playing phase of approximately 120 min, and a structured debriefing. The briefing introduces the objectives, ground rules, safety constraints, and the fictional starting situation. After the bunker door is closed, a visible countdown reinforces the time pressure of the scenario.

The game comprises ten content-coordinated modules arranged in a predefined sequence. Each module acts as a gated stage that yields the items or information required for subsequent modules, preventing participants from skipping critical tasks. Throughout the playing phase, the game master intervenes only when necessary to facilitate progress, while continuously observing activities via cameras. Security-relevant behaviors, key decisions, and mistakes are documented using a standardized observation protocol. In several modules, specific player actions trigger predefined interventions (e.g., controlled system reactions,

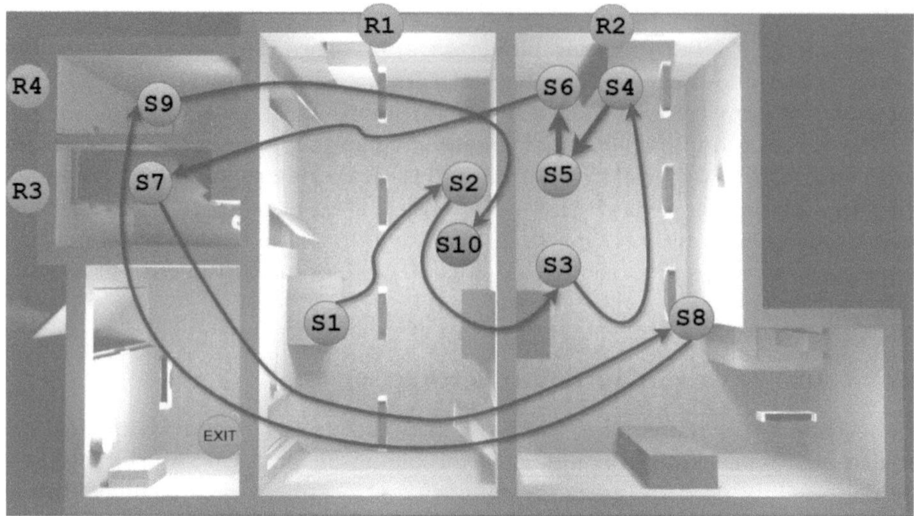

Fig. 2. Overview of the game settings and module sequence

manipulation of network services, or demonstrations of known vulnerabilities). These interventions serve both as didactic impulses and as measurement points for data collection (timestamp, triggering action, system response, and impact on progress). During the debriefing, the game master moderates a structured reflection on observed actions and errors. These observations are linked to real-world policies and best practices and interpreted through common human-factor mechanisms (e.g., routine, time pressure, trust, and distraction) to derive actionable, security-compliant behavior for everyday work [13,14]. Figure 3 summarizes the sequence of the ten modules.

5   Design of Adventures

The following section describes five modules that address different aspects of IT security and gameplay: authentication and data hygiene, near field communication (NFC), physical attacks via human interface devices (HID), email security and emergency communication and a locker with adhesive tape. The modules are designed as thematic clusters that integrate several puzzles and short tasks into one coherent learning episode. This structure follows common escape-room practice, but is adapted for training: within one module, participants solve multiple linked challenges (e.g., discovery tasks, decoding steps, and system interactions) that reinforce the same security concept from different angles. Each module therefore delivers both a gameplay artifact (e.g., a code or key) and an explicit security takeaway that is revisited during debriefing.

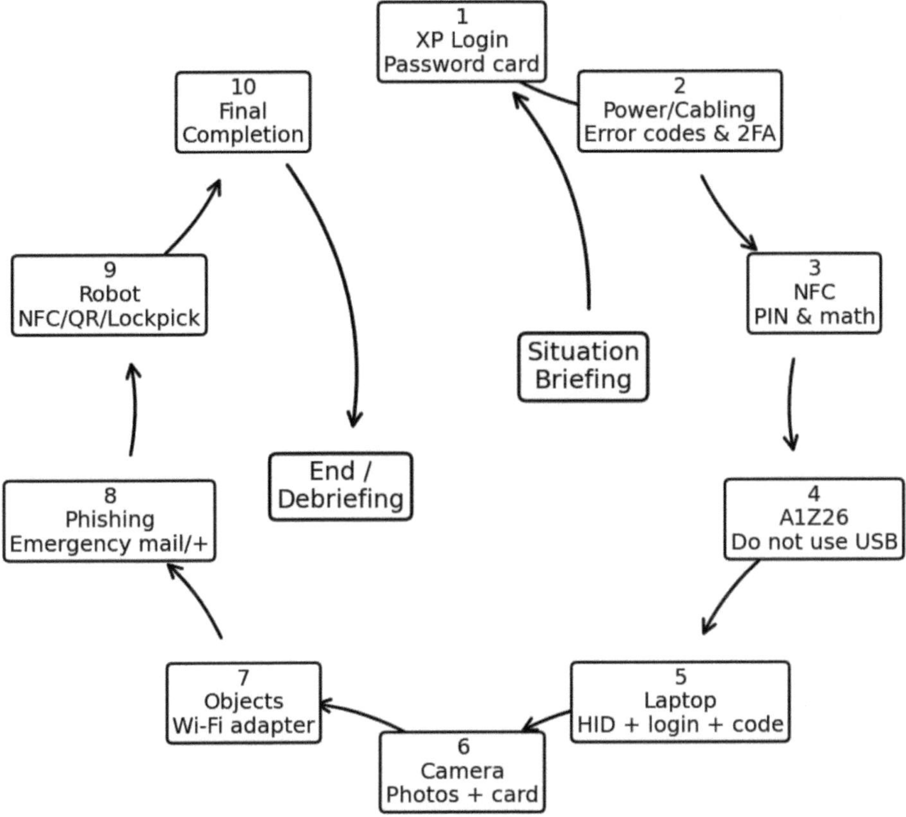

Fig. 3. Module flow of the IT security escape game

5.1   Module 1: PC with Authentication

This module focuses on authentication, password security, and data hygiene. Players encounter a locked PC whose outdated operating system simulates typical legacy systems in control centers or offices. Login details are scattered around both physically and digitally, for example in the form of printouts in the printer queue, sticky notes, or hidden files. An inconspicuous USB keylogger is installed and records keystrokes.

The module addresses insecure password handling, the danger of manipulated peripheral devices, and the careless use of removable media. Corresponding risks are explicitly addressed in standards and recommendations for handling data carriers and end devices [27,29]. In the debriefing, observed errors—such as passwords left lying around or the use of unknown USB devices—are compared with these guidelines and recommendations for action are derived.

5.2   Module 3: NFC-Interaction with a Mobile Phone

This module focuses on the use of NFC tags and mobile devices. It was developed to familiarize players with the implications of Near Field Communication (NFC) and the critical evaluation of digital information sources. It emphasizes the need to always question the reliability of digital information from unknown sources as well as from supposedly known sources. NFC tags are hidden in a drawer; these must first be recognized as such and read with a cell phone. The information they contain forms an equation that must be solved with the help of a book on the table. The result of the equation is a combination of numbers that can be used to open another cabinet. The aim is to teach interaction with a smartphone and several NFC tags that encrypt clues or provide access to information. The cybersecurity risk lies in manipulated or counterfeit tags, and there are signs that some of the tags are risky.

Tags pose a risk; technical recommendations and studies on NFC systems in practical use describe risks such as unauthorized reading, cloning, or the introduction of manipulated content [26]. This module is designed to raise awareness of the manipulability of NFC systems, the risks of contactless authentication and payment methods, and the danger of uncritically trusting the output of digital assistance systems. In the debriefing, the situations experienced in the game are linked to real-life use cases from mobile payment and access control scenarios.

5.3   Module 4: Locker with Adhesive Tape

The fourth module focuses on a classic escape room puzzle that is deliberately less technical and primarily addresses the fun of playing, teamwork, and detail-oriented problem solving. After completing the NFC module, players arrive at a previously locked cabinet where they find a folding rule. This seemingly simple tool forms the starting point for further progression in the game.

The central task is to use the folding rule to measure the lengths of stickers attached to another cabinet and assign these lengths to positions in the alphabet (1 = A, 2 = B, etc.). The letters obtained in this way result in a combination of numbers or characters that can be used to open the next locker. The puzzle is designed as a typical escape game element: it requires observation skills, communication, and the ability to connect pieces of information, without requiring any special IT knowledge. The module thus primarily strengthens the "play" dimension of the game and ensures a high degree of immersion and cooperation within the team.

In terms of IT security, the module pursues a specific, clearly defined goal: raising awareness of the dangers of unknown USB data carriers. The open locker contains deliberately placed USB sticks of unknown origin, which players are expressly *not* allowed to use. This requirement is taken up in the debriefing and linked to real attack vectors – such as the spread of malware via seemingly harmless storage media – as well as corresponding recommendations from guidelines and basic protection modules. The module thus makes it clear that not every device found may be "tried out" and that deliberately refraining from using a data carrier is the security-compliant course of action in many situations.

5.4   Module 5: Laptop with HID-Attack-Mouse

This module deals with physical IT security and the handling of removable media and peripheral devices. Players find an unsecured laptop with a seemingly inconspicuous mouse. This mouse has been opened and modified for the game. When the mouse is connected, an integrated microcontroller identifies itself as a keyboard and automatically executes previously stored commands. As a result, the laptop's integrated keyboard can no longer be used. This problem can only be solved by restarting the computer. After restarting, the laptop is locked, and players must find the password for the previously logged-in user in the user's locker. Due to the colored lighting in the room, this password is not visible and must be made visible with the help of LED lamps. This is intended to make players realize that unknown hardware can always pose a threat, even if it appears normal and inconspicuous. This is a classic HID attack scenario that can only be detected with disproportionate effort [28].

The module illustrates how little effort is required for successful hardware attacks and underscores the importance of clear guidelines for handling external devices and removable media, as well as for security policies to check equipment for manipulation. Corresponding recommendations are included in the IT baseline protection modules and guidelines for the use of removable media [27]. The debriefing discusses how such attacks can be prevented or at least made more difficult in real environments.

5.5   Module 7: Sleeping Room and Emergency E-Mail

The seventh module of the escape game was designed to raise participants' awareness of the dangers of phishing attacks and how to handle emails and digital information securely. Players use an emergency laptop to set up a connection via a Wi-Fi adapter, reset a password, and receive several emails. Except for one email, all other messages contain misinformation that players must identify. Sender details, links, and content must be critically examined in order to detect phishing and social engineering attacks. The correct email contains a secure link to a phishing quiz that players must answer. These patterns are the focus of many awareness campaigns – and therefore form the basis of this exercise [12,22].

At the same time, the game master simulates technical malfunctions, such as the deletion of the Wi-Fi profile, to address availability issues and their impact on communication security. In addition, techniques such as plus addressing are introduced to detect data leaks. The module thus combines technical, organizational, and behavioral aspects of secure email use.

6   Evaluation

To assess the effectiveness of Count2zero, a multi-stage evaluation design was implemented that combines qualitative and quantitative methods. In several rounds with participants from military and university environments, pre-game and post-game surveys were conducted, and observations were made during the game. The evaluation is based on the principles of design-based research [18] and the evaluation of serious games [3].

The initial survey captured participants' self-assessed IT knowledge, prior exposure to IT security incidents, and attitudes toward different training formats. Responses indicated a heterogeneous competence profile across the cohort, which supports the use of an escape room format that can accommodate mixed-ability teams through collaborative problem solving. At the same time, participants reported a high personal relevance of IT security topics particularly in relation to mobile devices, password practices, and email communication highlighting a strong intrinsic motivation for the training content.

During the game, mistakes, team processes, and problem-solving patterns were systematically documented. It was noticeable that under time pressure, security-related simplifications were often chosen, such as ignoring warnings or using insecure passwords in order to progress more quickly, a pattern that is also described in the literature on dealing with security requirements [13,14]. Note that in the debriefing, these situations were specifically addressed and linked to real guidelines and threat scenarios.

The post game survey showed a high level of acceptance of the training format. The fun factor was consistently rated highly, which is consistent with findings from motivation and game-based learning research by Ryan [19]. Participants with little prior knowledge reported a high increase in knowledge, while those with a high affinity for IT particularly appreciated the realism, technical authenticity, and focus on behavior. These results are consistent with studies on other security-related serious games by e.g., Hart [9]. Figure 4 depicts evaluation of all responses collected in the nine games to selected questions. Each bar represents the mean value of the ratings across all participants (n=37 participants) for the respective question on a Likert scale from 1 to 10 (1 = very low agreement or very negative rating, 10 = very high agreement or very positive rating). Question 1 (Did you enjoy the escape room?) and question 12 (Would you recommend the escape game to a colleague or friend who wants to increase their IT security awareness?) ask about acceptance and recommendation. These received a very high level of agreement with 9.11 points for question 1 and 9.16 for question 12, with a moderate spread of 1.58 for question 1 and 1.46 for question 12. This is a clear signal of a positive gaming experience and a high perceived benefit of the game. Questions 5 (Were you able to increase your awareness of IT security risks?) with an average rating of 7.27 points and a standard deviation of 2.19 points, and question 7 (Has your understanding of IT security improved as a result of the escape room?) with 6.84 points and a standard deviation of 2.24 points, need to be viewed in a different way. Depending on the level of knowledge of the respective player before the game, the game may only impart a moderate amount of new knowledge to a person who already has a very high level of knowledge in the field of IT security, which is reflected in the rating. However, the trend in the answers to both questions is clearly positive, with a slightly higher dispersion due to the heterogeneous prior knowledge of the players. A similar response pattern can be seen in the two questions 8 (Do you believe that your ability to recognize IT security risks has improved as a result of the game?), which was rated at an average of 6.7 points with a standard deviation of 2.31, and question 9 (Have you become more attentive to how you handle your personal data?), which was rated at an average of 6.89 points with a standard deviation of 2.16 points. Both questions are clearly in the positive range, but here too the variance is slightly greater due to the different levels of knowledge among the participants. The rating for question 13 (Was the duration of the escape room too short (1 Points) or too long (10 Points)?) is close to the middle of the scale with 5.56 Points and a relatively low dispersion of 0.95, which indicates that the duration of the game is perceived as predominantly appropriate but minimally too long.

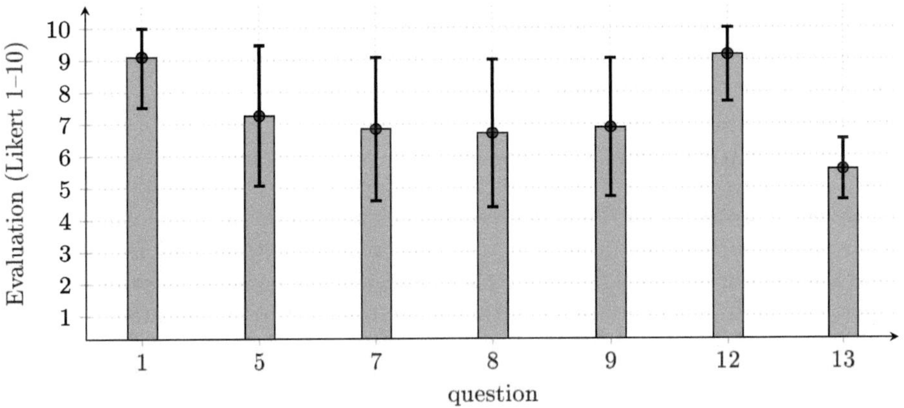

Fig. 4. Mean values of selected questions with standard deviation (errors clipped to 1 – 10)

7   Discussion

The evaluation results support the assumption that immersive, realistic learning environments offer added value compared to traditional awareness formats. In particular, the opportunity to make decisions under stress and time pressure allows for an analysis of the discrepancy between declarative knowledge and actual behavior, as discussed in models of policy compliance and safety behavior [13–15]. Count2zero makes this discrepancy visible and, in the debriefing, provides a framework for developing alternative, safety-compliant courses of action.

From a motivational perspective, the positive feedback on motivation and engagement can be reconciled with concepts from self-determination theory and game-based learning research [19]. The game offers autonomy in problem solving, experienced competence through successfully completed tasks, and social integration in the team—key determinants of intrinsic motivation. Studies on escape rooms in education and digital escape rooms confirm that these formats promote motivation and collaboration [6].

With regard to institutional implementation, references can be made to diffusion and technology acceptance models. The introduction of an escape game format as a regular awareness measure requires organizational support, resources, and embedding in a comprehensive security strategy [20,21]. At the same time, positive experiences and word-of-mouth propaganda within the organization can promote acceptance and dissemination.

The limitations of this approach arise primarily from the costs associated with premises, technology, and personnel. A physical escape room is considerably more resource-intensive than purely digital solutions. At the same time, existing concepts for virtual and hybrid escape rooms demonstrate that elements of the approach can be transferred to digital environments [8–10]. Count2zero can serve as a reference for the design of such formats.

8   Conclusions and Outlook

The work presented Count2zero as a serious escape game for promoting IT security awareness in security-critical contexts. Based on a design science approach, a realistic, cyber-physical learning environment was created in which real IT infrastructure, IoT devices, and digital communication tools are integrated. Four exemplary modules illustrate how specific security-related topics – authentication, data hygiene, NFC and mobile communication, physical attacks on end devices, and email security – can be trained in an experience-based and behavior-oriented manner.

The initial evaluation indicates that the escape game format generates high motivation, leads to intensive team interaction, and addresses both knowledge and behavior in dealing with security requirements. The results are consistent with studies on serious games, educational escape rooms, and gamified security awareness approaches [2]. At the same time, they make it clear that stress, time pressure, and complexity are key factors influencing security-compliant behavior and should be explicitly taken into account in awareness measures [13].

Future planned work includes an in-depth, quantitatively based analysis of the behavioral data collected during the game in order to more precisely identify determining factors such as security-compliant or risky behavior. Furthermore, the development of hybrid or virtual variants of Count2zero is a good idea in order to increase scalability and facilitate use in different organizational contexts [9,10]. Finally, additional modules can be developed or existing ones adapted to focus even more strongly on topics such as incident response, crisis communication, or the protection of critical infrastructure [22].

Acknowledgments. This work was carried out in the context of dtec.bw (Digitalization and Technology Research Center of the Bundeswehr) and was supported by the European Union-NextGenerationEU. The author thanks all participants from military and university environments for their time, engagement, and feedback during the evaluation runs.

References

1. Abt, C.C.: Serious games. Am. Behav. Sci. **14**(1), 129 (1970). https://doi.org/10.1177/000276427001400113
2. Connolly, T.M., Boyle, E.A., MacArthur, E., Hainey, T., Boyle, J.M.: A systematic literature review of empirical evidence on computer games and serious games. Comput. Educ. **59**(2), 661–686 (2012). https://doi.org/10.1016/j.compedu.2012.03.004
3. Ravyse, W.S., Seugnet Blignaut, A., Leendertz, V., Woolner, A.: Success factors for serious games to enhance learning: a systematic review. Virtual Real. **21**(1), 31–58 (2017). https://doi.org/10.1007/s10055-016-0298-4
4. Nicholson, S.: Peeking Behind the Locked Door: A Survey of Escape Room Facilities. White Paper (2015)
5. Borrego, C., Fernández, C., Blanes, I., Robles, S.: Room escape at class: escape games activities to facilitate the motivation and learning in computer science. J. Technol. Sci. Educ. **7**(2), 162–171 (2017). https://doi.org/10.3926/jotse.247
6. Makri, A., Vlachopoulos, D., Martina, R.A.: Digital escape rooms as innovative pedagogical tools in education: a systematic literature review. Sustainability **13**(8), 4587 (2021). https://doi.org/10.3390/su13084587
7. Beguin, E., et al.: Computer-security-oriented escape room. IEEE Secur. Priv. **17**(4), 78–83 (2019). https://doi.org/10.1109/MSEC.2019.2912700
8. Löffler, E., Schneider, B., Zanwar, T., Asprion, P.M.: CySecEscape 2.0 – a virtual escape room to raise cybersecurity awareness. Int. J. Serious Games **8**(1), 59–70 (2021). https://doi.org/10.17083/ijsg.v8i1.413
9. Hart, S., Margheri, A., Paci, F., Sassone, V.: Riskio: a serious game for cyber security awareness and education. Comput. Secur. **95**, 101827 (2020). https://doi.org/10.1016/j.cose.2020.101827
10. Zhao, T., Gasiba, T., Lechner, U., Pinto-Albuquerque, M.: Raising awareness about cloud security in industry through a board game. Information **12**(11), 482 (2021). https://doi.org/10.3390/info12110482
11. Sykosch, A.: Zur Messbarkeit von IT-Sicherheitsbewusstsein: ein nutzerverhaltensbasierter Ansatz. Dissertation, Universität Bonn (2022)
12. Sharif, K.H., Ameen, S.Y.: A review of security awareness approaches with special emphasis on gamification. In: 2020 International Conference on Advanced Science and Engineering (ICOASE) (2020). https://doi.org/10.1109/ICOASE51841.2020.9436595
13. Moody, G.D., Siponen, M., Pahnila, S.: Toward a unified model of information security policy compliance. MIS quarterly **42**(1), 285–311 (2018). https://doi.org/10.25300/MISQ/2018/13853
14. D'Arcy, J., Herath, T., Shoss, M.K.: Understanding employee responses to stressful information security requirements: a coping perspective. J. Manag. Inf. Syst. **31**(2), 285–318 (2014). https://doi.org/10.2753/MIS0742-1222310210

15. Vance, A., Siponen, M.T.: IS security policy violations. J. Organizational End User Comput. **24**(1), 21–41 (2012). https://doi.org/10.4018/joeuc.2012010102

16. Hevner, A.R., March, S.T., Park, J., Ram, S.: Design science in information systems research. MIS Q. **28**(1), 75–105 (2004)

17. Lee, J.S., Pries-Heje, J., Baskerville, R.: Theorizing in design science research. In: Jain, H. et al. (eds.) Service-Oriented Perspectives in Design Science Research, LNCS 6629, pp. 1–16. Springer, Heidelberg (2011). https://doi.org/10.1007/978-3-642-20633-7_1

18. Wang, F., Hannafin, M.J.: Design-based research and technology-enhanced learning environments. Education Tech. Res. Dev. **53**(4), 5–23 (2005). https://doi.org/10.1007/BF02504682

19. Ryan, R.M., Deci, E.L.: Self-determination theory and the facilitation of intrinsic motivation, social development, and well-being. Am. Psychol. **55**(1), 68–78 (2000). https://doi.org/10.1037/0003-066X.55.1.68

20. Venkatesh, V., Morris, M.G., Davis, G.B., Davis, F.D.: User acceptance of information technology: toward a unified view. MIS Q. **27**(3), 425–478 (2003). https://doi.org/10.2307/30036540

21. Rogers, E.M.: Diffusion of Innovations, 4th edn. Free Press, New York (1995)

22. Bundesamt für Sicherheit in der Informationstechnik (BSI): Die Lage der IT-Sicherheit in Deutschland 2021. BSI, Bonn (2021)

23. Bundesamt für Sicherheit in der Informationstechnik (BSI): Die Lage der IT-Sicherheit in Deutschland 2022. BSI, Bonn (2022)

24. Bundesministerium der Verteidigung (BMVG): Dritter Bericht zur Digitalen Transformation des Geschäftsbereichs des Bundesministeriums der Verteidigung. BMVG, Berlin (2021)

25. Philipp, A.: IT-Security in IIoT-Umgebungen. ZWF Zeitschrift für wirtschaftlichen Fabrikbetrieb **114**(4), 226–229 (2019). https://doi.org/10.3139/104.112067

26. Bundesamt für Sicherheit in der Informationstechnik (BSI): NFC-Systeme im Praxiseinsatz. BSI, Bonn (2020)

27. Bundesamt für Sicherheit in der Informationstechnik (BSI): SYS.4.5 Wechseldatenträger, IT-Grundschutz-Baustein, Edition 2023 (2023)

28. PricewaterhouseCoopers: HID attacks explained. https://www.pwc.com/mt/en/publications/technology/hid-attacks.html. Accessed 09-01-2025

29. Rheinland, T.Ü.V.: GS-Leitfaden zur zuverlässigen Datenhygiene und sicheren Datenentsorgung. TÜV Rheinland, Köln (2012)

30. Rieb, A., Lechner, U.: Towards a cybersecurity game: operation digital chameleon. In: Havarneanu, G., Setola, R., Nassopoulos, H., Wolthusen, S. (eds.) CRITIS 2016. LNCS, vol. 10242, pp. 283–295. Springer, Cham (2017). https://doi.org/10.1007/978-3-319-71368-7_24

31. Rieb, A.: IT-Security Awareness MIT Operation Digitales Chamäleon. Dissertation, Universität der Bundeswehr München, Neubiberg (2018). https://d-nb.info/1153067870

32. Ng, C.Y., Hasan, M.K.B.: Cybersecurity serious games development: a systematic Review. Comput. Secur. **150**, 104307 (2025). https://doi.org/10.1016/j.cose.2024.104307

33. Sanchez, E., Plumettaz-Sieber, M.: Teaching and learning with escape games from debriefing to institutionalization of knowledge. In: Gentile, M., Allegra, M., Söbke, H. (eds.) Games and Learning Alliance, LNCS 11385, pp. 242–253. Springer, Cham (2019). https://doi.org/10.1007/978-3-030-11548-7_23

34. Hänsch, N., Benenson, Z.: Specifying IT security awareness. In: 25th International Workshop on Database and Expert Systems Applications (DEXA), pp. 331–335. IEEE (2014). https://doi.org/10.1109/DEXA.2014.71
35. Penttilä, K.: History of Escape Games. Master's Thesis, University of Turku (2018)
36. Botturi, L., Babazadeh, M.: Designing educational escape rooms: validating the Star Model. Int. J. Serious Games **7**(3), 41–57 (2020). https://doi.org/10.17083/ijsg.v7i3.367

Cyberincident Detection and Response

The CONTAIN Response Canvas: A Template for Cyber Incident Response

Judith Strussenberg$^{(\boxtimes)}$, Ulrike Lechner , and Mandy Balthasar

University of the Bundeswehr Munich, Neubiberg, Germany
{judith.strussenberg,ulrike.lechner,mandy.balthasar}@unibw.de

Abstract. Ransomware attacks on mobile devices pose complex challenges that span individual behavior, organizational processes, and technological contexts for both professional and private use. Although cybersecurity training measures, such as serious games, are effective in raising awareness, they often lack mechanisms to transfer experiential knowledge into operational practice. In contrast, established incident response and business continuity frameworks are comprehensive, but typically text-heavy and difficult to apply under time pressure. This article introduces the CONTAIN Response Canvas (CRC), a visual, canvas-based artifact that adapts principles of the Business Model Canvas to ransomware incident response for personal mobile devices. The CRC structures technical, organizational, and communicative response measures in a compact format, supporting both orientation during incidents and structured reflection after training. The article also presents the serious game "A Question of Security", which embeds a reference response model that describes an ideal-typical procedure for handling a ransomware incident on a mobile device. This reference response model is part of the game design and was iteratively clarified and refined during 16 game sessions with 96 participants. Phases 2 – 4 of this model are represented using three phase-specific CONTAIN Response Canvases. The CRC thus serves as a structured visual representation of the reference response model and as a means of transferring the training results into reusable documentation artifacts. Finally, the article outlines how the CRC can be integrated into organizational awareness and training programs to support knowledge transfer, organizational learning, and sustained preparedness beyond the game-based setting.

Keywords: Business continuity management · Business Model Canvas · Cybersecurity · Incident response · Ransomware · Serious games

1 Introduction

Personal mobile devices, such as smartphones and tablets, are indispensable in both professional and private settings. They store sensitive data, provide access to corporate systems, and serve as central communication and coordination tools.

K. Kirchner et al. (Eds.): I4CS 2026, CCIS 3007, pp. 137–156, 2026.
https://doi.org/10.1007/978-3-032-27096-2_8

Consequently, ransomware attacks targeting these devices can disrupt individual users and organizational processes alike, particularly when there is a dual professional and private use of mobile devices as we address in our scenario. If ransomware compromises such a device, clear procedures are needed to limit damage, quickly restore operational capability, and involve relevant stakeholders. This requires not only suitable emergency processes at the organizational level, but also individuals who can act confidently under time pressure.

Training measures such as awareness programs or serious games can prepare individuals for incident response, but often lack mechanisms to transfer experiential knowledge into reusable operational practice. Conversely, incident response and business continuity frameworks are frequently text-heavy and difficult to apply in crisis situations, especially for non-experts. This gap between experiential learning and actionable documentation can hinder effective response and recovery.

This article introduces the *CONTAIN Response Canvas* (CRC), a structured visual artifact inspired by the Business Model Canvas [17]. The CRC adapts the canvas concept to ransomware incident response on mobile devices used in both private and professional contexts. It provides a structured representation of technical, organizational, and communicative measures while explicitly accounting for stakeholders and responsibilities. The CRC is designed to support orientation during incidents and structured reflection after training.

In addition, this article presents the serious game "A Question of Security", which was developed to train employees without in-depth cybersecurity expertise to respond appropriately to ransomware incidents on their mobile devices. The game embeds a reference response model that describes an ideal-typical procedure for handling such incidents. This reference response model is part of the game design and serves as the normative baseline against which player decisions are discussed during gameplay. Over 16 game sessions involving 96 participants, the model was iteratively clarified and refined.

Phases 2 – 4 of the reference response model are represented using three phase-specific CONTAIN Response Canvases. The CRC thus functions as a structured visual notation of the reference response model and provides a bridge between serious-game-based learning and reusable incident documentation. By making decisions, responsibilities, communication paths, and assumptions explicit, the CRC supports the transfer of experiential learning into organizational awareness and business continuity contexts.

This paper addresses the following research question:

RQ: How can the outcomes of serious game – based cybersecurity training be translated into structured and reusable incident response documentation using a visual canvas-based approach?

This article makes four contributions:

- We introduce the CONTAIN Response Canvas (CRC), a canvas-based notation template for documenting and communicating ransomware incident response scenarios on mobile devices.

- We present the serious game "A Question of Security" and its embedded reference response model as a structured training environment for mobile ransomware incidents.
- We demonstrate how the reference response model can be represented using phase-specific CRCs, thereby translating serious-game learning outcomes into structured incident documentation.
- We outline an implementation roadmap showing how CRC-based debriefing artifacts can be integrated into organizational awareness programs and information security management processes.

This article extends previous work on the serious game "A Question of Security" [8,25,26]. Although earlier publications focused on game design and alternative scenarios, the primary contributions of this paper are the explicit formulation of the reference response model and the design of the CONTAIN Response Canvas as its structured visual representation.

The paper is structured as follows. Section 2 presents related work, followed by the research method in Sect. 3. Sections 4 to 6 introduce the serious game, the CRC, and the reference response model, while Sect. 7 discusses implementation aspects and Sect. 8 concludes.

2   Related Work

2.1   Business Model Canvas

The Business Model Canvas (BMC) is a widely used framework for describing, analyzing, and designing business models. Developed by Osterwalder and Pigneur, it consists of nine elements that capture, e.g., customer value creation and communication [16,17]. Beyond its original economic focus, the BMC has inspired numerous adaptations in areas such as innovation, organizational change, and ethics, demonstrating the versatility of canvas-based approaches. The BMC is often used in interactive workshops to generate a shared understanding, structure, visualize, and facilitate discussions in the areas of business model development, analysis, and innovation. The nine-field canvas focuses on stakeholders and relationships, specific performance, resources, costs, and activities. We list the nine steps in the recommended order of completion, starting with the customers, from whom every next step is conceived, be it products, services or their further development [15]:

1. **Customer Segments** describe the groups of users or organizations the business model addresses and serves.
2. **Value Proposition** defines the products or services that create value for the customer segments by solving problems or satisfying needs.
3. **Channels** specify how the value proposition is delivered to and communicated with the customer segments.
4. **Customer Relationships** describe the types of relationships an organization establishes and maintains with its customers.

5. **Revenue Streams** represent the ways in which the organization generates income from each customer segment.
6. **Key Resources** identify the most important assets required to create and deliver the value proposition.
7. **Key Activities** describe the essential actions the organization must perform to operate the business model successfully.
8. **Key Partnerships** outline the network of external partners and suppliers that support the business model.
9. **Cost Structure** captures the major costs incurred in operating the business model.

Together, these building blocks provide a holistic and visual representation of a business model and support shared understanding, analysis, and innovation through structured discussion.

Although extensive textual documentation can capture complex processes, it often becomes difficult to navigate in time-critical situations. If this leads to the instructions, report, or explanation not being read, it can result in incorrect assumptions, decisions, or even dangerous behavior. In addition to texts, learning, understanding, decision-making, and documentation are always supported by visualization of contexts, whether real or virtual, from blackboards to slides, whiteboards, Kanban boards, and canvases. Transparency and clarity are created in a limited space, requiring a focus on the essentials and thus the analysis, understanding, evaluation, classification, and visual presentation of the subject matter. The scarcity of space, thus, leads to a restriction of the essentials, which brings clarity to both the designer and the users. A sequence of individual elements, on the other hand, provides structure. Examples include boxes arranged next to and below each other on a canvas, such as the BMC. At the same time, the arrangement of the individual topics within the boxes clarifies the relationships with other elements. Although a process can be approached step by step by examining the individual boxes, this does not imply hierarchy or ranking. If, for example, a necessary area, such as the key activities for a business model, cannot be developed from the outset, this does not block the entire process of creating a canvas. In addition, the given structure allows numerous variants to be developed, compared, and analyzed. Even those not involved in the creation process can quickly identify the core issues, connections, and requirements. This successful combination of focus, analysis, classification, and understanding has already been used in numerous scenarios, both for those involved in the development and, thanks to the documentation of the process in a structured overview, also for those using the results. The BMC can also be specifically used by companies operating in the social sector. Whether as a lean canvas for innovation-driven start-ups, as a business model with a value proposition design, as a change canvas for the process of organizational change, or as an ethics canvas for considering the ethical implications of research or innovation projects, the strategy is always based on structured quality rather than text-heavy quantity [18,19,23].

2.2   Frameworks for Business Continuity Management

The German Federal Office for Information Security (BSI) describes business continuity management (BCM) in standard 200-4 as a way for institutions to protect themselves from the effects of damaging events, such as cyber incidents or natural disasters, that could significantly affect business operations or even threaten their existence [3]. According to BSI, the aim of BCM is to ensure that business operations can continue even in the event of massive damage, or can be resumed in a reasonable time at a defined minimum level. BCM, according to BSI Standard 200-4, comprises organizational, technical, structural, and personnel measures. For sustainable organizational resilience, the BSI considers the integration of information security management, crisis management, and BCM to be essential. In addition to BSI Standard 200-4, there is a range of relevant international standards for BCM such as ISO 22301:2019, Capability Maturity Model Integration (CMMI) V2.0, COBIT, ITIL 4, and the National Fire Protection Association (NFPA) 1600 standard [1,4,5,12,20].

Most of the BCM standards are text-heavy. To the best of our knowledge, there are only a few frameworks that incorporate visual elements beyond tables or process models. One of them was proposed by Gibb and Buchanan [7]. The steps in this framework are Program initiation, Project initiation, Risk analysis, Selecting risk mitigation strategies, Monitoring and control, Implementation, Testing, Education and training, and Review. Each of these steps is represented in a visual element that includes input, key activities, and output. There are some more visually oriented attempts using business process modeling notation (BPMN) to model business continuity processes. E.g., Winkler and Gilani present a model-driven approach to generate a business continuity process using model-transformation chains to connect data across the different phases in BCM [2,27].

When talking about ways to document information on how to respond appropriately to cybersecurity incidents, playbooks are essential. Playbooks, also known as script, automation, runbook, checklist, standard operating procedure, workflow, or process, are guidelines to help security operations personnel gain an overview and respond quickly to specific threat scenarios. Schlette et al. point out that there is no common definition and propose security context, Process representation, and technology integration as the three main characteristics of a playbook [21]. Although playbooks are commonly used in security and in the core of Security Orchestration, Automation and Response (SOAR) platforms that automate security operations, there is a lack of research on their effectiveness in incident response situations [21,24].

2.3   Serious Games

Serious games blend educational or training content with games, creating learning experiences that go beyond pure entertainment [6,9,14]. Research shows that well-designed games can be effective in boosting motivation, participation, and knowledge retention in various fields, including education, healthcare, and business [11,13,22]. In the realm of incident management, serious games provide a prime opportunity to recreate real-life situations. Participants can learn to effectively handle realistic scenarios, such as the management of security incidents, within a safe environment [14]. This approach not only raises awareness of risks and challenges, but also improves understanding of decisions and their impacts, encouraging reflection on personal actions [6,13]. Through repetition of these scenarios, people can continually develop and internalize these skills [14]. In addition, collaborative methods can promote teamwork and communication [22].

In summary, existing BCM frameworks and incident response playbooks provide comprehensive guidance but are often text-heavy and designed primarily for operational security teams. Serious games, in contrast, support experiential learning, but often lack lightweight artifacts that preserve and transfer outcomes beyond the training setting. The CRC addresses this gap by offering a compact visual structure for capturing incident-response measures, roles, and communication paths in a form suitable for debriefing, documentation, and organizational learning.

3   Method

This research follows a Design Science Research (DSR) approach according to Hevner et al. [10] and focuses on the design and examination of the CONTAIN Response Canvas (CRC) as a socio-technical artifact. The objective was to address a practical problem observed in cybersecurity training while introducing the proposed solution to the existing theory, standards, and empirical experience of serious game sessions.

The starting point of this work is the design process, which included design phases and game events with evaluations of the serious game"A Question of Security", which supports awareness and learning in the context of cybersecurity incidents. A total of 16 game sessions with 96 players from different organizational backgrounds were held between September 2024 and October 2025. As part of the design process, we looked for a way to document the game results in a structured and accessible form. This documentation should serve as a tool for the game facilitator and as a record of individual games for players and facilitators.

This observation of a need to document the game output both for the game facilitator as well as the game participants is the most important element of the problem identification phase in DSR. To address this problem, we explored methods to represent the outcomes of serious game sessions in a concise and comprehensible manner. Based on its widely known structure, the focus on relationships, and its suitability to support reflection, a canvas-based approach was selected. Building on these considerations, we designed the CONTAIN Response Canvas (CRC) as an innovative, visually structured artifact to document and reflect incident response scenarios. A key design decision was to represent the incident response as phase-specific canvases, separating goals, stakeholders, and measures per phase to preserve clarity under time pressure. The design of the CRC adapts the principles of the Business Model Canvas. This step represents the artifact design phase of the DSR process.

To examine the suitability of the CRC, we used the reference response model of "A Question of Security", which describes an ideal response to a ransomware incident on a personal mobile device used for both professional and private purposes. The reference response model was embedded in the game design as an intended solution space and was iteratively refined during repeated gameplay. It reflects the response steps practiced during the game rounds and serves as a normative baseline. It incorporates content derived from established information security standards, including BSI IT-Grundschutz and ISO/IEC 27001. We applied these steps to three canvases of the CRC to assess whether the intended sequence of organizational, communicative, and technical measures could be represented in a clear and structured way using the canvas format. This application corresponds to an initial demonstration and formative examination of the artifact within its intended context.

Following this application, the CRC was considered with regard to its practical usefulness for facilitation and result documentation. In this stage of research, the canvas seems to be a promising tool to structure debriefings and capture key game outcomes in a compact and transparent form. In this sense, the CRC supports both facilitators and participants in securing and transferring the results of serious game sessions beyond the immediate training context.

The evaluation of the suitability of the CRC is qualitative and exploratory in nature, which is appropriate for early-stage design science research. The examination focused on the clarity, completeness, and usefulness of the canvas format for documenting and transferring game outcomes (Fig. 1).

4   The Serious Game "A Question of Security"

The game in which the CRC is applied is "A Question of Security". The board game includes a total of five rounds in which four to eight players can experience the case of ransomware on a personal mobile device, used both professionally and privately, or the case of ransomware on an ERP system [25, 26].

The game is structured as follows: In round 1,"Take a deep breath and think," the players express their fears and concerns in case the mobile device becomes unusable by a ransomware. In rounds 2 to 4, the focus is on responding properly to the incident. In these rounds, the players consider the important steps to be taken, which are then compared by the game facilitator at the end of the round with the respective steps of the reference response model. In round 5, called "Role-based Evaluation," the participants identify the internal and external stakeholders involved in the scenario. Rounds 1 and 5 do not provide a pre-made solution, as both the concerns and stakeholders can vary depending on the size and form of the organization.

Rounds 2 to 4 correspond each to a CONTAIN Response Canvas that represents the measures practiced. The reference process for the appropriate response

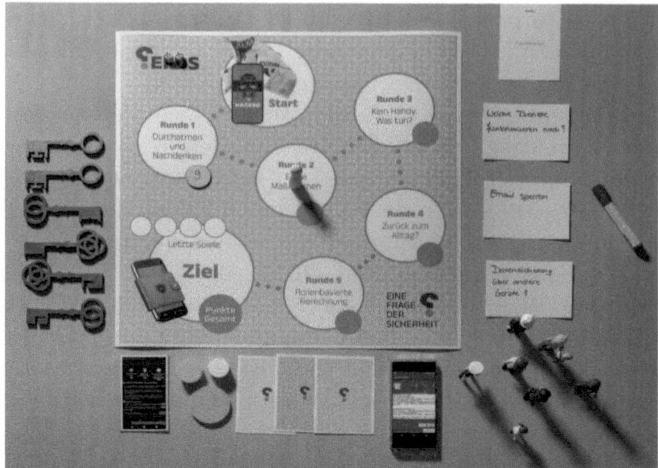

Fig. 1. Game material from "A Question of Security". In addition to the game board there are keys which form a mini puzzle. Between rounds, players can earn clues for the next round by solving it. There are mockups showing how ransomware on a mobile device looks like, tiles that are labeled with the respective score achieved, game cards and Playmobil figures who serve as stakeholders during the last game round. The white cards are labeled by the players with the actions they would take in each round. Photographer: Martin Bolle

to ransomware on an individual device is fundamentally based on the research of important IT security frameworks, such as NIST and BSI. The so derived measures are implemented by insights from the CONTAIN research consortium, and suggestions from experts as well as from the serious game implementations.

5 CONTAIN Response Canvas: Keeping Track in the Event of a Ransomware Incident

In this section, we present the CONTAIN Response Canvas. The Business Model Canvas by Osterwalder and Pigneur [15] is the starting point of our design. The CONTAIN Response Canvas is structured into nine panels, and there is a sequence according to which this canvas should be filled. The panels of the CONTAIN Response Canvas are described and presented in the order in which they are filled. The name, the important questions to be answered, and a brief description of each element are provided below (Fig. 2):

1. Internal/external customers (target group)
   - Who am I doing this for?
   - What is important to the customer?

   The target group (to which the Business Model Canvas refers as the customer) refers to the person or persons and roles for which incident response activities

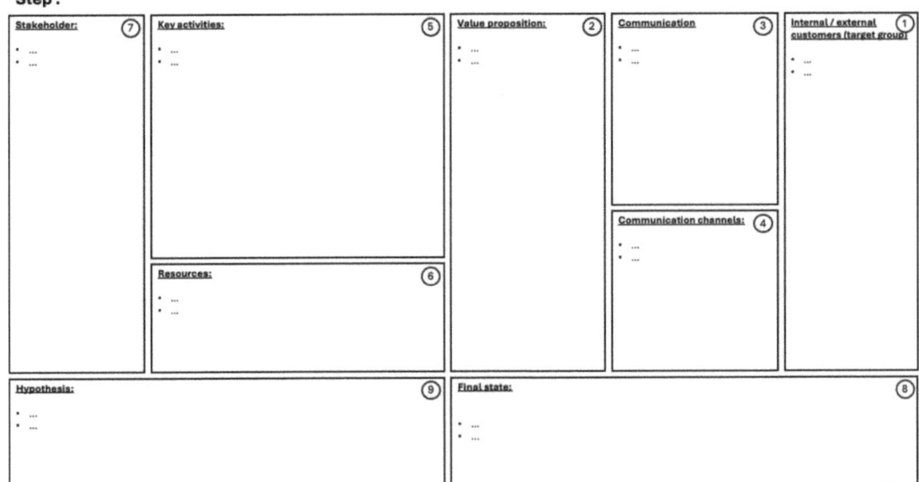

Fig. 2. This image depicts the CONTAIN Response Canvas (CRC).

are carried out. The people who are typically at the center here are "myself", external customers (such as end customers or business partners), Internal customers (such as business owners or management and the people in IT support and the people with roles and responsibilities for IT security, and information security or forensics)

2. Value proposition
   - How do I benefit my customer?
   - What value do I provide to the customer?

   The value proposition specifies the guidelines that incident response actions follow. Typical value propositions are related to containing damage, reliability, and orientation toward internal policies and compliance with legal regulations.

3. Communication
   - How and what do I communicate?
   - How do we deliver our products or services?

   The communication element captures information flows, including reporting, escalations, as well as the topic and the regularity. It also includes the documentation of the events.

4. Communication channels
   - What channels do I use?

   The communication channels section lists the initial and redundant media available and defined for communication. These include, for example, face-to-face meetings, telephone, email, or systems that are provided as redundancy in case of an emergency. This may include the communication channels of colleagues (telephones, messaging, email) that may be used as the own smartphone is not available and important channels may also be compromised.

5. Key activities

– What do I do?

Key activities refer to incident response tasks and represent the main steps in the investigation of the incident. Activities describe the actions taken to identify the cyber incident, contain and eliminate malware, and restore operations. In addition, measures are identified to increase security standards and eliminate vulnerabilities. This also includes documentation of observations and activities in incident response, and data collection for forensics to prepare for restoration, as well as law enforcement or legal procedures and the recovery of the device.

6. Key resources

– What information and resources are available to me?

Key resources include all people, roles, and internal and external service providers available to handle the incident. In organizations, this is the incident response desk. Resources also include insurance companies that provide advice or commission special service providers, as well as redundant systems and IT security specialists.

7. Stakeholders

– Who are my partners?

– Who are my stakeholders?

Partners or stakeholders refer to individuals or roles that are considered in incident response. These can include the company itself, for which the ability to deliver and the availability of products and services are important; authorities to which reports must be made; law enforcement agencies; data protection officers; IT security officers; and friends and family whose private information must be protected and who may be endangered by the incident itself.

8. Hypothesis

– What is my working assumption?

The working hypotheses reflect assumptions about the ransomware incident. They include, for example, the assumption regarding the spread of an incident within the network or among various personal IT. Assumptions are "the ransomware is only on my personal device and will not spread", "the ransomware did not exfiltrate personal data", "The ransomware spreads and has infected the organizations network". This part of the canvas urges the user to verbally state implicit assumptions.

9. Final state

– What is my goal?

This panel describes the "end state" of the endeavor. End states or goals are, e.g., to "to contain the malware" or "to resume normal operations for business as usual". This ninth and final panel may include the goal of identifying lessons learned and raising the level of security so that such an incident may not happen again. This includes, e.g., resolutions concerning the backup or password strategy can be part of this panel as well.

Note that the structure of the Canvas with the nine panels resembles the structure of the Business Model Canvas by Osterwalder and Pigneur. Also, the process that Osterwalder and Pigneur suggest remains unchanged. The meaning of several panels has changed: Customer segments (field 1) have become internal/ external customers (target group), Customer Relationship (Field 3) was changed to Communication and field 4 Channels was clarified to Communication Channels. Key Partners (field 7) were altered to Stakeholder. The greatest changes were made to fields 8 and 9, where revenue streams became final state, and cost structure serves as the field where the hypothesis about the actual state of the incident is put. The working assumption and the end state are new and particular to incident response. The Working Hypothesis guides and also delimits Actions in the Response Canvas. Actions and decisions that are adequate under the assumption that the malware has not spread from the personal device to the network are not sufficient once the malware has spread. Furthermore, the course of actions that suffice in cases where the ransomware only blocks access and encrypts data needs to be enriched when there is reason to believe that the ransomware has exfiltrated data.

6   Incident Response of "A Question of Security" A Reference Model

This section presents the reference response model for ransomware incidents affecting personal mobile devices used in both professional and private contexts. The reference response model is embedded in the design of the serious game "A Question of Security" and serves as the normative baseline against which player decisions are discussed during gameplay. Over 16 game sessions involving 96 participants, the model was iteratively clarified and refined through structured facilitation and reflection.

The model structures incident handling into five phases that reflect the temporal progression of a ransomware incident and its organizational implications. Phases 2 to 4 are represented using CRCs because they contain operational incident response actions, while Phases 1 and 5 frame the process and therefore do not require canvas representation. The CRC functions as a structured notation that makes explicit the relationships between stakeholders, communication, activities, assumptions, and the desired outcomes within each phase. The canvases therefore represent the model but do not constitute the model itself.

6.1   Model Structure

The reference response model follows a phase-oriented logic consisting of:

1. Situational awareness
2. Containment and initial response
3. Continuity without compromised device
4. Recovery and hardening
5. Role-based evaluation and organizational learning

The phases are sequential, but interdependent. Each phase produces structured outputs that serve as preconditions for the next phase. Across all phases, three recurring structural dimensions are emphasized:

- Stakeholder orientation
- Explicit communication structures
- Articulation of working assumptions

These dimensions form the conceptual backbone of the reference response model and are consistently represented within the CRC notation.

6.2   Phase 1 – Situational Awareness

Objective. Establish a shared understanding of the ransomware incident, its potential impact, and its urgency.

Core Focus. This phase captures perceived risks and consequences across the professional and private domains. It includes functional limitations (e.g., communication, financial access, mobility), potential data exfiltration scenarios, and broader implications consistent with contemporary ransomware tactics, including double and triple extortion.

Output. A consolidated perception of risks and priorities that informs containment decisions in Phase 2 (Fig. 3).

6.3   Phase 2 – Containment and Initial Response

Objective. Limit further damage and initiate coordinated incident handling.

Structural Characteristics. Phase 2 is characterized by rapid technical intervention combined with immediate stakeholder communication. The CRC representation emphasizes the coordination of containment measures, the escalation to IT or security roles, the documentation of observed events, and the explicit articulation of assumptions about the scope and impact of the incident.

Output. The device is isolated or handed over to responsible roles, containment measures are initiated, and responsibilities are clarified (Fig. 4).

6.4   Phase 3 – Continuity Without the Compromised Device

Objective. Maintain professional and personal functionality while the compromised device is unavailable.

Step 2: First steps

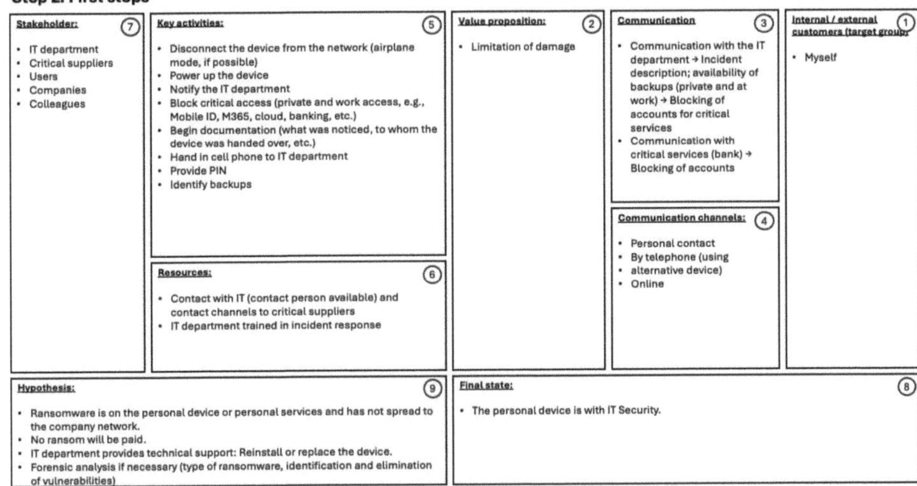

Fig. 3. CRC representation of Phase 2 – Containment and Initial Response

Structural Characteristics. This phase shifts focus from technical containment to organizational coordination and communication. The CRC representation highlights alternative communication paths, stakeholder transparency, redistribution of responsibilities, and preparation for device replacement or restoration.

Output. Stabilized workflows and reduced uncertainty among affected stakeholders.

6.5 Phase 4 – Recovery and Hardening

Objective. Restore normal operations and increase resilience to future incidents.

Structural Characteristics. Phase 4 integrates restoration, credential renewal, security enhancement measures, and monitoring activities. The CRC makes visible the alignment between recovery actions, stakeholder communication, and preventive hardening measures.

Output. Restored operational capability and strengthened security posture (Fig. 5).

6.6 Phase 5 – Role-Based Evaluation and Organizational Learning

Objective. Clarify responsibilities and derive institutional learning from the incident.

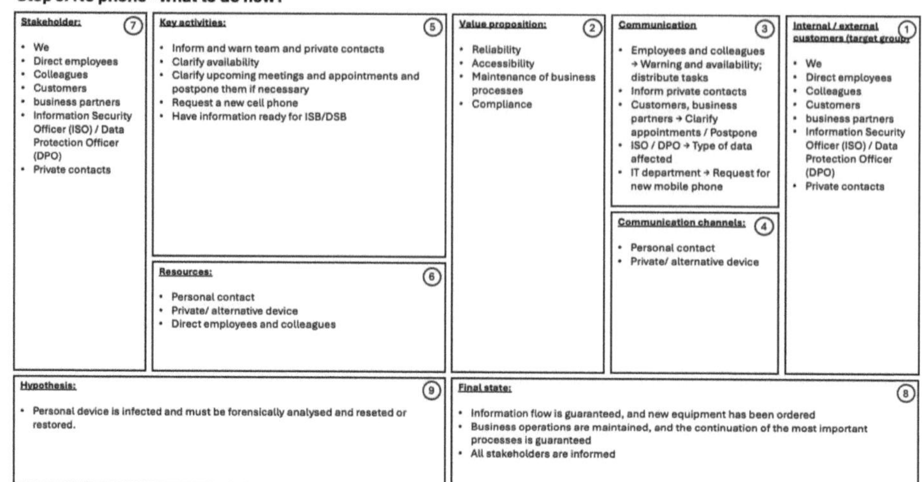

Fig. 4. CRC representation of Phase 3 – Continuity without Device

Structural Characteristics. This phase explicitly maps internal and external stakeholders, identifies dependencies, and supports reflection on decision-making processes. It provides the bridge from incident response to organizational improvement.

Output. Documented responsibilities, identified lessons learned, and input for policy adaptation and awareness programs.

7 Roadmap to Implementation and Organizational Learning

This section operationalizes Phase 5 of the reference response model by outlining how the outputs of the CONTAIN Response Canvases can be integrated into organizational information security management and awareness processes. Although the reference response model conceptually structures incident handling, this roadmap translates its results into organizational practice.

Figure 6 illustrates how the structured output of the CRC-based debriefing can serve as input to organizational learning and policy adaptation.

To implement the serious game "A Question of Security" in an organization, the first step is to analyze the organizational requirements, e.g., the needs, the information security, guidelines, and compliance requirements. The rationale is that, to maximize the take-away for the game participants, the game should resemble the everyday context. The game material, as well as the evaluation material, eventually needs to be refined. After gameplay validation of the results and evaluation of the game and game experience take place. The feedback from

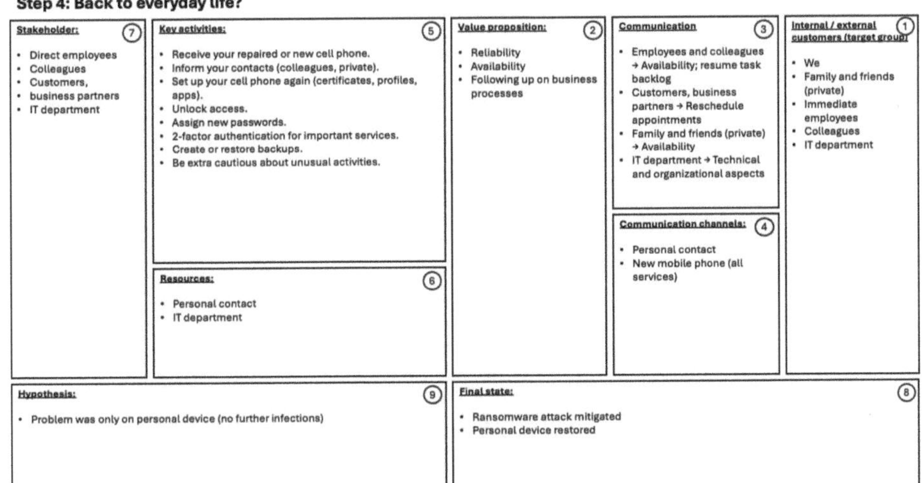

Fig. 5. CRC representation of Phase 4 – Recovery and Hardening

the evaluation informs the management of information security in the organization and provides impulses for the adaptation of policies, guidelines, and further awareness measures.

Regarding "A Question of Security", the canvas should be filled in during or after the game. The insights gained from the serious game "A Question of Security" go beyond the knowledge about ransomware and how individuals should behave in an emergency situation. The serious game offers valuable information about how security awareness is actually practiced in an organization. Discussions, decisions, and observations during game rounds reveal how well existing processes work, where uncertainties exist, and what assumptions or misunderstandings prevail about responsibilities and procedures. An analysis of these results can identify actionable insights for the organization. Incorporated into the continuous improvement process of the information security strategy, the feedback provided can result in concrete measures that require technical or organizational adjustments. These include, for example, the introduction of new security or collaboration tools, the optimization of IT structures and hardware, or physical security measures in the working environment. This feedback may also include decisions to speed up incident response and business continuity.

The following examples illustrate how CRC-based debriefings make implicit organizational decisions explicit and reveal structural gaps in incident response policies. What to do when the ransomware sends its notice? The options include disconnecting the device from the networks (mobile and organizations' WiFi), keeping the power supply, or turning off the device. This depends on the backups and applications on the network. Keeping the device powered and offline might be an option when one hopes to restore the device without a backup. A patchy backup strategy and the mixed use of the device for business and private purposes

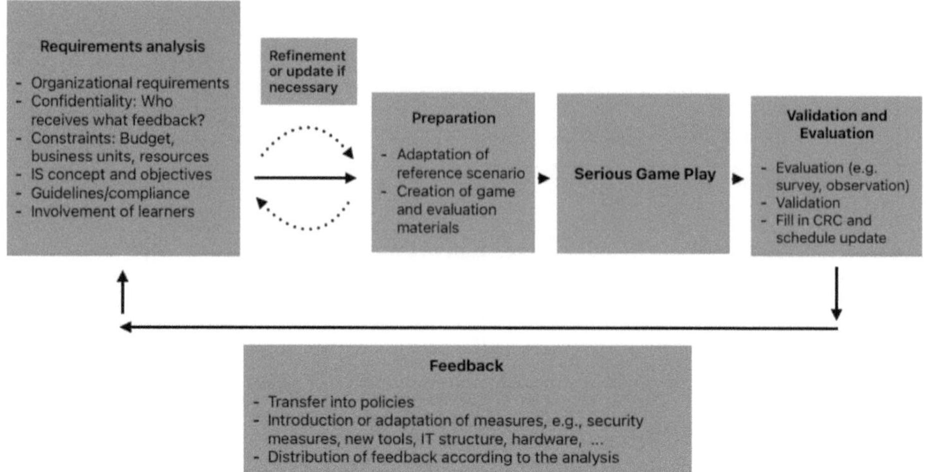

Fig. 6. If "A Question of Security" is to be used in an organization, the following process is recommended, to ensure that the knowledge gained from the serious game can be transferred back into the organization.

would be reasons to opt for this strategy. A strong backup and mobile device management would make a "switch it off and set it back to the initial settings" an option. In addition, the decision to hand over the device to the service desk might only be an option when there is no significant private use and private data and apps. Handing the device over to external IT security staff might be preferred when the data is sensitive or private. When the game results in the insight that all processes are too tedious and long, an investment in mobile device management might be an option.

To achieve a lasting effect, it is important to distribute feedback in a targeted manner and prepare it in a way that is appropriate for the recipient: operational findings should be passed on to IT and support teams, strategic ideas for information security management, and organizational recommendations for managers or human resource development. In this sense, the roadmap does not extend the reference response model, but demonstrates how its structured representation can trigger organizational adaptation and continuous improvement.

8 Conclusions, Limitations, and Next Steps

8.1 Conclusions

This article addresses the challenge of preparing individuals and organizations for ransomware incidents affecting personal mobile devices, particularly where private and professional responsibilities overlap. Existing approaches often struggle to connect experiential training with usable documentation in crisis conditions. The CONTAIN Response Canvas (CRC) is proposed to address this gap.

The CRC illustrates how the principles of the Business Model Canvas can be adapted to incident response and business continuity management. By providing a compact visual structure that integrates technical, organizational, and communicative measures, the CRC supports orientation and prioritization in stressful situations. This suggests the suitability of canvas-based artifacts as socio-technical tools in cybersecurity contexts.

The CRC bridges serious-game-based training and operational documentation. Although serious games effectively raise awareness, their impact can remain situational if learning outcomes are not consolidated. The CRC captures decisions and measures developed during gameplay and translates experiential learning into a reusable structure, supporting individual preparedness and shared understanding within organizations.

Applying the CRC as a representation of the reference response model illustrates how it supports individual, organizational, and role-based perspectives. By explicitly addressing both private and professional considerations, the CRC reflects real-world mobile device usage and encourages reflection on responsibilities, communication paths, and escalation mechanisms.

Finally, the proposed implementation approach highlights how the CRC can contribute to organizational learning. Rather than treating the serious game as a standalone intervention, the CRC enables insights from game play to inform policies, responsibilities, and awareness measures, supporting continuous improvement and organizational resilience.

In general, the CRC complements established incident response frameworks by improving accessibility and applicability at the human – organizational interface, particularly under time pressure and distributed responsibility.

8.2 Limitations

Cybersecurity is a constantly evolving field. Novel threats, particularly ransomware threats, novel cybersecurity technology, organizational frameworks, security technologies, and, in particular, changes in regulations will make it necessary to reconsider and refine both the game and the reference response model. The Canvas and the reference response model are also the result of a design process, and further discussions, applications, or game events may lead to the necessity to refine all these models. This is inherent in reference modeling research design; albeit we can claim that we have designed a useful artifact.

The CRC was developed and examined in close connection with the serious game "A Question of Security". The generalizability to other types of threats and to other types of IT-infrastructure is not discussed in this article. The evaluation of the Canvas is qualitative and exploratory and does not aim to provide evidence of effectiveness. Furthermore, the CRC focuses on ransomware incidents affecting personal mobile devices; its transferability to other types of incidents remains to be investigated. Evaluating the artifact in scenarios such as a serious game or a cyber range must be left to future research. Finally, as a complementary human-centered artifact, the CRC does not replace detailed incident response playbooks, and its effectiveness may depend on organizational context and facilitation.

8.3 Next Steps

Future work will focus on the empirical evaluation of the canvas in diverse settings. Interviews with practitioners will be conducted to assess perceived usefulness, required adaptations, and adoption barriers. In addition, the CRC should be adjusted to additional incident types. However, the Canvas design can build on the Business Model Canvas as a well established structure and expects that employees and end users transfer their understanding of the business model canvas to the new field of ransomware incident response, allowing them to ask the right questions.

Acknowledgments. This work originates from the CONTAIN and LIONS research projects. We acknowledge the funding for CONTAIN by the Bundesministerium für Forschung, Technologie und Raumfahrt (BMFTR) (grant number 13N16581-13N16587) as part of the SIFO program. LIONS is funded by dtec.bw—Digitalization and Technology Research Center of the Bundeswehr, which we gratefully acknowledge. dtec.bw is funded by the European Union—NextGenerationEU. We thank Dr. Stefanie Frey and Michael Bartsch from Deutor Cyber Security Solutions GmbH for helpful comments and insights.

References

1. Agutter, C.: ITIL Foundation Essentials ITIL 4 Edition-The Ultimate Revision Guide. IT Governance Publishing Ltd (2020)
2. Anne, K.M.: Agile Business Continuity Planning using Business Process Modeling Notation. Ph.D. thesis, Pace University New York (2012)
3. Bundesamt für Sicherheit in der Informationstechnik: BSI-Standard 200-4: Business Continuity Management. Bundesamt für Sicherheit in der Informationstechnik (2023). https://www.bsi.bund.de/SharedDocs/Downloads/DE/BSI/Grundschutz/BSI_Standards/standard_200_4.pdf. zugriff am 19.02.2026
4. Bundesamt für Sicherheit in der Informationstechnik (BSI): BSI-Standard 200-4: Business Continuity Management (2023). https://www.bsi.bund.de/DE/Themen/Unternehmen-und-Organisationen/Standards-und-Zertifizierung/IT-Grundschutz/BSI-Standards/BSI-Standard-200-4-Business-Continuity-Management/bsi-standard-200-4_Business_Continuity_Management_node.html. Version 1.0
5. Calder, A.: ISO 22301: 2019 and business continuity management-Understand how to plan, implement and enhance a business continuity management system (BCMS). IT Governance Publishing (2021)
6. Djaouti, D., Alvarez, J., Jessel, J.P.: Classifying serious games: the g/p/s model. In: Handbook of research on improving learning and motivation through educational games: Multidisciplinary approaches, pp. 118–136. IGI global (2011). https://doi.org/10.4018/978-1-60960-495-0.ch006
7. Gibb, F., Buchanan, S.: A framework for business continuity management. Int. J. Inf. Manage. **26**(2), 128–141 (2006). https://doi.org/10.1016/j.ijinfomgt.2005.11.008

8. Greiner, M., et al.: Scared? Prepared? Toward a ransomware incident response scenario. In: Phillipson, F., Eichler, G., Erfurth, C., Fahrnberger, G. (eds.) Innovations for Community Services, pp. 289–320. Communications in Computer and Information Science, Springer (2024). https://doi.org/10.1007/978-3-031-60433-1_17

9. Hamari, J., Shernoff, D.J., Rowe, E., Coller, B., Asbell-Clarke, J., Edwards, T.: Challenging games help students learn: an empirical study on engagement, flow and immersion in game-based learning. Comput. Hum. Behav. **54**, 170–179 (2016)

10. Hevner, A.R., March, S.T., Park, J., Ram, S.: Design science in information systems research. MIS Quarterly, 75–105 (2004)

11. Hofstede, G.J., De Caluwé, L., Peters, V.: Why simulation games work-in search of the active substance: a synthesis. Simul. Gaming **41**(6), 824–843 (2010)

12. Information Systems Audit and Control Association: COBIT® 2019 Framework: Governance and Management Objectives. ISACA (2018)

13. Kerres, M., Bormann, M., Vervenne, M.: Didaktische Konzeption von Serious Games: Zur Verknüpfung von Spiel- und Lernangeboten. MedienPädagogik: Zeitschrift für Theorie und Praxis der Medienbildung, pp. 1–16 (2009). https://doi.org/10.21240/mpaed/00/2009.08.25.X

14. Lameras, P., Arnab, S., Dunwell, I., Stewart, C., Clarke, S., Petridis, P.: Essential features of serious games design in higher education: linking learning attributes to game mechanics. Br. J. Edu. Technol. **48**(4), 972–994 (2017). https://doi.org/10.1111/bjet.12467

15. Osterwalder, A., Pigneur, Y.: Business model generation: a handbook for visionaries, game changers, and challengers. John Wiley & Sons (2010)

16. Osterwalder, A., Pigneur, Y.: Aligning profit and purpose through business model innovation. Responsible Manag. Prac. 21st Century, 61–76 (2011)

17. Osterwalder, A., Pigneur, Y.: Designing business models and similar strategic objects: the contribution of IS. J. Assoc. Inf. Syst. **14**(5) (2013). https://doi.org/10.17705/1jais.00333

18. Pepin, M., Tremblay, M., Audebrand, L.K., Chassé, S.: The responsible business model canvas: designing and assessing a sustainable business modeling tool for students and start-up entrepreneurs. Int. J. Sustain. High. Educ. **25**(3), 514–538 (2024). https://doi.org/10.1108/IJSHE-01-2023-0008

19. Reijers, W., Koidl, K., Lewis, D., Pandit, H.J., Gordijn, B.: Discussing ethical impacts in research and innovation: the ethics canvas. In: IFIP International Conference on Human Choice and Computers, pp. 299–313. Springer (2018). https://doi.org/10.1007/978-3-319-99605-9_23

20. Russo, N., Reis, L., Silveira, C., Mamede, H.S.: Towards a comprehensive framework for the multidisciplinary evaluation of organizational maturity on business continuity program management: a systematic literature review. Inf. Secur. J. Global Persp. **33**(1), 54–72 (2024). https://doi.org/10.1080/19393555.2023.2195577

21. Schlette, D., Empl, P., Caselli, M., Schreck, T., Pernul, G.: Do you play it by the books? A study on incident response playbooks and influencing factors. In: 2024 IEEE Symposium on Security and Privacy (SP), pp. 3625–3643. IEEE (2024). https://doi.org/10.1109/SP54263.2024.00060

22. Serrano-Laguna, Á., Martínez-Ortiz, I., Haag, J., Regan, D., Johnson, A., Fernández-Manjón, B.: Applying standards to systematize learning analytics in serious games. Comput. Standards Interfaces **50**, 116–123 (2017). https://doi.org/10.1016/j.csi.2016.09.014

23. Sparviero, S.: The case for a socially oriented business model canvas: the social enterprise model canvas. J. Soc. Entrepreneurship **10**(2), 232–251 (2019). https://doi.org/10.1080/19420676.2018.1541011

24. Stevens, R., et al.: How ready is your ready? Assessing the usability of incident response playbook frameworks. In: Proceedings of the 2022 CHI Conference on Human Factors in Computing Systems, pp. 1–18 (2022). https://doi.org/10.1145/3491102.3517559

25. Strussenberg, J., Henkel, A., Rudel, S., Lechner, U.: Simulating ERP cyber incidents: a serious game for awareness and incident management. In: Herzwurm, G., Petrik, D., Strobel, G., Kude, T., Block, L. (eds.) Software Business 16th International Conference, ICSOB 2025, Stuttgart, Germany, 24–26 November 2025, Proceeding, pp. 77–91. Lecture Notes in Business Information Processing, Springer Cham (2026). https://doi.org/10.1007/978-3-032-14518-5

26. Strussenberg, J., Seidenfad, K., Greiner, M., Riesel, K., Biermann, J., Lechner, U.: From paper to pixel: the digitalization of a serious game. In: Phillipson, F., Eichler, G., Erfurth, C., Fahrnberger, G. (eds.) International Conference on Innovations for Community Services, pp. 307–329. Communications in Computer and Information Science, Springer (2025). https://doi.org/10.1007/978-3-031-94263-1_18

27. Winkler, U., Gilani, W.: Model-driven framework for business continuity management. In: Service Level Agreements for Cloud Computing, pp. 227–250. Springer (2011). https://doi.org/10.1007/978-1-4614-1614-2_14

Comparison of the Endpoint Detection and Response (EDR) Solutions From CrowdStrike and SentinelOne

Christoph Eigner[1] and Günter Fahrnberger[2(✉)]

[1] University of Applied Sciences BFI Vienna, Vienna, Austria
[2] University of Hagen, Hagen, North Rhine-Westphalia, Germany
`guenter.fahrnberger@studium.fernuni-hagen.de`

Abstract. Endpoint Detection and Response (EDR) solutions serve as a cornerstone of modern cybersecurity, tackling the growing complexity and frequency of cyberattacks that target corporate networks. This paper compares two leading EDR platforms, CrowdStrike and SentinelOne, to evaluate their effectiveness in detecting common attack patterns such as phishing, malware, and ransomware. Furthermore, the study analyzes how each solution handles vulnerabilities including insecure authentication and outdated software. Both products employ advanced technologies such as Artificial Intelligence (AI) and Machine Learning (ML), which strengthen threat detection and response capabilities. The research seeks to deliver organizations actionable insights that guide the selection of an EDR solution matching their specific security requirements.

Keywords: CrowdStrike · Cybersecurity · Endpoint Detection and Response (EDR) · Malware detection · Phishing protection · Ransomware prevention · Security · SentinelOne · Threat detection

1 Introduction

In today's digital world, Endpoint Detection and Response (EDR) solutions hold a crucial role in protecting corporate networks and data. The growing complexity and frequency of cyberattacks highlight the urgent need for effective cybersecurity measures. Endpoints rank among the most common and vulnerable vectors for cyberattacks, with the expansion of remote and hybrid work further increasing the overall risk [16].

CrowdStrike and SentinelOne rank among leading vendors in the EDR market, recognized by Gartner as top performers in endpoint security. Given the diversity of available solutions and the complexity of the threat landscape, companies must clearly grasp the strengths and weaknesses of different EDR providers [11].

This study aims to obtain insights through a detailed comparison of the EDR solutions from CrowdStrike and SentinelOne, helping companies and cybersecurity professionals select and implement suitable security measures. The analysis

K. Kirchner et al. (Eds.): I4CS 2026, CCIS 3007, pp. 157–182, 2026.
https://doi.org/10.1007/978-3-032-27096-2_9

focuses on the effectiveness of detecting and countering common attack patterns, along with the capacity to handle critical vulnerabilities. Existing research often covers individual products or general EDR concepts, yet lacks a comprehensive comparison of the specific approaches taken by CrowdStrike and SentinelOne. This study fills that gap by systematically contrasting the advantages and limitations of the two leading solutions.

The relevance of this study stems from the ongoing evolution of cyberthreats and the growing influence of EDR in today's cybersecurity environment. Both companies employ advanced technologies such as Artificial Intelligence (AI) and Machine Learning (ML) to detect and counter threats [5,31]. A thorough comparison of these leading EDR solutions helps organizations make informed decisions for protecting their digital infrastructure while highlighting which specific approaches deliver the most effective defense against modern threats.

Therefore, this paper raises the research question of how the EDR solutions from CrowdStrike and SentinelOne differ in their ability to detect common attack patterns such as phishing, malware, and ransomware, and how they address vulnerabilities such as insecure authentication or outdated software.

The investigation builds upon a literature review that examines existing scientific publications and technical reports in order to compare the approaches of the two providers systematically. The study relies on an extensive analysis of current literature and reports on EDR solutions as well as the attack patterns addressed in them.

Accordingly, Sect. 2 outlines the methodological approach and the analytical framework of the study. Section 3 builds the theoretical foundation by explaining EDR systems and related attack patterns such as phishing, malware, and ransomware. Section 4 presents the comparison of the approaches from CrowdStrike and SentinelOne for threat detection and vulnerability remediation. The findings in Sect. 5 discuss how CrowdStrike and SentinelOne perform in different aspects of threat detection and mitigation as well as reflect on the limitations of the study. Section 6 summarizes the results and offers an evaluation framework and recommendations for selecting EDR solutions.

2   Methodology

This study follows a qualitative comparative research design grounded in a structured literature review. The investigation compares the EDR solutions from CrowdStrike and SentinelOne with regard to their capacity to detect common attack patterns such as phishing, malware, and ransomware, and to address vulnerabilities such as insecure authentication and outdated software.

2.1   Research Design

The comparison applies a document-based comparative approach. Instead of relying on laboratory experiments or field tests, the study examines and contrasts both EDR platforms through the systematic analysis of scientific literature, technical reports, vendor documentation, market analyses, and practitioner-oriented publications. This design supports a broad comparison of technical approaches, product capabilities, and operational characteristics across both vendors.

2.2   Data Collection

The literature search focused on publications related to EDR, CrowdStrike, SentinelOne, phishing, malware, ransomware, identity protection, and vulnerability management. Relevant sources came from academic databases, scholarly search engines, official vendor resources, analyst reports, and cybersecurity publications. The search prioritized recent sources in order to reflect the current development of both platforms.

The search process used combinations of the keywords provided in the metadata of this document. Additional sources entered the sample through backward reference tracking from relevant publications.

2.3   Inclusion and Exclusion Criteria

Sources entered the analysis when they addressed EDR concepts, functions, or evaluation criteria, contained information about CrowdStrike or SentinelOne, and discussed one or more focal comparison dimensions, namely phishing, malware, ransomware, authentication-related risks, or outdated software and vulnerability management. The selection also favored publications that reflected recent developments within the EDR market and originated from academic, professional, analyst, or official vendor contexts.

Sources remained outside the analysis when they lacked topical relevance to the research question, offered only general cybersecurity information without reference to EDR capabilities, duplicated information already covered by more recent or more detailed publications, or lacked sufficient accessibility for critical examination.

2.4   Analytical Framework

To support a structured comparison, the study defined several evaluation categories in advance. These categories covered the detection of phishing attacks, malware, and ransomware, the handling of authentication-related vulnerabilities, the management of outdated software and vulnerabilities, and architectural as well as operational characteristics such as cloud dependence, autonomy, threat intelligence, and automation. In addition, the analysis captured strengths and weaknesses reported across the reviewed sources.

The study then applied qualitative content analysis. Relevant statements on product capabilities, technological approaches, and operational characteristics underwent extraction, categorization, and comparison across both vendors. The analysis paid particular attention to recurring themes such as AI-supported detection, behavioral analytics, Indicator of Attack (IoA)- versus Indicator of Compromise (IoC)-oriented detection, automated response, rollback capabilities, and vulnerability prioritization.

2.5   Procedure of Comparison

The comparison followed four steps. First, the study established a theoretical foundation on EDR and common attack patterns. Second, the research collected and screened relevant sources on CrowdStrike and SentinelOne. Third, the extracted information underwent organization according to the predefined analytical categories. Fourth, the study synthesized and interpreted similarities and differences between both platforms with reference to the research question.

Whenever possible, the analysis contrasted information from vendor sources with academic publications, analyst assessments, or independent technical discussions in order to reduce one-sided interpretations. This triangulation strengthened the robustness of the comparison.

2.6   Methodological Rationale

A literature-based methodology suits this study because the research question concerns the comparative positioning, technical approaches, and documented capabilities of two commercial EDR platforms. Product documentation and industry analyses describe many relevant aspects such as threat intelligence models, cloud architecture, identity protection features, and ransomware rollback mechanisms, while academic literature contributes conceptual and theoretical grounding. The combination of these perspectives enables a broad and current comparison.

2.7   Validity and Limitations

The study strengthens validity through the use of multiple source types and a predefined comparison framework. Nevertheless, the methodology includes several limitations. The study does not include empirical performance testing in a controlled environment, and some sources originate from vendor materials that may present products in a favorable light. In addition, the rapid pace of product development in cybersecurity may reduce the long-term timeliness of specific findings. Subsection 5.2 addresses these limitations through critical reflection.

3   Theoretical Background

3.1   Endpoint Detection and Response (EDR): Definition and Concept

EDR has emerged as a key component within the modern cybersecurity landscape. EDR solutions aim to identify, analyze, and counter threats on endpoints such as desktops, laptops, and servers [16]. Because of the growing complexity and frequency of cyberattacks that often penetrate networks through endpoints, effective EDR protection serves a crucial function.

EDR denotes an integrated security solution that unites continuous real-time endpoint monitoring, advanced threat detection, automated response, and forensic analysis. EDR systems outperform traditional antivirus tools, applying behavioral analytics, ML, and threat intelligence to detect both known and unknown threats [31].

EDR systems typically include the following functions.

Realtime Monitoring. A key characteristic of EDR technologies involves continuous realtime observation of endpoints. These systems function to monitor them continuously while collecting telemetry related to system events, network connections, active processes, and file operations. In addition, they analyze endpoint logs to detect system changes, registry key modifications, and other potentially security-relevant actions [16]. By combining these datasets with advanced detection technologies such as ML, behavioral analysis, and threat intelligence, EDR solutions facilitate the identification of suspicious activities, Indicators of Compromise (IoCs), and security incidents [4]. Continuous monitoring enables organizations to recognize threats at an early stage and react swiftly, which helps contain attacks during their earliest stages.

Behavior Analysis. A key feature of modern EDR systems relies on behavior analysis powered by AI and ML. These technologies enable the detection of suspicious activities through the examination of anomalies in process operations and user interactions. Unlike traditional signature-based security solutions limited to known threats, behavior-based detection allows early recognition of new and previously unseen attacks [31].

Threat Detection. Threat detection serves as a core capability within EDR solutions, helping organizations detect and handle security incidents. One of the most advanced approaches to threat detection in modern EDR systems uses Indicators of Attacks (IoAs), key elements for efficiently identifying both known and unknown threats [18].

Unlike traditional approaches that rely on IoCs and focus on already discovered attack patterns or recognized malware variants, IoAs concentrate on attacker behavior [4]. The goal involves recognizing not only specific malware signatures but also the Tactics, Techniques, and Procedures (TTPs) employed to compromise systems. Such a perspective enables detection of new attack techniques not yet cataloged in threat databases and, therefore, possibly overlooked by classical signature-based processes.

A key advantage of IoA-based detection arises from AI and ML. These technologies allow EDR systems to identify attacks in realtime and respond quickly. AI-driven IoAs undergo training using large threat databases and behavioral analytics, allowing EDR platforms to adapt dynamically to emerging threats.

Through this adaptive mechanism, detection covers not only established threats but also newly developing attack strategies across diverse scenarios [18].

Automated Response. A key component within EDR solutions involves the capability for automated actions against detected threats. Such reactions help prevent attack propagation and reduce the overall impact on the network. EDR frameworks employ a mix of AI-driven analysis, threat intelligence, and pre-defined security policies to recognize and respond to threats instantly, without manual intervention [30].

Forensic Analysis. Within EDR platforms, forensic analysis holds a crucial function during investigations of security incidents. It allows understanding of the cause, scope, and consequences of attacks and forms the foundation for identifying additional potential threats across the system.

3.2   Common Attack Patterns: Phishing, Malware, Ransomware

This subsection provides an overview of the most common attack patterns that companies face today. Understanding these threats proves crucial for grasping the necessity and functionality of EDR solutions.

Phishing. Phishing represents a fraudulent method in which attackers attempt to obtain sensitive information such as usernames, passwords, credit card data, or other confidential details by impersonating trustworthy entities. These attacks exploit social engineering to persuade victims to disclose their information or perform harmful actions. Hadnagy emphasizes that phishing presents a relatively simple way to reach others and prompt them to act without thinking [15].

Phishing attacks can take various forms, with e-mail as the most common channel. In this method, attackers send fake e-mails that appear to originate from legitimate organizations such as banks, online shops, or government agencies. The e-mails often contain links to counterfeit websites that closely resemble the originals. Victims receive prompts to enter their personal data on these fraudulent websites, which attackers then steal.

Hadnagy explains that successful phishing attacks often rely on psychological principles that influence human behavior. These include creating urgency, exploiting authority, and establishing trust. By understanding and applying these principles, attackers can increase the likelihood of victims falling for their schemes.

The following types of phishing occur.

- **Spearphishing** denotes targeted attacks aimed at specific individuals or groups within an organization. These attacks often exhibit greater sophistication and utilize personalized information to gain the victim's trust.

- **Whaling** refers to phishing attacks targeting high-ranking executives or prominent individuals. These attacks aim at people with privileged access to sensitive information.
- **Vishing** revolves around phishing attacks carried out through phone calls.

Malware. Malware, a blend of *malicious* and *software*, functions as a collective term for any program designed to damage computers, networks, or devices, to disrupt operations, or to gain unauthorized access without the owner's knowledge or consent [2]. It ranks among the most serious threats to cybersecurity and may cause major financial losses, data breaches, and reputational harm.

Malware spreads through the following channels.

- **Infected Websites and Downloads:** Users unknowingly download malware when they visit compromised websites or obtain infected files.
- **Phishing E-Mails:** Attackers send messages that look legitimate but include harmful attachments or links that install malware.
- **Social Engineering:** Attackers trick users into installing malware or revealing sensitive information [14].
- **Exploiting Software Vulnerabilities:** Malware exploits security gaps in programs to gain access to systems and spread further [2].

One classifies the following types of malware.

- **Viruses:** Malicious programs that attach to existing files, spread through user actions such as opening infected files, and infect other data on the system. They normally require human interaction for activation.
- **Worms:** Malicious programs that spread across networks without user involvement. Unlike viruses, they spread without a host file and transfer themselves to other systems, as in the case of WannaCry.
- **Trojans:** Malicious programs that disguise themselves as useful software while secretly performing harmful actions.
- **Ransomware:** Malicious programs that encrypt data and demand payment for decryption. Due to its importance, the subsequent subsubsection focuses on the topic of ransomware.
- **Spyware:** Malicious programs that monitor user activity and steal information.
- **Adware:** Malicious programs that display unwanted advertisements.
- **Rootkits:** Malicious programs that hide deep in the system and grant unauthorized access [7].

Ransomware. Ransomware represents a type of malicious software that encrypts data on an infected system or blocks access to it, demanding payment to restore or unlock the information [19]. The term combines the English words *ransom* and *software*.

Ransomware attacks typically proceed through the following steps.

- **Infection:** The malware often spreads through phishing e-mails, infected advertisements, or compromised websites.
- **Encryption:** After activation, the malware starts encrypting files or entire systems.
- **Ransom Demand:** A message notifies the victim about the encryption and demands payment of a ransom, usually in cryptocurrency.

One can distinguish the following types of ransomware.

- **File Encrypter:** This type of ransomware enciphers files on the Hard Disk Drive (HDD) and targets specific file extensions such as *.doc*, *.docx*, or *.jpeg*. After encryption, the file extension changes to a ransomware-specific suffix like *.locked*, *.xxx*, or *.aaa*.
- **Master Boot Record (MBR) Encrypter/Overwriter:** This software overwrites or encrypts the MBR and demands a ransom for the password that unlocks the original MBR. When the MBR gets overwritten with a corrupted version, forensic tools may recover the old MBR. Encryption of the MBR complicates recovery because the entire HDD ends up encrypted, making the system unbootable.
- **Wiper/Disk Erasure:** Instead of encrypting data, this variant destroys the HDD by infecting the MBR and corrupting the New Technology File System (NTFS) file table. Even payment of ransom offers no chance of recovery.
- **Fake Encrypter:** This malware simulates encryption by changing file extensions. The files remain intact and can be restored through renaming.
- **Screen Locker:** This variant locks only the screen without encrypting files. Usually, termination of the related process removes the lock.
- **Leakware/Double Extortion:** The attacker threatens to publish stolen data to force ransom payment. In some cases, data also undergoes encryption to intensify pressure on the victim.
- **Triple Extortion:** Along with data encryption and publication of stolen material, this variant employs additional pressure tactics such as Distributed Denial of Service (DDoS) attacks or direct contact with customers and partners.

3.3   Overview of CrowdStrike and SentinelOne

CrowdStrike and SentinelOne rank among leading providers in the field of EDR. Both companies deliver advanced security solutions designed to protect organizations from cyberthreats. Although both pursue similar goals, key distinctions exist in their methods and technologies.

Comparison Between IoAs and IoCs. In cybersecurity, IoAs and IoCs represent two essential concepts for detecting and countering threats. Although both approaches aim to identify cyberattacks, they differ in focus and methodology.

IoAs follow a proactive approach by identifying suspicious activities that suggest an ongoing attack before damage occurs [18]. They analyze the behavior of threat actors in realtime, which allows an early defense against cyberattacks. The following list illustrates examples of IoAs.

– Unusual access attempts targeting sensitive systems
– Use of legitimate tools for malicious purposes (e.g., PowerShell in attacks)
– Uncommon privilege escalations within a network
– Modification of security policies or disabling of protection mechanisms

The key advantage of IoAs stems from their preventive impact. They allow the detection of attacks at an early stage and the initiation of countermeasures before a system becomes compromised. Growing integration of AI into security platforms further enhances IoAs. Modern AI models process vast volumes of data and continuously learn new attack patterns, which improves threat detection accuracy and decreases false alarms.

IoCs denote digital traces signaling that an attack already occurred or a system suffered compromise [4]. They rely on forensic data and assist security teams in analyzing incidents and implementing suitable countermeasures. The following list presents examples of IoCs.

– Unusual network traffic
– Irregularities in user accounts (e.g., unexpected login attempts)
– Modifications to system files or registry values
– Use of unknown or unexpected programs
– Large volumes of compressed data in uncommon storage locations

The main drawback of IoCs lies in their reactive character. Because they focus on attacks that have already occurred, detection usually happens only after damage has taken place.

Table 1 demonstrates the differences between IoAs and IoCs.

Table 1. Comparison between IoAs and IoCs

Criterion	Indicators of Attack (IoAs)	Indicators of Compromise (IoCs)
Detection Timing	Proactive, during the attack	Reactive, after the attack
Examples	Suspicious actions, unexpected privilege escalation	Unusual network traffic, altered files
Focus	Detection of an ongoing attack	Proof of a completed attack
Objective	Early defense against attacks	Analysis and damage containment
Disadvantages	Requires continuous monitoring and analysis	Late detection, often after damage

CrowdStrike. CrowdStrike, founded in 2011, has evolved quickly into a leading player within the EDR field [11]. The company gained recognition through its cloud-based Falcon platform, which delivers a wide range of security capabilities such as incident response, threat detection and hunting [5].

A key element of CrowdStrike technology involves using AI and ML for detection and prevention of threats. CrowdStrike highlights the significance of IoAs for identifying advanced intrusions ahead of traditional IoCs. The cloud-based architecture allows CrowdStrike to gather and analyze threat data from numerous sources, enabling rapid response to emerging risks [11].

SentinelOne. SentinelOne launched in 2013 and gained recognition as another key player within the EDR market. The company follows a slightly different approach than CrowdStrike, focusing on autonomous, AI-driven endpoint security [31].

The SentinelOne Singularity platform employs advanced AI algorithms to detect and block threats in realtime, even when the endpoint operates offline. One major advantage of SentinelOne involves its ability to identify and neutralize attacks automatically without constant human supervision. Its so-called behavioral AI not only searches for known threats but also continuously monitors and analyzes application and process behavior. Suspicious actions such as unexpected file modifications, unusual network connections, or processes attempting access to sensitive system areas get detected and evaluated in realtime. This AI functions independently of signatures and builds context-based models that uncover previously unknown threats. SentinelOne emphasizes the importance of behavioral analytics for recognizing malicious activity that traditional signature-based methods might overlook. Through a combination of static analysis (e.g., examining code characteristics) and dynamic behavioral observation, SentinelOne delivers a holistic detection method capable of uncovering even zero-day attacks with high reliability.

4   Analysis

4.1   Detection of Common Attack Patterns

This subsection compares the capabilities of CrowdStrike and SentinelOne in detecting frequent attack patterns such as phishing, malware, and ransomware.

Phishing. Phishing ranks among the most frequent and effective techniques used by cybercriminals to steal login credentials or sensitive data. Phishing attacks can take various forms, including e-mails, short messages (smishing), or fraudulent websites [17].

CrowdStrike applies advanced technologies to detect and prevent phishing attacks. The company employs a mix of AI, ML, and behavioral analytics to refine detection and defense against such threats. CrowdStrike's Falcon platform continuously examines e-mails, websites, and other communication channels for suspicious patterns that often indicate phishing attempts. These patterns include forged logos, spelling mistakes, implausible requests, or unusual Uniform Resource Locators (URLs) that cybercriminals use to mislead their targets. CrowdStrike's AI-driven technology learns continuously from features and behavioral patterns linked to phishing attacks, enabling more precise predictions and faster identification of new threats. ML empowers the platform to locate abnormal patterns and anomalies that suggest a potential attack, using both supervised and unsupervised learning techniques. During supervised learning, the AI trains on known examples of phishing e-mails to automatically recognize similar threats in the future. Unsupervised learning allows the platform to scan new data for deviations from normal communication behavior, even without predefined classifications, which helps uncover unknown or sophisticated phishing tactics. According to CrowdStrike, this combination enables early detection of zero-day and targeted social-engineering attacks. The Falcon platform detects traditional and emerging phishing methods, providing stronger protection than conventional security tools. Another key pillar of CrowdStrike's approach involves threat intelligence. By merging realtime threat data, CrowdStrike can identify and block known phishing campaigns and attackers at an early stage. Security analysts around the globe collect these insights, forming a solid foundation for countermeasures against current and evolving phishing threats. Threat intelligence supports recognition of targeted attacks where criminals impersonate trusted organizations or individuals. CrowdStrike follows a proactive philosophy, focusing not only on responding to phishing but also on blocking it before execution. The platform continuously processes data and communication channels to spot phishing indicators and trigger immediate counteractions before users face exposure. This strategy limits phishing impact and strengthens protection of endpoints, networks, and confidential data.

SentinelOne relies on a mix of AI and ML to detect and prevent phishing attempts. The Singularity platform from SentinelOne enables realtime analysis of e-mails, websites, and other communication channels to identify suspicious content and behavior. A key feature of SentinelOne involves the use of *Deep File Inspection*, a technique designed specifically to detect and block malicious attachments in phishing messages. The system analyzes the behavior of files and programs before execution to prevent harmful activity [31]. SentinelOne employs both static and dynamic analysis. Static analysis examines file attributes, metadata, and code structure to locate malicious content without execution, while dynamic analysis monitors runtime behavior to find compromising actions. The ML capabilities inside the platform allow SentinelOne to continuously learn and recognize previously unknown threats that do not rely on traditional signatures. Phishing attacks distributed through manipulated attachments or fake URLs undergo early detection through this technology, before any damage occurs. SentinelOne follows a proactive approach, reacting not only to known risks but also uncovering new behavioral patterns and attack techniques with its AI. A major component of the technology includes behavioral AI, which delivers an in-depth assessment of file and application activity on endpoints. Avoiding external cloud connections grants significantly faster threat recognition. During a phishing attempt, the platform checks a malicious attachment not only by its signature but also by monitoring its execution behavior. When the file performs abnormal tasks such as launching shell commands or downloading data from the Internet, SentinelOne blocks it instantly, preventing any potential spread of harm.

Malware. CrowdStrike employs ML to detect malware without relying on traditional methods such as hash comparison. Over the years, CrowdStrike has built an extensive collection of malicious files gathered from various sources, including attacker activities within customer environments, the dark web, and security research data. This information forms the foundation for developing ML models designed to identify harmful software early across diverse Information Technology (IT) environments, including container images and serverless functions [1].

The CrowdStrike Falcon platform gives teams the capability to check container images for malware before deployment. This feature holds particular importance in modern Development and Operations (DevOps) environments, where software undergoes continuous development and moves into production systems. Pre-deployment scanning helps security staff detect potential threats early, well before any software reaches production. Through this process, analysts can identify malicious code within container images and serverless functions without executing them. The method allows teams to address vulnerabilities beforehand and reduces the likelihood that malware infiltrates the environment after deployment and causes damage.

CrowdStrike's behavioral analysis approach relies on the detection of IoAs to identify advanced attacks at an early stage, long before traditional IoCs appear. This proactive method allows more effective threat detection and defense [18].

The core technology of SentinelOne relies on behavior-based AI focused on analyzing how processes act on endpoints. Unlike traditional security solutions that depend mainly on file inspection, the behavior-based AI monitors every process and all their interactions in realtime, regardless of duration. Through this approach, the AI detects attacks that do not manifest as classic malware, including fileless intrusions, scripts, crafted documents, and zero-day exploits. The behavioral analysis operates in a vector-agnostic manner, meaning the detection logic concentrates on malicious behavior itself rather than on the specific type of threat. This technology tracks and records every activity on an endpoint and provides a complete timeline of events known as a *Storyline*. That continuous tracking enables identification of all relevant behaviors linked to security incidents without relying on signatures or predefined patterns [31].

The Static AI Engine from SentinelOne functions as a key element of the company's Cloud Workload Protection Platform (CWPP), which operates through AI. The engine applies ML to examine files before execution. In essence, the Static AI Engine replaces traditional signature-based malware detection with file classification driven by structural attributes and historical patterns linked to malicious behavior [6]. Its operation relies on supervised ML algorithms that inspect files without executing them. This approach allows the engine to classify a file as benign, suspicious, or malicious before introduction into a system. Classification depends on decision-tree algorithms that deliver predictive confidence regarding a file's harmful potential. SentinelOne trained its ML models with nearly one billion samples collected during the past decade, while the company's threat researchers continually refine these models to stay aligned with emerging threats.

Ransomware. Ransomware constitutes a highly dangerous type of malware designed to block a victim's data through encryption. To regain access, the attacker usually demands a ransom [19]. Such attacks can cause severe consequences for businesses, including the loss of critical information, heavy financial strain, and lasting damage to reputation.

CrowdStrike delivers multilayer defense against ransomware by employing the Falcon platform's broad range of technologies and detection mechanisms. Core techniques include behavioral analysis focused on identifying suspicious actions that signal potential ransomware activity. A common indicator involves mass encryption of files, a hallmark of ransomware operations [3]. CrowdStrike relies on exploit-prevention technologies that block ransomware from leveraging software vulnerabilities attackers could use for infiltration. Behavioral detection ranks among the most effective approaches for ransomware identification because it depends not only on known signatures but also uncovers new and previously unseen attack patterns. Such a method provides an important advantage. Many ransomware samples get noticed only after data encryption, which often leads to major damage when early detection fails. The Falcon platform incorporates a proactive security strategy monitoring unusual data traffic connected with ransomware behavior, such as data exfiltration before encryption. Another major benefit of CrowdStrike technology involves rapid containment. Once infection indicators emerge, automatic protection isolates impacted systems and initiates restoration to stop further harm. Ransomware does not necessarily demand root privileges to inflict damage. Many modern variants focus on encrypting files within the user context accessible through standard permissions. Because numerous users hold broad write rights in production environments, substantial harm can occur even without administrative access. Particularly serious issues arise when ransomware encrypts network drives or shared folders accessible with the infected user's write permissions.

SentinelOne employs an innovative and patented technology called the Ransomware Protection Engine (RPE) to safeguard organizations from the severe consequences of ransomware attacks. This technology holds a central role in ransomware defense by focusing on the behavior of processes and files to detect and block suspicious activity. The RPE demonstrates a remarkable ability to identify new or previously unknown ransomware variants without any prior classification as threats in a database. Through realtime behavioral analysis, the RPE detects potential attacks at an early stage and prevents major damage [24]. The uniqueness of SentinelOne technology comes from its independence from signature-based methods and its reliance on proactive, behavior-driven detection mechanisms that capture even new and sophisticated attack strategies. Such an approach carries great importance in today's threat landscape, where adversaries regularly craft fresh, unidentified ransomware variants to evade security measures. The SentinelOne RPE delivers a high level of effectiveness, allowing rapid identification and neutralization of novel threats. In addition, SentinelOne includes an automated rollback function that enables organizations to recover systems and data after a successful ransomware intrusion. If an infection occurs despite preventive defenses, the rollback feature restores affected data and systems to their previous secure state, minimizing downtime and greatly lowering the risk of data loss.

4.2   Addressing Authentication Vulnerabilities

CrowdStrike relies on Falcon Identity Protection, a solution for monitoring and securing user identities. AI-driven algorithms establish baselines for normal user behavior, allowing early detection of anomalies such as stolen credentials or unauthorized access. Realtime prevention blocks suspicious actions such as credential stuffing or pass-the-hash attacks. CrowdStrike also provides extensive visibility into authentication attempts and enables forensic analysis during identity-related incidents [28].

SentinelOne addresses insecure authentication through the integration of behavior-based AI and dedicated identity-protection capabilities. The Singularity Identity Posture Management (SIPM) solution analyzes Active Directory (AD) and Azure AD for weaknesses, uncovering potential attack paths such as privilege escalation or lateral movement following an initial compromise. SIPM reviews configurations, detects misconfigurations, and issues realtime alerts for suspicious activities. SentinelOne enables the deployment of Multi-Factor Authentication (MFA) and enforces the least-privilege principle to restrict access strictly to what users require [23].

4.3   Outdated Software: Strategies for Management

CrowdStrike delivers a comprehensive solution for managing outdated software and vulnerabilities with Falcon Spotlight. The latter enables continuous, scan-free vulnerability assessment across endpoints, allowing organizations to identify outdated software in realtime [8]. A key feature, the ExPRT.AI algorithm, prioritizes vulnerabilities according to the likelihood of exploitation, helping IT teams focus on the most critical security risks [29]. CrowdStrike's cloud-based architecture simplifies software version and security update management, allowing centralized control and easier update distribution. The solution includes automated patch-management capabilities that accelerate the remediation of security gaps. Organizations manage patches from a central location and apply them automatically to affected systems, which speeds up the vulnerability-fixing process. Falcon Spotlight integrates seamlessly with the CrowdStrike Falcon platform and uses its unified, lightweight agent architecture, eliminating any need for extra scans or agents [20].

CrowdStrike's Falcon Spotlight uses the ExPRT.AI model for vulnerability prioritization. Unlike the static Common Vulnerability Scoring System (CVSS), a numeric system that rates vulnerability severity on a 010 scale (with 0 indicating no threat and 10 indicating a critical one), ExPRT.AI provides a dynamic assessment that adapts to the current threat landscape. This technology leverages CrowdStrike's proprietary threat intelligence and identifies roughly twice as many critical Common Vulnerabilities and Exposures (CVEs) as CVSS.

ExPRT.AI targets a smaller fraction of vulnerabilities regarded as truly critical, which greatly reduces workload.

The efficiency of ExPRT.AI appears in its accuracy rate. With only 10% of vulnerabilities under review, it prioritizes around 60% of those actually exploited, compared with roughly 20% under CVSS. Figure 1 illustrates the contrast between CVSS and ExPRT.AI by showing how ExPRT.AI creates a more focused prioritization process that helps security teams allocate resources with greater precision [29].

Fig. 1. Falcon Spotlight's ExPRT.AI [29]

SentinelOne delivers a comprehensive approach to managing outdated software through its Singularity Vulnerability Management solution. The tool provides continuous, realtime visibility into vulnerabilities within applications and operating systems, regardless of whether they operate on physical, virtual, or cloud environments. SentinelOne applies a mix of active and passive scanning techniques to examine the network for EDR deployment gaps and potentially risky devices. A key feature involves dynamic vulnerability prioritization based on the likelihood of exploitation by threat actors and the business impact level. This focus allows security teams to address the most consequential weaknesses first and reduce overall exposure [26]. SentinelOne Ranger, a dedicated tool within the platform, assists with mapping existing assets and their software versions. The function proves highly useful for organizations that still run legacy products such as older Windows releases or discontinued applications like Adobe Flash. The solution functions as an add-on to existing EDR deployments, eliminating the need for additional isolated security tools or resource-intensive scheduled scans [22].

4.4 Comparison of Strengths and Weaknesses Between CrowdStrike and SentinelOne

CrowdStrike and SentinelOne EDR solutions differ in their capacity to detect common attack patterns such as phishing, malware, and ransomware, while addressing vulnerabilities like weak authentication or outdated software. A key element of CrowdStrike technology involves AI and ML for threat recognition and defense. CrowdStrike highlights IoAs as a method for identifying advanced attacks before traditional IoCs appear [18]. Its cloud-driven architecture allows the collection and analysis of threat data from multiple sources, enabling rapid reactions to emerging threats.

SentinelOne has gained recognition as another significant player in the EDR market and follows a slightly different path. The company focuses on autonomous endpoint protection powered by AI. The SentinelOne Singularity platform employs AI algorithms for realtime detection and threat blocking, considering endpoint operation even without network access [31]. One major strength of SentinelOne lies in automated attack detection and neutralization without continuous human supervision. In addition, SentinelOne emphasizes behavioral analytics to reveal malicious actions that traditional signature-based methods might miss.

Regarding identification of specific attack patterns, both platforms aim to safeguard enterprises from cyberthreats, yet they rely on distinct architectures and methodologies.

CrowdStrike Strengths. The Falcon platform from CrowdStrike stands out through its powerful cloud-based threat intelligence network. This network collects and analyzes threat data from millions of global endpoints, enabling rapid identification of new attack attempts and allowing precise, efficient responses [5]. With the help of AI and ML, the system processes this information in realtime, detecting threats and preventing them proactively.

IoA-based detection represents a crucial leap forward in cybersecurity. While traditional security measures often rely on IoCs, which signal that an attack already occurred, IoA-based detection allows a proactive security approach. By identifying attack patterns and suspicious behavior at an early stage, companies can counter threats before they cause damage [18].

The Falcon platform delivers a wide range of security capabilities, including EDR, Next-Generation Anti-Virus (NGAV), threat intelligence, vulnerability management, and IT hygiene. This integration provides comprehensive endpoint protection and lowers the complexity of security management [5].

The CrowdStrike Falcon platform functions as a fully cloud-based security solution that gives organizations a flexible and highly scalable foundation adapting seamlessly to the constantly shifting IT landscape. Through its agentless approach, the platform enables automatic detection and monitoring of cloud-native assets (from host to cloud) across a wide range of operating systems and environments, including physical, virtual, and cloud-based endpoints [10].

CrowdStrike Weaknesses. Through this architecture, companies gain comprehensive transparency, effective enforcement of security policies, and continuous compliance monitoring across hybrid and multi-cloud environments. In addition, the solution enables flexible scaling of security measures without affecting system performance, resulting in an efficient and cost-effective security infrastructure. Gartner confirms the platform's strong qualities, especially scalability, flexibility, and user-friendliness, based on independent user reviews [12].

Using a cloud-based architecture within the CrowdStrike Falcon platform provides many advantages, such as centralized administration and strong scalability. However, dependence on the cloud also introduces drawbacks, especially in situations involving unstable or slow Internet connections. Because realtime threat detection and response rely on constant communication with the cloud, poor connectivity reduces the efficiency of the security solution. When the Internet connection fails or experiences heavy latency, identification and response to threats may suffer delays. Such circumstances create potential risks for organizations that depend on continuous, uninterrupted monitoring to detect and halt cyberattacks quickly [5].

A major drawback of the CrowdStrike Falcon platform lies in its relatively high pricing compared with other EDR solutions. For large enterprises handling many endpoints, expenses can increase quickly. CrowdStrike's licensing model often introduces complexity because various features come as separate modules that require individual purchase. Companies must select the security functions relevant to their needs and pay for each module separately, which drives total costs upward. Organizations with limited budgets or those seeking a more economical option may find this a significant disadvantage. Figure 2 illustrates that when choosing modules, buyers must consider that the solution can vary greatly in price depending on the breadth of required security capabilities [9].

SentinelOne Strengths. SentinelOne's Singularity Platform delivers an advanced approach to autonomous endpoint protection powered by AI and ML. It detects and blocks threats in realtime. A major benefit of this technology comes from its ability to perform effectively even when an endpoint operates offline, ensuring protection for systems without a constant network link. This capability allows the platform to identify and neutralize threats independently, without reliance on a central cloud or external security infrastructure, which maintains continuous defense regardless of network or connection status [31]. An important strength of this autonomous solution lies in its reduction of the need for continuous human oversight. Traditional security solutions often require manual intervention and constant attention from IT security teams, while the Singularity Platform acts independently and responds automatically to incidents. Such automation ensures immediate threat detection and blocking, dramatically

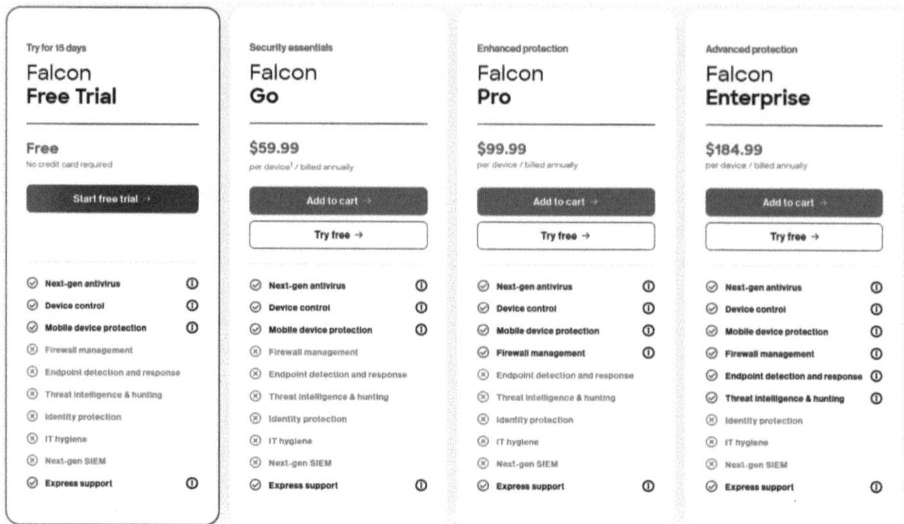

Fig. 2. CrowdStrike pricing [9]

shortening response times during security events. As a result, organizations can monitor endpoints in realtime and prevent attacks before they cause major harm.

SentinelOne employs a behavioral detection technology that enables identification of malicious activity often missed by traditional signature-based security solutions. Conventional security tools rely mainly on known threat signatures to detect harmful software or actions. This approach proves inadequate against new, unknown, or fileless attacks, because such threats leave no recognizable signatures. In these situations, SentinelOne's behavioral detection operates through analysis of behavioral patterns within system processes and user interactions.

The Singularity platform gains recognition for its straightforward deployment and operation. Its interface feels intuitive and user-friendly, helping users learn quickly and configure efficiently.

A distinctive capability of SentinelOne allows automatic reversal of modifications caused by an attack, restoring the system to its original condition [25]. This feature, known as Ransomware Rollback, enables rapid recovery after a ransomware incident without paying the demanded ransom. It relies on continuous monitoring of file activities and employs advanced technologies such as ML and behavioral analytics to detect file changes. In the event of a ransomware attack that encrypts files, the platform can return affected data to its pre-attack state, preventing permanent loss or damage. The mechanism minimizes downtime and limits the financial impact of an incident. In addition, it maintains the integrity and confidentiality of data by undoing all malicious alterations introduced by malware. This rollback capability forms part of the SentinelOne Singularity platform, an advanced eXtended Detection and Response (XDR) solution that expands beyond traditional EDR functionality to deliver comprehensive protection against multiple threat types. Through this technology, organizations gain stronger cyber resilience and can resume normal operations quickly after an attack without relying on ransom payments.

SentinelOne Weaknesses. Compared with several other providers such as CrowdStrike, SentinelOne maintains a less extensive threat-intelligence network. CrowdStrike enjoys a strong reputation for its broad collection of threat data and its large community of security researchers, which enables the company to identify and counter new or unknown threats more quickly. SentinelOne implements advanced mechanisms for threat detection as well, yet the scale and depth of its threat-intelligence network appear narrower in comparison. In certain situations, this limitation may cause slower recognition and mitigation of emerging or previously unknown threats [12,13].

Although SentinelOne's AI algorithms deliver strong performance, they occasionally generate False Positives (FPs). Such events mark legitimate actions as malicious, creating unnecessary alerts and disruptions. Conversely, the system may face False Negatives (FNs), leaving real threats undetected. SentinelOne reports ongoing model training and behavioral detection techniques to keep FPs and FNs at a minimal level [21].

Compared with CrowdStrike, SentinelOne delivers a slightly smaller range of features. While the platform covers essential security capabilities, certain scenarios may demand additional tools or integrations to address every specific security requirement of an organization. Companies with more complex IT infrastructures may need to combine multiple security solutions to achieve full protection. Such situations may require extra resources and greater administrative effort, since SentinelOne lacks some of the necessary functions [13].

5   Discussion of the Results

5.1   Synthesis of Insights Within the Research Framework

The present study aims to compare the EDR solutions from CrowdStrike and SentinelOne regarding their capacity to detect common attack patterns such as phishing, malware, and ransomware, as well as their effectiveness in addressing vulnerabilities like insecure authentication and outdated software. The analysis of available literature and technical reports revealed several important findings.

Table 2 summarizes the central differences between CrowdStrike and SentinelOne across the main comparison dimensions of this study.

Effectiveness in Detecting Attack Patterns. Both EDR solutions demonstrate strong performance in detecting and countering common attack patterns. CrowdStrike's Falcon platform employs advanced AI and ML algorithms to identify IoAs, enabling proactive threat detection [5]. SentinelOne's Singularity platform also relies on AI-driven behavioral analysis to detect and neutralize threats in realtime, even when endpoints remain offline [26].

Table 2. Comparison between CrowdStrike and SentinelOne

Aspect	CrowdStrike	SentinelOne
Overall Approach	Cloud-based, intelligence-driven protection with strong AI/ML and IoA detection	Autonomous, behavior-based endpoint protection with strong AI/ML and offline capability
Phishing	Strong detection through AI, behavioral analytics, and global threat intelligence	Strong detection of malicious attachments and phishing behavior via Deep File Inspection and behavioral AI
Malware	Excels in ML-based malware detection, including containers and serverless workloads	Excels in behavior-based detection, including fileless and zero-day attacks
Ransomware	Strong behavioral detection, exploit prevention, and rapid containment	Strong behavioral detection plus standout rollback recovery capability
Authentication	Focuses on identity monitoring and anomaly detection with Falcon Identity Protection	Focuses on AD/Azure AD posture management, MFA, and least-privilege enforcement
Outdated Software / Vulnerabilities	Falcon Spotlight with scan-free assessment and strong AI-based prioritization (ExPRT.AI)	Singularity Vulnerability Management with realtime visibility and asset discovery via Ranger
Key Strength	Broad threat intelligence network and highly integrated cloud platform	Autonomous protection, offline defense, and automated remediation
Key Weakness	Higher cost and reliance on stable cloud connectivity	Smaller threat-intelligence network and slightly narrower feature set
Best Fit	Enterprises wanting cloud-scale intelligence and broad integrated security	Organizations wanting autonomous endpoint protection and fast recovery from attacks

For phishing detection, both solutions present effective methods. CrowdStrike technology analyzes e-mail content and URLs for suspicious patterns, while SentinelOne's autonomous endpoint protection identifies unusual activity directly on the device. Regarding ransomware, both platforms deliver strong defensive measures. CrowdStrike Falcon employs behavior-based indicators to detect ransomware actions at an early stage, while SentinelOne's rollback function allows rapid restoration of infected systems.

Mitigation of Vulnerabilities. Regarding the handling of weaknesses such as insecure authentication or outdated software, both solutions demonstrate different strengths. CrowdStrike's Falcon platform delivers extensive capabilities for vulnerability management and patch handling, which proves advantageous when dealing with legacy software. SentinelOne follows an approach focused on autonomous detection and defense against attacks that exploit vulnerabilities. A notable trend revealed by the analysis points toward a shift to integrated security strategies. Both CrowdStrike and SentinelOne provide comprehensive platforms that extend beyond traditional EDR functions and include components such as threat intelligence, network protection, and cloud workload defense. This holistic strategy enables stronger identification and mitigation of complex, multi-stage attacks.

Automation and Response Speed. Another crucial aspect concerns the automation of security processes. SentinelOne's autonomous approach allows rapid, automatic threat response without human intervention. CrowdStrike's Falcon platform also delivers automated response capabilities but emphasizes the inclusion of human expertise in decision-making.

Cloud-Native Architecture. The cloud-native architecture of both solutions provides a decisive advantage. It supports faster threat intelligence updates, greater scalability, and enhanced flexibility for adapting to evolving threat environments.

5.2   Methodological Limitations and Critical Reflection

Despite the insights gained, the present study reveals several methodological limitations that require attention during the interpretation of the results.

Limitation to Literature Analysis. The study relies solely on the examination of existing literature and technical reports. Although this approach enables a broad overview of the current state of research, it lacks practical tests or first-hand empirical data. The addition of hands-on evaluations within real corporate environments could strengthen the validity of the results.

Rapid Technological Development. The EDR landscape evolves quickly, which may reduce the timeliness of some findings. Both CrowdStrike and SentinelOne update their products on a regular basis, so certain analyzed features might no longer reflect the latest versions.

Independence of Sources. While objectivity guided the selection of sources, part of the information originates from vendor documentation and marketing materials. Such content may introduce bias favoring specific products. A stronger emphasis on independent research and user reports could balance this limitation.

Context Dependence of Effectiveness. The effectiveness of EDR solutions can vary significantly with their deployment context. Factors such as company size, industry, and existing IT infrastructure influence overall performance. The current analysis considered these contextual differences only to a limited extent.

Focus on Technical Aspects. The study emphasized technical attributes of the EDR solutions. Other relevant factors like user experience, integration with existing systems, or cost-effectiveness received less attention. Broader evaluation of these dimensions could support a more comprehensive understanding of the solutions.

Despite these limitations, the paper provides meaningful insight into the strengths and distinctions of the EDR platforms from CrowdStrike and SentinelOne, offering a solid foundation for further, more detailed research and practical evaluations within specific organizational environments.

6   Conclusion

6.1   Summary of Key Findings

Both EDR platforms demonstrate advanced capabilities in threat detection and defense, while each follows a distinct approach. CrowdStrike relies heavily on cloud-driven analytics and threat intelligence. SentinelOne applies a more autonomous, AI-supported method directly on the endpoint.

Regarding phishing detection, both platforms deliver effective protection. CrowdStrike technology analyzes e-mail content and URLs for suspicious patterns, while SentinelOne's autonomous endpoint defense identifies abnormal behavior on the device.

For ransomware protection, both solutions display solid effectiveness. CrowdStrike Falcon employs behavioral indicators for early identification, while SentinelOne's rollback function enables swift recovery of infected systems.

In malware detection, both vendors apply advanced AI and ML algorithms. CrowdStrike focuses on recognizing IoAs, while SentinelOne follows a behavioral strategy that can detect even unknown threats.

With vulnerability management, CrowdStrike provides broader capabilities for assessment and patch control. SentinelOne focuses more on autonomous identification and neutralization of attacks that exploit weaknesses.

Both solutions deliver strength in automating security processes. SentinelOne grants a higher level of independence, while CrowdStrike emphasizes deeper integration of human expertise.

The cloud-native architecture of both platforms provides a decisive advantage in scalability, flexibility, and rapid updates to threat intelligence.

6.2   Addressing the Research Question

The introductory Sect. 1 formulates the research question regarding how the EDR solutions from CrowdStrike and SentinelOne differ in detecting common attack patterns such as phishing, malware, and ransomware, and how they handle vulnerabilities such as insecure authentication or outdated software.

Based on the conducted analysis, both EDR solutions demonstrate effective, yet distinct approaches for detecting and countering common attack patterns while addressing vulnerabilities.

CrowdStrike employs a more cloud-focused strategy that leverages global threat intelligence and advanced analytics, granting a broad threat perspective and allowing rapid adaptation to emerging attack patterns. Its strength centers on identifying complex, multi-stage attacks and incorporating human expertise into the analytical process.

SentinelOne, by contrast, follows a more autonomous, AI-driven strategy that operates directly at the endpoint. This design enables swift, automated threat responses, even when endpoints stay offline. The platform excels in autonomous detection and neutralization of attacks without continuous human supervision.

Regarding specific attack patterns, the following observations follow.

Both solutions provide effective phishing detection mechanisms. CrowdStrike concentrates on e-mail and Uniform Resource Locator (URL) analysis, while SentinelOne identifies suspicious endpoint activity.

Both leverage AI and ML for malware handling. CrowdStrike highlights IoAs, while SentinelOne applies a broader behavior-driven methodology. CrowdStrike uses behavior-based indicators for early ransomware detection, while SentinelOne enables rapid recovery through its rollback function.

When handling vulnerabilities, CrowdStrike provides broader capabilities for vulnerability management and patch handling, while SentinelOne focuses more on autonomous detection and defense against attacks exploiting those weaknesses.

6.3 Evaluation Framework and Recommendations for Selecting EDR Solutions

The analysis of CrowdStrike and SentinelOne shows that effective evaluation and selection of EDR systems requires more than feature checklists or vendor claims. Robust assessments should rely on a structured framework rooted in adversary techniques, business context, and operational workflows. The Massachusetts Institute of Technology Research and Engineering (MITRE) Adversarial Tactics, Techniques, and Common Knowledge (ATT&CK) framework offers a widely accepted foundation for describing and testing adversary behavior drawn from real-world incidents [27]. However, security teams should avoid interpreting ATT&CK coverage alone as a proxy for overall protection, since not every technique produces the same business risk or detection challenge.

An actionable evaluation framework should incorporate at least five dimensions.

- **Detection Effectiveness:** Does the solution identify adversary activity spanning phishing, malware, credential access, privilege escalation, or ransomware steps?
- **Protection and Response:** How rapidly and automatically does the product prevent, contain, or remediate malicious behavior?
- **Analytical Quality:** Does the system provide precise telemetry, useful context, forensic value, and clear alerts?

- **Operational Efficiency:** What False Positive (FP) rates, alert volumes, case-handling requirements, and automation options emerge during production use?
- **Architectural and Organizational Fit:** Does deployment succeed across hybrid or remote environments, support offline capability, integrate with existing tools, and meet regulatory needs?

For benchmarking, organizations should derive test scenarios from their own threat model and target relevant ATT&CK techniques and common attack paths. Testing should cover not only initial detection, but also prevention, containment speed, analyst workload, and post-alert workflows. Comparing both out-of-the-box and tuned configurations yields more representative insights, since some platforms require policy adjustments after deployment. Mature benchmarks should also track FPs, alert consolidation, and Security Operations Center (SOC) impact. Key metrics include detection rates, prevention rates, mean time to respond, number of actionable alerts per incident, and analyst effort.

Threat and vulnerability prioritization should align with organizational risk rather than rely solely on technical scores. Security teams should identify high-value assets such as privileged accounts, identity infrastructure, and critical business applications, then map likely attack paths involving phishing, credential compromise, lateral movement, or ransomware propagation. In the same way, vulnerability management should consider exploitability, system exposure, business impact, control gaps, and operational relevance. Missing MFA, insecure authentication, outdated business-critical software, or excessive permissions may therefore deserve higher priority than raw CVSS values suggest.

For practical validation, organizations should combine atomic tests, multi-step adversary emulation, and purple-team exercises. Such testing should simulate realistic campaigns and evaluate not only whether a system detects each attack step, but also how quickly and effectively it contains or remediates malicious activity.

These criteria also guide the selection between CrowdStrike and SentinelOne. Organizations should evaluate their current IT infrastructure, desired level of automation, internal cybersecurity expertise, integration requirements, compliance obligations, scalability needs, and budget. CrowdStrike may offer stronger advantages for highly connected, cloud-based environments and for organizations seeking broad threat intelligence and deep analytical support. SentinelOne may prove more suitable for decentralized or frequently offline environments and for organizations that prefer stronger autonomous protection and automated remediation. A careful cost-benefit analysis, ideally combined with pilot deployments or trial phases, provides the most reliable basis for determining which platform best fits long-term security and operational requirements.

Acknowledgments. Many thanks to Bettina Baumgartner from the University of Vienna for proofreading this paper!

References

1. Asthana, K.: CrowdStrike uses proven detection logic for pre-deployment malware scanning (2024). https://www.crowdstrike.com/en-us/blog/crowdstrike-falcon-pre-deployment-malware-detection/
2. Babulak, E.: Malware – Detection and Defense. IntechOpen (2022). https://ssrn.com/abstract=4146732
3. Baker, K.: What Is Ransomware Detection? (2023). https://www.crowdstrike.com/en-us/cybersecurity-101/ransomware/ransomware-detection/
4. Baker, K.: Indicators of compromise (IOC) security explained (2025). https://www.crowdstrike.com/en-us/cybersecurity-101/threat-intelligence/indicators-of-compromise-ioc/
5. Benacci, K.: CrowdStrike introduces industry's first AI-powered indicators of attack for crowdstrike falcon platform to uncover the most advanced attacks (2022). https://www.crowdstrike.com/en-us/press-releases/crowdstrike-introduces-industrys-first-ai-powered-indicators-of-attack/
6. Bosworth, R.: Decrypting SentinelOne?s Cloud Detection – The static AI Engine in real-time CWPP (2023). https://www.sentinelone.com/blog/decrypting-sentinelones-detection-an-in-depth-look-at-our-real-time-cwpp-static-ai-engine/
7. Carvey, H.A.: Windows Forensic Analysis DVD Toolkit: Incident Response and Cybercrime Investigation Secrets. Syngress, 2nd edn. (2009)
8. CrowdStrike: embrace the future of risk-based vulnerability management (2025). https://www.crowdstrike.com/en-us/platform/exposure-management/risk-based-vulnerability-management/
9. CrowdStrike: pricing (2025). https://www.crowdstrike.com/en-us/pricing/
10. CrowdStrike: secure everything you build and deploy in the cloud (2025). https://www.crowdstrike.com/en-us/platform/cloud-security/cspm/
11. Frida, S.: CrowdStrike named a leader in 2024 Gartner magic quadrant for endpoint protection platforms (2024). https://www.crowdstrike.com/en-us/blog/crowdstrike-named-leader-2024-gartner-magic-quadrant-endpoint-protection/
12. Gartner peer insights: crowdstrike falcon cloud security reviews (2025). https://www.gartner.com/reviews/market/cloud-native-application-protection-platforms/vendor/crowdstrike/product/crowdstrike-falcon-cloud-security
13. Gartner peer insights: singularity mobile likes and dislikes (2025). https://www.gartner.com/reviews/market/mobile-threat-defense/vendor/sentinelone/product/singularity-mobile/likes-dislikes
14. Hadnagy, C.: Social Engineering: The Science of Human Hacking. Wiley, 2nd edn. (2018)
15. Hadnagy, C., Fincher, M.: Phishing Dark Waters: The Offensive and Defensive Sides of Malicious Emails. Wiley, 1st edn. (2015)
16. Kaur, H., et al.: Evolution of endpoint detection and response (EDR) in Cyber security: a comprehensive review. E3S Web Conf 556, 1–7 (2024). https://doi.org/10.1051/e3sconf/202455601006
17. Lenaerts-Bergmans, B.: Introduction to Phishing (2024). https://www.crowdstrike.com/en-us/cybersecurity-101/social-engineering/phishing-attack/
18. Lenaerts-Bergmans, B.: Indicators of Attack (IOAs) Explained (2025). https://www.crowdstrike.com/en-us/cybersecurity-101/threat-intelligence/indicators-of-attack-ioa/
19. Narula, J., Narula, A.: Breaking Ransomware: Explore ways to find and exploit flaws in a ransomware attack. BPB Online, 1st edn. (2023)

20. Roeckl, A.: Patch Management (2024). https://www.crowdstrike.com/en-us/cybersecurity-101/exposure-management/patch-management/
21. SentinelOne: SentinelOne Sets the Standard with 100
22. SentinelOne: singularity network discovery – cloud-delivered network visibility & control (2024). https://assets.sentinelone.com/iotranger/singularity-network-discovery-en
23. SentinelOne: what is identity security posture management (ISPM)? (2025). https://www.sentinelone.com/cybersecurity-101/identity-security/identity-security-posture-management-ispm/
24. SentinelOne: what is ransomware? – Examples, prevention & detection (2025). https://www.sentinelone.com/cybersecurity-101/cybersecurity/ransomware/
25. SentinelOne: What is Ransomware Rollback? (2025). https://www.sentinelone.com/cybersecurity-101/cybersecurity/what-is-ransomware-rollback/
26. SentinelOne: what is vulnerability assessment? Types & Benefits (2025). https://www.sentinelone.com/cybersecurity-101/cybersecurity/vulnerability-assessment/
27. Strom, B.E., et al.: Finding cyber threats with ATT&CK^{TM}-based analytics. Technical report, Massachusetts Institute of Technology Research and Engineering (MITRE) Corporation (2017). https://apps.dtic.mil/sti/trecms/pdf/AD1107945.pdf
28. Terry-March, R.: Identity threat detection and response (ITDR) explained (2025). https://www.crowdstrike.com/en-us/cybersecurity-101/identity-protection/identity-threat-detection-and-response-itdr/
29. Tran, K.: Falcon spotlight is changing the game: vulnerability management with ever-adapting AI (2025). https://www.crowdstrike.com/en-us/blog/introducing-falcon-spotlight-exprt-ai/
30. Trellix: what is endpoint detection and response? (2025). https://www.trellix.com/security-awareness/endpoint/what-is-endpoint-detection-and-response/
31. Vaas, L.: Behavioral AI: an unbounded approach to enterprise security (2020). https://www.sentinelone.com/blog/behavioral-ai-an-unbounded-approach-to-protecting-the-enterprise/

Artificial Intelligence for Work Processes

Application Scenarios for the Examination of the Impact of Artificial Intelligence in Industrial Procurement 4.0 Challenges and Processes

Karl-Heinz Lüke[1] and Gerald Eichler[2]

[1] Ostfalia University of Applied Sciences, Siegfried-Ehlers-Str. 1, 38440 Wolfsburg, Germany
ka.lueke@ostfalia.de

[2] Deutsche Telekom AG, Products – Innovation – Experience, Deutsche-Telekom-Allee 9, 64295 Darmstadt, Germany
gerald.eichler@magenta.de

Abstract. Artificial intelligence (AI) is undoubtedly a critical technology that has been widely adopted in various fields, especially in business, art, and science. AI algorithms perform tasks that require human-like intelligence. These tasks include machine learning, deep learning, and complex decision-making processes. AI applications are used across all industries, particularly in industrial procurement 4.0, which is derived from logistics 4.0. This area is important for optimizing processes. An empirical analysis of AI use cases in industrial procurement shows that supplier selection, supplier performance measurement, and negotiation technologies are among the most frequently used and effective applications.

Keywords: AI governance · Artificial intelligence · Industrial procurement · Machine and deep learning · Social influence · Supply chain management · UTAUT analysis

1 Motivation and Related Work

This study provides a detailed analysis of Artificial Intelligence (AI) applications in industrial procurement, examining the use of AI in various functional areas such as supplier selection, negotiation, expenditure analysis, commodity group management, supplier performance measurement, and risk management. Additionally, the study emphasizes the role of AI in fostering sustainable practices in industrial procurement.

Against this background, this study aims to identify, document, and categorize AI application scenarios and examples of AI usage in industrial procurement. Additionally, it seeks to determine the current and future state of AI implementation in the procurement sector and analyze the impact of AI usage on business processes, process management, corporate management, resource availability, and user acceptance.

This study will provide valuable insights, including a better understanding of how AI technologies can be used in real-world procurement environments, identification of

K. Kirchner et al. (Eds.): I4CS 2026, CCIS 3007, pp. 185–202, 2026.
https://doi.org/10.1007/978-3-032-27096-2_10

challenges and best practices in AI implementation in procurement, and development of new AI methods and models to address specific procurement problems. Additionally, new insights may emerge regarding AI-induced changes in the work environment, the roles of procurement experts, and the impact of AI on the economic efficiency, sustainability, and resilience of supply chains.

A previous study on Supply Chain Management (SCM) [1] serves as the basis for the customer survey. That study focused on a broader examination of use cases throughout the SCM, including:

- Inventory management and forecasting,
- Transportation and traceability,
- Supplier management,
- Logistics,
- Risk management,
- Sustainability.

This paper will examine inventory and supplier management in greater detail. These practices are classified as part of procurement and have received high approval ratings. SCM is a management approach that deals with the design, optimization, and control of comprehensive logistics chains. It is rather broad in scope. Procurement, on the other hand, plays a central role in the supply of organizations. It focuses not only on supplier selection, but also on intelligent supplier performance measurement [2].

2   From Fundamentals of Industrial Procurement Towards Appliance of Modern Features of AI Technologies

2.1   The Roadmap to Procurement 4.0

In the future, industrial procurement and AI technologies will form a remarkable partnership to serve latest Industry 4.0 trends. The term "Industrie 4.0" originated in Germany and was introduced at the 2011 Hanover Fair as a high-tech strategy for digitizing the manufacturing sector. This strategy promotes integrating the Internet of Things (IoT), Cyber-Physical Systems (CPS), and smart factories to boost competitiveness, flexibility, and automation. It is an early nod to the Fourth Industrial Revolution (4IR) and is now known worldwide as Industry 4.0 [3].

Step by step, industrial sub-domains adopted 4.0 key paradigms. These include networking, decentralization, real-time capability, and service orientation. Logistics 4.0, a key driver, refers to the potential application of information technology and smart connected objects in logistics, very similar to the Industry 4.0 concept, which has been widely adopted in operations and manufacturing.

A more recent sub-domain (2016–2018) is Procurement 4.0. Today, it mainly targets the digital transformation of purchasing by applying the latest AI and big data technologies to real-time data analysis to enhance efficiency, transparency, and strategic decision making. Procurement 4.0 shifts the focus from manual tasks to proactive, data-driven supplier management, sustainability, and resilient supply chains. The development stages of procurement are primarily technology driven:

- Procurement 1.0:

  - Single tasks, manual work,

- Procurement 2.0:

  - Material Requirements Planning (MRP) systems as internal stand-alone implementation,

- Procurement 3.0:

  - Enterprise Resource Planning (ERP) eProcurement with Electronic Data Interface (EDI) towards suppliers and markets,

- Procurement 4.0:

  - Integration of cloud, big data analytics, and AI-based control.

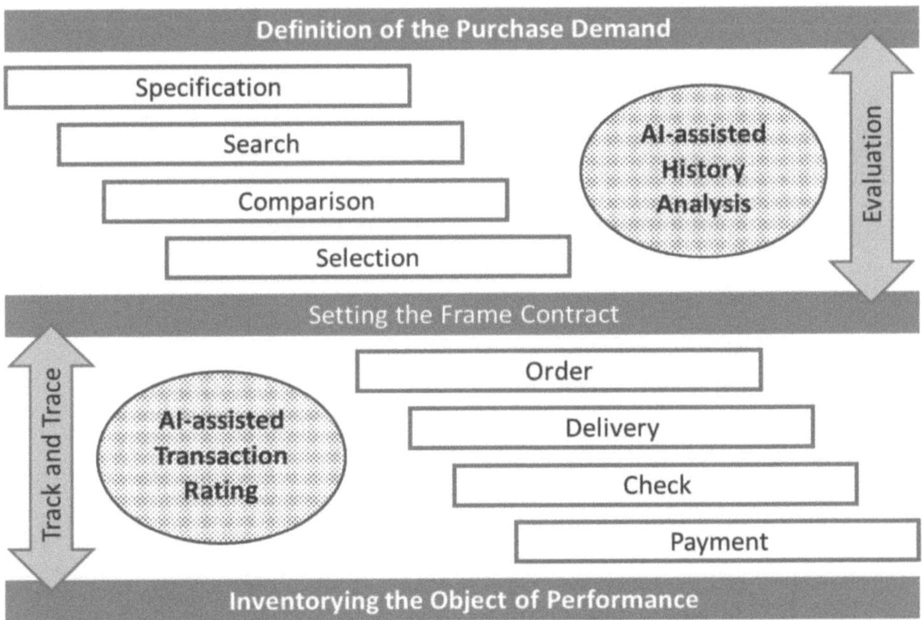

Fig. 1. Detailed sequence of a purchase process

Procurement 4.0 is characterized by an increased influence of strategic elements, such as objects, networks, and innovation, as well as an increased influence on operational and autonomous processes for managing all types of assets [4]. It encompasses every step of the process, from defining the purchase demand and transforming it into a precise request to signing a contract and ensuring final delivery.

The steps remain the same, but the commercial setting and observation are subject to change. Figure 1 summarizes the intermediate steps of the preparation and execution phases. Both can be supported by analytic and generative AI.

The digital transformation of procurement leads to a complex framework that aligns operational, tactical and strategic actions in order to balance cost, time and quality criteria. Figure 2 illustrates these dimensions in relation to internal and external impact.

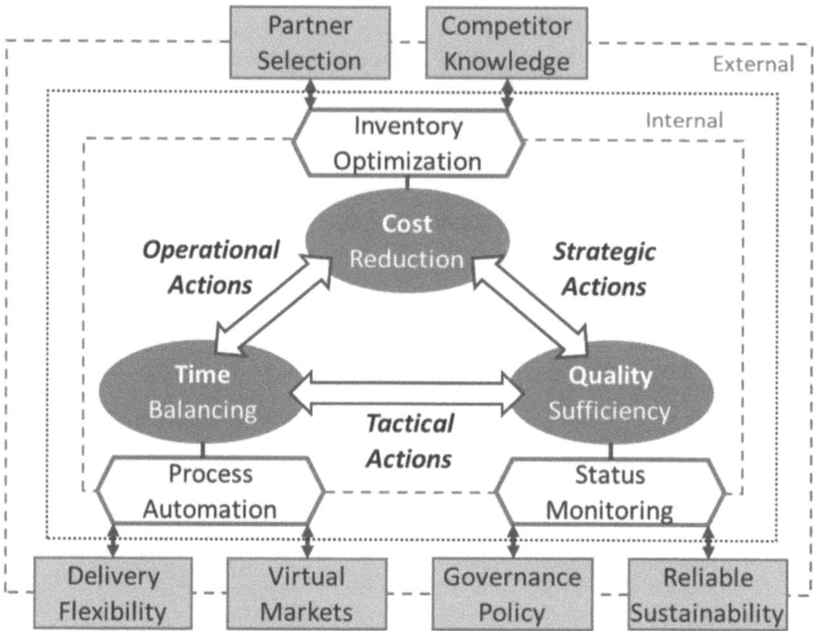

Fig. 2. Framework for the digital transformation of procurement

With the restructuring of departments or even entire enterprises, the management is looking mainly for four things:

- Cost reduction,
- Process optimization,
- Business flexibility,
- Inventory optimization.

The company's view must be reflected in the procurement view at different levels of abstraction. This affects both the qualifications of the people involved and the application of modern technologies, as depicted in Fig. 3. The traditional image of business people, office administrators, and business managers is evolving into that of highly qualified purchasing managers with enhanced skills in process engineering, data analytics, and AI tools.

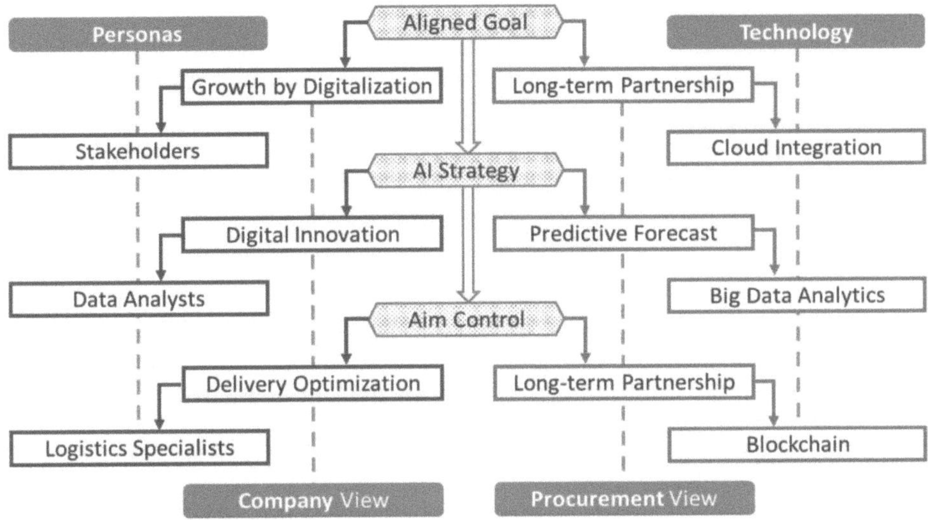

Fig. 3. People and technology – a mediation by management and procurement

2.2 AI Exploitation Within Closed Web Domains

In the context of "artificial intelligence," the term "intelligence" does not mean "message," but rather "intelligence" in the sense of understanding, learning, and problem-solving. The term "artificial intelligence" therefore describes systems that perform tasks that normally require human cognitive abilities. This includes, among other things, text generation, but it is only one aspect of AI. Large Language Models (LMM) have made a huge fund of words, phrases, and grammar, as well as their combination with semantics, available for solving daily problems. This can be achieved by enriching the training materials on a certain domain with methodologies of Machine Learning (ML) and Deep Learning (DL) [6]. Neural networks are a central approach in modern AI and have enabled significant advances, particularly in the processing of unstructured data. Structured data can be converted into information and contextualized, thereby generating actionable knowledge. Domain-specific taxonomies can be expanded into knowledge ontologies to formally represent relationships and make them available for machine use.

Companies have a huge fund of exploitable training materials, starting from technical specifications and process descriptions to research materials. Sources are not limited to structured written documents, but can also include video/audio conferencing scripts, as well as chat and email communications. Several companies are piloting the use of these for internal messaging. For security and legal reasons, it is important to stay within the intranet. This is especially true for the application of modern AI tools, which are usually provided by external vendors.

The procurement domain has its own specific documentation records, which are characteristic for several phases:

- Market: partner repository, opponent list, product rating, reliability analysis,
- Contract: frame contract, agreement, terms of condition,
- Pre-sales: demand, offer, bundle, discount, order,

- Delivery: track and trace data, transport insurance,
- Post-sales: invoice, receipt, goods issue slip, warranty document,
- Maintenance: Service Level Agreement (SLA), operation and recovery concept.

The generation of flexible, but proven contacts is one main target for the text-based AI application [5]. Manual decision-making processes can be supported by new, AI-generated, real-time dashboards. In addition to Key Performance Indicators (KPI) as well as Objectives and Key Results (OKR), which are part of an agile management framework, real-time market analyses optimize procurement triggers.

3 AI Application Scenarios in Industrial Procurement

3.1 Definition of the Application Scenarios for the Questionnaire

Literature sources are used to identify and analyze specific application scenarios and use cases for AI in industrial procurement [3, 5, 7–9]. To the author's knowledge, no systematic and comprehensive study has yet been completed on the current and planned future implementation status of selected procurement-related AI application scenarios, nor on their business processes, process management, corporate management, resource availability or user acceptance. In consideration of the particular requirements of the industry, six use cases of AI were developed to reflect the particular characteristics of procurement in an industrial context.

1. *AI technologies in supplier selection:* AI algorithms enhance supplier selection processes by analyzing performance and reliability data from diverse sources and databases to identify suitable suppliers for the supply chain. AI systems evaluate risks such as financial stability, sustainability and geopolitical influences associated with supplier selection.
2. *AI technologies in negotiations:* AI technologies support negotiations by analyzing data to predict optimal outcomes, understanding sentiment through Natural Language Processing (NLP) to gauge counterpart emotions, and suggesting strategies based on historical negotiation patterns. Machine learning models identify favorable terms and potential risks, helping negotiators make data-driven decisions.
3. *AI technologies in spend analysis and category management:* AI enhances spend analysis and category management by analyzing purchasing data to identify savings opportunities and improve cost efficiency. Machine learning categorizes complex spending patterns, while NLP reviews contracts to ensure compliance and highlight cost-saving terms.
4. *AI technologies in procurement sustainability:* AI supports procurement sustainability by enabling organizations to assess suppliers based on environmental and ethical criteria, ensuring alignment with sustainability goals. Additionally, it analyses data to identify inefficiencies and track carbon footprints, helping organizations make informed, eco-friendly purchasing decisions.
5. *AI technologies in supplier performance measurement:* AI technologies streamline supplier performance measurement by automating data collection and providing real-time insights into supplier behavior. Machine learning models predict risks and flag potential delays, while NLP helps to assess supplier relationships and compliance.

Automated dashboards and predictive analytics support proactive decision making, allowing businesses to address issues before they escalate.

6. *AI technologies in risk management:* AI enhances risk management by automating data analysis, predicting potential issues and identifying anomalies in real time. Machine learning models forecast risks, while NLP analyses reports for hidden threats.

3.2 Questionnaire Methodology and Evaluation Criteria

The online survey *"Application Scenarios for Artificial Intelligence (AI) in Industrial Procurement"* was conducted in March and April 2025. As part of the study, an online survey was sent to 512 companies from various industries. Only 29 of those companies participated in the survey. Of those, 19 responses could be considered for evaluation. Ten companies either discontinued the survey prematurely or completed it incorrectly. Therefore, the response rate that could be used for evaluation is 3.7%.

1. AI technologies in supplier selection

AI algorithms enhance supplier selection processes by analysing performance and reliability data from diverse sources and databases to identify suitable suppliers for the supply chain. AI systems evaluate risks such as financial stability, sustainability and geopolitical influences associated with supplier selection.

Questions about AI technologies in supplier selection	do not agree at all	rather disagree	partly/partly	partially agree	fully agree
This AI technology application is already being used in my company.	☐	☐	☐	☐	☐
The (further) implementation of this AI technology application is interesting for my company.	☐	☐	☐	☐	☐
If this AI technology application is available, I can very well imagine (further) implementation in my company.	☐	☐	☐	☐	☐
The implementation of this AI technology application improves company processes.	☐	☐	☐	☐	☐
The integration of this AI technology application simplifies the management of company processes.	☐	☐	☐	☐	☐
My company provides the necessary resources (e.g. financial resources, infrastructure) for the expansion of this AI technology application.	☐	☐	☐	☐	☐
Employees/colleagues influence me in the use of this AI technology application.	☐	☐	☐	☐	☐

Fig. 4. Example: Questionnaire for use case *AI technologies in supplier selection*

The IPM AG[1] provided the panel for the survey. The companies in the IPM panel were selected, based on the following industry sectors: the automotive industry, the electrical engineering industry, and the mechanical engineering industry. Among other activities, the IPM regularly conducts surveys in various industry sectors. The composition of the

---

[1] IPM AG, URL: http://www.ipm.ag/, accessed February 2026.

panel with regard to the representation of various industrial sectors and their inclusion of representatives from middle and upper management positions is an accurate reflection. Consequently, despite the low response rate that is generally associated with online surveys, it can be inferred that the utilization of this panel ensures a representative sample.

As illustrated in Fig. 4, use case 1 concerns the application of AI technologies in demand forecasting. The response scale, ranging from "do not agree at all" (1) to "fully agree" (5), follows the standard approach used for multi-item scales. For a more thorough exposition of the methodological framework. In principle, it can be posited that the utilized Likert scale, which is a form of multi-item scale, adequately fulfills the criteria for interval scaling [1, 10].

User acceptance of AI application scenarios in industrial procurement is analyzed using the Unified Theory of Acceptance and Use of Technology (UTAUT). The UTAUT model combines the best-known models for technology acceptance. It identifies significant factors influencing behavioral intention and usage behavior. The most important constructs include performance expectation, effort expectation, social influence, and facilitating conditions. This method of technology acceptance research is consistently applied in this study to investigate the acceptance of AI use cases in industrial procurement. The significant influence factors are identified and a corresponding question is formulated for each factor [11, 12].

The key influence factors from the UTAUT analysis are shown as questions, used for all use cases. While the use of multiple items (questions) per factor is customary for the purpose of capturing different dimensions, a review of the questionnaire demonstrated that a single item per factor was sufficient [1, 13].

4   Results of the AI Application Scenarios Study

4.1   Survey Participants' Profile

The present study focuses on companies in the automotive industry (37%), the electrical engineering industry (26%), and the mechanical engineering industry (37%). The majority of the study participants, more than three-quarters, employ a maximum of 500 people, and only approximately two companies employ more than 5,000 people. At the level of the supply chain, approximately one-third of the companies are original equipment manufacturers (OEMs). Meanwhile, one-third of the respondents are 1st-tier suppliers, 10% are 2nd-tier suppliers, and 16% are 3rd-tier and n-tier suppliers, see Fig. 5.

The automotive sector especially emphasizes clearly defined procedures for industrial procurement, which are subject to continuous optimization. New opportunities for the use of AI methods are opened up by the application of innovation management practices [14].

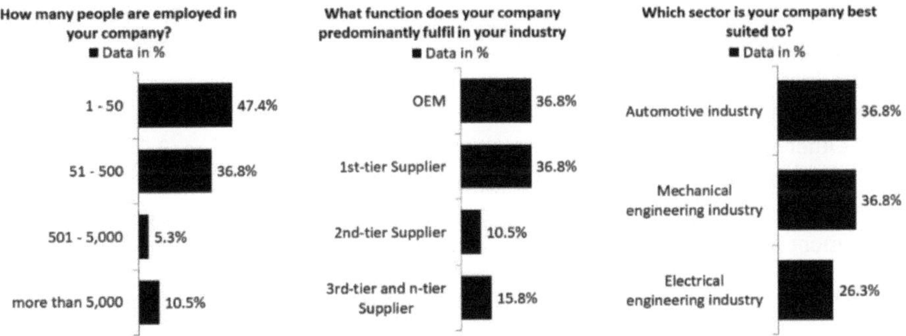

Fig. 5. Survey profile "AI application scenarios in industrial procurement"

4.2   Specific Evaluation of Application Scenarios

The study examined which industrial procurement functions in the companies are of interest for further implementation (Fig. 6(a)), whether implementation is possible given the availability of technology (Fig. 6(b)), and to what extent AI-induced improvements in business processes (Fig. 7(a)) and process management (Fig. 7(b)) have been achieved.

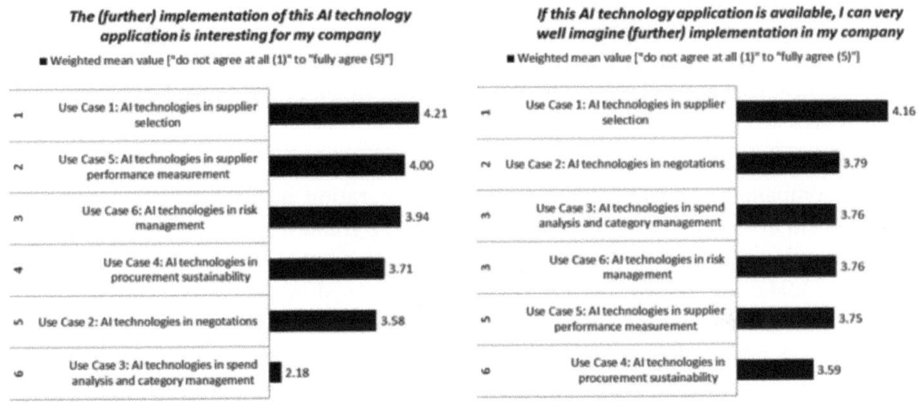

Fig. 6. (a) Upcoming AI use in industrial procurement (b) AI implementation when technology is available

Furthermore, it was determined whether the companies intend to use AI in the future if the necessary technologies are available and whether they plan to provide the resources necessary for technology expansion, e.g., financial resources and infrastructure (Fig. 8(a)). Finally, the influence of employees and colleagues on the use of AI technology in industrial procurement was surveyed (Fig. 8(b)).

Asking the management, the companies surveyed expressed a strong interest in implementing AI applications in various functional areas of industrial procurement in the future. This applies in particular to AI support for supplier selection (4.21), performance measurement (4.00), and risk management (3.94). The companies surveyed showed less interest in AI integration in the context of sustainable procurement (3.71) and conducting negotiations (3.58). The least interest was shown in AI support for expenditure analysis and product group management (2.18).

Participating companies can imagine further use in industrial procurement if AI technologies are available. This applies in particular to AI support for supplier selection (4.16). Other areas of application include negotiations with suppliers (3.79), expenditure analysis and category management (3.76) and risk management (3.76). Companies consider AI implementation for performance measurement (3.75) and to support sustainable procurement processes (3.59) to be less of a priority.

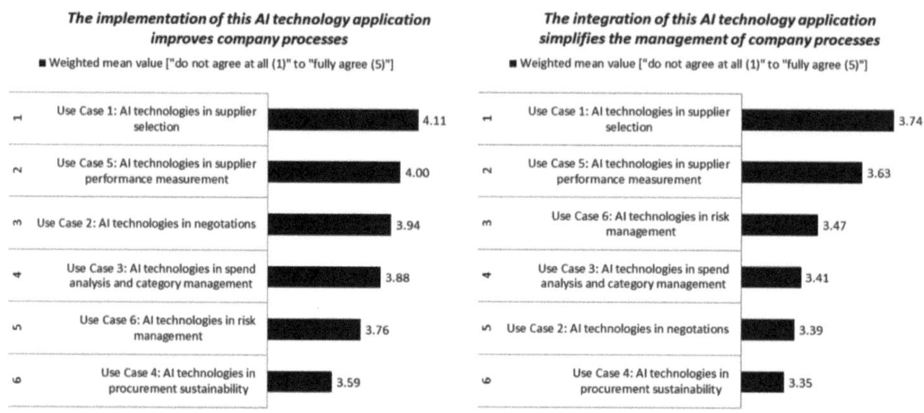

Fig. 7. (a) AI-driven improvement of business processes (b) Process management improvement, driven by AI

The companies surveyed confirm that AI integration in procurement leads to an improvement in business processes, see Fig. 7(a). The greatest AI effects in this regard are seen in supplier selection (4.11), performance measurement (4.00), and negotiations with suppliers (3.94). In contrast, the improvements achieved in the context of expenditure analysis and category management (3.88) are less pronounced. These principles apply equally to risk management (3.76) and sustainable procurement (3.59).

The integration of AI in the industrial procurement areas examined leads to a simplification of business process management, see Fig. 8(b). The use of AI optimizes supplier selection (3.74), supplier performance measurement (3.63), and risk management (3.47) in particular. To a lesser extent, this also applies to negotiations with suppliers (3.39), sustainable procurement (3.35), and expenditure analysis and commodity group management (3.41).

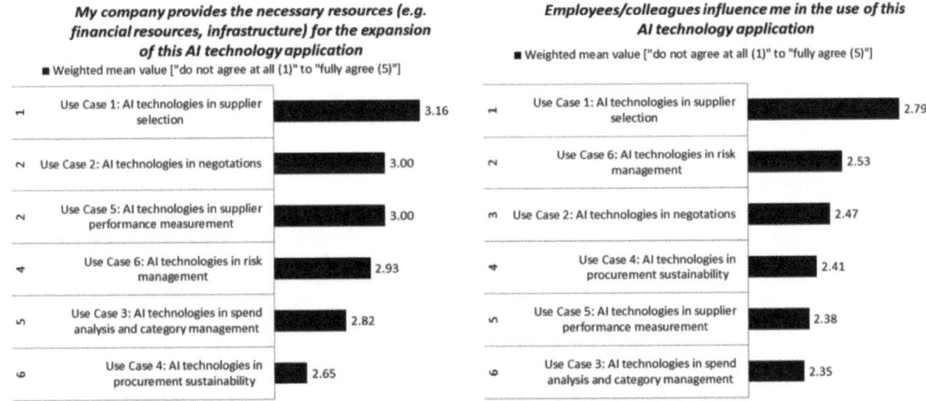

Fig. 8. (a) Availability of resources for AI implementation (b) Social influence on AI usage

The level of corporate resources allocated to further AI implementation e.g., financial resources and infrastructure is comparatively low, see Fig. 8(a). The allocation of resources needed to promote further AI use in industrial procurement focuses primarily on supplier selection (3.16), supplier negotiations (3.00), and performance management (3.00). Conversely, there is a lower level of availability of resources for risk management (2.93), expenditure analysis and category management (2.82), and sustainable procurement (2.65).

The social influence of employees and colleagues on the individual AI use of respondents can be classified as relatively low, see Fig. 8(b). A comprehensive collegial influence on AI use exists, particularly in the fields of supplier selection (2.79), risk management (2.53), and supplier negotiations (2.47). However, there is less influence in the context of sustainable procurement (2.41), performance management (2.38), expenditure analysis, and category management (2.35).

4.3 Ranking Over All UTAUT Questions

Taking into account the ranking values based on the specific questions of the UTAUT analysis, use case 1, *AI technologies in supplier selection*, achieves the highest ranking in the hierarchy. Based on the weighted mean value ranking, this results in a value of 1, as depicted in Fig. 9.

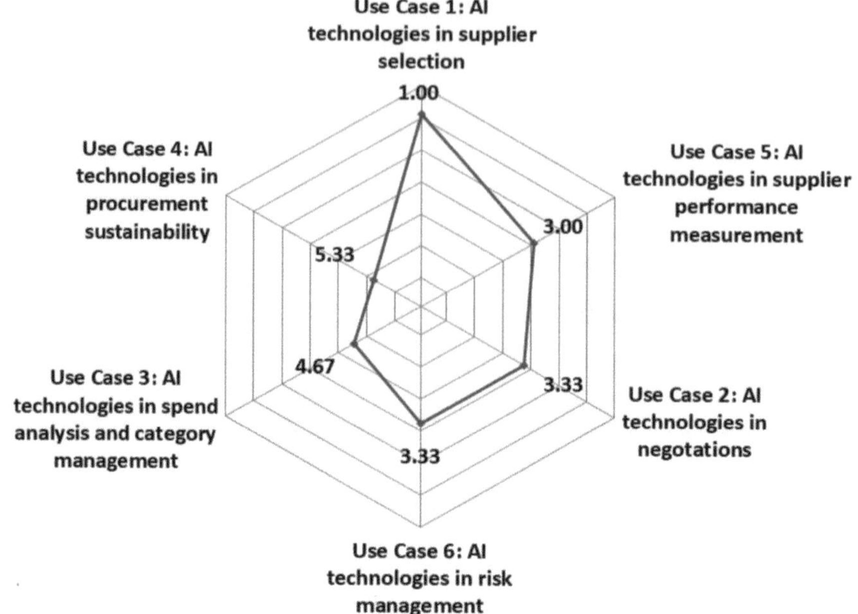

Fig. 9. Weighted mean value ranking based on all UTAUT-specific questions

AI algorithms can effectively enhance supplier selection processes. These AI algorithms can analyze performance and reliability data from various sources and databases, identifying suitable suppliers for the supply chain. AI systems evaluate risks associated with supplier selection, including financial stability, sustainability, and geopolitical influences. Therefore, the focus for a possible initial implementation should be on this use case.

Use case 4, AI technologies in procurement sustainability, ranks lowest in the hierarchy. Participants in the online survey tend to attach little importance to sustainability aspects in industrial procurement. Evaluating suppliers based on environmental and ethical criteria to ensure compliance with sustainability goals is a secondary objective for respondents and should not be pursued as a high priority at this stage.

4.4 Customer-Specific Assessment

This study focuses on the implementation of distance measures structured within a metric system. These are essential for facilitating the calculation of similarities and dissimilarities. In this context, the Minkowski metric is frequently used as a distance measure. It should be noted that if the calculated distance between two objects (a, b) is smaller than the distance between another pair of objects (a, c), it can be hypothesized that the former pair has a higher degree of similarity. Conversely, a larger distance indicates a lower similarity between the objects in question [1, 15].

$$b_{k,l} = \left[\sum_{m=1}^{M} \left| x_{k,m} - x_{l,m} \right|^p \right]^{\frac{1}{p}} \tag{1}$$

$b_{k,l}$:	distance value of the objects k and l $b_{k,l}^{max} = max\{b_{1,1}, \ldots, b_{k,l}, \ldots, b_{n,n}\};$ $b_{k,l}^{min} = min\{b_{1,1}, \ldots, b_{k,l}, \ldots, b_{n,n}\}; \forall k \neq l$
	$b_{k,l} = b_{l,k}; b_{k,l} = 0 \forall k = l;$ number of objects n $(n = 1, \ldots, N);$ $\forall k \neq l : b_{k,l} \in \mathbb{R}_0^+$
$x_{k,m}, x_{l,m}$:	value of the variable (weighted mean value) m of objects $k, l(m = 1, \ldots, M), M$: number of questions in the UTAUT analysis of the relevant use case, $\forall k, l : x_{k,m}, x_{l,m} \in \mathbb{R}^+$
X :	weighted mean value matrix $X = \begin{pmatrix} x_{1,1} & x_{1,2} & \cdots & x_{1,m} \\ x_{2,1} & x_{2,2} & \cdots & x_{2,m} \\ \vdots & \vdots & \ddots & \vdots \\ x_{n,1} & x_{n,2} & \cdots & x_{n,m} \end{pmatrix}$
A :	distance matrix $A = \begin{pmatrix} b_{1,1} & \cdots & b_{1,n} \\ \vdots & \ddots & \vdots \\ b_{n,1} & \cdots & b_{n,n} \end{pmatrix}$
p :	Minkowski constant $(p \geq 1)$, here: $p = 2$

Table 1. Minkowski metric for use case *AI technologies in supplier selection* in two different customer segments: (a) position in the supply chain, (b) company size

Position	OEM	1st-tier	2nd-tier	3rd-n-tier
OEM	0.00	1.78	2.31	3.88
1st-tier		0.00	1.54	3.18
2nd-tier			0.00	3.81
3rd-n-tier				0.00

Size	1-50	51-500	501-5.000	>5.000
1-50	0.00	1.36	2.53	2.57
51-500		0.00	1.98	2.55
501-5.000			0.00	1.41
> 5.000				0.00

The differences in distance demonstrate significant differences in the level of evaluation of use cases between the various customer segments. The use case of AI technologies in supplier selection serves as an ideal example in this context, as it can be used to examine customer segments in terms of their "position in the supply chain" ("OEM," "1st-tier supplier," etc.) and "company size" (number of employees, "1–50," "51–500," etc.). The Minkowski metric is calculated using the independent variables as shown in Table 1. The distance matrix A allows the following statements to be derived, see Table 1(a) and Table 1(b). In the present study, the customer segments "3rd-tier suppliers" and "n-tier suppliers" are combined into one segment due to diverging group sizes in the original survey, see Table 1(a).

The following conclusions can be drawn from Table 1:

- Table 1(a): In this study, it was found that the customer segments "OEM" and "3rd-n-Tier" show the highest distance ($b_{k,l}^{max}$) in the evaluation of the use case *AI technologies in supplier selection*, with a result of 3.88. The smallest gap $\left(b_{k,l}^{min}\right)$ can be observed between the customer segments "1st-tier" and "2nd-tier" (1.54) and between 'OEM' and "1st-tier" (1.78). It can be seen that there is a positive correlation between the distance level and the position in the supply chain. From this, it can be deduced that optimizing the coordination between the supply stages leads to a convergence of the evaluation for the use case.
- Table 1(b): The highest distance level ($b_{k,l}^{max}$) between the customer segments "1–50" and " > 5,000" is 2.57. The smallest distance $\left(b_{k,l}^{min}\right)$ is between the customer segments "1–50" and "51–500" (1.36). It is clear that the significant differences in the size of the companies, measured by the number of employees, lead to a high distance value.

5   Insights and Trends

5.1   Methodology of a Questionnaire

Previous surveys have already led to the successful implementation of certain lessons:

- Choices should be always named, not numbered to be clear in the right answers,
- The number of choices should be five or six, depending on, whether an average is of interest,
- In some cases, a "no answer option" is useful to omit random choices in non-applicable scenarios.

Furthermore, people who often faced different types of questionnaires emphasized the following:

- The target of the survey and who is processing the answers, should be clearly stated,
- A time estimation, how long the survey takes should be clear in advance to decrease the number of dropouts,
- During the execution of the survey, a progress bar keeps people on track,
- Participants of a survey should be informed about the plain results afterwards.

Further improvements are needed to identify the key criteria for quickly creating an optimal survey, particularly to increase the response rate. Clearly, there is a need to improve the balance and expand the scope of the survey.

5.2 Key Results and Comparison with Previous Studies

The response rate for this study was slightly higher than that of the SCM study from 2024. Despite the generally low response rate associated with online surveys, it can be concluded that using this panel ensures a representative sample. To verify the results in the long term, a follow-up study should be conducted at a later date using a different panel.

As the topic of procurement investigated by the 2025 survey, is more specific than SCM, under review in 2024, the divergence of ratings is lower, as proven by the calculation of the Minkowski metrics, see Table 1.

The highest rating in the UTAUT scale got the AI technology application in supplier selection use case, which is a decision of continuous market analyses, see Fig. 9. Using AI technologies for supplier selection is highly relevant because traditional evaluation methods often cannot keep up with the growing complexity and volume of data in modern supply chains. AI can process and analyze large, diverse datasets much faster and more consistently than humans can, leading to more transparent, evidence-based decisions. This reduces subjectivity and the risk of overlooking critical information. Additionally, AI enables companies to evaluate suppliers not only based on cost and quality, but also on critical risk factors such as financial stability, sustainability performance, and geopolitical exposure [5, 8].

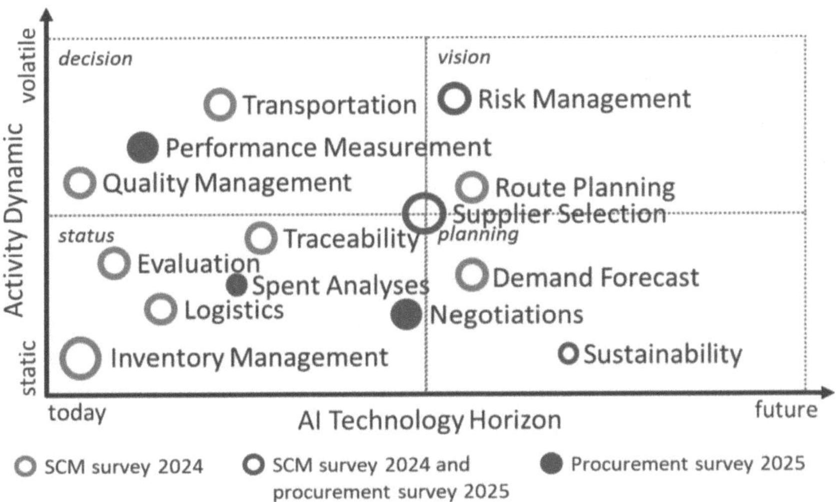

Fig. 10. AI Technology horizon (x-axis), dynamics (y-axis) and relevance (circle size)

The world markets become more volatile and require higher flexibility against the 2024 SCM survey [1]. Risk management is becoming increasingly important in supply chain management and procurement because supply chains have grown more global and complex, making them more vulnerable to disruptions. Concurrently, geopolitical tensions, climate-related events, and the consequences of crises such as the pandemic of 2020 have demonstrated the vulnerability of supply networks. Furthermore, companies often rely on a limited number of suppliers, and digitalization introduces new cyber risks. Consequently, organizations require robust risk management strategies to maintain stability [16].

Sustainability again got the lowest attention. One can assume that short term profits still dominate responsible long-term thinking.

Figure 10 combines the results of the 2024 SCM survey and 2025 procurement survey on application of AI technologies. Some of the topics examined in 2024 are specific to SCM e.g., transportation, while other use cases focus on procurement in 2025 e.g., performance management. Therefore both, common areas e.g., risk management and the respective specific areas for 2024 (SCM) and 2025 (procurement) have been presented.

5.3   Trends and Challenges in Industrial Procurement

The detailed examination of trends and challenges for AI in procurement can be facilitated by a strategic management tool such as a SWOT analysis. A SWOT analysis is a strategic management tool used to assess a situation based on four key factors: strengths (internal advantages), weaknesses (internal limitations), opportunities (external opportunities for improvement or growth), and threats (external risks or challenges). SWOT analysis enables informed decisions to be made, risks to be identified, and effective strategies to be developed [17].

Our SWOT analyses summarize the findings for the paradigm change with Procurement 4.0, for details refer to Fig. 11.

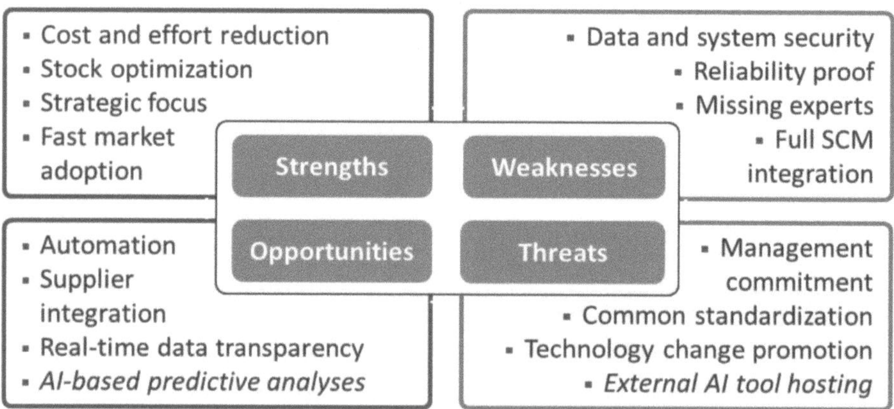

Fig. 11. Industrial procurement SWOT analyses with respect to AI appliance

AI can be both, a driver or a barrier. Mobile objects management in Logistics 4.0, as part of the SCM, is a clear driver for Procurement 4.0. However, the application of AI technologies takes more time than expected, even in big enterprises.

AI in procurement offers significant strengths, including reduced costs, a stronger strategic focus, and faster market adoption. However, companies must also be aware of the weaknesses. These include, for example, concerns about data and system security, the need to demonstrate the reliability of AI, the shortage of qualified professionals, and the complexity of fully integrating AI into the supply chain. AI also opens up promising opportunities such as process automation, better supplier integration, real-time data transparency, and predictive analytics that support proactive decision-making. Other threats include the lack of standardization, rapid technological change, and risks associated with hosting external AI tools. Overall, a thorough SWOT analysis helps companies effectively leverage AI in procurement while minimizing potential risks.

5.4 Conclusion

AI is on the path to fundamentally transforming the procurement process. During the initial implementation phase, the focus should particularly be on the use cases *AI technologies in supplier selection* and *AI technologies in supplier performance measurement*, as these received the highest level of support in the present study. Future research should focus on optimizing AI applications, increasing the transparency of decision-making processes and critically examining the broader societal implications of AI-driven automation.

Additionally, the proposed use case ranking should be validated in a follow-up study within a broader community with an independent sample to test the robustness and generalizability of the results.

References

1. Lüke, K.-H., Eichler, G., Royer, D.: Artificial intelligence application scenarios considering objective and subjective influence factors. In: Conference Proceedings of Innovations for Community Services (I4CS), pp. 94–112, Springer, Heidelberg (2025)
2. Goudz, A., Erdogan, S.: Künstliche Intelligenz im Supply Chain Management – Potenziale und Grenzen der KI. Springer Nature, Wiesbaden (2024)
3. Tatini, P.R.: Transforming sourcing and supply chain management: the evolution of AI agents in modern procurement. Int. J. Sci. Res. Comput. Sci. Eng. Inf. Technol. **11**(1) (2025). https://ijsrcseit.com/index.php/home/article/view/CSEIT251112131/CSEIT2 51112131. Accessed Feb 2026
4. Kleemann, F.: Einkauf 4.0 – Digitale Transformation der Beschaffung, Springer Nature, Wiesbaden (2024)
5. Guida, M., Caniato, F., Moretto, A., Ronchi, S.: The role of artificial intelligence in the procurement process: State of the art and research agenda. J. Purchas. Supply Manag. **29**(2) (2023). https://www.sciencedirect.com/science/article/pii/S14784092230 00079. Accessed Feb 2026
6. Thakur, M., Patel, P., Gupta, K., Kumar, M., Sathishkumar, A.S.: Applications of artificial intelligence and machine learning. In: Supply Chain Management: A Comprehensive Review.: Eur. Chem. Bull. **12** (Special Issue 8), 2838–2851 (2023)

7. Hof, A., Schulz, C.: Generative KI im Lieferketten-Management (2024). https://beschaffung-aktuell.industrie.de/einkauf/generative-ki-im-lieferketten-management. Accessed Feb 2026
8. Allal-Chérif, O., Simón-Moya, V.; Ballester, A.C.C.: Intelligent purchasing: how artificial intelligence can redefine the purchasing function. J. Bus. Res. **124**, 69–76 (2021)
9. Deloitte (Ed.): The AI opportunity in sourcing and procurement: Opportunities in the market today (2020). https://www.deloitte.com/ca/en/services/consulting/perspectives/ai-opportunity-sourcing-procurement.html. Accessed Feb 2026
10. Kuß, A.: Marktforschung, 4th edn. Springer Gabler, Wiesbaden (2012)
11. Venkatesh, V., Morris, M.G., Davis, G.B., Davis, F.D.: User acceptance of information technology: toward a unified view. MIS Q. **27**(3), 425–478 (2003)
12. Venkatesh, V., Davis, F.D.: A theoretical extension of the technology acceptance model: four longitudinal field studies. Manag. Sci. **46**(2), 186–204 (2000)
13. Lüke, K.-H., von Hugo, D., Eichler, G.: 5G network quality of service supporting adequate quality of experience for industrial demands in process automation. In: Conference Proceedings of Innovations for Community Services (I4CS), pp. 201–222. Springer, Heidelberg (2021)
14. Lüke, K.-H., Walther, J., Wäldchen, D., Royer, D.: innovation management methods in the automotive industry. In: Conference Proceedings of Innovations for Community Services (I4CS), pp. 125–141, Springer, Heidelberg (2019)
15. Backhaus, K., Erichson, B., Plinke, W., Weiber, R.: Multivariate Analysemethoden. Springer, Berlin/Heidelberg (2018)
16. Bungartz, O., Schwarz, G.: Überwachung der Leistung des Risikomanagements. In: Bungartz, O. (ed.) Risikomanagement in Supply Chains, pp. 241–266. Erich Schmidt Verlag, Berlin (2025)
17. Paul, H., Wollny, V.: Instrumente des strategischen Managements: Grundlagen und Anwendung. De Gruyter Oldenbourg, Berlin (2025)

Extending AI-Assisted Software Development Beyond Vibe Coding

Siniša Nešković[1] and Kathrin Kirchner[2(✉)]

[1] IT University of Copenhagen, Rued Langgaards Vej 7, 2300 Copenhagen, Denmark
[2] Technical University of Denmark, Lautrupvang 15, 2750 Ballerup, Denmark
sinn@itu.dk, kakir@dtu.dk

Abstract. The adoption of Generative AI (GenAI) in software development is currently dominated by the discussion of "vibe coding," in which developers describe the desired functionality in natural language and let large language models generate the corresponding code with minimal review. This describes a fundamental shift in how software is developed and in the competencies necessary for a software developer. Vibe coding reduces the need for manual coding, leaving the software developer to focus on high-level design and code evaluation. While effective for prototypes, this approach is insufficient for complex software systems, where development spans analysis, architecture, design, testing, and deployment, and where every phase requires human understanding and evaluation.

In this position paper, we argue that AI-assisted development of complex systems requires methodology encoding: the systematic translation of a project's adopted methodology (architecture, patterns, workflows, standards, and roles) into AI tool configuration. This creates a configured agentic development environment that enables consistent AI assistance across the entire software development lifecycle. We define a new professional role, the Agentic Architect, who is responsible for designing this environment. We illustrate the concept using Claude Code and discuss implications for developer competencies and organizational roles.

Keywords: AI agent · Generative AI · Software development · Vibe coding

1 Introduction

Recent advances in Artificial Intelligence, especially the widely available Generative AI (GenAI), are already changing the way we work, make decisions, and communicate. GenAI has also opened new possibilities for automating and extending tasks in software engineering, e.g., code generation and completion, test generation, and user interface design [1]. The adoption of GenAI influences how software is developed, and tools like GitHub Copilot, Claude Code, and Amazon CodeWhisperer already boost efficiency, reduce manual programming effort, and foster creative programming practices [2]. The use of GenAI for software development can thus lead to higher job satisfaction, as it can eliminate repetitive tasks, help retain flow, provide quick help, aid understanding of code, and enable learning [3].

K. Kirchner et al. (Eds.): I4CS 2026, CCIS 3007, pp. 203–215, 2026.
https://doi.org/10.1007/978-3-032-27096-2_11

The most visible manifestation of this shift is vibe coding, a term coined by Andrej Karpathy referring to building software by formulating requirements in natural language and accepting AI-generated code with minimal comprehension or review [4]. It has its roots in the need for efficient prototype development and a shortage of skilled programmers [5].

While vibe coding works well for rapid prototyping, it carries an implicit assumption that is problematic for complex systems: that developers do not need to deeply understand the generated output. For a quick prototype or a personal tool, this assumption may be acceptable. For a production system with domain complexity, architectural constraints, quality requirements, and team coordination, it is inadequate and potentially dangerous. Complex software demands that every phase of development, from requirements analysis through architecture, design, implementation, testing, and deployment, involves human understanding and evaluation of AI-generated artifacts.

Moreover, the current discussion of vibe coding focuses mostly on the implementation phase, specifically on generating source code. But software development produces far more than code. It produces many other valuable deliverables, e.g., requirements specifications, domain models, architecture documentation, design decisions, process documentation, development plans, deployment configurations, and test strategies. Source code is just one artifact among many, and arguably a derived one, since it implements the knowledge captured in all the others. AI-assisted development of complex systems must address the entire lifecycle, not just the coding phase. But how can AI support be leveraged and synthesized across the lifecycle, and how should the interplay between human software engineers and GenAI be developed further [6]?

In this position paper, we investigate how GenAI can be systematically integrated into all phases of software development for complex systems. We make three contributions:

First, we introduce the concept of methodology encoding, that is, the systematic translation of a project's adopted software development methodology (architecture, patterns, workflows, standards, roles, and quality gates) into the configuration of an AI development tool. This creates a persistent, hierarchical, project-wide configuration that enables consistent AI assistance across the entire software development lifecycle. Methodology encoding differs from ad hoc prompting or vibe coding. It creates a configured agentic development environment, not a series of interactions with GenAI.

Second, we illustrate methodology encoding using Claude Code, a GenAI development tool by Anthropic. We show how its extensibility mechanisms (context files, skills, subagents, hooks, and plugins) map to the components of a software development methodology.

Third, we define the Agentic Architect as a new professional role. The Agentic Architect does not architect the software product itself; that remains the Software Architect's responsibility. Instead, the Agentic Architect architects the agentic development environment: the configured AI setup that embodies the methodology of the software project and enables the development team to work efficiently with GenAI assistance.

The remainder of this position paper is structured as follows. Section 2 reviews related work. Section 3 introduces the concept of methodology encoding and illustrates it using Claude Code. Section 4 defines the new Agentic Architect role. Section 5 discusses implications and limitations. Section 6 concludes with future work directions.

2 Background and Related Work

2.1 Limitations of Vibe Coding

Vibe coding allows not only programmers but also subject matter experts to describe their requirements to a software system in natural language or refer to existing examples (such as a website or user interface), while the coding is done by GenAI [7]. Treude and Gerosa [8] provide a taxonomy of ways developers can use GenAI for various tasks, ranging from auto-completing code to receiving assistance via conversational interaction with GenAI. Gadde [9] presents three current ways of vibe coding: 1) conversational code generation, where users interact with a GenAI tool in natural language and provide feedback that can lead to modifications; 2) multimodal expression processing, where users combine natural language text with diagrams or reference examples; and (3) context-aware generation, where GenAI systems additionally possess data about typical project structures, existing codebases, and application context.

However, practical experience shows several limitations of vibe coding. In a study with practitioners, Yu [10] found that GenAI can enhance daily programming work efficiency but offers fewer benefits for complex or domain-intensive work. Repeated re-prompting, limited domain-specific knowledge, and the lack of integration with design rules lead to lower time efficiency for non-trivial tasks. This finding is crucial: the limitation of vibe coding for complex systems is not necessarily that the AI generates poor code; rather, it is that ad hoc, interactive prompting cannot capture the persistent, structured knowledge that complex software projects require.

The integration of GenAI into existing workflows is a core driver of its adoption in software engineering. As Russo [11] points out, successful adoption depends not on the AI's raw capability but on how well it integrates with established development practices. This observation motivates our proposal: rather than adapting workflows to AI capabilities, we propose encoding existing methodology into an AI configuration.

2.2 Related Approaches

Several researchers have begun to address the integration of GenAI beyond the coding phase. Banh et al. [5] developed a conceptual framework for integrating GenAI into software engineering. They argue that GenAI can do more than assist with coding; it can also support architectural design or code analysis. The proposed framework remains at an abstract level, offering no concrete implementation suggestions.

The question of how GenAI changes the role of software developers has already been discussed. Kam et al. [12] found that when developers use AI to complete repetitive work more quickly and with less effort, the time savings enable them to spend more time in the early stages of the software development lifecycle. They conclude that a future AI-enhanced developer would need the skills and knowledge of today's senior developer to design good systems and make technical decisions. Our work makes this insight concrete by specifying what "senior-level skills" means in an AI-assisted context and defining the new competency of methodology encoding.

Based on an extensive literature review, Nguyen-Duc et al. [13] identify open research questions about GenAI in software engineering, including: How can GenAI improve software process automation? How does the adoption of GenAI impact the required skills for software engineers? Our approach directly addresses both questions: process automation through methodology encoding, and skill impact through the Agentic Architect role.

Beyond academic literature, the industry has produced several relevant proposals. Concepts such as Adaptive Intent-Driven Development (using multiple specialized AI agents for architectural debates [14]) or intent-driven IDEs (structuring development around intent, knowledge, execution, and oversight layers, e.g., Kiro [15]) point toward a similar evolution. However, these proposals share a common gap: they describe what AI can do across the software development lifecycle but not how to systematically configure AI to follow a specific project's methodology. Our concept of methodology encoding addresses this gap.

2.3 Software Development Methodology

To ground our proposal, we briefly define what a software development methodology comprises. Following established software engineering literature [16], a methodology defines the structured approach by which software is developed. Its components include:

- Activities: the tasks that are performed during development (e.g., domain analysis, architectural design, code review, testing, deployment).
- Workflows: the sequences of and dependencies between activities, defining how development proceeds through phases.
- Roles: the responsibilities assigned to team members, specifying who performs which activities with what expertise (e.g., domain expert, architect, reviewer).
- Artifacts: the deliverables produced during development (e.g., domain models, architecture documents, source code, test plans, deployment configurations). Standards: the conventions and quality criteria that artifacts must satisfy (e.g., coding style, naming conventions, documentation requirements).
- Quality gates: the mandatory checks that must be passed before the development can proceed (e.g., code review, test coverage thresholds, security scans).

This vocabulary is important because, as we will show in Sect. 3, each methodology component maps to a specific type of AI configuration mechanism. Methodology encoding is the process of translating these components into an AI tool configuration.

3 From Vibe Coding to Methodology Encoding

3.1 AI Across the Software Development Lifecycle

We claim that GenAI will become part of the entire software development process, where at every step the developer will work closely with the GenAI tool. Table 1 summarizes this claim. In every phase, both humans and AI are needed to achieve meaningful results. The human developer provides intent, domain knowledge, and evaluative judgment; the AI provides generation capability, pattern consistency, and scalable execution.

While each phase can be AI-assisted through conversational prompting, complex systems pose a challenge. Different developers may prompt differently, leading to inconsistent outputs. Architectural decisions made in one phase may not carry through to

Table 1. Human-GenAI collaboration in the software development phases

Phase	Traditional (Developer)	AI-Assisted Approach (Developer -GenAI - Collaboration)
Requirements	Elicit and document requirements	Developer describes intent, GenAI helps to structure and refine specifications
Analysis	Manual domain analysis and modeling	Developer describes the domain, GenAI proposes domain models and dependencies
Architecture	Design architecture and document design decisions	Developer describes constraints and qualities, GenAI makes design decisions and proposes architecture
Design	Create a detailed component design	Developer describes the desired behavior, GenAI generates designs
Implementation	Write code	Developer describes behavior, GenAI generates code
Testing	Write test cases	Developer describes scenarios, and GenAI generates tests
Documentation	Write documentation manually	GenAI generates from code and intent
Deployment & Operations	Manual Continuous Integration/Continuous Deployment (CI/CD) setup, deployment scripts, and monitoring configurations	Developer describes infrastructure needs, GenAI generates CI/CD pipelines and operational automation

another. Coding standards may be followed in one session and forgotten in the next. For complex systems, ad-hoc prompting is insufficient. What is needed is a persistent, structured way to configure the AI tool with the project's methodology, so that every interaction, by every developer, follows the same architecture, patterns, workflows, and standards.

3.2 The Concept of Methodology Encoding

We define methodology encoding as the systematic translation of a project's adopted software development methodology, including architectural decisions, design patterns, development workflows, quality standards, role responsibilities, and enforcement rules, into the configuration of an AI development tool.

Methodology encoding is different from related practices. Prompt engineering is per-interaction and short-lived: each prompt must re-establish context, and there is no persistence across sessions or developers. Template-based code generation produces fixed output structures without adaptive behavior; it can scaffold but not reason. IDE configuration (code analysis and formatting) constrains tool behavior but does not encode domain knowledge, workflows, or role-specific expertise. Methodology encoding is persistent (it survives across sessions), hierarchical (different levels of specificity for different parts of the project), and project-wide (shared by the entire team).

3.3 Illustration: Claude Code

To make methodology encoding concrete, we illustrate it using Claude Code, an AI-powered development tool by Anthropic. Claude Code, at the time of writing this paper, had already provided a set of extensibility mechanisms that, taken together, constitute a methodology encoding platform. Claude Code is publicly available and well-documented, so our proposal could be evaluated in practice later. However, we do not claim that Claude Code is the only or best platform for methodology encoding.

Table 2 shows how each methodology component (defined in Subsect. 2.3) maps to a specific Claude Code mechanism.

Table 2. Mapping methodology components to Claude Code mechanisms

Methodology Component	Claude Code Mechanism	Explanation
Standards (always on)	CLAUDE.md (root level)	Loaded at session start, always in context. Encodes coding conventions, architecture terminology, and global constraints
Context-specific patterns	CLAUDE.md (path-based)	Placed in subdirectories. Loaded automatically when working in that path. Encodes location-specific design patterns
Workflows & activities	Skills	Reusable procedures, invoked by the developer or auto-loaded by the AI when the task matches. Encode step-by-step workflows
Roles & expertise	Subagents	Specialized AI assistants with custom prompts and isolated context. Encode the expertise of specific roles (e.g., domain architect, service designer)
Quality gates	Hooks	Deterministic scripts that run at specific lifecycle events. Unlike other mechanisms, hooks always fire; they do not depend on AI judgment
Distribution	Plugins	Bundle skills, subagents, and hooks into installable packages. Enable sharing encoded methodology across projects and teams

A critical distinction emerges from this mapping. The first four rows (CLAUDE.md, skills, subagents) represent probabilistic guidance: the AI reads instructions and should follow them, but compliance depends on the model's interpretation. Hooks, by contrast, represent deterministic enforcement: they always execute regardless of AI behavior. A well-encoded methodology uses both: hooks enforce hard constraints (code must be formatted, types must check) while context files, skills, and subagents provide the judgment-requiring guidance that shapes how the AI works within those constraints.

To illustrate how these mechanisms work together, consider a brief scenario. A developer working on a Domain-Driven Design (DDD) based platform types, "I need to create a Tasks domain for project management." The AI, configured through methodology encoding, responds as follows:

- the root CLAUDE.md provides global context (DDD terminology, coding conventions);
- a path-based CLAUDE.md in the domains folder loads the DDD decomposition pattern;
- the workflow encoded in a subdirectory-level CLAUDE.md directs the AI to invoke a domain-architect subagent;
- this subagent, with its DDD expertise prompt, designs the bounded context;
- a service-designer subagent design software services and corresponding APIs within the domain;
- and hooks deterministically enforce formatting and type-checking on API specifications.

The developer evaluates and approves each step. This is not vibe coding; the developer must understand and validate everything. But the process orchestration, pattern compliance, and quality enforcement are handled by the encoded methodology.

4 The Agentic Architect: A New Role

4.1 Definition

We define the Agentic Architect as a new professional role responsible for architecting the agentic development environment rather than the software product itself. While a Software Architect designs what gets built (system structure, components, integration patterns, technology stack), the Agentic Architect designs how AI builds it by translating the project's adopted methodology into AI tool configuration.

The output of the Agentic Architect's work is not a system design document. It is a configured AI development environment, a coherent set of context files, skills, subagents, hooks, and plugins that embodies the project's methodology and enables the development team to work efficiently with AI assistance. The Agentic Architect's core responsibilities are: (1) translating the project's adopted methodology into AI tool configuration, and (2) configuring AI to generate all artifact types, not just source code, but also domain models, architecture documentation, deployment configurations, and test plans.

4.2 Distinction from Existing Roles

The Agentic Architect is distinct from several existing roles that might appear similar at first glance. Table 3 clarifies these distinctions.

Table 3. Translating traditional roles into subagent configurations.

Existing Role	Traditional Primary Responsibility	Agentic Architect
Software Architect	Designs system structure and selects technology stack	Does not make these decisions; instead, encodes them into an AI configuration so the AI follows them consistently
CTO / Vice President of Engineering	Defines development methodology and team workflows	Does not define methodology, but translates the adopted methodology into an AI tool configuration
DevOps Engineer	Configures build pipelines and deployment infrastructure	Configures the AI development environment, not the operational infrastructure
Process Engineer	Documents and improves development processes	Goes beyond documentation to create executable process encodings, that is a methodology that the AI follows, not just what humans read

The distinctive competency of the Agentic Architect is translation: understanding both the project's methodology deeply enough to encode it faithfully, and the AI tool's configuration capabilities well enough to encode it effectively. This competency does not exist in current role definitions. A Software Architect may understand DDD perfectly but not know how to encode bounded context rules into AI subagent configurations. A DevOps engineer may be an expert in continuous integration and delivery pipelines, but not in translating architectural patterns into AI context files.

4.3 Encoding Roles as Subagents

In traditional software methodology, roles define who performs which activities and with what expertise. In methodology encoding, these roles are translated into subagent configurations. Table 4 illustrates this mapping.

Additionally, quality gate responsibilities that were traditionally role-dependent become hooks, that is, deterministic enforcement that does not rely on anyone, human or AI, remembering to check. For example, "code must be formatted before commit" becomes a hook that runs the formatter after every file edit. "No changes to production configuration without review" becomes a hook that blocks modifications to protected

Table 4. Translating traditional roles into subagent configurations

Traditional Role	Encoded as Subagent	Tasks of the subagent
Domain expert / DDD specialist	Domain-architect	Bounded context design, ubiquitous language definition, and domain classification
Database architect	DB-designer	Database schema design
Senior Developer/ Tech Lead	Service-designer	Service design, API specification, component structure, and integration patterns with domains
QA engineer	Test-engineer	Test scenario design, test code generation, coverage analysis

paths. This separation of concerns (probabilistic expertise in subagents, deterministic enforcement in hooks) is a key design principle of the methodology-encoding approach.

Humans do not disappear in this model. The shift is from performing to: (1) defining the role's expertise and procedures as a subagent configuration, (2) encoding quality gates as hooks, (3) delegating tasks to configured subagents, and (4) validating outputs. This requires the same domain expertise as the original role (the Agentic Architect must understand DDD to encode a domain-architect subagent), but the application of that expertise changes from doing to configuring and reviewing.

4.4 Organizational Implications

Who performs the Agentic Architect role depends on the organization. In a startup or small team, the CTO or tech leader who already defines both architecture and process is the natural candidate. In a medium-sized company, the software architect may take on expanded responsibilities. In a large enterprise, a dedicated role may emerge, potentially within a Software Engineering Process Group (SEPG).

The implications for developer competencies are significant. All developers working with a methodology-encoded AI environment need to understand the encoded methodology well enough to evaluate AI-generated outputs. As Kam et al. [12] argue, future AI-enhanced developers need senior-level skills. Our approach makes this concrete: the encoded methodology defines what "good software" looks like, but developers must still judge whether the AI output meets that standard.

The Agentic Architect specifically needs a new competency: the ability to translate methodology knowledge into AI configuration. This requires understanding both software engineering methodology (activities, workflows, roles, artifacts, standards, quality gates) and AI tool configuration capabilities (context management, skill design, subagent definition, hook engineering, plugin packaging). This competency is not present in current professional role definitions and is a new skill requirement created by the maturation of AI-assisted development.

5   Discussion

Before discussing the implications and limitations of our approach, Fig. 1 presents the three contributions of our position paper: The Agentic Architect (described in Sect. 4) is responsible for translating the project's development methodology into an AI tool configuration through methodology encoding, as introduced in Sect. 3. The resulting configured environment, illustrated in this paper using Claude Code's mechanisms, enables consistent AI assistance across the full software development lifecycle. The dashed arrow illustrates the developer's role in evaluating outputs and triggering further refinement of the encoded methodology.

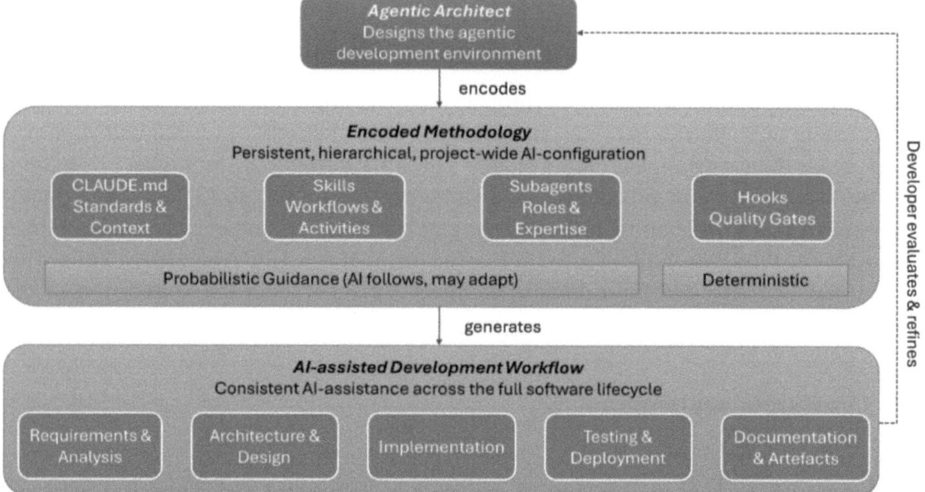

Fig. 1. Relationship between Agentic Architect, encoded methodology, and AI-assisted development workflow (Example: Claude)

5.1   Relation to Existing Work

Our approach addresses several gaps identified in the literature. Banh et al. [4] proposed a conceptual framework for integrating GenAI into software engineering, but it remained at an abstract level. Our methodology encoding concept goes beyond abstraction by providing a concrete mechanism mapping: we show specifically how architectural decisions become context files, how role expertise becomes subagent configurations, how quality gates become deterministic hooks, and how the entire configuration can be packaged as plugins for team distribution.

Nguyen-Duc et al. [13] identified two open research questions that our approach directly addresses. First, "How can GenAI improve software process automation?" Our study addresses this question through methodology encoding, where the development process itself is configured as AI agent instructions, with deterministic hooks for critical enforcement points. The process is not merely documented; it is made executable by the AI. Second, "How does the adoption of GenAI impact the required skills for software engineers?" Developers need senior-level evaluation skills, and, in addition, the new competency of methodology encoding emerges as a distinct professional capability.

Kam et al. [12] concluded that future developers need "the skills and knowledge of today's senior developer." Our approach makes this insight actionable. The encoded methodology captures senior-level knowledge (architectural patterns, design principles, quality criteria) and makes it available to every developer through AI assistance. But this does not reduce the need for understanding; rather, it shifts the developer's role from producing artifacts to evaluating them. A junior developer working with a methodology-encoded AI environment still needs to understand why the domain-architect subagent proposes a particular bounded context boundary, even if the developer did not design it.

A unique aspect of our approach is the distinction between probabilistic guidance and deterministic enforcement. Context files, skills, and subagents provide probabilistic guidance: the AI should follow the encoded patterns but may deviate, especially in edge cases or with complex instructions. Hooks provide deterministic enforcement: they always execute regardless of AI behavior. The Agentic Architect must decide which parts of the methodology require deterministic enforcement and which can rely on AI judgment. This is a design decision with no direct precedent in traditional process engineering, where all enforcement ultimately depends on human compliance.

The transition from vibe coding to methodology encoding increases maturity. Vibe coding, as Karpathy [4] defined it, demonstrated that natural language can drive code generation, which is a breakthrough. But for complex systems, "giving in to the vibes" is insufficient. Methodology encoding is the counterpart: AI generates artifacts from natural-language intent, within the constraints of an explicitly encoded methodology, with deterministic hooks enforcing critical quality gates, and with the developer understanding and evaluating every output. This is also in line with the Copenhagen Manifesto to embed GenAI into software engineering, as our methodology encoding approach ensures that GenAI enhances, rather than replaces, human decision-making and creativity [17].

5.2 Limitations

This position paper presents an approach that has not been empirically validated through controlled experiments or longitudinal studies. The illustrative example demonstrates the feasibility of the approach but not its effectiveness, efficiency, or scalability. Empirical validation is an important direction for future work.

Current AI development tools, including Claude Code, lack enterprise features needed for large-scale adoption: role-based access control (any developer can invoke any subagent), built-in approval workflows, comprehensive audit trails, and team collaboration features. Git-based workflows partially mitigate these gaps; pull requests serve as approval gates, and Git history provides a partial audit trail. However, local authorization, cost tracking, and AI decision logging remain unsolved.

A fundamental challenge is keeping the AI configuration synchronized with evolving project knowledge. When the team adopts a new pattern or makes an architectural decision, the documentation and the AI configuration must be updated to reflect it. Currently, this synchronization is manual, which creates a risk of configuration drift and causes the AI to follow outdated patterns. Automating bidirectional synchronization between project documentation and AI configuration remains an open problem.

Finally, even with methodology encoding, the AI's compliance with probabilistic guidance (context files, skills, subagent instructions) is not guaranteed. The model should follow the encoded patterns but may deviate. The balance between probabilistic guidance and deterministic enforcement is itself a design challenge for the Agentic Architect.

6   Conclusion and Future Work

This position paper has made three contributions to the evolving field of AI-assisted software development. First, we introduced the concept of methodology encoding, that is, the systematic translation of a project's adopted methodology into AI tool configuration, as an approach for extending AI assistance beyond vibe coding to the entire software development lifecycle. Second, we illustrated methodology encoding concretely through Claude Code's extensibility mechanisms, showing how context files, skills, subagents, hooks, and plugins map to the classical components of software development methodology. Third, we defined the Agentic Architect as a new professional role that architects the agentic development environment by translating adopted methodologies into AI configurations, different from the Software Architect, who designs the product itself.

These contributions are conceptual and require empirical validation. Future work should include empirical studies of methodology encoding in real projects, investigating effectiveness, developer productivity, and artifact quality. A tool-agnostic formalization of methodology encoding would identify the minimal set of mechanisms that any AI development tool must support. Longitudinal studies of the Agentic Architect role adoption would track how organizations create and evolve this role. Research into automated configuration synchronization, specifically detecting when documentation changes require configuration updates, would address the drift problem we identified. Finally, comparative studies across AI development tools would establish whether the patterns we identified in Claude Code generalize to other platforms.

The evolution from vibe coding to methodology encoding represents a maturation of AI-assisted software development. Vibe coding demonstrated that natural language can drive code generation. Methodology encoding extends this insight to the full lifecycle, with the discipline and structure that complex systems require. The Agentic Architect is the role that makes this possible, bridging between human methodology knowledge and AI configuration to create development environments where AI amplifies the team's expertise rather than replacing it.

7   Disclosure of Interests.

The authors have no competing interests to declare that are relevant to the content of this article.

References

1. Rico, S., Öberg, L.-M.: Challenges and opportunities for generative ai in software engineering: a managerial view. In: Proceedings of the 33rd ACM International Conference on the Foundations of Software Engineering, pp. 1338–1344. Association for Computing Machinery, New York (2025)
2. Kirchner, K., Bolisani, E., Kassaneh, T.C., Scarso, E., Taraghi, N.: Generative AI meets knowledge management: insights from software development practices. Knowl. Process. Manag. **32**, 223–235 (2025). https://doi.org/10.1002/kpm.70004
3. Kemell, K.-K., Saarikallio, M., Nguyen-Duc, A., Abrahamsson, P.: Still just personal assistants? – a multiple case study of generative AI adoption in software organizations. Inf. Softw. Technol. **186**, 107805 (2025). https://doi.org/10.1016/j.infsof.2025.107805
4. De Silva, D., et al.: Generative AI vibe coding for prototyping industrial systems. In: 2025 IEEE 34th International Symposium on Industrial Electronics (ISIE), pp. 1–6. IEEE, Toronto (2025). https://doi.org/10.1109/ISIE62713.2025.11124737
5. Banh, L., Holldack, F., Strobel, G.: Copiloting the future: how generative AI transforms software engineering. Inf. Softw. Technol. **183**, 107751 (2025). https://doi.org/10.1016/j.infsof.2025.107751
6. Abrahão, S., Grundy, John, Pezzè, M., Storey, M.-A., Tamburri, D.A.: Software engineering by and for humans in an AI era. ACM Trans. Softw. Eng. Methodol. **34** (2025). https://doi.org/10.1145/3715111
7. Elgendy, I.A., et al.: Responsible vibe coding: architecture, opportunities, and research agenda. J. Comput. Inf. Syst. 1–19 (2026). https://doi.org/10.1080/08874417.2026.2621186
8. Treude, C., Gerosa, M.A.: How developers interact with AI: a taxonomy of human-AI Collaboration in software engineering. In: 2025 IEEE/ACM Second International Conference on AI Foundation Models and Software Engineering (Forge), pp. 236–240. IEEE, Ottawa (2025). https://doi.org/10.1109/Forge66646.2025.00033
9. Gadde, A.: Democratizing software engineering through generative AI and vibe coding: the evolution of no-code development. J. Comput. Sci. Technol. Stud. **7**, 556–572 (2025)
10. Yu, L.: Paradigm shift on coding productivity using GenAI. In: Proceedings of the 29th International Conference on Evaluation and Assessment in Software Engineering, pp. 708–713. Association for Computing Machinery, New York (2025). https://doi.org/10.1145/3756681.3757081
11. Russo, D.: Navigating the complexity of generative AI adoption in software engineering. ACM Trans. Softw. Eng. Methodol. **33**, 135:1–135:50 (2024). https://doi.org/10.1145/3652154
12. Kam, M., et al.: What do professional software developers need to know to succeed in an age of Artificial Intelligence? In: Proceedings of the 33rd ACM International Conference on the Foundations of Software Engineering, pp. 947–958. Association for Computing Machinery, New York (2025). https://doi.org/10.1145/3696630.3727251
13. Nguyen-Duc, A., et al.: Generative artificial intelligence for software engineering—a research agenda. Softw. Pract. Exp. **55**, 1806–1843 (2025). https://doi.org/10.1002/spe.70005
14. Ayyagari, B.: From Agile to Adaptive Intent-Driven Development (AIDD): The AI-First Paradigm Shift. https://medium.com/@binoy_93931/from-agile-to-adaptive-intent-driven-development-aidd-the-ai-first-paradigm-shift-e07e5c7df1ec. Accessed 11 Feb 2026
15. Kiro: Agentic AI development from prototype to production. https://kiro.dev/. Accessed 11 Feb 2026
16. Sommerville, I.: Software Engineering. Pearson, Boston (2017)
17. Russo, D., et al.: Generative AI in software engineering must be human-centered: the copenhagen manifesto. J. Syst. Softw. **216**, 112115 (2024). https://doi.org/10.1016/j.jss.2024.112115

Toward GenAI-Based Contextual Metadata Generation for Reusability: Evaluating Metadata Extraction from Scientific Publications

Burak Toptas[1]([✉]) [iD], Richard Lenz[2] [iD], and Rainer Groß[1] [iD]

[1] Technische Hochschule Nuremberg Georg Simon Ohm, Keßlerplatz 12, 90489 Nuremberg, Germany
{burak.toptas,rainer.gross}@th-nuernberg.de
[2] Friedrich-Alexander-Universität Erlangen-Nuremberg, Martensstr. 3, 91058 Erlangen, Germany
richard.lenz@fau.de

Abstract. Metadata is crucial to improve the findability and reusability of research outputs, thereby contributing to a more efficient use of research resources. Their effectiveness increases as metadata goes beyond purely descriptive elements and captures richer contextual information. However, creating such context-rich metadata remains a time-consuming task for researchers. Recent advances in Large Language Models (LLMs) offer the potential to provide scalable, automated metadata annotation to support research communities. Therefore, we pursue the development of an LLM-based metadata annotation service that automatically generates structured metadata, aimed at reducing documentation effort for researchers while improving findability and reusability. The deployment of such a service, however, raises critical quality concerns. Manual metadata annotations are commonly treated as ground truth, despite being selective, potentially incomplete, and influenced by interpretation. Conversely, LLM-generated metadata may introduce additional uncertainties, including hallucinated metadata elements. To address this challenge, we conduct a comparative evaluation of metadata annotations generated by human annotators and one LLM (ChatGPT-5.2) from 22 scientific publications using an identical structured schema. Annotation quality is assessed along two complementary dimensions: completeness, capturing coverage of publication-supported metadata elements, and semantic correctness, measuring the degree to which annotated metadata values are textually grounded. Our analysis indicates that LLM-based annotations achieve higher completeness across most metadata categories, particularly for contextual and process-oriented elements that are frequently omitted in manual annotations. Importantly, although the higher completeness of LLM-based annotations might intuitively suggest lower semantic correctness and an increased risk of hallucinated metadata elements, our experimental results do not support this assumption. By operationalizing metadata quality through explicit dimensions, this work provides measurable criteria for evaluating automated metadata annotations.

Keywords: Automated metadata annotation · Large language models · Metadata quality assessment · Research data management

K. Kirchner et al. (Eds.): I4CS 2026, CCIS 3007, pp. 216–236, 2026.
https://doi.org/10.1007/978-3-032-27096-2_12

1 Introduction

Metadata is crucial to improve the findability, interpretability, and reusability of research outputs and thus supports a more efficient use of research resources [1]. Its value increases when metadata goes beyond descriptive fields and captures richer contextual information needed for reuse. Despite their importance, metadata creation is widely perceived as time-consuming and resource intensive [2, 3]. This so-called *metadata dilemma* reflects a misalignment of incentives: while metadata provide high collective value to the research community, they offer limited benefit to individual researchers, yet demand considerable effort [4]. As a result, widely adopted metadata standards were intentionally designed to be simple and generic to ensure broad acceptance [5]. However, this simplicity comes at the cost of expressiveness when reuse requires detailed context (e.g., methodology, experimental setup, or used instruments) [2]. A considerable proportion of reuse-relevant context is already documented in scientific publications but remain largely unstructured and therefore difficult to integrate into metadata records at scale. Chao [2] demonstrates that methodological sections of scientific papers contain valuable information on sampling, instruments, and procedures that can be systematically mapped to metadata fields. Against this background, we developed in our prior study the Contextually Comprehensive Metadata Model (CCMM), which extends Dublin Core with four additional categories [6]. The model extends bibliographic elements with contextual knowledge and thus bridges the gap between generic and domain-specific standards. Beyond this, the model is designed to serve as a target schema for Large Language Models (LLMs) to enable automated metadata extraction. It defines, which metadata should be extracted, how it should be structured, and provides semantic anchors that guide LLMs during prompting and parsing of unstructured sources. Building on this schema-first design, we pursue the vision of an LLM-based metadata annotation service that automates CCMM-based metadata annotation. In a final scenario, the service ingests a research output, generates draft metadata for each CCMM element, and exposes the extracted values together with their textual evidence to the user. Researchers can then review, correct, or accept suggestions and export the resulting metadata record into RDM systems or repositories. Such a service aims to reduce documentation effort while improving the coverage of reuse-relevant context. Conceptually, this approach integrates LLM-based information extraction into digital research infrastructures. Its evaluation therefore extends beyond metadata quality and addresses broader questions of system reliability, performance, transparency, and trust in AI-supported applications. However, while LLM-based metadata extraction promises efficiency gains and improved coverage, it raises methodological questions how the quality of LLM-generated metadata can be assessed in the absence of a reliable ground truth. Existing evaluation approaches often implicitly treat human annotations as a ground truth. Yet, prior work in annotation research highlights that manual annotations are frequently incomplete, selective, and influenced by individual expertise, attention, and subjective interpretation [7]. This is particularly critical for complex and context-rich metadata elements, where relevant aspects may be overlooked rather than explicitly judged as irrelevant. Consequently, treating human annotations as ground truth risks interpreting missing annotations as missing information. Preliminary observations in our ongoing research suggest that LLM-generated metadata exhibit higher details than human annotation, capturing methodological and contextual aspects that are not documented by human annotators. While this may initially appear as superior performance, such findings cannot be interpreted uncritically. Increased details may also introduce inaccuracies, redundancies, or misinterpretations. This creates a paradoxical situation, where LLM-generated metadata may be more comprehensive, yet their completeness and correctness remain uncertain without a validated reference. Based on this observation, we hypothesize that LLMs can systematically identify relevant contextual metadata elements that are overlooked or not explicitly considered by human annotators. Importantly, this hypothesis does not presuppose higher overall quality of LLM-generated metadata but frames completeness and correctness as an empirically testable dimension.

Considering the aforementioned challenges, our evaluation of LLM-based metadata annotation should adhere to four requirements. First, the evaluation must avoid implicitly treating human annotation as ground truth and instead account for potential incompleteness in manual annotations. Second, it should distinguish between different quality dimensions, rather than consolidating quality into a single metric. Third, the evaluation must operate at the level of individual metadata elements to enable detailed comparison between human and LLM-generated annotations. Finally, the assessment process should be transparent to support future extensions toward validated reference metadata. Against this backdrop, this paper addresses the following research question: *How can differences between human and LLM-based annotations be evaluated without assuming human annotations as ground truth?* Rather than positioning either approach as inherently superior, this study adopts a self-critical perspective and treats ground truth construction as an explicit research challenge. We make the following main contributions. First, we propose a schema-driven evaluation design for LLM-based contextual metadata annotation that operationalizes completeness and semantic correctness at metadata-element level. Second, we apply this design to 22 publications and provide element-level evidence that human and LLM-based annotations differ systematically in coverage of publication-supported aspects and in semantic correctness across elements. Finally, we derive implications for a metadata service and outline the concept of a potential service.

2   Background Context

2.1   Contextual Metadata and the CCMM

Metadata provides structured descriptions that support discovery, interpretation, and reuse of research data. In RDM, the practical challenge is not the absence of metadata standards directly, but the difficulty of capturing sufficient context without imposing tedious documentation effort on researchers. Generic standards such as Dublin Core provide an interoperable baseline but remain limited in representing rich contextual information for reuse [8]. This motivates extensions that preserve interoperability while adding structured context. Although a notable amount of context relevant to reuse is documented in scientific publications but remains unstructured and therefore difficult to integrate into metadata records on a large scale [2]. To address this tension while maintaining compatibility with established standards, the CCMM extends Dublin Core with four additional categories that operationalize recurring potentially reuse-relevant documentation elements. In Fig. 1 the Dublin Core-based elements are retained as descriptive core to support cross-domain interoperability.

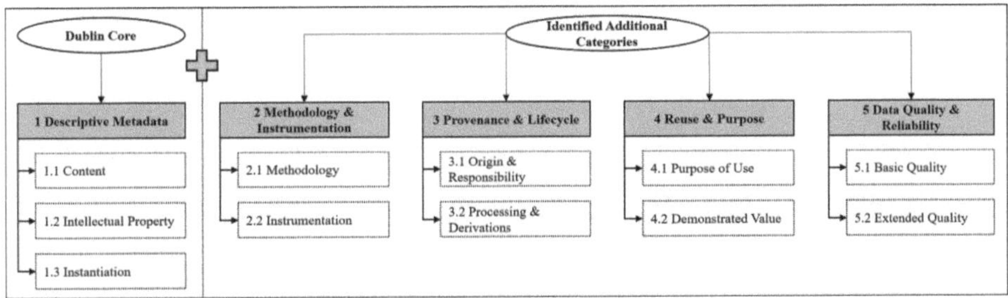

Fig. 1. The Contextually Comprehensive Metadata Model (CCMM) [6]

As illustrated in Fig. 1, the CCMM is organized hierarchically into categories, subcategories, and metadata elements. Across the four contextual categories, the model comprises $n = 29$ metadata elements, which serve as the unit of analysis in the evaluation metrics reported in Subsect. 3.5. The additional contextual categories capture complementary reuse perspectives: *Methodology & Instrumentation* captures methodological and technical conditions of data creation (e.g., methodology, instruments, computational methods). *Provenance & Lifecycle* captures origin, responsibility, and processing history (e.g., where/when data were created and how they were processed). *Reuse & Purpose* captures intended use and demonstrated value (e.g., use cases, reuse examples). *Data Quality & Reliability* captures indicators of trust, robustness, and integrity (e.g., validation, uncertainty measures, fixity/integrity checks). For extraction, metadata elements can be decomposed into fine-grained contextual aspects, which represent the smallest analytical unit in this study. For instance, the subcategory *2.2 Instrumentation* includes elements such as *data collection method,* or *equipment/materials*, each of which may comprise multiple explicit aspects (e.g., device type, software, measurement setting) distributed across the publication text. Moreover, the subcategories can be extended according to domain-specific needs. This enables the definition of metadata elements without requiring a complete reinvention of metadata structures. For instance, the subcategory *Instrumentation* can be extended in the context of fracture mechanics with elements such as *temperature, moisture,* or *test velocity* [9]. Importantly, the schema defines explicit extraction targets and thereby supports transparent, element-level assessment of LLM-based metadata generation.

2.2 LLM-Based Metadata Extraction and Evaluation

Recent research has increasingly explored the use of LLMs for automated metadata extraction from scientific publications. This is motivated by the high cost and limited scalability of manual metadata curation. Early work in this area focused on identifying bibliographic entities. Watanabe et al. [10] analyze how well LLMs can extract dataset-related metadata (e.g., name, usage, description) from conference papers. Their evaluation of Llama 3 and Mistral 7B across 777 papers shows that while LLMs can scale extraction across documents, a trade-off between coverage and accuracy is evident through quantitative evaluation. The authors highlight systematic error sources, including the misclassification of model or method names as datasets and difficulties in correctly linking metadata elements to the corresponding dataset entity. This work provides early empirical evidence that LLM-based metadata extraction tends to be expansive but not necessarily reliable, underscoring the need for more detailed evaluation strategies. In highly specialized domains, Turner et al. [11] examine the use of GPT-4 for extracting structured metadata from neuroimaging publications. Focusing on annotation tasks in a domain ontology, they report performance levels comparable to trained human annotators across several metadata categories. Importantly, their analysis explicitly questions the assumption of human annotations as unquestioned ground truth. They note that even carefully curated human labels contain inconsistencies, omissions, and interpretative ambiguities. More recently, Alyafeai et al. [12] propose MOLE, a schema-driven framework for large scale metadata extraction and validation from scientific papers across multiple languages. Their work expands the number of extractable metadata attributes and introduces a benchmark with manually annotated reference metadata. MOLE incorporates explicit validation mechanisms, such as type checking, option constraints, and length enforcement and evaluates performance across a wide range of LLMs. While the framework represents an important step toward standardized evaluation, its assessment still relies on human generated reference annotations as the ground truth. The authors acknowledge that some metadata attributes may not be explicitly stated in the publication text, but the evaluation framework does not systematically distinguish between missing annotations and absent information.

In line with this, research in annotation studies and natural language processing consistently challenges the assumption that human annotations can be treated as unquestioned ground truth. Arstein and Poesio [13] emphasize that human labels and agreement outcomes depend on task framing, guidelines, specificity, and annotator judgment and therefore cannot be interpreted as a direct ground truth. Moreover, Pavlick and Kwiatkowski [14] show that disagreement can be systematic and irreducible even among competent annotators, suggesting that a single hard reference label may not exist for content-rich constructs. Building on this perspective, we formulate two hypotheses to guide our evaluation. H1: *LLM-based annotations tend to achieve higher completeness for context-rich metadate elements, capturing publication-supported aspects that are more likely to be omitted in manual annotations.* H2: *Higher completeness in LLM-based annotations may be accompanied by a higher number of unsupported aspects (e.g., hallucinations), potentially resulting in lower correctness for some metadata elements.*

2.3 Quality Dimensions for Metadata

Research in information quality consistently identifies completeness as a core quality dimension. Early conceptualizations by Wang and Strong [15] as well as Wand and Wang [16] describe completeness as an intrinsic property of information quality, independent of specific application contexts. A recent scoping review by Kumar et al. [17], synthesizing 55 metadata quality studies, further confirms completeness as the most frequently operationalized quality dimension in metadata assessment. In addition to completeness, this study considers correctness as a complementary quality dimension. While correctness is less frequently operationalized in prior metadata quality assessments [17], it is theoretically well-established in the information quality literature as a measure of factual validity and truthfulness of information [18, 19]. In the context of LLM-based metadata extraction, correctness becomes particularly relevant, as increased annotation coverage may introduce metadata values that are not explicitly covered by the source text. Therefore, correctness is included to systematically assess hallucination effects and determine whether annotated metadata values are actually reflected in the scientific publication.

Building on this foundation, we further specify completeness and correctness for our evaluation context. *Completeness* refers to whether all information necessary to describe a real-world phenomenon is present. Wand and Wang [16] define completeness as the ability of an information system to represent all meaningful states of the represented real-world system, rather than merely the presence or absence of specific data values. In the context of metadata quality, completeness may be assessed at different levels, including schema level completeness (i.e., whether all required metadata fields are defined) and data-level completeness (i.e., whether values are provided for these fields). Since this study aims to evaluate the quality of metadata annotations extracted from scientific publications, we focus exclusively on data-level completeness relative to the publication text. *Correctness* refers to the intellectual distance to which metadata values accurately represent the resource they describe. Literature distinguishes two levels of correctness: syntactic and semantic correctness [18, 19]. Syntactic correctness refers to the conformity of metadata values with grammatical rules, formatting constraints, and the specifications of a metadata standard or application profile. Common issues at this level include misspellings, invalid value ranges, or inconsistent formatting. Semantic correctness refers to the extent to which metadata values truthfully represent the underlying reality of the resource described, reflecting the absence of misrepresentation. This level of correctness requires comparison against a reliable reference source [14]. Since metadata annotations in our study are generated using a predefined schema with controlled input fields, syntactic correctness is ensured by design and is therefore not evaluated as a separate quality dimension. Instead, we focus on semantic correctness. In our context of metadata extraction from scientific publications, semantic correctness is defined as the degree to which annotated metadata values are factually supported by and consistent with the information stated in the publication text. This perspective is particularly relevant for evaluating LLM-based annotations, where increased completeness may introduce additional metadata elements that are not explicitly described in the source text.

3   Research Design

To systematically compare human and LLM-based metadata annotations without assuming human annotation as ground truth, this study adopts a structured evaluation design. Therefore, we combine a comparative annotation workflow with a Goal Question Metric (GQM) approach. The methodology is designed to enable an element-level assessment of metadata quality grounded in the source publication text.

3.1 Metadata Annotation

Human metadata annotations were collected through a survey-based annotation process using SoSci Survey [20]. Authors of scientific publications were invited to annotate their own papers according to the CCMM schema in order to leverage their domain knowledge and familiarity with the underlying research context. Participants were recruited across multiple research domains to ensure cross-domain applicability of the evaluation framework. In total, 22 publications were included in the study, each annotated by its corresponding author. No cross-annotation between participants was conducted. The survey provided predefined input fields and brief descriptions of each metadata element to support consistent interpretation across annotators. In a second step, we generated LLM-based metadata annotations for the collected set of publications using ChatGPT (web interface) with the GPT-5.2 model in Auto mode. For each publication, the corresponding full-text PDF was provided as input to ChatGPT and served as the source document for metadata extraction. To align the LLM task with the human survey instrument, we used a standardized prompt template that reflected the SoSci Survey structure. First, the prompt assigned a fixed metadata analyst role and explicitly restricted extraction to information explicitly stated in the PDF. Second, it presented the same element wording as the survey, and third, enforced the same response structure by combining controlled answer options with free-text fields where applicable. In addition, the prompt implemented two conservative control mechanisms to reduce unsupported additions: it instructed the model to output "Not available" if no reliable textual evidence could be identified, and allowed "Other…" only when the PDF explicitly contained information not covered by the predefined options. Human and LLM outputs were recorded for each metadata element and served as the basis for the subsequent aspect-level evaluation.

3.2 Overview of the GQM Approach

The GQM approach is a hierarchical model that begins with the definition of goals specifying the purpose of measurement, the object to be measured, the issue of measurement, and the viewpoint from which the measurement is conducted [21, 22]. During this process, the objectives are gradually refined into several questions that typically break down the problem into its main components. Each question is then refined into metrics. In some cases, a single metric can be used to address multiple questions. The resulting evaluation model comprises three levels [22]:

- *Conceptual level:* At this level, evaluation goals are defined for a specific object of measurement, taking into account the assessment purpose, viewpoint, and contextual environment.
- *Operational level:* A set of questions is derived to characterize how the defined evaluation goals can be addressed.
- *Quantitative level:* A dataset is associated with questions from the operational level to answer it quantitatively. These questions can be objective or subjective and depend on the object being measured and the viewpoint.

Although the GQM approach was originally proposed in software engineering, it has since been applied in a variety of other domains, including data quality assessment

[21]. In the following sections, we describe how the GQM approach is applied in this study.

3.3 Goal Definition

Following the GQM approach by Basili et al. [22] and Behkamal et al. [21], we define the primary goal of this study, derived from the research question, as follows: *Assessment of the quality of contextual metadata annotations extracted from scientific publications, comparing human- and LLM-based annotations with respect to their suitability for reuse, without assuming human annotation as ground truth.* This goal specifies the purpose of measurement (quality assessment), the object of measurement (contextual metadata annotations), the issue of measurement (differences in annotation quality between human and LLM-based approaches), and the viewpoint (RDM and reuse).

3.4 Question Formulation

At the operational level, the evaluation goal is refined into a set of guiding questions addressing the quality dimensions of metadata annotations. We formulate the questions for each quality dimension as follows. *Completeness* is defined as the degree to which contextual metadata elements explicitly supported by the publication are represented in the metadata annotation. Given that both human and LLM-based annotations are generated using an identical structured schema with predefined fields, completeness can be operationalized at the element level by assessing whether metadata elements covered by the publication are included in the annotation. Therefore, we formulate the following question: *To what extent are contextual metadata elements explicitly described in the scientific publication represented in the metadata annotation?*

Semantic correctness is defined as the degree to which selected metadata values are factually supported by the publication text, thereby distinguishing between improved coverage and potentially hallucinated or unsupported content. Accordingly, we formulate the following question to guide this dimension: *To what extent are the selected metadata values factually supported by the information stated in the publication?*

3.5 Quality Metrics

At the measurement level of the GQM approach, we operationalize completeness and semantic correctness using two metrics defined at the level of metadata elements.

As the CCMM is structured hierarchically into categories, subcategories, and metadata elements, each element (e.g., *Equipment & Materials*) can comprise multiple fine-grained contextual aspects. For example, a single metadata element such as *Equipment & Materials* may involve several aspects, such as the *used instruments*, *materials*, or *devices*. Both, completeness and semantic correctness are assessed at the aspect level, but aggregated at the level of metadata elements.

To describe the metrics used in our evaluation, we introduce the following notation. We denote the CCMM metadata elements by e_i with $i = 1, \ldots, n$, where n is the number of metadata elements in the CCMM. Publications in the evaluated corpus are denoted by p_j with $j = 1, \ldots, m$, where m is the number of annotated publications. For each metadata element e_i and publication p_j, we identify the set of contextual aspects that are explicitly stated in the publication text and belong to e_i. The number of such text-supported aspects is denoted by $A_{text}(e_i, p_j)$. To account for different annotation sources, we introduce z_k with $k = 1, \ldots, l$, representing the annotation source. In this study, $l = 2$, corresponding to a human annotator (z_1) and one LLM-based annotator (z_2). Therefore, we denote by $A_{covered}(e_i, p_j, z_k)$ the number of text-supported aspects that are covered by the corresponding annotation.

The text-supported aspect sets underlying $A_{text}(e_i, p_j)$ were constructed prior to evaluation by two authors of this study. Both reviewed the full text of each publication and extracted all contextual aspects relevant to the respective CCMM elements. Differences were resolved through discussion until consensus was reached. This reference construction was performed independently of both the human survey annotations and the LLM outputs. The resulting aspect sets represent a text-grounded decomposition of publication-supported information and serve as a structured reference for evaluation. Accordingly, they do not constitute a traditional external ground truth, but a structured representation of the textual evidence available for each (e_i, p_j) pair.

Completeness captures the extent to which text-supported aspects are represented in an annotation. For each metadata element e_i, publication p_j, and annotator source z_k, completeness is defined as the proportion of text-supported aspects covered by the annotation:

$$Comp\left(e_i, p_j, z_k\right) = \frac{A_{covered}(e_i, p_j, z_k)}{A_{text}(e_i, p_j)}$$

To obtain an element-level completeness score for each annotator type, we average publication-level completeness across the m publications:

$$Comp(e_i, z_k) = \frac{1}{m} \sum_{j=1}^{m} Comp\left(e_i, p_j, z_k\right) = \frac{1}{m} \sum_{j=1}^{m} \frac{A_{covered}(e_i, p_j, z_k)}{A_{text}(e_i, p_j)}$$

A completeness value of 1 indicates that all aspects explicitly reported in the publication for the respective metadata element are covered by the annotation, whereas lower values indicate partial or selective coverage. Since both human and LLM-based annotations were produced under identical schema constraints, differences in completeness reflect differences in aspect coverage rather than schema validity.

Semantic correctness captures whether the aspects selected in an annotation are factually supported by the publication text. For each metadata element e_i, publication p_j, and annotator source z_k, we assess each selected aspect with respect to the availability of explicit textual evidence in the corresponding publication. Selected aspects are classified as covered if they can be grounded in the publication text and as uncovered if no corresponding evidence can be identified. Using the notation introduced above, $A_{covered}(e_i, p_j, z_k)$ denotes the number of selected aspects that are supported by the publication, and $A_{uncovered}(e_i, p_j, z_k)$ denotes the number of selected aspects that are not supported. Semantic correctness is then defined as the proportion of selected aspects that are covered:

$$Corr(e_i, p_j, z_k) = \frac{A_{covered}(e_i, p_j, z_k)}{A_{covered}(e_i, p_j, z_k) + A_{uncovered}(e_i, p_j, z_k)}$$

To obtain an element-level semantic correctness score for each annotator type, we average publication-level correctness across the m publications:

$$Corr(e_i, z_k) = \frac{1}{m} \sum_{j=1}^{m} Corr(e_i, p_j, z_k) = \frac{1}{m} \sum_{j=1}^{m} \frac{A_{covered}(e_i, p_j, z_k)}{A_{covered}(e_i, p_j, z_k) + A_{uncovered}(e_i, p_j, z_k)}$$

A semantic correctness value of 1 indicates that all selected aspects for a given metadata element are textually supported. Lower values indicate the presence of unsupported selections and thus potential over-interpretation or hallucinated additions.

Since semantic correctness depends on which and how many aspects an annotator selects, it is inherently annotator-dependent and must be interpreted jointly with completeness. Element-level results are reported separately for each annotation source z_k using the element-level mean scores $Comp(e_i, z_k)$ and $Corr(e_i, z_k)$, each obtained by averaging publication-level scores across the m publications. The annotation sources correspond to a human annotator (z_1) and an LLM-based annotator (z_2). To facilitate direct element-level comparison between these two sources, we compute delta values as the differences between their mean scores:

$$\Delta_{Comp}(e_i) = Comp(e_i, z_1) - Comp(e_i, z_2),$$

$$\Delta_{Corr}(e_i) = Corr(e_i, z_1) - Corr(e_i, z_2).$$

Negative delta values therefore indicate higher mean scores for LLM-based annotations, while positive values indicate higher mean scores for humans. Considering both metrics together enables distinguishing different annotation strategies, such as conservative behavior characterized by high correctness but limited coverage, and more expansive annotation behavior characterized by broader coverage with potential correctness trade-offs. Importantly, joint analysis allows evaluating whether increased completeness is accompanied by sustained semantic correctness, indicating more detailed yet text-grounded annotation, or whether higher coverage is achieved at the expense of unsupported or potentially hallucinated content. This combined perspective is particularly relevant for evaluating LLM-based metadata extraction, where LLMs may systematically differ from human annotators in both coverage and selection behavior.

4 Results

4.1 Dataset and Sample Characteristics

To establish an empirical basis for this study, data was collected from December 12, 2025 to February 9, 2026, resulting in 25 completed surveys. Prior to analysis, three documents were excluded from the sample: one manuscript that had not yet been formally published at the time of data collection, one doctoral dissertation, and one contribution that did not meet common peer-review criteria. The final dataset therefore comprises 22 scientific publications. To contextualize the annotation setting, descriptive characteristics of the annotated publications were recorded. The publications originate from a heterogeneous set of academic disciplines. Specifically, 15 publications originate from computer science, followed by three from engineering, and one publication each from chemistry, humanities, medicine, and physics. Regarding academic roles, the majority of annotations were provided by PhD candidates ($n = 14$), followed by postdoctoral researchers ($n = 5$). Additionally, two professors and one lecturer participated in the study. These descriptive characteristics were collected to contextualize the annotation process and the resulting metadata but were not used as control variables in the subsequent analysis. Table 1 shows the heterogeneous set of academic disciplines for the collected publications.

Table 1. Disciplinary distribution of the annotated publications

Academic discipline	Publication
Computer science	[23–37]
Engineering	[38–40]
Chemistry	[41]
Humanities	[42]
Medicine	[43]
Physics	[44]

In addition to generating metadata annotations, participants assessed the perceived suitability of the proposed metadata schema for supporting research data reusability. Specifically, respondents evaluated the statement *"The presented metadata schema promotes the reusability of research data in accordance with the FAIR principles"* on a five-point Likert scale ranging from *strongly disagree* to *strongly agree*. Overall, responses indicate a predominantly positive assessment. Of the 22 respondents, 16 agreed *(rather agree: n = 10; strongly agree: n = 6)*, while five were neutral. Only one participant strongly disagreed, and no responses were recorded for rather disagree. These findings suggest that the schema is largely perceived as supportive of data reusability, but does not constitute a direct measure of annotation quality.

4.2 Evaluation Results

This section reports the results of the element-level comparison between human and LLM-based metadata annotations. Results are presented in separate sections for completeness and semantic correctness and are complemented by a joint analysis examining the relationship between both quality dimensions. Table 2 summarizes the mean values of completeness and semantic correctness for both annotation approaches across the

CCMM metadata elements and reports the corresponding mean differences. Negative delta values therefore indicate higher scores for LLM-based annotations.

Table 2. Element-level mean values of semantic correctness and completeness for human and LLM-based annotations

Subcategory	Metadata Elements (e_i)	Means Semantic Correctness ($Corr(e_i, z_k)$)			Means Completeness ($Comp(e_i, z_k)$)		
		Human (z_1)	LLM (z_2)	Δ	Human (z_1)	LLM (z_2)	Δ
2.1 Methodology	(e_1) Methodology	0.89	0.89	0.00	0.66	0.96	−0.30
	(e_2) Data collection method	0.89	1.00	−0.11	0.62	0.96	−0.34
	(e_3) Experimental design	0.64	0.91	−0.27	0.50	0.95	−0.45
	(e_4) Sample types	0.84	0.95	−0.11	0.68	0.92	−0.24
2.2 Instrumentation	(e_5) Equipment & Materials	0.95	1.00	−0.05	0.83	0.98	−0.15
	(e_6) Computational/analytical app	0.66	0.97	−0.31	0.49	0.91	−0.42
	(e_7) System/environment	0.43	0.89	−0.46	0.41	0.80	−0.39
	(e_8) Technical dependencies	0.71	0.86	−0.15	0.59	0.80	−0.21
3.1 Origin & Responsibility	(e_9) Location	0.95	1.00	−0.05	0.93	0.98	−0.05
	(e_{10}) Context of creation	0.75	0.98	−0.23	0.83	0.98	−0.15
	(e_{11}) Project/funding	0.80	1.00	−0.20	0.80	1.00	−0.20
	(e_{12}) Data origin	0.80	1.00	−0.20	0.69	0.91	−0.22
	(e_{13}) Date (collected/published)	0.44	0.98	−0.54	0.37	0.96	−0.59
3.2 Processing & Derivations	(e_{14}) Activity workflow steps	0.80	0.98	−0.18	0.45	0.97	−0.52
	(e_{15}) Data processing/analysis type	0.48	0.91	−0.43	0.36	0.88	−0.52
	(e_{16}) Relations to works/datasets	0.67	0.95	−0.28	0.52	0.86	−0.34
	(e_{17}) Dependency	0.80	0.86	−0.06	0.74	0.85	−0.11
4.1 Purpose of use	(e_{18}) Intended use	0.95	1.00	−0.05	0.95	1.00	−0.05

(continued)

Table 2. (*continued*)

Subcategory	Metadata Elements (e_i)	Means Semantic Correctness ($Corr(e_i, z_k)$)			Means Completeness ($Comp(e_i, z_k)$)		
		Human (z_1)	LLM (z_2)	Δ	Human (z_1)	LLM (z_2)	Δ
	(e_{19}) Reuse potential	0.86	1.00	−0.14	0.86	1.00	−0.14
4.2 Demonstrated value	(e_{20}) Example reuse cases	0.50	1.00	−0.50	0.49	0.98	−0.49
	(e_{21}) Recommended uses	0.52	0.98	−0.46	0.42	0.91	−0.49
	(e_{22}) Possible analyses/patterns	0.80	0.83	−0.03	0.60	0.61	−0.01
	(e_{23}) Notable observations	0.50	0.98	−0.48	0.41	0.87	−0.46
5.1 Basic quality	(e_{24}) Validation & Issues	0.83	0.97	−0.14	0.62	0.86	−0.24
	(e_{25}) Replicates/samples	0.75	0.95	−0.20	0.65	0.82	−0.17
	(e_{26}) Error & Uncertainty measures	0.91	0.91	0.00	0.88	0.91	−0.03
5.2 Extended quality	(e_{27}) Completeness & Structure	0.55	0.68	−0.13	0.55	0.68	−0.13
	(e_{28}) Quality procedure	0.73	0.98	−0.25	0.59	0.76	−0.17
	(e_{29}) Fixity & Integrity checks	0.91	1.00	−0.09	0.91	1.00	−0.09

The reported values reflect the average performance across the studied corpus at the granularity of contextual aspects. Across the majority of metadata elements, LLM-based annotations achieve higher completeness and equal or higher semantic correctness compared to human annotations. Importantly, the observed differences are not confined to a single CCMM category but occur across methodological, provenance-related, processing-oriented, purpose-related, and quality-related elements, suggesting systematic differences in annotation behavior rather than isolated element specific deviations.

4.3 Completeness of Metadata Annotations

The analysis of the completeness metrics indicates pronounced differences between human and LLM-based annotations. For nearly all metadata elements, LLM-based annotations yield higher completeness values (negative Δ), indicating broader coverage of contextual aspects that are supported by the publications. Since completeness is defined relative to $A_{text}(e_i, p_j)$, higher completeness reflects that a larger share of the publication-supported aspects is captured in the annotation, rather than merely indicating that more fields are populated. This pattern is illustrated in Fig. 2, which shows the mean values of completeness for human and LLM-based annotations across all metadata elements.

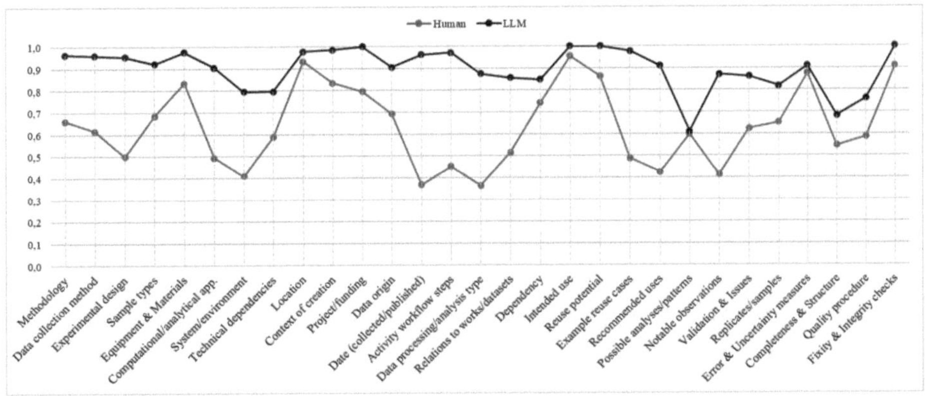

Fig. 2. Element-level mean values of completeness for human and LLM-based annotations

Large completeness gaps are particularly evident for elements that comprise multiple fine-grained aspects and require integrating information distributed across different sections of a paper. Notable examples include *Activity workflow steps* ($\Delta = -0.52$), *Data processing/analysis type* ($\Delta = -0.52$), *Example reuse cases* ($\Delta = -0.49$), and *Recommended uses* ($\Delta = -0.49$). In contrast, elements with more standardized and clearly stated reporting show smaller differences (e.g., *Location, Intended use*), although LLM-based annotations still attain equal or higher completeness in these cases. Overall, the results suggest that omissions in human annotations concentrate in elements where relevant evidence is explicit but fragmented, whereas the LLM more consistently captures dispersed contextual aspects.

4.4   Semantic Correctness of Metadata Annotations

The semantic correctness results largely mirror the patterns observed for completeness. Across most metadata elements, LLM-based annotations achieve equal or higher correctness values than human annotators, indicating that broader coverage is not systematically associated with reduced textual evidence. In other words, the completeness advantage of the LLM is overall accompanied by stable or improved text-grounded selection of aspects. Under this operationalization, lower correctness values indicate the presence of selected aspects for which no explicit supporting evidence can be identified in the publication text ($A_{uncovered}(e_i, p_j, z_k) > 0$). Figure 3 visualizes this pattern.

The strongest differences in the mean values of semantic correctness occur for elements related to temporal, procedural, and system-level information, for which evidence is often fragmented yet explicitly stated. Examples include *Date (collected/published)* ($\Delta = -0.54$), *Example reuse cases* ($\Delta = -0.50$), *Notable observations* ($\Delta = -0.48$), and *Recommended uses* ($\Delta = -0.46$). For elements with precise and clearly reported information, correctness values converge between both approaches (e.g., *Methodology*

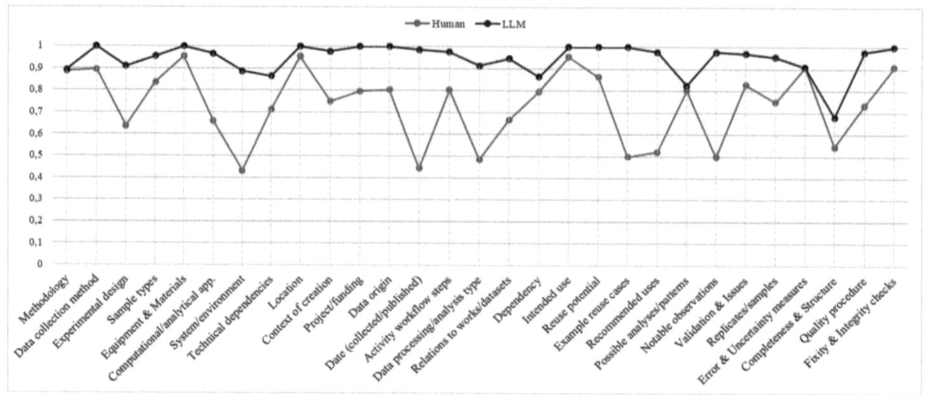

Fig. 3. Element-level mean semantic correctness for human and LLM-based annotations

with $\Delta = 0.00$; *Error & Uncertainty measures* with $\Delta = 0.00$), suggesting comparable text-evidence when information is explicitly and unambiguously reported. Given the bounded (0,1) scale and near-ceiling semantic correctness value for several elements, some differences may be conservative estimates.

4.5 Joint Analysis of Completeness and Semantic Correctness

To examine the relationship between completeness and semantic correctness, we conducted a joint analysis based on element-level differences of the mean values between human annotators and the LLM for both dimensions. Figure 4 plots these deltas across metadata elements and reveals a strong positive linear association between completeness and semantic correctness.

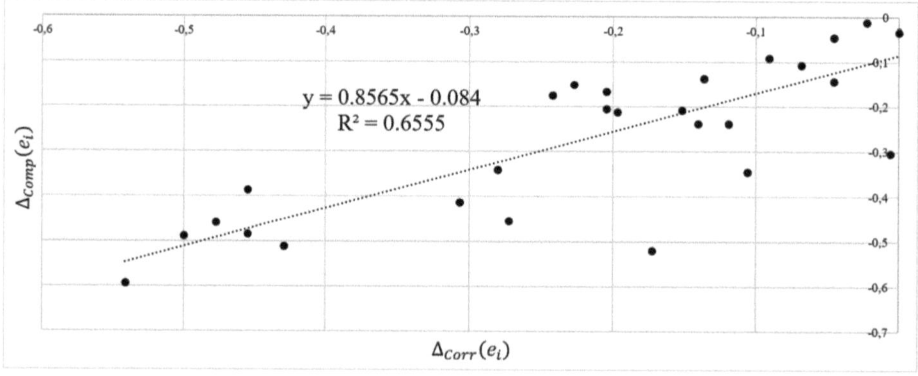

Fig. 4. Association between element-level deltas in semantic correctness and completeness

Pearson´s correlation coefficient is $r = 0.81$, indicating that metadata elements with larger LLM advantages in semantic correctness tend to also exhibit larger LLM advantages in completeness. Consistent with this association, the linear regression model accounts for a substantial share of the variance in completeness Δ ($R^2 = 0.66$). The estimated slope ($= 0.86$) indicates that differences in semantic correctness Δ are associated with proportionally similar differences in completeness Δ at the element level. Taken together, the joint analysis suggests that, within this dataset and scoring scheme, broader coverage in LLM-based annotations typically co-occurs with equal or higher semantic correctness. This pattern is consistent with an expansive annotation behavior that remains largely text-grounded at the element level.

5 Conclusion

This study sets out to compare human and LLM-based contextual metadata annotations. Across most CCMM metadata elements, the results show higher mean values of completeness for LLM-based annotations and equal or higher mean values of semantic correctness. A key interpretation is that, within the present scoring scheme, LLM-based annotation tends to exhibit broader coverage of publication-supported aspects. This is particularly visible for elements where relevant contextual information is typically distributed across a publication. In such cases, human annotators appear more prone to omission, which is consistent with the practical challenge of consolidating dispersed evidence under time constraints. By contrast, when information is precise and clearly stated, completeness and semantic correctness values converge. Importantly, the results should not be interpreted as demonstrating that LLM annotations are better in general sense. Instead, the findings highlight that the two annotation sources produce systematically different coverage profiles under identical schema constraints. In particular, higher completeness values for LLMs indicate that LLMs populate a larger number of aspects that are supported by the publication text. Whether this additional detail is beneficial for specific reuse scenarios depends on individual needs. In other words, the empirical pattern can be interpreted as grounded expansion in selected aspects rather than as a universal claim of quality superiority. Moreover, a central implication of the results concerns the ground truth problem in evaluating automated metadata extraction. If human annotations are incomplete, treating them as unquestioned ground truth risks interpreting missing human selections as absent information. This study addresses this methodological tension by explicitly separating two quality dimensions. The combined perspective makes it possible to distinguish between different error types and behaviors: selective omission (low completeness but high correctness), grounded expansion (high completeness with stable correctness), and unsupported expansion (high completeness with reduced correctness). The observed pattern in this study aligns primarily with the second case. Consistent with *H1*, LLM-based annotations cover more publication-supported aspects, while *H2* is not supported at the aggregate level, as the completeness gains do not coincide with a systematic decrease in semantic correctness. This framing is particularly relevant for human-centered AI because it emphasizes how LLMs can support the automation of metadata generation under clear constraints and human oversight. Rather than positioning either humans or LLMs as inherently superior, the results suggest that value arises from two sources: understanding how each differs in coverage and evidence, and designing review processes that make these differences actionable. In conclusion, the proposed evaluation design operationalizes the requirements outlined in the introduction through a text-grounded, element-level comparison across two complementary quality dimensions and provides a transparent basis for more robust reference formation in future work.

5.1 Research Contributions

The theoretical contributions of this study rely on contextual metadata, RDM, and human-centered evaluation of AI-assisted annotations. First, it proposes an evaluation approach for LLM-based contextual metadata annotation that does not implicitly assume human annotations as ground truth. By placing evaluation in publication text and assessing both coverage and textual support, the approach addresses a methodological gap in current extraction benchmarks that rely on manual reference labels. Second, the study operationalizes metadata quality at the fine-grained contextual aspects within metadata elements. This aspect-level operationalization aligns measurement with the structure of contextual metadata and enables element-level comparability across annotation sources. As a result, completeness is interpreted as coverage of publication-supported aspects, and semantic correctness is interpreted as textual evidence of selected aspects. Third, the findings provide empirical evidence for a recurring annotation pattern under schema constraints. Specifically, LLM-based annotations tend to achieve broader coverage without showing a systematic reduction in textual support at the element level.

From a practical perspective, the results suggest that LLM-based annotation can serve as a scalable method for increasing contextual metadata coverage, particularly for elements where relevant information is dispersed across publications. At the same time, the need for human oversight remains important, not because LLM output is necessarily undergrounded in aggregate, but due to varying metadata quality requirements across reuse contexts and the risk of unsupported expansion (e.g., hallucinations). Therefore, we make three design recommendations for human-centered, AI-oriented metadata services. First, *LLM-first drafting with evidence-linked review*: LLM output should be presented as suggested aspects accompanied by explicit textual evidence (e.g., quoted spans or pointers to sections). This supports transparency and enables rapid verification of evidence rather than requiring researchers to re-read full documents. Second, *risk-based human-in-the-loop verification*: Review effort can be prioritized toward metadata elements that show large completeness gaps between human and LLM annotations, or are known to require consolidation of dispersed context (e.g., activity workflow steps, processing details). This focuses human attention where omission and misinterpretation risks are highest. Third, *schema-first constraints as a safety mechanism*: Constraining LLM annotation through a structured schema and explicit option sets helps prevent unconstrained free-text generation and supports auditability. In practice, this implies standardized prompt templates, consistent parsing rules, and versioned model configurations to ensure reproducibility and accountability.

5.2 Limitations and Future Work

Several limitations should be considered when interpreting the results. First, completeness depends on the identification of publication supported aspect sets. Although evidence evaluation in the publication text increases transparency, aspect identification remains a manual and potentially interpretative step. The approach should therefore be understood as a structured decomposition of explicit text evidence rather than a ground truth of the underlying research reality. Second, the reported element-level means are aggregated across publications. This improves stability for element-level patterns but limits conclusions about variability across individual papers, domains, or annotators. In addition, the joint analysis is conducted across metadata elements rather than across publications, which constrains statistical inference and requires cautious interpretation of correlation and regression results as descriptive associations. Third, human annotations were provided by paper authors, which leverages domain knowledge but may introduce self-reporting biases and differences between what authors implicit know and what is explicitly reported. The semantic correctness metric mitigates this risk by evaluating evidence strictly relative to the publication text, yet the process may still reflect selective reporting and interpretation. Finally, the study is based on a limited corpus and a single LLM under consistent prompt conditions. While this controlled design enables a stable comparison between human and LLM-based annotations, it restricts the generalizability of the quantitative findings. Results may depend on domain-specific reporting types, the prompt design, and the employed model. Importantly, the objective of this study was not to benchmark different LLMs, but to evaluate a schema-driven assessment framework under controlled conditions. Generalization to other schemas, documents, models, or extraction settings requires further research. Future work can extend the present study along several directions. First, analyses per publication should quantify variability and uncertainty rather than relying just on corpus-level means. Second, reliability checks for aspect identification and correctness judgments should be strengthened through additional raters. Third, a two-stage human-in-the-loop evaluation should be implemented in which LLM-generated aspects are reviewed by authors or independent curators. This would directly test whether aspects missing from human annotations are overlooked, judged irrelevant, or insufficiently supported by text. Fourth, future evaluations should include additional LLMs to assess cross-model robustness of the proposed evaluation framework. Finally, future work should evaluate schema fit and adaption across domains and investigate how metadata models can be tailored to reuse contexts without risking interoperability.

Disclosure of Interests. The authors have no competing interests to declare that are relevant to the content of this article.

References

1. Anger, M., Wendelborn, C., Winkler, E.C., Schickhardt, C.: Neither carrots nor sticks? Challenges surrounding data sharing from the perspective of research funding agencies—a qualitative expert interview study. PLoS ONE **17**(2), 1–25 (2022)
2. Chao, T.: Mapping methods metadata for research data. Int. J. Digit. Curation **10**(1), 82–94 (2015). https://doi.org/10.2218/ijdc.v10i1.347
3. Borgman, C.L.: The conundrum of sharing research data. J. Am. Soc. Inf. Sci. Technol. **63**(6), 1059–1078 (2012). https://doi.org/10.1002/asi.22634
4. Edwards, P.N., Jackson, S.J., Bowker, G.C., Knobel, C.P.: Understanding Infrastructure: Dynamics, Tensions, and Design. History & Theory of Infrastructure: Lessons for New Scientific Cyberinfrastructures, pp. 1–50 (2007)

5. DCMI Metadata Terms. https://www.dublincore.org/specifications/dublin-core/dcmi-terms/. Accessed 13 Feb 2026

6. Toptas, B., Lenz, R., Groß, R.: A contextually comprehensive metadata model: bridging simplicity and expressiveness for GenAI-based metadata generation. In: 19th International Conference on Metadata and Semantic Research (MTSR 2025), Thessaloniki, Greece (in press)

7. Aroyo, L., Welty, C.: Truth is a lie: crowd truth and the seven myths of human annotation. AI Mag. **36**(1), 15–24 (2015). https://doi.org/10.1609/aimag.v36i1.2564

8. Sugimoto, S., Baker, T., Weibel, S.L.: Dublin core: process and principles. In: Lim, E.-P., et al. (eds.) ICADL 2002. LNCS, vol. 2555, pp. 25–35. Springer, Heidelberg (2002). https://doi.org/10.1007/3-540-36227-4_3

9. Park, M.S., Park, H.: An examination of metadata practices for research data reuse: characteristics and predictive probability of metadata elements. Malays. J. Libr. Inf. Sci. **24**(3), 61–75 (2019). https://doi.org/10.22452/mjlis.vol24no3.4

10. Watanabe, Y., Ito, K., Matsubara, S.: Capabilities and challenges of LLMs in metadata extraction from scholarly papers. In: Oliver, G., Frings-Hessami, V., Du, J.T., Tezuka, T. (eds.) Sustainability and empowerment in the context of digital libraries, Communications in Computer and Information Science, pp. 280–287. Springer, Singapore (2025). https://doi.org/10.1007/978-981-96-0865-2_23

11. Turner, M.D., et al.: Large language models can extract metadata for annotation of human neuroimaging publications. Front. Neuroinform. **19**(1), 1–16 (2025)

12. Alyafeai, Z., Al-Shaibani, M.S., Ghanem, B.: MOLE: metadata extraction and validation in scientific papers using LLMs. arXiv, 1–29 (2025). https://doi.org/10.48550/arXiv.2505.19800

13. Artstein, R., Poesio, M.: Inter-coder agreement for computational linguistics. Comput. Linguist. **34**(4), 555–596 (2008). https://doi.org/10.1162/coli.07-034-R2

14. Pavlick, E., Kwiatkowski, T.: Inherent disagreements in human textual inferences. Trans. Assoc. Comput. Linguist. **7**, 677–694 (2019). https://doi.org/10.1162/tacl_a_00293

15. Wang, R.Y., Strong, D.M.: Beyond accuracy: what data quality means to data consumers. J. Manag. Inf. Syst. **12**(4), 5–33 (1996). https://doi.org/10.1080/07421222.1996.11518099

16. Wand, Y., Wang, R.Y.: Anchoring data quality dimensions in ontological foundations. Commun. ACM **39**(11), 86–96 (1996)

17. Kumar, V., Chandrappa, Harinarayana, N.: Exploring dimensions of metadata quality assessment: a scoping review. J. Librarianship Inf. Sci. **57**(3), 661–673 (2025). https://doi.org/10.1177/09610006241239080

18. Margaritopoulos, T., Margaritopoulos, M., Mavridis, I., Manitsaris, A.: A conceptual framework for metadata quality assessment. In: Proceedings of the 2008 International Conference on Dublin Core and Metadata Applications (DCMI 2008), pp. 104–113. Dublin Core Metadata Initiative, Berlin, Germany (2008)

19. Bugbee, K., et al.: Improving discovery and use of NASA's earth observation data through metadata quality assessments. Data Sci. J. **20**, 17 (2021). https://doi.org/10.5334/dsj-2021-017

20. Leiner, D. J.: SoSci Survey (version 3.5.02). Computer Software (2024). https://www.soscisurvey.de

21. Behkamal, B., Kahani, M., Bagheri, E., Jeremic, Z.: A metrics-driven approach for quality assessment of linked open data. J. Theor. Appl. Electron. Commer. Res. **9**(2), 11–12 (2014). https://doi.org/10.4067/S0718-18762014000200006

22. Basili, V.R., Caldiera, G., Rombach, H.D.: The goal question metric approach. In: Marciniak, J.J. (ed.) Encyclopedia of Software Engineering. Wiley, New York (1994)

23. Kott, A., Toptas, B., Schötteler, S., Gross, R., Brockmann, P., Kosch, H.: Sustainability tensions in generative artificial intelligence use. In: Proceedings of the European Conference on Information Systems (ECIS 2025) (2025)

24. Kott, A., Lehner, M., Groß, R., Kosch, H.: A systematic approach to quality scoring of AI-generated legal texts. In: Proceedings of the 3rd International Conference on AI-generated Content (AIGC 2025) (2025)

25. Kott, A., Rössler, A., Groß, R., Kosch, H., Ries, F.: AI regulates AI: an artifact for automated risk assessment. In: Proceedings of INFORMATIK 2025 (2025). https://doi.org/10.18420/INF2025_117

26. Kott, A., Brockmann, P., Marutschke, D.M., Kryssanov, V.: Global software engineering education: Students' experiences during the pandemic. Int. J. Learn. Teach. 10(4), 451–457 (2024). https://doi.org/10.18178/ijlt.10.4.451-457

27. Schwarzinger, T., Thoma, M., Preindl, T., Kjæer, M., Just, V.P., Steindl, G.: RDF fusion: an extensible SPARQL engine for hybrid data models. IEEE Access 13, 184297–184311 (2025). https://doi.org/10.1109/ACCESS.2025.3623639

28. Haller, D.: A query-driven approach for SHACL type inference. In: Proceedings of the International Conference on Very Large Data Bases (VLDB 2023) (2023)

29. Buttke, L., Schötteler, S., Seuring, S., Ebinger, F.: The German supply chain due diligence act: impacts on sustainable supply chain management from a stakeholder perspective. Supply Chain Manag. Int. J. 29(5), 909–925 (2024). https://doi.org/10.1108/SCM-01-2024-0058

30. Weinzierl, S., Zilker, S., Dunzer, S., Matzner, M.: Machine learning in business process management: a systematic literature review. Expert Syst. Appl. 253, 124181 (2024). https://doi.org/10.1016/j.eswa.2024.124181

31. Deinhard, J.-L., Lenz, R.: Practical problems in customer data — a use-case-driven classification. In: Proceedings of BTW 2025 (2025). https://doi.org/10.18420/BTW2025-24

32. Weber, L., Lenz, R.: Accelerating singular spectrum transformation for scalable change point detection. IEEE Access 13, 213556–213577 (2025). https://doi.org/10.1109/ACCESS.2025.3640386

33. Gumpert, F., Eitel, D., Helbig, U., Lohbreier, J.: Impact of nanotube length on electrical properties in PEMFCs: a coupled stochastic and numerical study for sustainable mobility. EPJ Web Conf. 334, 03011 (2025). https://doi.org/10.1051/epjconf/202533403011

34. Groß, R., Freudenthaler, K., Ulrich, T.: Best of both worlds: how can we usefully combine online and classroom teaching in the context of project-based learning within the framework of industry-university cooperation? In: Proceedings of the 15th International Conference of Education, Research and Innovation (ICERI 2022), pp. 3205–3213 (2022). https://doi.org/10.21125/iceri.2022.0799

35. Hall, K., Helmus, B., Eymann, T.: How to balance privacy and (health) benefits: privacy calculus and the intention to use health tracking at the workplace. Int. J. Hum. Comput. Interact. 41(10), 6235–6252 (2025). https://doi.org/10.1080/10447318.2024.2375704

36. Zobel, M., Fritz, M., Scholz, I.: Object tracking and pose estimation using light-field object models. In: Proceedings of the 7th International Fall Workshop Vision, Modeling, and Visualization, pp. 371–378 (2002)

37. Barbian, D.: Digitale Produktpässe in der chemischen Industrie. Zeitschrift für Stoffrecht 22(2), 100–108 (2025). https://doi.org/10.21552/stoffr/2025/2/4

38. Eitel, D., et al.: Insight into the formation of carbon-doped titanate nanotubes. Chem. Eng. J. Adv. 24, 100898 (2025). https://doi.org/10.1016/j.ceja.2025.100898

39. Eitel, D., et al.: Structural characterization of carbon-doped and carbon-coated TiO2 core-shell nanoparticles. Adv. Mater. Interfaces 13(2), e00770 (2026). https://doi.org/10.1002/admi.202500770

40. Mehta, K., Lwakatare, B., Zörner, W., Ehrenwirth, M.: Mini-grid performance in Sub-Saharan Africa: case studies from Tsumkwe and Gam. Namibia. Sustain. Energy Res. 12(1), 30 (2025). https://doi.org/10.1186/s40807-025-00174-y

41. Blahnik, J., Schuster, J., Müller, R., Müller, E., Kunz, W.: Surfactant-free micro-emulsions (SFMEs) as a template for porous polymer synthesis. J. Colloid Interface Sci. **655**, 371–382 (2024). https://doi.org/10.1016/j.jcis.2023.10.162
42. John, R., Catherine, B.-A., Henry, B., Reuben, G.H.-W., Marina, S.: Current research in Egyptology 2024. Archaeopress Access Archaeol. (2025). https://doi.org/10.32028/978180 5831136
43. Plank, A.-C., et al.: Comparison of C-reactive protein in dried blood spots and saliva of healthy adolescents. Front. Immunol. **12**, 795580 (2021). https://doi.org/10.3389/fimmu.2021.795580
44. Gumpert, F., Eitel, D., Kottas, O., Helbig, U., Lohbreier, J.: Multiscale simulations of three-dimensional nanotube networks: enhanced modeling using unit cells. Comput. Mater. Sci. **254**, 113891 (2025). https://doi.org/10.1016/j.commatsci.2025.113891

Artificial Intelligence for Decision Support

Neural Proposal Generation for Evolutionary Negotiation in Project Portfolio Selection

Andreas Fink[✉]

Helmut Schmidt University / University of the Federal Armed Forces Hamburg,
Hamburg, Germany
`andreas.fink@hsu-hh.de`

Abstract. Decisions about the provision of community services and infrastructure often involve multiple stakeholders with heterogeneous preferences. We formulate these problems as multi-agent, multi-constraint project portfolio selection tasks with private stakeholder utilities and propose an evolutionary negotiation mechanism for participatory coordination over feasible portfolios. In this approach, stakeholders are represented by software agents that negotiate over candidate solutions within a population-based search process. Proposal generation relies either on classical evolutionary variation operators or on learning-based strategies. Specifically, we iteratively retrain autoencoders and variational autoencoders on the evolving solution population to learn latent structural patterns induced by stakeholder preferences and resource constraints. New proposals are generated by recombining latent codes and decoding the resulting representations into candidate solutions. Computational experiments indicate that the learning-based proposal strategies produce solutions near the Pareto front, with variational autoencoders achieving the best performance in the studied scenarios.

Keywords: Autoencoders · Automated negotiation · Evolutionary algorithms · Project portfolio selection · Variational autoencoders

1 Introduction

Community service provision typically requires balancing the interests of multiple stakeholders with heterogeneous preferences. This motivates the design of participatory decision-making mechanisms that incorporate stakeholder input to enhance legitimacy, transparency, and public acceptance. Applications include participatory budgeting initiatives, which aim to involve citizens directly in public investment decisions [42], and the selection of project portfolios [34]. Typical portfolios comprise health or emergency facilities, sensor deployments, and other infrastructure that supports community resilience and livability. Existing approaches exhibit limitations when confronted with complex decision environments characterized by heterogeneous stakeholder preferences, combinatorial

K. Kirchner et al. (Eds.): I4CS 2026, CCIS 3007, pp. 239–259, 2026.
https://doi.org/10.1007/978-3-032-27096-2_13

choice spaces, and multiple resource constraints, such as in terms of budgets, capacities, or spatial limitations. These challenges motivate the investigation of digital decision-making mechanisms that are applicable to a broad class of coordination problems. In this work, we focus on project portfolio selection problems in community planning contexts, where mechanisms are required to identify mutually beneficial solutions in a fair way, while stakeholders do not need to fully disclose their preferences. Traditional optimization approaches would commonly presuppose complete knowledge of objective functions, which is incompatible with settings where parties act strategically and may misrepresent preferences if this promises individual advantage.

In the proposed automated coordination mechanism, stakeholders are represented by software agents that negotiate over feasible project portfolios while largely preserving preference privacy. To address the combinatorial complexity of the solution space, the negotiation process is embedded in an evolutionary approach that iteratively refines a population of candidate portfolios. This concept is based on the negotiation-driven evolutionary framework originally proposed for permutation-based sequencing problems in [25]. Conventional evolutionary operators such as crossover and mutation serve as a baseline for candidate generation. However, we focus on machine learning proposal strategies to exploit latent structural properties of the combinatorial solution space and the preference feedback during the negotiation. In particular, we consider neural network-based autoencoders and variational autoencoders to generate promising proposals for an efficient and fair exploration of high-dimensional solution spaces under conflicting stakeholder interests.

The main contributions of this paper are as follows. First, we adapt the evolutionary negotiation mechanism of [25] from permutation-based problems to binary project portfolio selection. Second, we investigate neural network-based proposal generation, with a particular focus on a novel use of variational autoencoders that iteratively learn latent structural patterns and generate proposals by recombining latent codes and decoding the resulting representations. Third, we experimentally evaluate conventional and learning-based proposal strategies in two- and three-agent scenarios on instances with up to 500 projects and up to 30 resource dimensions, and we analyze the scalability and effectiveness of the proposed methods.

The remainder of the paper is structured as follows. In Sect. 2 we review the background with related work. In Sect. 3 we describe the formal problem model, which is followed by a description of the proposed methodology in Sect. 4. This includes the evolutionary negotiation protocol and the proposal generation components based on autoencoders and variational autoencoders. Section 5 presents computational experiments on project portfolio selection scenarios and analyzes the results. Section 6 concludes the paper and discusses directions for future research.

2   Background and Related Work

Participatory decision-making in the public sector is a relevant topic in decision support systems (DSS) and group decision support systems (GDSS) research. Early DSS work focused on structured decision models, interactive exploration of alternatives, and computer-based support for managerial and public-sector decisions [37,41]. In public planning contexts, multi-criteria decision analysis and optimization-based DSS have been proposed to support collective choice, for instance by visualizing Pareto-efficient trade-offs or facilitating arbitration between conflicting objectives [12]. These approaches typically presuppose that stakeholder preferences can be elicited explicitly and reported truthfully. In practice, stakeholders may be unwilling or unable to articulate complete utility functions, especially when preferences are sensitive or only partially formed.

Digital participation platforms have been proposed to support citizen involvement in public planning, yet there are limitations in scalability, deliberation quality, and preference aggregation [32,33]. Voting and ranking mechanisms compress preferences into basic signals. In many settings, monetary incentives or transfer payments are infeasible, which restricts the use of related mechanisms [24,36]. Automated agent-based negotiation offers an alternative for addressing these challenges. Unlike single-shot aggregation methods such as traditional auctions, negotiations treat collective decision-making as an iterative exchange of proposals aimed at reaching agreement [15,16,27,29,30]. Automated negotiation has been considered in application fields such as electronic commerce, supply chain coordination, and distributed resource allocation, where agents operate under private information and bounded rationality [1,35]. Such systems can be viewed as decentralized decision support mechanisms that preserve stakeholder autonomy and preference privacy [5]. However, existing frameworks often target bilateral negotiation and operate in continuous or low-dimensional domains, which limits their suitability for decision problems that involve more than two groups and large combinatorial solution spaces.

Algorithmic decision-making should not only be evaluated in terms of economic efficiency, but also with regard to fairness, transparency, and accountability criteria [6,34,42,44]. Classical fairness concepts do not transfer directly to public project selection and participatory budgeting problems [10]. For instance, the core, defined as the set of allocations that are stable against deviations by coalitions, may be empty in related settings. These results suggest that outcome-only or axiomatic notions may be insufficient in this domain, strengthening the case for procedural accounts of fairness. Negotiation-based decision processes, in which stakeholders iteratively evaluate and respond to concrete proposals, support a procedural notion of fairness. Proposals and responses make the decision process explicit and auditable. In this context, we consider an evolutionary negotiation mechanism, where we assume that digital agents representing stakeholders are able to compare and choose among alternative proposals, which avoids full preference disclosure. For proposal generation, we employ learning-based procedures. Recent work has shown that autoencoders can be used within evolutionary optimization and estimation-of-distribution algorithms to derive adaptive variation operators that leverage structural properties of high-quality solutions instead of relying solely on random recombination and perturbation [9,11,14,21,31,38]. For studies focusing specifically on variational autoencoders in evolutionary search, see [3,4,18,26].

3   Problem Model

Addressing the selection of community service projects under shared resource constraints and private stakeholder preferences, we model the setting as a multi-agent, multi-constraint project selection problem with privately held utility parameters. There is a set of n candidate projects $i \in \{1, \ldots, n\}$. Each project can either be selected ($x_i = 1$) or not selected ($x_i = 0$), i.e., there is a binary decision vector $\mathbf{x} \in \{0,1\}^n$. The decision is subject to d resource constraints, representing, for example, budget, personnel, or equipment limitations. If project i is selected, it consumes $w_{i,r}$ units of resource $r \in \{1, \ldots, d\}$. Each resource r has a capacity limit b_r that must not be exceeded. The set of feasible project portfolios is thus given by

$$\mathcal{C} = \left\{ \mathbf{x} \in \{0,1\}^n \;\middle|\; \sum_{i=1}^{n} w_{i,r} x_i \leq b_r, \quad \forall r \in \{1, \ldots, d\} \right\}. \tag{1}$$

The decision problem involves m self-interested agents, indexed by $k \in \{1, \ldots, m\}$, each representing a stakeholder. Agent k assigns an individual utility value $v_{i,k}$ to project i. Assuming additive preference aggregation, the utility of portfolio $\mathbf{x}$ for agent k is given by

$$u_k(\mathbf{x}) = \sum_{i=1}^{n} v_{i,k} x_i. \tag{2}$$

The methodology described below allows the model to be extended to account for complementarity or substitutability among projects, which corresponds to super-additive or sub-additive utility calculations, or other non-linear functions.

In the single-agent case ($m = 1$), the problem reduces to the multi-dimensional knapsack problem [8,17,39]. For $m > 1$, agents have potentially conflicting preferences, and the outcome must be coordinated. Since the utilities $v_{i,k}$ are private and disclosure of cardinal preferences should be avoided, we focus on mechanisms that operate on ordinal preference information only (which also renders the approach independent of the particular utility function). Thus, we assume agents can compare two feasible portfolios. Given two feasible solutions $\mathbf{x}, \mathbf{x}' \in \mathcal{C}$, agent k (weakly) prefers $\mathbf{x}'$ over $\mathbf{x}$ if and only if

$$u_k(\mathbf{x}') \geq u_k(\mathbf{x}). \tag{3}$$

While we seek Pareto-efficient project portfolios, the solution space generally grows exponentially with n and the Pareto front typically contains multiple solutions. Under information asymmetry, enforcing an axiomatic outcome-selection rule is difficult. As mentioned above, we therefore emphasize procedural fairness. Assuming transferable utility, one can benchmark against utilitarian welfare maximization. However, aggregate welfare does not address distributional concerns. More generally, solution quality can be assessed by proximity to the Pareto front. Although the true Pareto front is unknown in practice, it can be approximated in experimental settings and used as a benchmark for comparative evaluation.

4 Methodology

4.1 Conceptual Framework

We consider a socio-technical decision support framework for participatory community service planning, where stakeholders are modeled as autonomous negotiation agents. Candidate project portfolios are produced through an evolutionary search process using learned proposal models. Figure 1 summarizes the layered conceptual architecture, which connects human stakeholders to negotiation agents and to computational components for coordination and learning. This structure keeps responsibilities separate and makes the system easier to scale and adapt. At the same time, it preserves a direct trace from stakeholder input to the resulting algorithmic proposals.

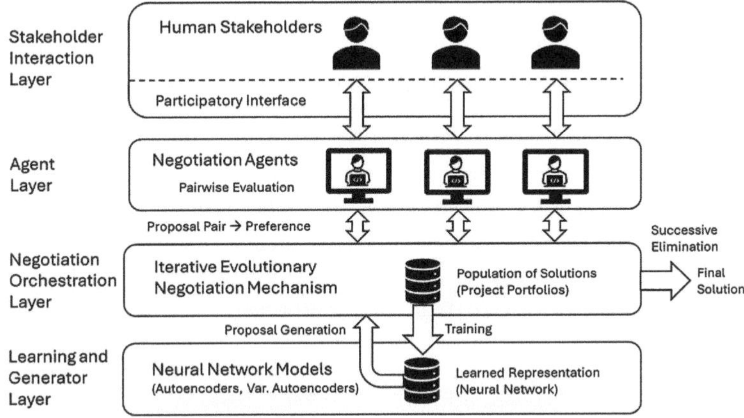

Fig. 1. Conceptual architecture of the evolutionary multi-agent negotiation framework for participatory project portfolio decision making

Human stakeholders interact with the system through a decision support interface that allows them to connect to a private software component holding the respective stakeholder's preference information. On the negotiation platform, this endpoint is represented in the agent layer by a negotiation agent that can access the stakeholder's private preference model as needed for interaction. Interaction is restricted to ordinal feedback, namely pairwise comparisons between presented project portfolios and, in the final elimination stage, identification of the least-preferred portfolio within a presented set. This design reduces cognitive load and avoids eliciting cardinal utilities. Utilities remain local to the agents and are not disclosed to the platform or to other agents.

Coordination among stakeholders is achieved through a multi-party, iterative negotiation protocol. In each iteration, candidate solutions are generated and agents express pairwise preferences in accordance with the problem model described in Sect. 3. At the negotiation orchestration layer, an evolutionary negotiation mechanism maintains a population of feasible portfolios. Embedded in this mechanism, a solution generator constructs project portfolios under shared resource constraints using only information available from the current population and ordinal agent feedback. In each iteration, the generator component proposes a candidate portfolio that may replace a solution from the population if all agents (weakly) prefer the candidate. We consider two generator approaches: classical evolutionary operators (crossover/mutation) and learned generators based on (variational) autoencoders trained online. The learned generators are trained on the evolving population of accepted portfolios and sample new candidates from a latent representation of the high-dimensional binary decision space. That is, the learning layer incorporates representation learning models in view of feasible and mutually beneficial solutions from the evolving population, with the aim to support efficient exploration of the combinatorial solution space.

After a fixed proposal budget (i.e., number of iterations), the population typically contains multiple portfolios. Therefore, we eventually apply a fair successive elimination procedure to select a single outcome.

4.2   Evolutionary Negotiation Protocol

Algorithm 1 presents the multi-agent evolutionary search negotiation protocol, which builds on the concept described in [25]. The algorithm maintains a population P of feasible solutions (project portfolios) that evolves through iterative candidate generation and replacement, which conforms to the general approach of evolutionary search [2, 19]. However, the multi-agent setting restricts the available information and procedures for selecting and refining solutions. The initial population is generated by a randomized construction procedure: projects are processed in random order and added whenever feasibility is maintained. At the core of the subsequent procedure, solution candidates (feasible project portfolios) are generated iteratively and may replace solutions from the population if the agents agree. Specifically, the algorithm involves, in case of a learning-based generator, an outer loop where a generator is trained on the current population, and the inner generation loop, where candidate solutions are produced and assessed for possible inclusion in the population. We consider three alternative generators: a traditional evolutionary generator (Subsect. 4.3) and two neural-network-based generators (Subsects. 4.4 and 4.5). The generator update step is absent for the evolutionary generator, which uses classical operators that do not rely on a learned model.

Algorithm 1. Evolutionary Negotiation Protocol

1: **procedure** (Agents, TrainingLoops, GenerationLoops, PopSize, GENERATOR)
2:     $P \leftarrow \emptyset$
3:     **for** $v = 1$ **to** PopSize **do**
4:         $P \leftarrow P \cup$ RANDOMFEASIBLESOLUTION()
5:     **end for**
6:     **for** $t = 1$ **to** TrainingLoops **do**
7:         GENERATOR.UPDATE(unique(P))   ▷ Train on current population
8:         **for** $g = 1$ **to** GenerationLoops **do**
9:             $\mathbf{s}' \leftarrow$ GENERATOR.GENERATE(P)
10:             $\mathbf{s}' \leftarrow$ REPAIRIFINFEASIBLE($\mathbf{s}'$)
11:             **for** $\mathbf{s} \in$ RANDOMSHUFFLE(P) **do**
12:                 **if** $\forall k \in$ Agents : k.PREFER($\mathbf{s}', \mathbf{s}$) **then**
13:                     $P \leftarrow P \cup \{\mathbf{s}'\} \setminus \{\mathbf{s}\}$
14:                     **break**
15:                 **end if**
16:             **end for**
17:         **end for**
18:     **end for**
19:     **return** SUCCESSIVEELIMINATION(P, Agents)
20: **end procedure**

As the generators may produce infeasible solutions, a repair procedure is applied if needed before the subsequent assessment. This is done by, in the first phase, randomly removing projects one-by-one until feasibility is restored and then, in the second phase, projects are greedily inserted in descending order of their weight efficiency subject to feasibility. The weight efficiency of a project i is defined as

$$e_i = \frac{1}{\bar{w}_i}, \quad \text{where } \bar{w}_i = \frac{1}{d} \sum_{r=1}^{d} w_{i,r}. \tag{4}$$

The random removal procedure in the first repair phase is a simple yet natural concept for neural generators to avoid introducing a heuristic bias that may conflict with the learned latent structure. We also use this random procedure for the evolutionary generators, since in our initial exploratory tests the alternative concept of a purposeful greedy removal according to the weight efficiency led to worse results, accompanied by a rapid loss of population diversity.

Let $\mathbf{s}'$ denote a solution (candidate portfolio) produced by the generator (and after a possible repair). As described in Algorithm 1, such a candidate may replace an incumbent $\mathbf{s} \in P$ only if it is (weakly) preferred by all agents:

$$\mathbf{s}' \text{ (weakly) dominates } \mathbf{s} \iff \forall k \in \{1, \ldots, m\} : u_k(\mathbf{s}') \geq u_k(\mathbf{s}). \tag{5}$$

This replacement rule guides the population toward Pareto-efficient portfolios without disclosing cardinal utilities; however, the effectiveness of the search ultimately depends on the quality of the generator.

After the negotiation loop, the eventual population typically contains multiple portfolios. To select a single implementable outcome, we use a successive elimination procedure in which agents take turns removing the individually least-preferred portfolio from the remaining set. The procedure terminates when one portfolio remains, and that portfolio is returned as the negotiation outcome.

4.3 Evolutionary Generator

The baseline generator uses well-established evolutionary operators for binary-encoded solutions [43]. Because fitness-based selection would require access to private utilities, we sample two parent portfolios uniformly at random. Then, we select from three crossover operators with equal probability: (i) with the uniform crossover, each bit is sampled from either parent with probability 0.5; (ii) two-point crossover with cut points $p_1 < p_2$ means that the offspring inherits bits from parent 1 outside the interval $[p_1, p_2)$ and from parent 2 within; (iii) union crossover implies that a project is selected in the offspring if it is selected by at least one parent. Subsequently, bit-flip mutation is applied with a mutation rate of $\mu = 1/n$, which corresponds to one expected bit flip per offspring on average.

4.4 Autoencoder Generator

Autoencoders (AEs) are neural network models for representation learning that learn a compact latent representation of high-dimensional input data while retaining essential structural information. By jointly training an encoder-decoder pair end-to-end to reconstruct the input in a self-supervised setting, autoencoders can capture correlations and regularities in the underlying data distribution [20, 23]. In our approach, the autoencoder-based generator learns a compressed latent representation of the current population of feasible project portfolios and generates new candidate solutions by recombining and then decoding latent vectors. This allows the negotiation mechanism to exploit learned structural patterns in the evolving population while respecting that agent utility functions remain private.

Architecture. The devised autoencoder consists of an encoder $f_{\mathrm{enc}} : \{0, 1\}^n \to [0, 1]^D$ and a decoder $f_{\mathrm{dec}} : [0, 1]^D \to [0, 1]^n$, where D denotes the dimensionality of the latent space. The encoder is implemented as a multilayer network with two hidden layers and ReLU activations. Unless stated otherwise, the size of each hidden layer is set to twice the latent dimensionality. For training stability and convergence, layer normalization is applied after each affine transformation, and dropout (probability 0.1) is applied after the first hidden activation for regularization. Thus, the encoder is defined as

$$\mathbf{h}_1 = \mathrm{ReLU}(\mathrm{LayerNorm}(W_1 \mathbf{x} + \mathbf{b}_1)), \tag{6}$$

$$\mathbf{h}_2 = \mathrm{ReLU}(\mathrm{LayerNorm}(W_2 \mathbf{h}_1 + \mathbf{b}_2)), \tag{7}$$

$$\mathbf{z} = \sigma(W_3 \mathbf{h}_2 + \mathbf{b}_3), \tag{8}$$

where $\mathbf{x} \in \{0,1\}^n$ denotes the solution vector (cf. Sect. 3) and $\sigma(\cdot)$ is the sigmoid activation function, ensuring bounded latent representations with respect to subsequent recombination in latent space. The decoder mirrors this architecture, i.e., with layer normalization and ReLU in the hidden layers, dropout after the initial layer, and a sigmoid activation in the final layer to produce selection probabilities for each project.

Training. The autoencoder is trained on the set of unique solutions currently contained in the population. Training minimizes the binary cross-entropy reconstruction loss, interpreting the decoder outputs as Bernoulli parameters for the individual selection decisions. To encourage robustness and reduce overfitting to individual population members, denoising training is employed. During training, each input solution is corrupted by independently flipping each bit with probability $\rho = 0.1$, while the reconstruction target remains the original, uncorrupted solution. This approach promotes the learning of stable latent representations that generalize beyond exact population instances.

Following common practice, we train the models using the Adam optimizer with a cosine-annealing learning-rate schedule. To exploit temporal continuity in the evolving population and to reduce computational overhead, we warm-start the model parameters from the preceding training iteration.

Latent Space Recombination. After training, all solutions in the population are encoded into the latent space. New latent representations are generated by convex interpolation between existing latent vectors:

1. Sample r from $\{2,3\}$ and then select r parent solutions uniformly at random (to balance coherence and diversity)
2. Sample non-zero weights $(\alpha_1, \ldots, \alpha_r)$ such that the weights add up to 1
3. Compute interpolated latent vector: $\mathbf{z}' = \sum_{j=1}^{r} \alpha_j \mathbf{z}^{(j)}$
4. Add Gaussian perturbation: $\mathbf{z}' \leftarrow \mathrm{clip}(\mathbf{z}' + \epsilon, 0, 1)$, where $\epsilon \sim \mathcal{N}(0, 0.05^2 I)$

Decoding with Temperature. The perturbed latent vector $\mathbf{z}'$ is decoded to obtain per-project selection probabilities $\hat{\mathbf{p}} = f_{\mathrm{dec}}(\mathbf{z}')$. To control the stochasticity of solution generation, we apply temperature scaling in logit space:

$$p_i = \sigma\left(\frac{\mathrm{logit}(\hat{p}_i)}{T}\right), \quad x_i' \sim \mathrm{Bernoulli}(p_i), \tag{9}$$

where $T = 0.8$ slightly sharpens the distribution relative to $T = 1$.

Multiple Sampling. To reduce sampling variance, multiple candidate solutions are generated from the same latent representation. Among these candidates, the solution with the highest number of selected projects is retained. While using project count as a proxy for quality is an approximation, this heuristic rule does not rely on specific project data or utility values.

4.5 Variational Autoencoder Generator

Variational autoencoders (VAEs) build on autoencoders by modeling the latent representation as a probability distribution instead of a single deterministic code, which aligns with the generative function within our algorithmic approach. That is, the main purpose is not compression, but probabilistic modeling of a data distribution in latent space. The encoder outputs the parameters of an approximate posterior over latent variables, and the decoder specifies the corresponding generative model that maps latent samples back to the data space. VAEs are commonly trained by maximizing the evidence lower bound (ELBO), which balances a reconstruction term (here a Bernoulli likelihood suited to binary selection vectors) against a regularization term that keeps the approximate posterior close to a chosen prior [28,40]. The result is a latent space that is more structured and typically smoother, which can be useful when the goal is to generate and sample a diverse set of candidate solutions in high-dimensional problems.

Architecture. The VAE architecture closely follows the autoencoder introduced in Subsect. 4.4, but replaces the deterministic latent encoding with a probabilistic one. Given an input solution $\mathbf{x}$, the encoder outputs the parameters of a diagonal multivariate Gaussian in latent space, namely a mean vector and a log-variance vector:

$$\boldsymbol{\mu} = W_\mu \mathbf{h} + \mathbf{b}_\mu, \tag{10}$$

$$\mathbf{v} = W_\sigma \mathbf{h} + \mathbf{b}_\sigma, \tag{11}$$

where $\mathbf{h}$ is the encoder's final hidden representation and $\mathbf{v} = \log \boldsymbol{\sigma}^2$. Latent samples are drawn using the reparameterization trick to enable backpropagation through the sampling operation [28]:

$$\mathbf{z} = \boldsymbol{\mu} + \boldsymbol{\sigma} \odot \boldsymbol{\epsilon}, \quad \boldsymbol{\epsilon} \sim \mathcal{N}(\mathbf{0}, I). \tag{12}$$

The decoder maps latent samples $\mathbf{z}$ back into the solution space and outputs Bernoulli parameters for each project-selection variable.

Training. As usual, we train the VAE by maximizing the ELBO, which combines a reconstruction term with a Kullback-Leibler regularizer [28,40]. To tune the influence of the regularizer, we use a β-VAE objective [22] with $\beta = 0.1$. As in the autoencoder case, we warm-start the parameters from the previous training iteration to take advantage of continuity across successive populations.

Latent Space Recombination. For the VAE-based generator, recombination operates on the parameters of the latent distributions rather than on a single point. Given k parent solutions with encoded parameters $(\boldsymbol{\mu}^{(j)}, \log \boldsymbol{\sigma}^{2(j)})$, we construct an offspring distribution by inheriting, for each latent dimension, the mean and log-variance from one randomly chosen parent from the population. An offspring latent vector is then sampled from $\mathcal{N}(\boldsymbol{\mu}', \mathrm{diag}(\boldsymbol{\sigma}'^2))$ and decoded to produce a candidate solution. We generate one candidate per recombination step, since the stochastic latent sampling already injects variability and supports exploration.

5 Computational Experiments

5.1 Data and Experimental Setting

We derive multi-agent instances from the single-agent multi-dimensional knapsack benchmark of [8]. Reusing original data, we generate additional utility coefficients for agents $k > 1$ using the same randomization procedure as in [8]. We study nine instances with (n, d) combinations where $n \in \{100, 250, 500\}$ denotes the number of projects and $d \in \{5, 10, 30\}$ the number of resource dimensions. For each (n, d) setting, we take the first instance from the corresponding benchmark file mknap$l$ ($l \in \{1, \ldots, 9\}$) generated with tightness ratio $\alpha = 0.5$ ($b_r = \alpha \sum_{i=1}^{n} w_{i,r}$, $r = 1, \ldots, d$), and label the resulting instances B1 through B9. As either n or d increases, we expect the instances to become more challenging. We note that, due to the exponential growth of the solution space, even for the smaller instances with $n = 100$ there are already up to $2^{100} \approx 10^{30}$ candidate solutions, which rules out approaches that do not selectively explore the solution space in a targeted manner.

All algorithms are implemented in Python, with neural network generators trained with PyTorch. Parts of the implementation were developed with assistance from Claude Opus. Experiments are run on Intel Xeon Platinum 8360Y processors; however, our implementation is predominantly single-threaded and Python-based, so faster runtimes are likely achievable with further engineering. The goal here is not to optimize absolute performance, but to evaluate the proposed algorithmic procedures under consistent experimental conditions.

To assess the outcomes of the negotiation simulations, we report both agent-level and aggregate indicators. Let a negotiation among $m \in \{2, 3\}$ agents result in a utility vector $\mathbf{u} = (u_1, \ldots, u_m)$, where $u_k \geq 0$ is the utility obtained by agent k (cf. (2)). The individual values u_k capture how the outcome is distributed across agents. For an overall efficiency view, we report the utilitarian sum (social welfare) $U(\mathbf{u}) = \sum_{k=1}^{m} u_k$, which is a standard aggregate measure in negotiation and social choice settings.

To put the negotiation results into context, we compute reference solutions based on a centralized version of the problem. Specifically, we suppose an omniscient planner that maximizes the utilitarian sum. The resulting combinatorial optimization problem is $\mathcal{NP}$-hard. We solve the mixed-integer programs (MIP) using the Gurobi Optimizer with a time limit of 600 s per run. The results are reported in Table 1. As shown, for the first four instances, and for both $m = 2$ and $m = 3$ agents, optimal solutions are obtained within the commonly used optimality tolerance of 0.01 %. For the remaining instances, the solver returns

Table 1. Results of the Gurobi MIP Solver for the simplified centralized planning model for $m = 2$ and for $m = 3$ agents (instances with n projects, d dimensions)

Problem			Instances with $m = 2$ agents				Instances with $m = 3$ agents				
	n	d	U	u_1	u_2	gap	U	u_1	u_2	u_3	gap
B1	100	5	83281	41177	42104	0.00%	123336	40210	42276	40850	0.00%
B2	250	5	210631	104763	105868	0.01%	310791	103557	104267	102967	0.01%
B3	500	5	419849	211065	208784	0.01%	618680	207752	205157	205771	0.01%
B4	100	10	79317	39647	39670	0.01%	118720	39061	38595	41064	0.01%
B5	250	10	212065	107210	104855	0.09%	311289	106313	103118	101858	0.08%
B6	500	10	416509	208340	208169	0.06%	614137	204735	205050	204352	0.05%
B7	100	30	78599	39105	39494	0.49%	116467	38305	38948	39214	0.69%
B8	250	30	206108	103794	102314	0.34%	303261	100987	102053	100221	0.38%
B9	500	30	413392	207448	205944	0.24%	607629	204120	200837	202672	0.25%

near-optimal solutions with MIP gaps mostly below 0.5 %, which provides us with useful upper bounds (note that we have a maximization problem).

In addition, the Pareto front of the corresponding multi-objective model provides a reference for the best outcome the negotiation could in principle achieve. We approximate this front using the ϵ-constraint method [13] and approximately solve a sequence of MIP models with the Gurobi Optimizer. For the two-agent case, we enforce a minimum utility level for agent 1 ($u_1 \geq L$) and maximize agent 2's utility u_2, where we sweep L over a suitable range. We repeat the same procedure with the agents' roles swapped to cover the front more evenly. Finally, we remove dominated solutions and keep only non-dominated points. The resulting set provides an approximation of the Pareto front, which we use to place the negotiation outcomes in context.

5.2 Results of the Negotiation Mechanism

Tables 2 and 3 report results obtained by applying Algorithm 1 with different generator components for $m = 2$ and $m = 3$ agents, respectively. For each configuration, we performed ten runs with different random seed values, each terminated after 300,000 iterations. For neural generators, the 300,000 iterations consist of 100 training phases with 3,000 generation iterations each. The autoencoders use a 50-dimensional latent space and are trained for 20 epochs. Typical wall-clock times per run are in the range of five to ten minutes, which is acceptable for the considered application domain. To compare aggregate utility outcomes for $m = 2$ and $m = 3$ agents with 300,000 iterations, we apply a one-sided Wilcoxon signed-rank test (90 paired observations per setting). The results confirm the pattern observed in the tables: both neural generators yield significantly higher aggregate utilities than the baseline using evolutionary operators ($p < 10^{-15}$). The difference between the AE and VAE generators is smaller, but still evident: the test indicates that the VAE achieves significantly higher outcomes than the AE ($p < 10^{-11}$).

To study the effect of reducing the number of iterations, Table 4 reports results for $m = 2$ agents obtained with 50,000 iterations (for the neural gen-

Table 2. Aggregate utility results for $m = 2$ agents (means $\pm$ std. dev. and percentage deviations in relation to the exact solver results for the hypothetical centralized planning) for different generators with 300,000 iterations (10 repetitions)

	Evolutionary Operators		Autoencoder		Variational Autoencoder	
B1	82818.6 $\pm$ 188.6	(0.6%)	82984.4 $\pm$ 128.7	(0.4%)	83054.5 $\pm$ 107.6	(0.3%)
B2	208647.8 $\pm$ 323.9	(0.9%)	209680.0 $\pm$ 213.9	(0.5%)	210095.9 $\pm$ 149.9	(0.3%)
B3	414543.3 $\pm$ 1081.4	(1.3%)	416160.1 $\pm$ 538.8	(0.9%)	418287.1 $\pm$ 221.0	(0.4%)
B4	78409.9 $\pm$ 330.2	(1.1%)	78819.5 $\pm$ 85.6	(0.6%)	78865.5 $\pm$ 170.0	(0.6%)
B5	209540.1 $\pm$ 333.0	(1.2%)	210811.5 $\pm$ 280.1	(0.6%)	211277.8 $\pm$ 167.3	(0.4%)
B6	409914.2 $\pm$ 727.8	(1.6%)	412068.4 $\pm$ 463.7	(1.1%)	414355.3 $\pm$ 529.0	(0.5%)
B7	77868.0 $\pm$ 365.2	(0.9%)	77983.7 $\pm$ 131.2	(0.8%)	78107.8 $\pm$ 155.4	(0.6%)
B8	203017.2 $\pm$ 735.6	(1.5%)	204461.5 $\pm$ 307.3	(0.8%)	204929.9 $\pm$ 266.4	(0.6%)
B9	403422.3 $\pm$ 1434.3	(2.4%)	408668.1 $\pm$ 561.5	(1.1%)	410947.8 $\pm$ 495.0	(0.6%)

Table 3. Aggregate utility results for $m = 3$ agents (means $\pm$ std. dev. and percentage deviations in relation to the exact solver results for the hypothetical centralized planning) for different generators with 300,000 iterations (10 repetitions)

	Evolutionary Operators		Autoencoder		Variational Autoencoder	
B1	122095.9 $\pm$ 270.4	(1.0%)	122780.7 $\pm$ 163.3	(0.5%)	122954.1 $\pm$ 216.0	(0.3%)
B2	307680.2 $\pm$ 823.7	(1.0%)	309467.3 $\pm$ 299.6	(0.4%)	309938.4 $\pm$ 360.6	(0.3%)
B3	611857.4 $\pm$ 1146.8	(1.1%)	613964.3 $\pm$ 546.2	(0.8%)	615516.0 $\pm$ 468.8	(0.5%)
B4	117419.6 $\pm$ 263.8	(1.1%)	117906.8 $\pm$ 254.5	(0.7%)	118014.8 $\pm$ 260.5	(0.6%)
B5	307136.9 $\pm$ 485.0	(1.3%)	309101.7 $\pm$ 352.7	(0.7%)	309480.8 $\pm$ 238.1	(0.6%)
B6	604127.1 $\pm$ 1336.1	(1.6%)	607805.4 $\pm$ 635.3	(1.0%)	609921.9 $\pm$ 716.1	(0.7%)
B7	114804.0 $\pm$ 489.6	(1.4%)	115390.1 $\pm$ 237.0	(0.9%)	115632.9 $\pm$ 253.6	(0.7%)
B8	296938.9 $\pm$ 1268.6	(2.1%)	300485.3 $\pm$ 437.9	(0.9%)	301110.4 $\pm$ 444.2	(0.7%)
B9	593152.5 $\pm$ 1692.5	(2.4%)	599971.8 $\pm$ 1180.1	(1.3%)	603000.3 $\pm$ 1107.6	(0.8%)

erators: 40 training phases with 1,250 generations each). We conducted analogous experiments also for 100,000 iterations ($50 \times 2,000$) and 200,000 iterations ($80 \times 2,500$) (tables omitted for brevity). The summary in Fig. 2 depicts the evolution of the average mean deviation across all instances for the considered generators under these configurations. The results indicate that all generators benefit from additional iterations within the examined range, yet the VAE generator needs a certain number of iterations to perform better than the AE generator.

This trend is further supported by Fig. 3, which illustrates intermediate solution sets from exemplary runs on instance B9. The VAE population initially lags behind but eventually achieves the best outcome. Note that this experiment uses 100 training phases with 3,000 generation iterations each, which makes the search relatively explorative in the early stages. Consequently, the intermediate AE and VAE populations at 50,000 iterations are worse than those obtained under configurations tailored to shorter negotiations (e.g., 40 training phases with 1,250 generation iterations in runs that terminate after 50,000 iterations). In the example in Fig. 3, AE converges relatively quickly (only 27 unique solutions by 300,000 iterations) while achieving a high mean aggregated utility of 408,670. VAE obtains the best observed aggregated utility overall (410,566)

Table 4. Aggregate utility results for $m = 2$ agents (means $\pm$ std. dev. and percentage deviations in relation to the exact solver results for the hypothetical centralized planning) for different generators with 50,000 iterations (10 repetitions)

	Evolutionary Operators		Autoencoder		Variational Autoencoder	
B1	82501.8 ± 158.9	(0.9%)	82919.9 ± 120.4	(0.4%)	82929.6 ± 105.8	(0.4%)
B2	207296.9 ± 512.3	(1.6%)	209258.3 ± 280.6	(0.7%)	208754.6 ± 306.6	(0.9%)
B3	411661.3 ± 587.9	(2.0%)	414550.7 ± 661.4	(1.3%)	413026.3 ± 802.1	(1.6%)
B4	77865.7 ± 413.7	(1.8%)	78627.3 ± 125.5	(0.9%)	78591.5 ± 230.0	(0.9%)
B5	208043.0 ± 394.2	(1.9%)	210212.4 ± 245.5	(0.9%)	209479.0 ± 465.7	(1.2%)
B6	406759.5 ± 780.7	(2.3%)	410396.0 ± 843.8	(1.5%)	408310.8 ± 1094.1	(2.0%)
B7	77252.0 ± 367.4	(1.7%)	77907.9 ± 249.8	(0.9%)	77977.1 ± 242.0	(0.8%)
B8	201143.1 ± 687.6	(2.4%)	203926.4 ± 351.4	(1.1%)	203275.1 ± 629.1	(1.4%)
B9	399417.4 ± 877.2	(3.4%)	406883.8 ± 936.8	(1.6%)	404406.4 ± 1412.9	(2.2%)

while maintaining greater diversity (69 unique solutions). The baseline generator remains diverse (eventually 99 unique solutions) but at lower utility levels (mean aggregated utility: 402,656).

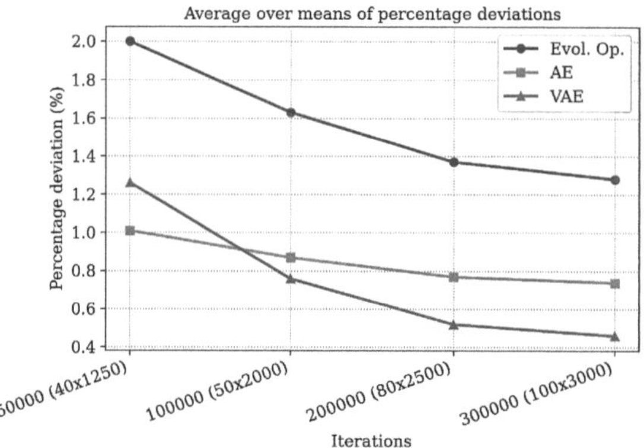

Fig. 2. Average performance of the generators with increasing iterations

Figure 4 visualizes the negotiation outcomes for $m = 2$ agents and 300,000 iterations alongside the corresponding Pareto front approximations. For each generator, the scatter plot shows results from ten independent runs. We also report the mean utility vector and draw covariance ellipses to give a compact summary of the empirical distributions.

5.3   Discussion

Across all benchmark instances and both agent configurations, the autoencoder and the variational autoencoder generators consistently produce solutions closer to the Pareto front than the baseline evolutionary operators. For 300,000 iterations (Tables 2 and 3), the baseline achieves solutions with deviations ranging

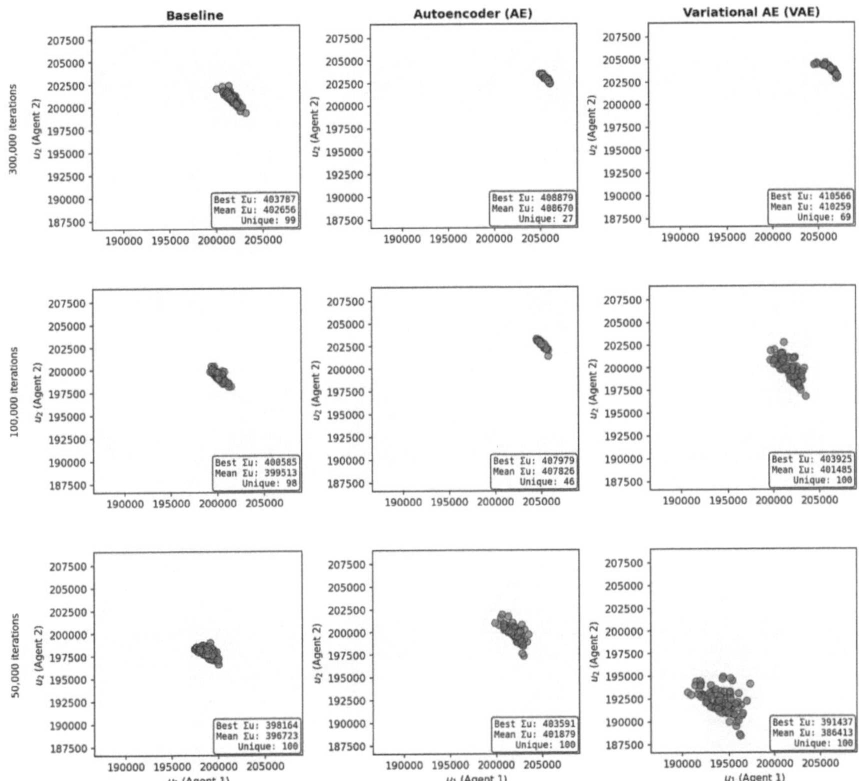

Fig. 3. Exemplary development of the population for instance B9 at different stages of the negotiation (for the case of 300,000 iterations with 100 training phases and 3,000 generation iterations)

from 0.6% to 2.4% from the centralized planning bound, while the neural generators reduce these deviations to 0.4%–1.3% (AE) or 0.3%–0.8% (VAE). The improvement is attributable to the neural generators' capacity to learn latent representations that capture structural regularities in the evolving population of high-quality solutions, enabling more targeted exploration of the solution space compared to the considered evolutionary operators. The relative advantage of neural generators increases with problem size. On the smallest instance (B1, $n = 100$, $d = 5$), the VAE improves upon the already quite good baseline by 0.3 and 0.7% points (for 2 agents and 3 agents, respectively); on the largest instance (B9, $n = 500$, $d = 30$), the improvement grows to 1.8 and 1.6% points. This scaling behavior suggests that learned representations become increasingly valuable as the combinatorial complexity of the solution space grows. While both neural models yield substantial improvements over the baseline, the variational

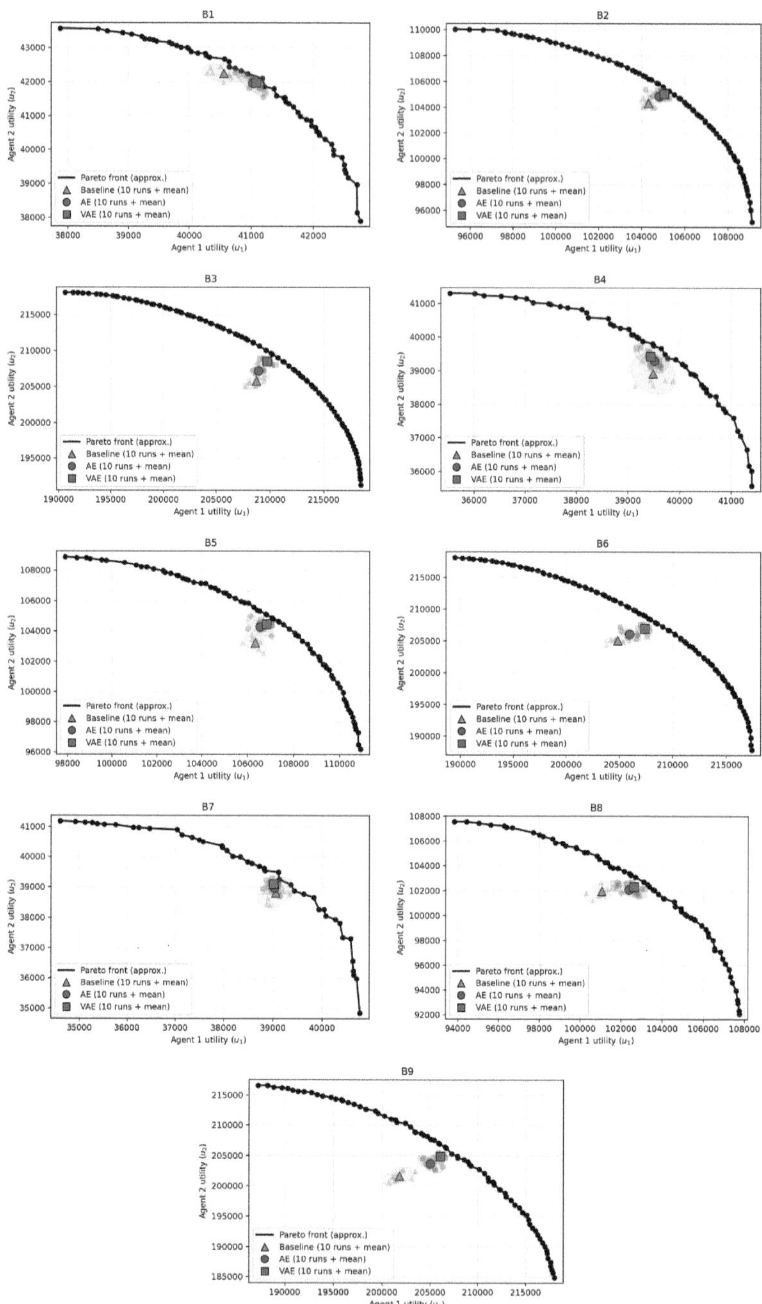

Fig. 4. Comparison of negotiation results for different generators (evolutionary operators as baseline, autoencoder (AE), and variational autoencoder (VAE)) within the bounds of approximated Pareto fronts (for $m = 2$ agents, 300,000 iterations)

autoencoder achieves the best results. Nevertheless, the differences between AE and VAE are smaller compared to the gap between either neural generator and the baseline, indicating that the primary benefit stems from learned latent representations rather than the specific architectural choice.

As shown in Tables 2 and 4 and Figs. 2 and 3, solution quality improves with additional iterations for all generator types, yet the gains are particularly pronounced for the VAE generator. The VAE generator requires a certain number of iterations and corresponding training loops to achieve high-quality results (as illustrated for the case of 50,000 iterations, where the AE performs better than the VAE). A plausible explanation is that variational representation learning typically entails a higher training effort before converging to a high-quality latent structure.

Figure 4 provides a visual confirmation of the quantitative analysis. For all instances, the solutions produced by neural generators cluster near the estimated Pareto front, whereas the baseline solutions are more scattered and typically lie further away from the front, indicating both lower efficiency and higher variability across runs. The covariance ellipses illustrate the reduced variance of neural generator outcomes. Notably, even for the most constrained instances (B7–B9 with $d = 30$ dimensions), the neural generators identify solutions near the Pareto front.

A limitation of the present evaluation is that it used instances that are synthetically derived from the multidimensional knapsack benchmark. This supports controlled comparisons, but may not capture preference structures observed in real-world settings. Moreover, our experiments are restricted to small negotiating groups (two and three agents), whereas practical applications may involve larger and more heterogeneous stakeholder groups. We also note that we did not study the impact of strict versus weak preference responses in the step where agents are asked whether they accept replacing an incumbent population member. In our experiments, the diverse scenario data almost never produced situations where this distinction would matter, so there was little empirical basis for a meaningful comparison. Furthermore, the set of methodological design choices explored in this study is limited. We did not perform systematic hyperparameter tuning, and we only tested a few architectural and algorithmic variants. A more comprehensive ablation study, covering both model design and optimization settings, is therefore an important direction for future work.

6   Conclusions

This paper presented a negotiation mechanism for project portfolio selection in community service planning contexts. The approach addresses the challenge of coordinating stakeholders with heterogeneous and partially private preferences under shared resource constraints, a setting that remains underexplored in the decision support systems and automated negotiation literature, despite its relevance to public-sector planning. The studied solution approach integrates negotiation and machine learning into an evolutionary optimization loop.

256   A. Fink

Autonomous agents represent stakeholders, repeatedly evaluate candidate portfolios, and accept only proposals that are Pareto-improving. This mechanism enforces monotonic progress toward more efficient outcomes. At the same time, it supports preference privacy, since agents communicate only pairwise judgments rather than disclosing cardinal utility values. Methodologically, the main contribution is the investigation of neural solution generators, in particular the variational autoencoder, on the basis of the considered application type with binary vector solutions. These models successively learn compact latent representations of the evolving population and exploit them to propose promising candidate portfolios. Computational experiments on benchmark instances with up to 500 projects, 30 resource dimensions, and two or three agents demonstrate that the neural generators substantially outperform conventional evolutionary operators. The variational autoencoder obtained the best results, in particular for larger and more constrained instances. These findings suggest that learned probabilistic representations can provide an effective mechanism for exploiting structural regularities in high-dimensional combinatorial solution spaces.

From a practical point of view, the approach has several strengths for participatory governance and has the potential to be generalized to other applications. First, it can coordinate decisions among multiple stakeholders in a fair way without requiring them to reveal their full preferences, which preserves preference privacy and reduces incentives for strategic misreporting that may complicate centralized optimization. Second, the protocol is easy to explain: stakeholders can simply reject any proposal that would leave them worse off. This veto mechanism makes the process transparent, which in turn increases acceptance of the outcome. Third, the framework is modular, so different solution generators can be plugged in and the system can be adjusted to the needs and constraints of a given application.

Several directions for future research emerge from this work. First, the experimental evaluation could be extended to settings with larger numbers of agents and to instances derived from real-world community planning scenarios. This may involve accounting for interdependencies between projects beyond resource contention [7] and studying whether the benefit of learned proposal generators persists in particularly hard instances with less exploitable structure (e.g., by varying tightness and related structural parameters). Second, alternative neural architectures, such as transformer-based models, generative adversarial networks, or graph neural networks that explicitly represent project dependencies, may be worth considering. Third, the framework could be extended to accommodate additional constraints, such as minimum requirements for specific project categories (e.g., environmental sustainability targets) or fairness constraints that guarantee minimum utility levels for all stakeholders. Finally, integration with interactive decision support interfaces would enable empirical evaluation with human stakeholders, providing insights into usability, trust, and perceived fairness of algorithmically supported participatory decision-making.

Acknowledgement. This work originates from the LIONS research project. LIONS is funded by dtec.bw – Digitalization and Technology Research Center of the Bundeswehr, which we gratefully acknowledge. dtec.bw is funded by the European Union – NextGenerationEU.

References

1. Baarslag, T., Hendrikx, M.J.C., Hindriks, K.V., Jonker, C.M.: Learning about the opponent in automated bilateral negotiation: a comprehensive survey of opponent modeling techniques. Auton. Agent. Multi-Agent Syst. **30**(5), 849–898 (2016)
2. Bäck, T.: Evolutionary Algorithms in Theory and Practice: Evolution Strategies, Evolutionary Programming, Genetic Algorithms. Oxford University Press (1996)
3. Bentley, P., Lim, S.L., Arcaini, P., Ishikawa, F.: Using a variational autoencoder to learn valid search spaces of safely monitored autonomous robots for last-mile delivery. In: Proceedings of the Genetic and Evolutionary Computation Conference, pp. 1303–1311 (2023)
4. Bhattacharjee, S., Gras, R.: Estimation of distribution using population queue based variational autoencoders. In: 2019 IEEE Congress on Evolutionary Computation, pp. 1406–1414. IEEE (2019)
5. Bui, T., Yen, J., Zeleznikow, J.H.J., Sankaran, S.: A multi-attribute negotiation support system with market signaling for electronic markets. Group Decis. Negot. **10**(6), 515–537 (2001)
6. Busuioc, M.: Accountable artificial intelligence: holding algorithms to account. Public Adm. Rev. **81**(5), 825–836 (2021)
7. Carazo, A.F.: Multi-criteria project portfolio selection. In: Schwindt, C., Zimmermann, J. (eds.) Handbook on Project Management and Scheduling Vol. 2. IHIS, pp. 709–728. Springer, Cham (2015). https://doi.org/10.1007/978-3-319-05915-0_3
8. Chu, P.C., Beasley, J.E.: A genetic algorithm for the multidimensional knapsack problem. J. Heurist. **4**(1), 63–86 (1998)
9. Churchill, A.W., Sigtia, S., Fernando, C.: A denoising autoencoder that guides stochastic search. arXiv preprint arXiv:1404.1614 (2014)
10. Conitzer, V., Freeman, R., Shah, N.: Fair public decision making. In: Proceedings of the 2017 ACM Conference on Economics and Computation, pp. 629–646 (2017)
11. Cui, M., Li, L., Zhou, M.: An autoencoder-embedded evolutionary optimization framework for high-dimensional problems. In: 2020 IEEE International Conference on Systems, Man, and Cybernetics (SMC), pp. 1046–1051. IEEE (2020)
12. Efremov, R.V., Insua, D.R., Lotov, A.: A framework for participatory decision support using Pareto frontier visualization, goal identification and arbitration. Eur. J. Oper. Res. **199**(2), 459–467 (2009)
13. Ehrgott, M.: Multicriteria Optimization. Springer (2005)
14. Feng, L., Zhou, W., Liu, W., Ong, Y.S., Tan, K.C.: Solving dynamic multiobjective problem via autoencoding evolutionary search. IEEE Trans. Cybern. **52**(5), 2649–2662 (2022)
15. Fink, A., Gerhards, P.: Negotiation mechanisms for the multi-agent multi-mode resource investment problem. Eur. J. Oper. Res. **295**(1), 261–274 (2021)
16. Fink, A., Homberger, J.: Decentralized multi-project scheduling. In: Schwindt, C., Zimmermann, J. (eds.) Handbook on Project Management and Scheduling Vol. 2. IHIS, pp. 685–706. Springer, Cham (2015). https://doi.org/10.1007/978-3-319-05915-0_2
17. Fréville, A.: The multidimensional 0–1 knapsack problem: an overview. Eur. J. Oper. Res. **155**(1), 1–21 (2004)

18. Garciarena, U., Santana, R., Mendiburu, A.: Expanding variational autoencoders for learning and exploiting latent representations in search distributions. In: Proceedings of the Genetic and Evolutionary Computation Conference, pp. 849–856 (2018)
19. Goldberg, D.E.: Genetic Algorithms in Search, Optimization, and Machine Learning. Addison Wesley (1989)
20. Goodfellow, I., Bengio, Y., Courville, A.: Deep Learning. MIT Press (2016)
21. Grantham, K., Mukaidaisi, M., Ooi, H.K., Ghaemi, M.S., Tchagang, A., Li, Y.: Deep evolutionary learning for molecular design. IEEE Comput. Intell. Mag. **17**(2), 14–28 (2022)
22. Higgins, I., et al.: β-VAE: learning basic visual concepts with a constrained variational framework. In: International Conference on Learning Representations (2017)
23. Hinton, G.E., Salakhutdinov, R.R.: Reducing the dimensionality of data with neural networks. Science **313**(5786), 504–507 (2006)
24. Homberger, J., Fink, A.: Generic negotiation mechanisms with side payments - design, analysis and application for decentralized resource-constrained multi-project scheduling problems. Eur. J. Oper. Res. **261**(3), 1001–1012 (2017)
25. Homberger, J., Fink, A.: Deep representation learning for generating candidate solutions in multi-agent negotiation evolutionary search. In: Amen, M., et al. (eds.) Operations Research Proceedings 2025. Lecture Notes in Operations Research. Springer (2026, to appear)
26. Hottung, A., Bhandari, B., Tierney, K.: Learning a latent search space for routing problems using variational autoencoders. In: International Conference on Learning Representations (2021)
27. Jennings, N.R., Faratin, P., Lomuscio, A., Parsons, S., Sierra, C., Wooldridge, M.: Automated negotiation: prospects, methods and challenges. Group Decis. Negot. **10**(2), 199–215 (2001)
28. Kingma, D.P., Welling, M.: Auto-encoding variational Bayes. In: International Conference on Learning Representations (2014)
29. Kraus, S.: Strategic Negotiation in Multiagent Environments. MIT Press, Cambridge (2001)
30. Lang, F., Fink, A.: Learning from the metaheuristics: protocols for automated negotiations. Group Decis. Negot. **24**(2), 299–332 (2015)
31. Li, Y., et al.: Generative models in decision making: a survey. arXiv preprint arXiv:2502.17100 (2025)
32. Macintosh, A.: Characterizing e-participation in policy-making. In: Proceedings of the 37th Annual Hawaii International Conference on System Sciences, pp. 1–10. IEEE (2004)
33. Medaglia, R.: eParticipation research: moving characterization forward (2006–2011). Gov. Inf. Q. **29**(3), 346–360 (2012)
34. Mogbojuri, A., Olanrewaju, O.: An integrated AHP-GP-GA approach for public project portfolio selection problem. Ain Shams Eng. J. **16**(10), 103644 (2025)
35. Oliver, J.R.: A machine-learning approach to automated negotiation and prospects for electronic commerce. J. Manag. Inf. Syst. **13**(3), 83–112 (1996)
36. Papadimitriou, C., Schapira, M., Singer, Y.: On the hardness of being truthful. In: Proceedings of the 49th Annual IEEE Symposium on Foundations of Computer Science, pp. 250–259. IEEE (2008)
37. Power, D.J.: Decision Support Systems: Concepts and Resources for Managers. Greenwood Publishing Group (2002)
38. Probst, M., Rothlauf, F.: Harmless overfitting: using denoising autoencoders in estimation of distribution algorithms. J. Mach. Learn. Res. **21**(78), 1–31 (2020)

39. Puchinger, J., Raidl, G.R., Pferschy, U.: The multidimensional knapsack problem: structure and algorithms. INFORMS J. Comput. **22**(2), 250–265 (2010)
40. Rezende, D.J., Mohamed, S., Wierstra, D.: Stochastic backpropagation and approximate inference in deep generative models. In: International Conference on Machine Learning, pp. 1278–1286 (2014)
41. Shim, J.K., Warkentin, M., Courtney, J.F., Power, D.J., Sharda, R., Carlsson, C.: Past, present, and future of decision support technology. Decis. Support Syst. **33**(2), 111–126 (2002)
42. Wampler, B.: Participatory budgeting: core principles and key impacts. J. Public Deliberation **8**(2) (2012)
43. Whitley, D.: A genetic algorithm tutorial. Stat. Comput. **4**(2), 65–85 (1994)
44. Wirtz, B.W., Weyerer, J.C., Geyer, M.: Artificial intelligence and the public sector-applications and challenges. Int. J. Public Adm. **42**(7), 596–615 (2019)

LLM-Supported Excerpt-Level Maturity Assessment
A Conceptual and Technical Proof of Concept

Wesley Preßler[1]([✉]), Patrick Seidel[2], and Steffen Späthe[3]

[1] Ernst-Abbe-Hochschule Jena, 07745 Jena, Germany
Wesley.Pressler@eah-jena.de
[2] Friedrich Schiller University Jena, 07745 Jena, Germany
patrick.seidel@uni-jena.de
[3] Navimatix GmbH, 07745 Jena, Germany
steffen.spaethe@navimatix.de

Abstract. Maturity models are widely used as instruments for assessing the current state of transformations within organizations. However, traditional assessment approaches are often resource-intensive, subjective, and difficult to scale across domains. Recent advances in large language models (LLMs) and structured reasoning techniques, such as Chain of Thought (CoT) prompting, offer new possibilities for automating and augmenting such assessments. Despite this potential, systematic approaches that leverage LLMs for maturity level determination remain underexplored. In this paper, we propose a concept for LLM-based maturity assessment grounded in a custom-developed maturity model. We design and evaluate a two-stage proof-of-concept pipeline in which a BERT-based encoder performs category-level classification, followed by a fine-tuned LLM decoder, adapted using LoRA+ and Parameter-Efficient Fine-Tuning (PEFT), that generates structured Chain of Thought reasoning sequences to derive maturity ratings and also explains the determination of the maturity level. We further critically examine the conditions under which such a system can and should be deployed, addressing the question of whether full automation is appropriate or whether hybrid human-AI oversight models are preferable. Our results demonstrate the technical feasibility of the proposed approach while surfacing important limitations regarding data quality. We argue that CoT-supported reasoning can improve the verifiability of model outputs for human evaluators and can serve as a key mechanism for calibrating confidence in partially or even fully automated maturity assessments. This work contributes an initial research paper that fundamentally addresses the application of LLMs in the determination of maturity levels.

Keywords: AI co-creation · Automated assessment · Chain-of-thought reasoning · Decoder-based model · LLM · Maturity model

1   Introduction

Maturity models have become a recognized instrument for the methodical evaluation of transformative processes. Software development, process management, and social and community-focused situations all utilize maturity models. Simultaneously, massive language models offer creative suggestions for text analysis, classification, and justification generation, which may also be applicable for executing maturity evaluations. Nonetheless, both advancements face an inherent conflict: maturity assessments necessitate clear, methodologically sound evaluations, whereas massive language models are frequently perceived as opaque systems with decision-making processes that are challenging to validate. This tension prompts an inquiry into the situations under which LLM-based analyses of maturity levels are methodologically warranted and how such integration may be practically implemented. The current literature has thus far only examined this subject in a disjointed fashion. There is a growing discourse around the utilization of LLMs in qualitative research, mostly focusing on concerns related to data quality, validation, and epistemic limitations. Conversely, research on maturity models exhibits methodological diversity; however a detailed analysis has largely overlooked the potential benefits and risks associated with generative AI systems. A detailed analysis that systematically connects the normative inquiry on the justification of LLMs in maturity assessment and the technical question of their architectural integration is lacking. This study seeks to bridge this gap by integrating two complementary viewpoints. A normative framework is established to define procedural prerequisites for the systematic application of LLMs in qualitative maturity evaluation. Second, we present a technical implementation that operationalizes these conditions through architectural design choices. The emphasis is on Chain-of-Thought-style rationales as inspectable outputs for human review. Rather than claiming fully valid automated maturity assessment, the paper examines whether LLMs can support bounded, excerpt-level judgments within a predefined maturity framework. The organization of the current document is as follows: Sect. 2 offers a summary of the fundamental principles utilized in this academic paper. Section 3 establishes the normative framework and delineates procedural guidelines for the methodical and prudent utilization of LLMs. Section 4 delineates the technological implementation comprehensively, encompassing system architecture and training. Section 5 examines the efficacy of the trained model in relation to expert assessment. Section 6 examines the alignment of technical design decisions with normative criteria and identifies any restrictions present. Section 7 encapsulates the findings and delineates avenues for subsequent scientific inquiries. The guiding question is therefore not whether LLMs can replace qualitative maturity assessment, but under which conditions they can support narrowly defined assessment tasks without overstating their epistemic status.

2   Background

2.1   Maturity Model

In a previous paper for the I4CS in Munich 2025, we provided already an overview of what maturity models are. For a better understanding, the following is a brief description of the 'maturity model' tool. For a more comprehensive discussion of the topic, we recommend the following sources: Preßler, W., Schmidt, L. (2025) [9]. Maturity models are methodically structured assessment tools that systematically record the development status of structures, technologies, processes and capabilities and convert them into comparable levels. Their added value lies less in the mere description of the current situation and more in the diagnostic consolidation: maturity models make transformation progress visible, identify bottlenecks and allow measures to be prioritized as the next plausible steps. In this way, they function in the scientific support of digital transformation projects both as an orientation framework (for control/intervention) and as an evaluation grid (for comparison over time, sub-areas and stakeholders). The maturity model we have further developed originated from the 'Multi-Generation Smart Community' research project at Ernst Abbe University of Applied Sciences in Jena, which was funded by the Zeiss Foundation. The Smart City Wheel [4] served as a heuristic frame of reference for dimensions of urban digitalization in the initial model and was used as a methodological basis in the project context. The decisive factor here was the shift from the 'Wheel' as a set of predefined dimensions to a framework that can be operationalized in a project- and context-specific manner: the model should enable statements and measurements that are not tied to a single use case, but rather support the accompaniment of transformation processes in changing environments. Three special features characterize the mGeSCo maturity model: (1) the possibility of generalization, (2) clear scaling, and (3) consideration of social integration conditions. The model is therefore not only used to evaluate a single transformation project, such as a smart neighborhood, but was designed from the outset as an adaptable framework for any conceivable digital transformation by capturing the model logic (dimensions + levels + measurement points) as an adaptable and/or reusable structure. In the current logic, which we intend to further develop in this paper, work is carried out along the dimensions of working, housing, living and caring, in line with the 'mGeSCo' architecture. The assessment is carried out on a six-point scale (0–5), ranging from 'no implementation' to 'full integration'. This creates a transparent development logic that supports both project planning and monitoring. The application is explicitly designed as an iterative research and accompanying process: (a) assessment of the current situation, (b) definition of objectives, (c) planning/implementation of measures, (d) continuous monitoring through quantitative and qualitative surveys, (e) needs-based model adaptation in co-production. The feedback loops in particular are not an 'add-on' but a methodological core, as they link the transformation back to the needs and experiences of those involved. A central innovation of the model is the extension of classic maturity logic, which often focuses on factual implementation status (degree of implementation), to include digital literacy, technology acceptance and interpretation patterns. This is done in order to understand the sustainability of digital transformation as a socio-technical integration achievement – including the assumption of mutual influence between these dimensions. The aim is to make "maturity" operationalizable not as a mere "increase in technology", but as an interplay of competence, willingness to use and attributions of meaning/legitimacy [9].

The previous chapters of the paper describe the further development of the existing model based on the Smart City Wheel: dimensions were tailored to the project logic, the 0–5 scale was established as a comparable progress logic, and social integration conditions were added as independent evaluation axes. This results in a maturity model that is both theoretically sound in terms of content and methodologically compatible – especially for technical implementation that systematically maps qualitative and quantitative evidence to the model logic. For the following chapter, the maturity model serves as a semantic backbone that structures excerpt-level evidence within predefined dimensions and levels, without equating single excerpts with full organizational maturity. At the same time, it remains open how exactly this classification is technically implemented (prompting, classification pipeline, validation logic) without subordinating the social science model logic to the technical process.

2.2 Large Language Models

Large language models (LLMs) are typically based on transformer architectures, which enabled major advances in natural language processing through parallelized self-attention mechanisms [12]. The processing of extensive data sets was accomplished, for instance, through the use of "self-attention," which is employed by LLMs. The establishment of connections among words is intended to influence the generation of responses [12]. These features allowed the language models to comprehend the context of texts and formulate a potential response accordingly. It is essential to differentiate between encoder and decoder models, each of which has distinct applications. Encoder-only models, like BERT, excel at comprehending texts and executing tasks such as text categorization and entity recognition because of their bidirectional methodology, [1]. They can, owing to the bidirectional method, evaluate the meaning depending on the context both to the left and right of the target word. This suggests that decoder-only models like GPT, specifically designed for text production, are better suited for this task. These models consider the most recently produced content and construct the subsequent most probable token accordingly. As a result, they are unidirectional and are less appropriate for the classification of text samples or entities inside texts. These two model types can be trained according to the use case to yield improved outcomes in a particular domain. The complete corpus does not require retraining; instead, it enhances the existing knowledge, allowing for further material to be integrated into the model. The models are therefore pre-trained and can be refined by fine-tuning [1,12]. Through this training, LLMs can adhere to human instructions and deliver suitable responses by techniques like "Instruction Tuning" and "Reinforcement Learning from Human Feedback

(RLHF)." Strategies like few-shot learning, reasoning, or self-consistency can enhance these models. These strategies allow models to learn from patterns or instances, apply them, build sequences of reasoning, draw conclusions, or devise multiple solutions and subsequently select the most appropriate one [13,14]. This seeks to render LLMs accessible to additional domains and to instruct them in human cognitive patterns. Moreover, these strategies aim to alleviate or even eradicate the existing issues and challenges associated with LLMs. The text generation of these models relies on probabilities, which may result in the creation of realistic yet fabricated content. This phenomenon is referred to as "hallucination" and presents a considerable challenge in the application of these models [8]. False information can yield differing repercussions based on the context, thereby necessitating human evaluation. Moreover, pure language models are constrained by the knowledge available at the time of their training [8]. This guarantees that new information is excluded from consideration when formulating responses without supplementary instruments. Supplementary techniques such as web search or retrieval-augmented generation (RAG) can alleviate these significant issues. Ultimately, these models remain imperfect and are now undergoing further development. Nonetheless, they demonstrate considerable potential to automate many domains and execute repetitive activities.

3   Methodological Reflection

With a view to the desired combination of LLM's and maturity models based on qualitative survey methods, it is essential to first clarify the epistemic and methodological requirements that can or must legitimately be asserted when using transformer-based language models in qualitative interview analysis. We draw on our contribution to the 2025 conference, where we fine-tuned a pure encoder transformer model to assign interview excerpts to four predefined dimensions of a maturity model for examining digital transformation in four dimensions ("Housing", "Working", "Living", "Caring") [11]. In this setting, the classifier achieved high performance on the inputs (e.g., 22 out of 23 excerpts were correctly assigned by GottBERT Large), but two structural challenges also came to the fore: the opacity of the decision paths and the limited scope of automatable conclusions in qualitative workflows [11]. Building on that empirical baseline, this chapter asks: "Which analytical tasks can be delegated to LLM-based systems in qualitative research, under which epistemic obligations, and with what limits?" The central issue is therefore not whether model outputs appear "good" or "bad", but what status they can legitimately have within a qualitative research design—and where the boundary between classification and interpretation must be drawn. Our previous work addressed the central problem of time-consuming and error-prone manual categorization of text segments in qualitative surveys such as maturity analyses. For this reason, we proposed an encoder-based transformer classification as a solution to reduce the effort involved while maintaining quality where possible. The goal of automation was deliberately limited: the aim was to assign text segments to a predefined category system rather than attempting to classify and interpret the text segments analytically. Methodologically, this means that the model we developed performs pure basic pattern recognition without interpreting the data in any way. All assigned segments had to be not only checked by a person but also assigned a maturity value within the dimensions of the model [11]. However, even within this limited framework, two caveats are important for further discussion. First, the distribution of categories in our labelled dataset is uneven (e.g., "housing" occurs more frequently than "work", "life", and "care"). In our empirical setting, this bias is not automatically a problem of data quality; it may reflect substantial salience effects in the interview material, i.e., participants disproportionately articulate transformation-related experiences through the lens of topics related to living. If this distribution were to be regarded as "noise" and mechanically balanced out, there would be a risk of imposing artificial symmetry on an empirically asymmetrical phenomenon. At the same time, the prevalence has consequences for content analysis: if one topic dominates the material, there is an increased risk that a coding instrument – whether human or model-based – will stabilize the majority logic as the standard and oversimplify less frequently articulated interpretations. In the logic of content analysis, which structures content, it is therefore essential to review and refine the category system in such a way that it depicts contrasts, deviations and borderline cases in a rule-based manner (coding guidelines, anchor examples, coding rules) and that the internal study quality is ensured through targeted cross-checks. This becomes clear in our evaluation, in which ModernBERT variants assign almost all entries to the category "housing", which we interpret less as "empirical truth" and more as a combination of abbreviations of the majority class and a discrepancy between domain and language (English pre-training vs. German interview data). The second concern is that the original paper explicitly points out the partial opacity of the internal decision paths in encoder models and identifies interpretability (XAI) as an open problem [11]. In view of the aforementioned findings, it is evident that encoder-based classification can serve as a high-throughput, limited assignment of text to an existing category system – provided that the outputs are validated and distortions and error patterns are systematically analyzed. The situation becomes critical when a model is expected to do more than just categorization and is also required to perform a kind of qualitative interpretation of the data. This gives rise to entirely new considerations for practical application. In reflexive qualitative traditions, meaning is not treated as something that can be extracted from data as an objective property. Instead, it is produced through situated, theory-informed engagement with participants accounts and with the research process itself. Friese articulates this constructivist stance by contrasting positivist assumptions of "objective meaning" with constructivist grounded theory, where meaning is co-constructed by researchers, participants, and analytic procedures [3]. This implies two immediate implications for LLM-supported analysis:

1. Qualitative interpretation is method-bound, not merely output-bound. In interpretive approaches, validity depends not only on what is claimed about

the data, but on whether the claim is produced through recognizable analytic procedures – e.g., iterative coding and constant comparison, memoing, case-based contrasts, and explicit handling of researcher assumptions.
2. Interpretation is reflexive and positioned, not merely semantic. Reflexivity requires accounting for how assumptions, values, and experiences shape coding and theorizing. Friese stresses that curiosity, abductive moves, and the impulse to challenge preconceptions cannot be outsourced to the model; they remain the responsibility of the human analyst [3].

From the perspective of qualitative research, it is therefore clear that model outputs cannot be treated as equivalent to methodologically sound interpretations. Even plausible-sounding "analyses" may fail to meet the epistemic requirements of a particular interpretation method, as plausibility is not synonymous with procedural adequacy. A related debate concerns whether generative LLMs can reliably enact method-specific interpretive procedures (e.g., variants of hermeneutics) when prompted to do so. In exploratory tests with common chat-based LLMs (prior to building our encoder-based classifier), we observed frequent variation across runs and procedural drift: outputs differed substantially even under comparable prompts, and method steps were inconsistently reproduced. This illustrates how hallucinations and unstable reproduction of structured knowledge can directly threaten the trustworthiness of automated qualitative "evaluations". This is crucial for methodological reflection because it points to a problem of methodological conformity: the model's inability to guarantee adherence to the procedural steps that constitute a qualitative method. If results vary strongly across runs or deviate from defined procedures, the output cannot be treated as a reproducible application of that method – even if its narrative form resembles qualitative reasoning [10]. For this reason, in the initial version, we pursued the path of mere category assignment and initially rejected the idea of assistance for the evaluation and interpretation of qualitative data [11]. This is not only a technical criticism, but also an epistemic one. In method-driven qualitative analysis, the credibility of claims is linked to (I) the traceability/replicability of interpretations of or in the data, (II) procedural discipline, and (III) reflexive accountability. If procedural discipline cannot be demonstrated, the epistemic status of the model's "interpretation" shifts: LLM results must be treated as heuristic statements (possible readings), not as methodologically certified interpretations [10]. Based on these considerations, a clear premise for the further development of our analysis model can be established: If LLMs in the present design are used not as an interpretative authority but as a limited analytical tool, governance requirements must become part of the method itself: task delimitation, transparency of data flows, validation logic and protection concepts for interview material are not downstream "compliance" issues, but prerequisites for the epistemic validity of the results [10]. By defining the epistemic and methodological framework conditions in advance, we were able to incorporate these important considerations into the design and implementation of the model from the outset during the final implementation.

4   Implementation

A two-stage system was developed to ascertain the maturity level, which initially identifies the relevant primary category and subsequently offers a recommendation for it based on an interview excerpt. In the initial phase, classification is performed using a BERT model (encoder-only), with the resultant data being directly applied to the subsequent phase, which involves assessing the maturity level. This is executed through the utilization of a Llama-3.1-8B-Instruct (Decoder-Only), for which a Lora adapter was trained. This adapter can provide a maturity level suggestion utilizing the Chain of Thought approach (Fig. 1).

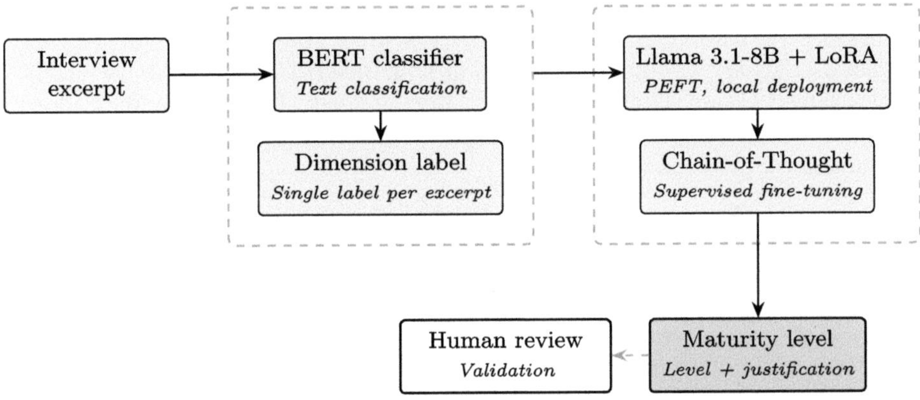

Fig. 1. Two-stage pipeline for automated maturity assessment

In the current proof of concept, each excerpt is assigned one primary dimension for operational simplicity, although some passages may plausibly relate to more than one dimension. The precise procedure is as follows:

1. Raw data in the form of interview excerpts
2. Classification of the main category of the interview excerpt
3. CoT generation through the LoRA decoder
4. Proposal for a maturity level

The training data underpins both tiers of the proposed architecture, with its structure and quality significantly impacting the system's overall efficiency. This academic study will focus solely on the training data of the LoRA decoder, as the data foundation of the BERT classifier has been thoroughly addressed in a separate scholarly effort [11]. The decoder's objective is to produce a recommendation for a maturity level that can act as a foundation for an expert. The model will assess interview fragments to generate a relevant suggestion for a maturity level. Fourteen data points were utilized for model training, each comprising the following segments:

- instruction: The system prompt aims to enhance the model's guidance on when to reference the trained model component.
- input: The unmodified segment from the interview, which will be examined to formulate the maturity level suggestion, is included.
- output: The text contains the rationale and essential facts needed for a fundamental evaluation of the maturity level.

The data were produced by an expert who conveyed his cognitive processes as training data. Thus, each data point signifies an evaluation of a particular interview segment, encompassing the relevant text excerpts and rationales for the maturity level. An excerpt from such an interview may appear as follows:

- In this respect, the mobility topics at the moment are indeed more about this electric wheelchair, which we are now launching with the company Carqueville. To try it out, someone rents it as needed. Yes, so the service is, I just talked about the nursing service management, I've already mentioned a bit, like emergency call button systems, etc. But that is all fundamentally available in principle.

The expert's methodology for interpreting the excerpt was included in the "Chain of Thought" framework for model training. The rephrasing of the aforementioned interview extract is as follows:

- ### Step 1: Inventory of the Material First, I check whether the section describes (a) planning/ideas, (b) concrete planning with initial tests, (c) pilot implementation, (d) broad implementation, or (e) full integration. Additionally, I check whether it concerns access/networking to health services (e.g., emergency call, nursing service, availability of services). ### Step 2: Collect relevant text signals I extract the statements about the implementation status from the text.: - Planned offer with external company: "... with that one company ... wants to launch." - Test character / trial: "To try it out ..." - Usage logic as needed (rental): "... someone rents it as needed." - Health service reference: "... emergency call button systems, etc." - Availability statement: "... everything ... generally available." ### Step 3: Comparison with the level definition $0 - -5$ I compare the hints with the levels: - Level 0: does not fit, as services are mentioned. - Level 1: would fit if it's just about ideas/interest. Here, however, an experimentation is already described, and services are available. - Level 2: fits because a specific project with testing/trial is mentioned (trying out the electric wheelchair). - Level 3: would fit if it were clear that the offer is already running as a pilot in a specific area (e.g., defined user group/neighborhood/regular process in the pilot). - Level 4/5: would require widespread use or complete integration. That is not substantiated. ### Step 4: Logical Decision In the section, two signals are placed side by side: 1) The electric wheelchair is being "launched" and is to be "tested" $\rightarrow$ this indicates an early implementation phase (testing/trial). 2) Emergency call button systems are described as "generally available" $\rightarrow$ this sounds like basic provision is available, but there is no indication of widespread use or integration. Since the text does not provide evidence of widespread establishment or integration and the wheelchair is explicitly described as a trial, the safest classification is a concrete plan with initial testing. ### Result: Caring = Level 2 ### Textual evidence - "To try that out ..." - "... emergency button systems, etc. ... generally available."

The expert's methodology for interpreting the excerpt was included in the "Chain of Thought" framework for model training. The rephrasing of the aforementioned interview extract is as follows: The example illustrates how the trained decoder converts a dimension-specific prompt and an interview excerpt into a bounded maturity-level proposal with an explicit rationale. To facilitate the model's generation of such a proposal, a modification of its weights is necessary, a process referred to as model training or fine-tuning. Nonetheless, comprehensively training such a model would be impractical with standard hardware and within a reasonable duration. Consequently, the choice was made to utilize optimized model training, facilitated by Unsloth [5]. This framework enhances model training by utilizing PEFT, namely Lora+. This work utilizes Parameter-Efficient Fine-Tuning (PEFT) approaches [6] to meet the substantial resource demands for adapting big language models. PEFT freezes the bulk of model parameters while updating only a minor subset, therefore considerably diminishing memory demands and computational workload. Additionally, Low-Rank Adaptation (LoRA) facilitates the training of compact adapters that may be toggled on and off as required [7]. Consequently, it is unnecessary to comprehensively train the large base model; just smaller pieces require training. This provides the further benefit that previously learned knowledge remains intact, allowing the model to utilize existing knowledge even after the weights have been modified. This training is mostly governed by established parameters, which can be distinguished for adapter training, model training, and resource efficiency. The subsequent parameters were utilized for the adapter's training:

- LoRA Rank (r = 32): The dimensionality of the LoRA matrices is established, dictating the level of expressiveness. The chosen value surpasses the typical range (8–16) due to the necessity for a more intricate adjustment in the creation of CoT, which concurrently elevates memory demands.
- LoRA Alpha (lora_alpha = 32): This pertains to the LoRA rank and mitigates training instability caused by excessively large or small updates.

Alongside the adapter training, overarching training parameters were defined:

- Learning Rate (2e-4) & LR Scheduler (linear): The learning rate has been optimized for LoRA and exceeds that of traditional model training techniques. The linear scheduler reduces the probability of overfitting to the training dataset.
- Warmup Steps (10) & Max Steps (100): The learning rate must be incrementally elevated to the goal value to initially avert erratic updates. The steps were intentionally minimized owing to the restricted volume of training data.

To enhance training efficacy, the subsequent parameters were also considered:

- Batch Size (2) & Gradient Accumulation (4)
- Optimizer (adamw_8bit): Reduces storage requirements without significant loss of quality.
- fp16 / bf16 (automatically): Automatic selection of the precision format based on the available hardware.

These training settings are formulated to facilitate training despite constrained hardware capabilities. The Unsloth framework facilitated the training process, enabling completion in under 10 minutes on an Nvidia RTX 4080 Super equipped with 16 GB of VRAM. In conclusion, the advanced language model, through the use of PEFT and LoRA, can assess maturity levels based on interview excerpts and produce an appropriate recommendation. Moreover, the thinking process is presented, enabling an assessor to comprehend the rationale and integrate it into their judgment.

5 Evaluation

This section presents an illustrative example of system behavior rather than a benchmark-style evaluation. The aim is to show how the pipeline processes one interview excerpt and how the resulting output can be compared with expert judgment.

Person 1: (...) Not really. So, the coworking is on the operator's side. So, the premises are difficult for coworking spaces. So, we have also spoken with various coworking space providers. The room heights and room volumes in such a, let's say, system building are really not optimal for the areas and the way of working. Let's put it this way, and um, the point is that Jena Wohnen is not allowed to do this. So, we are not allowed to operate something like that, we would have had to find an operator, and unfortunately, it just didn't work out. In this respect, one can certainly benefit from the now, let's say, very well-established fiber optic connection. So, we have internet in large quantities in the apartments, meaning fiber optic is available all the way to the apartment, so mobile working from home is basically possible without any issues. And we do have a common room that can be booked if, let's say, another workspace beside the home couch is more sensible. But otherwise? Nothing more. No. (2709-SL-24, Pos. 35–36)

Probability Distribution:

- Working : 97.74%
- Housing: 1.29%
- Living: 0.68%
- Caring: 0.29%

This resolution has now been incorporated into the system prompt used for decoder analysis, which is detailed as follows:

"Determine the maturity level (0–5) for the dimension Working based on the following passage. Justify the classification step by step and support it with text passages."

The outcome of the second model (maturity level) is as follows:

Step 1: Inventory of the material First, I look at which of the four dimensions I can assign the section to and whether the section contains indications of a maturity level (a) pure ideas/planning, (b) tests/initial implementations, (c) pilot operation, (d) widespread use, or (e) full integration. ### Step 2: Collect Relevant Text Signals Step 2: Collect relevant text signals I mark the statements that show the implementation status of Working/Smart Cities: - Problems with coworking space -Operators and premises: "... premises ... difficult ... System construction ... areas ... not optimal." - Healthy home office possible thru fiber optics: "... Internet ... in the apartments ... easily possible." - Alternative workspace bookable: "... common room ... book ... another workplace ... makes sense." - Status as a limitation/No implementation: "... is not allowed to do ... should have found an operator ... unfortunately didn't fit." - No further measures/infrastructure: "... nothing more. No." ### Step 3: Comparison with the Level Definition (0–5) I check the levels based on the signals: - Level 0 (no implementation): does not fit completely because there is concrete infrastructure (fiber optic) and a usable workspace. - Level 1 (initial planning): only partially fits, because while operators were discussed and premises were sought, the conditions for home office are already realistically in place. - Level 2 (concrete planning + initial tests): the text does not describe any tests or new implementations; rather, it utilizes an existing infrastructure (fiber optic). - Level 3 (Pilot implementation): no pilot operation or broad establishment is described. - Stage 4/5: no indications of widespread use or integration. ### Step 4: Logical Decision Step 4: Logical Decision The section describes an existing infrastructure (fiber optic internet in the apartments) that enables remote work. Additionally, a common room can be booked, providing an alternative workspace. However, no independent coworking infrastructure is operated, and no pilot implementation/broad establishment is described. Thus, the status in the area of Working/Smart Cities remains at the level of early planning/initial implementation. ### Result Working (Smart Cities) = Level 1 ### Textual evidence - "... Internet ... in the apartments ... easily possible." - "... common room ... book ... different workplace ..." - "... is not allowed to do ... should have found an operator ..."

The following text presents a study of an interview segment with a human expert, comparing the model output to the human interpretation in the final phase.

- **Categorization:** Working
- **Search for key passages:** "Not really. Coworking is on the operator side.";
  "We also spoke to various coworking providers and operators."; "In that respect, you can certainly use the fiber optic connection, which is now very good, in my opinion. We have internet in the flats, so fiber optic runs right into the flats."; 'And we have a common room that you can book if, let's say, a different place to work than your sofa at home makes sense, so to speak. But otherwise? Nothing more. No.'
- **Interpretation:** The remarks given by the test subject indicate that the co-working space was conceptualized but could not be executed due to multiple factors (system construction, operator, etc.). All apartments possess fiber optic internet, not as a result of the smart neighborhood, but rather as a fundamental infrastructure of the residential building. The common room (a room that can be booked by all residents in the neighborhood) is promoted as an alternate workspace; however, it is inadequate for this function (contextual insights from the interviewees). Classification based on maturity: The remarks indicate that preliminary preparations for co-working spaces have been established, suggesting a maturity level beyond 0. No co-working area has been established, and the internet in the apartments is solely infrastructural and not associated with the 'smart neighborhood' initiative. No additional planning, trialing, or testing has occurred.
- Result: Working, maturity level of 1

In this case, the model output aligns with the expert judgment, illustrating feasibility but not yet establishing robust performance.

6   Discussion

6.1   Human Reflexivity in Analytical Evaluation

The epistemic boundary discussed above raises a practical question: if LLM outputs must be treated as heuristic statements rather than certified interpretations, what legitimate function can they serve in qualitative analysis without replacing reflexive work? A recurring answer in the methodological debate is a dialogical one: LLMs may act as an additional voice that provokes contrasts and alternative readings, while interpretive accountability remains with the researcher [2]. On closer inspection, this dialogical proposal splits into two positions that pull in different directions: (A) rejection on the grounds of non-negotiable costs, and (B) conditional use within a constructivist, reflexively governed workflow.

Position A: Skepticism/Rejection Due to "Absolute Costs". A frequent argument is not primarily technical but responsibility-based: LLM use is linked to external effects (e.g., environmental impact, exploitative working conditions in data processing, and appropriation of intellectual work as training material), and these costs are treated as inseparable from scientific practice. A second concern is methodological and social: automating coding work may deprive research teams of learning and training opportunities, especially for student assistants who often acquire qualitative skills through collaborative coding and discussion. The guiding question then shifts from "Is it feasible?" to "Why should it be done at all under these conditions?", including the claim that potential epistemic gains do not justify hidden costs [2].

Position B: Conditional Use Through Joint Construction of Meaning. Friese offers a constructive alternative that does not deny the risks but changes the framework: within a constructivist, grounded theory, meaning is not extracted as an objective property but is jointly constructed through multiple perspectives. AI-generated readings can then be treated as an additional voice in a pluralistic interpretive process – neither superior nor methodologically privileged, but potentially useful for broadening perspective and promoting reflexivity [3]. Drawing on Friese's notion of "fluid positionality", we treat LLM responses as the generation of simulated viewpoints derived from large-scale textual corpora rather than as situated interpretation [3]. A dialogical framework becomes methodologically relevant as soon as it is associated with concrete risks and countermeasures. Friese identifies modes of error that are particularly prominent in qualitative work: **Risk of subservience/echo chamber.** Interactive chat models show a tendency towards user orientation (sycophancy), which can stabilize rather than disrupt existing theoretical assumptions. For the analysis, this means that the workflow must systematically enforce contradiction and case contrast (e.g. "best counter-reading", "disconfirming evidence") [3]. **Common sense orientation.** Because generative models optimize for likely continuations, they can privilege dominant, conventional framings and thereby reduce sensitivity to counter-intuitive or contradictory evidence – an issue Friese describes as the "proving the obvious" tendency [3]. To mitigate this, he recommends interaction patterns that explicitly look for contradictions, blind spots, differences between cases, and "unexpected" observations. These measures imply a change in the concept of "help": LLMs are not primarily used to shorten the interpretation process, but to generate friction in the most productive way possible. By inserting contrasts, alternative readings, and critical prompts that force analysts to re-examine assertions based on data and context. This is consistent with practical workflow suggestions in QualCoder, where AI outputs refer to source passages and offer different analysis modes ("Code Critic", "Analyze Unexpected", "Analyze Differences") proposed by Friese 2025 [3], turning the system into a structured dialogue partner rather than an interpretive authority. **Operationalization of so-called "acceptable roles" in the analysis process** To move from theoretical principle to our research design, the roles of LLM were specified along a graded spectrum of epistemic delegation:

- High congruence: Support for limited, verifiable tasks such as retrieval ("Find instances of X"), reformatting, summarizing code coverage with links to source passages, or procedural classification under a fixed category system (as in our use case for mapping a maturity model of digital transformation) [11].
- Conditional congruence: Idea generation and abductive provocation as possible interpretations – explicitly formulated as hypotheses that must be tested using raw data, memos, and case comparisons, with interaction patterns designed to counteract bias.
- Low congruence: Delegating methodologically bound interpretations (e.g., claiming that the model "applied" a hermeneutic procedure) when adherence to the methodology cannot be proven and the results may deviate or vary without a comprehensible procedure.

Taken together, the discourse suggests an integration: rejection can be justified where absolute costs or project values preclude LLM use, while conditional use requires explicit methodological governance if it is pursued. This is not only a methodological issue but also an infrastructural one. In many non-profit and community contexts, qualitative data concern vulnerable groups and sensitive life situations, which raises the bar for trust, transparency, and data protection. The feasibility of LLM support therefore depends on governance requirements that combine task selection, validation, transparency, and protection of interview material. The central thesis is that tasks involve heterogeneous risks and that interpretive tasks are particularly hard to reconcile with LLM use where suitable validation may be unavailable. This motivates a procedural rule: before using an LLM, researchers should enumerate candidate tasks, decide on suitability, and specify a validation plan to prevent drift from narrow support functions (e.g., retrieval or formatting) into interpretive claims the workflow cannot validate [10]. Codifying these considerations into a small set of enforceable procedural rules allows us to specify when LLM support is methodologically congruent, how it must be validated, and where it must be excluded to protect epistemic claims.

The prior analysis outlines a series of procedural prerequisites, task selection, validation, transparency, and data protection that any methodologically consistent LLM integration must fulfill. The following parts describe how these requirements might be met through architectural and operational design decisions instead of depending exclusively on external governance protocols.

6.2   Task Selection and Risk Differentiation

The necessity for clear task enumeration and risk-based appropriateness determinations is evident in the two-stage pipeline architecture. The system exemplifies task separation at the structural level by decoupling categorization (BERT) from interpretive reasoning (LoRA-adapted decoder with Chain of Thought). The classification stage does a relatively simple, low-risk job of putting inputs into established categories. The reasoning stage, on the other hand, does a more complicated and epistemically sensitive job of coming up with maturity-level reasons. This separation guarantees that the interpretive element is not merged with standard processing but is instead isolated as a separate phase that can be independently assessed and regulated. Accordingly, downstream maturity recommendations should be understood as conditional on the upstream dimension assignment rather than as exhaustive interpretations of the excerpt.

6.3   Validation and Transparency Through CoT

A definable validation procedure is supported, but not completed, by Chain-of-Thought rationales. Rather than validating the assessment by themselves, these rationales provide inspectable outputs that can be reviewed against source passages and level criteria by human experts. This architecture converts the model's output into an auditable artifact, enabling domain experts to assess both the plausibility of the given maturity level and the methodological soundness of the underlying reasoning. The Chain-of-Thought outputs serves a narrower role: they externalizes a rationale that can be inspected, criticized, and compared with the underlying material.

6.4   Protection Against Interpretive Overreach

The restricted output architecture mitigates the concern that LLM utilization may transition from specific support roles to unverifiable interpretive assertions. The model generates bounded assessment rationales within a predefined maturity framework. This mapping constrains the output space, although it does not eliminate ambiguity or upstream classification error. The system functions inside a confined interpretive framework, mitigating the possibility of epistemic overreach identified by procedural literature as a primary threat.

6.5   Data Protection and Portability

The deployment architecture mitigates infrastructure-level issues pertaining to data privacy and trust, particularly in scenarios involving vulnerable populations. The model is trained and executed locally, guaranteeing that sensitive assessment data remains within the organizational environment and is not subjected to third-party processing. This mitigates a substantial category of governance issues linked to cloud-based LLM services. Furthermore, the methodology is crafted for transferability: while the fine-tuning pipeline utilizes parameter-efficient techniques (LoRA adapters) and open-weight basic models, the system can be duplicated on other local infrastructures without reliance on proprietary platforms. This transferability reduces the obstacles to adoption in resource-limited environments, such as nonprofit organizations and community-based initiatives, where data sovereignty and cost-effectiveness are essential criteria.

The implementation converts the aforementioned procedural rules into specific technical mechanisms: task differentiation via pipeline architecture, validation through Chain of Thought transparency, interpretive constraint through structured output mapping, and data protection through local deployment. Nonetheless, it does not address the prior normative inquiry regarding the appropriateness of LLM-assisted assessment in a specific context – a determination that rests with the researchers and stakeholders involved. After reaching a decision, the design enables the implementation of methodologically consistent LLM support.

7   Conclusion

This study integrates two views on the employment of LLM in maturity assessments: a normative analysis of the methodological requirements and a technological implementation illustrating how these requirements can be architecturally achieved. The normative study has elucidated that the application of LLMs in evaluative contexts is contingent upon procedural stipulations, specifically an explicit task selection, a definable validation strategy, transparency in reasoning pathways, and the safeguarding of sensitive information. The technical implementation demonstrates that these requirements can be concretely realized rather than remaining abstract: the division of classification and justification via a two-stage pipeline, the generation of inspectable rationales through chain-of-thought reasoning, the restriction of interpretative flexibility through structured output mapping to predefined maturity levels, and the safeguarding of sensitive data through local training and deployment. This provides three fundamental contributions. The paper offers a normative framework that delineates procedural criteria for the systematic application of LLMs in evaluative contexts, differentiating between acceptable support roles and concerning interpretative intrusions. Secondly, the technical implementation illustrates the feasibility of a transparent, locally operable, and transferable LLM architecture that supports excerpt-level maturity recommendations that remain subject to expert review. Thirdly, the study illustrates that methodological governance requirements and technical architectural decisions should not be regarded as distinct discourses but can be effectively interconnected. These findings are accompanied by other limitations. The paper's contribution is therefore not a claim of fully automated maturity assessment, but a bounded proof of concept for human-supervised support within a predefined framework. The approach shows how methodological constraints, local deployment, and structured output can be combined in one architecture. At the same time, broader validation, multi-excerpt aggregation, and robustness testing remain tasks for future work.

References

1. Devlin, J., Chang, M.W., Lee, K., Toutanova, K.: BERT: pre-training of deep bidirectional transformers for language understanding (2019). https://doi.org/10.48550/arXiv.1810.04805
2. Friese, S.: Response to open letter that opposes the use of generative ai for reflexive qualitative research - qeludra blog (2025). https://qeludra.com/blog/response-to-open-letter-opposing-the-use-of-generative-ai-for-reflexive-qualitative-research
3. Friese, S.: From coding to conversation: a new methodological framework for AI-assisted qualitative analysis. Qual. Inquiry, 10778004251412871 (2026). https://doi.org/10.1177/10778004251412871
4. Giffinger, R., Gudrun, H.: Smart cities ranking: an effective instrument for the positioning of the cities? ACE: architecture. City Environ. 4(12), 7–26 (2010). https://doi.org/10.5821/ace.v4i12.2483
5. Han, D., Han, M.: Unsloth team: Unsloth. Unsloth AI (2023)
6. Han, Z., Gao, C., Liu, J., Zhang, J., Zhang, S.Q.: Parameter-efficient fine-tuning for large models: a comprehensive survey (2024). https://doi.org/10.48550/arXiv.2403.14608
7. Hu, E.J., et al.: LoRA: low-rank adaptation of large language models (2021). https://doi.org/10.48550/arXiv.2106.09685
8. Minaee, S., et al.: Large language models: a survey (2025). https://doi.org/10.48550/arXiv.2402.06196
9. Preßler, W., Schmidt, L.: Ein interdisziplinares reifegradmodell zur begleitung digitaler transformationsprozesse in einem smarten quartier. In: Opielka, M., Erfurth, C. (eds.) Soziale Digitalisierung: Perspektiven zu den Schnittstellen von Technik und Gesellschaft, pp. 99–121. Springer Fachmedien, Wiesbaden (2025). https://doi.org/10.1007/978-3-658-46328-1_5
10. Schroeder, H., Aubin Le Quéré, M., Randazzo, C., Mimno, D., Schoenebeck, S.: Large language models in qualitative research: uses, tensions, and intentions. In: Proceedings of the 2025 CHI Conference on Human Factors in Computing Systems, pp. 1–17. CHI '25, Association for Computing Machinery, New York, NY, USA (2025). https://doi.org/10.1145/3706598.3713120
11. Seidel, P., Preßler, W.: Automated text classification in maturity models using transformer architectures: an encoder-based approach. In: Zielinski, S., Eichler, G., Erfurth, C., Fahrnberger, G. (eds.) Innovations for Community Services, pp. 51–60. Springer Nature Switzerland, Cham (2025). https://doi.org/10.1007/978-3-031-94263-1_4
12. Vaswani, A., et al.: Attention is All You Need (2023). https://doi.org/10.48550/arXiv.1706.03762
13. Wang, X., et al.: Self-Consistency Improves Chain of Thought Reasoning in Language Models (2023). https://doi.org/10.48550/arXiv.2203.11171
14. Wei, J., et al.: Chain-of-thought prompting elicits reasoning in large language models (2023). https://doi.org/10.48550/arXiv.2201.11903

Smart Urban Infrastructure

Distributed Supercapacitor-Based Charging Infrastructure for Urban Micromobility Integrated into Public Lighting Poles

Michal Hodoň[(✉)], Peter Ševčík, Matúš Formanek, and Peter Šarafín

Department of Technical Cybernetics, University of Žilina, Univerzitná 8215/1, 010 26 Žilina, Slovakia
{michal.hodon,peter.sevcik,matus.formanek,
peter.sarafin}@fri.uniza.sk

Abstract. This paper investigates the integration of supercapacitor-based energy storage directly into public street lighting poles to enable distributed charging of urban micromobility platforms. The proposed architecture transforms existing lighting infrastructure into spatially distributed energy nodes that accumulate energy at low, feeder-friendly power levels and deliver short-duration charging pulses to electric scooters, e-bikes, and small electric vehicles. Based on realistic volumetric and gravimetric constraints of standard lighting poles, the achievable supercapacitor storage capacity per pole is estimated to be approximately 0.1–1 kWh using current technology. While this capacity represents only incremental range extension for passenger electric vehicles, it is sufficient for full or near-full recharging of many urban micromobility devices within a single charging session. The operating principle relies on temporal decoupling between grid energy intake and charging delivery. Energy is gradually stored from the distribution grid, surplus photovoltaic sources, or adaptive lighting dimming, and subsequently released as short charging pulses in the 3–8 kW range. This approach increases charging point density without imposing high instantaneous loads on the distribution network. The paper presents storage dimensioning methodology, energy-to-range analysis for different mobility classes, and power-flow considerations relevant to distributed urban deployment. The results indicate that supercapacitor-integrated lighting poles represent a technically feasible and grid-friendly pathway toward scalable micromobility charging infrastructure in dense urban environments.

Keywords: Distributed pulsed charging · Public lighting infrastructure · Supercapacitor energy storage · Urban electromobility

1 Introduction

The rapid growth of urban micromobility, particularly electric scooters, e-bikes, and light electric vehicles, has introduced new demands on charging infrastructure in dense city environments. Unlike highway-oriented fast charging for passenger electric vehicles, micromobility platforms typically require smaller energy transfers but at high spatial density and with high frequency. In many cities, the lack of accessible, distributed

K. Kirchner et al. (Eds.): I4CS 2026, CCIS 3007, pp. 281–297, 2026.
https://doi.org/10.1007/978-3-032-27096-2_15

charging points limits operational flexibility for shared mobility fleets and private users alike. Conventional approaches to charging infrastructure deployment rely on dedicated charging stations connected to medium- or high-power grid feeders. While effective for centralized applications, such solutions require civil works, new cabling, permitting procedures, and grid reinforcement. These barriers are particularly significant in historic or densely built urban areas. At the same time, public lighting infrastructure represents one of the most spatially distributed and standardized electrical systems in cities. Lighting poles are already connected to the distribution network, are regularly spaced along streets and parking zones, and increasingly incorporate smart control capabilities as part of smart-city deployments. This work explores the integration of supercapacitor-based energy storage directly into public street lighting poles to enable distributed micromobility charging. Instead of drawing high instantaneous power from the grid during charging events, each pole operates as a localized energy buffer. Energy is accumulated gradually at feeder-friendly power levels and subsequently delivered as short charging pulses when a vehicle is connected. This temporal decoupling between grid power intake and charging power delivery reduces peak stress on the distribution network while increasing the density of available charging points. Based on realistic volumetric and mass constraints of standard lighting poles, the achievable supercapacitor storage capacity per pole is estimated to be on the order of 0.1–1 kWh using current technology. Although such capacity is insufficient for full charging of passenger electric vehicles, it is well aligned with the energy requirements of electric scooters and e-bikes, whose typical battery capacities range between approximately 0.4–0.8 kWh. Consequently, a single charging session can provide full or near-full recharging for micromobility devices, while still offering incremental range extension for larger electric vehicles. Supercapacitors are selected as the storage technology due to their high power density, rapid charge–discharge capability, long cycle life, and wide operating temperature range. These characteristics are particularly advantageous for outdoor, high-frequency charging applications integrated into public infrastructure. Unlike lithium-ion batteries, supercapacitors are optimized for frequent short-duration energy exchange, making them suitable for distributed buffering at the pole level. The main contribution of this paper is a feasibility-oriented analysis of distributed supercapacitor-enhanced lighting poles as micromobility charging nodes. The work presents storage dimensioning methodology, energy-to-range evaluation for different vehicle classes, and power-flow considerations relevant to grid-friendly deployment. The proposed architecture aims to provide a scalable, infrastructure-efficient pathway toward increasing urban charging density without requiring extensive grid reinforcement.

The transformation of EV charging infrastructure is increasingly driven by the integration of intelligent control, cybersecurity mechanisms, distributed energy resources, and high-performance power electronics. A recent framework combining artificial intelligence and quantum-key-based security mechanisms demonstrates how resilient, decentralized charging ecosystems can be achieved through predictive maintenance, secure peer-to-peer transactions, and advanced load balancing strategies [1]. This highlights the growing importance of cyber-resilience and intelligent grid coordination in large-scale EV deployment. Infrastructure diversification is addressed through complementary charging paradigms. The integration of stationary charging stations with wireless dynamic charging roads has been shown to significantly reduce detours and dwell time in dense urban mobility scenarios [2]. Similarly, standardized inductive charging systems for autonomous fleets have demonstrated high transfer efficiencies and enable automated, bidirectional power exchange with minimal user interaction [3]. Power electronic optimization remains fundamental to efficient charging. High-efficiency converter topologies and advanced thermal management strategies are critical for reliable high-power operation [4]. Wireless renewable-powered charging architectures with adaptive battery-state estimation further demonstrate that stable high-voltage output and high efficiency can be achieved in distributed environments [5]. Ultra-fast charging supported by supercapacitor buffering has been experimentally validated in public transportation applications, achieving high peak power delivery within short time intervals while limiting grid stress through local energy storage [6]. The suitability of supercapacitors for burst-power and high-cycle applications is further supported by studies investigating storage sizing trade-offs and adaptive strategies in mobility-dependent energy systems [7]. Practical implementation of distributed renewable-powered infrastructure with intelligent control mechanisms has also been demonstrated in urban traffic systems [8]. From a macro-infrastructure perspective, modeling studies indicate that even moderate EV penetration can substantially increase urban electricity demand, potentially requiring significant grid reinforcement investments under unfavorable charging scenarios [9]. Optimized heterogeneous charging network design, including endogenous charging duration modeling, is therefore essential to avoid diminishing returns in infrastructure expansion [10]. Converter control and power flow management remain active research topics. Advanced DC–DC converter control strategies ensure stable and efficient fast charging under grid constraints [11]. Supercapacitor sizing and characterization for urban charging nodes have been investigated in the context of shuttle-bus routes, linking operational energy demand to infrastructure requirements [12]. Intelligent charging systems incorporating supercapacitor control schemes enable constant-power transfer and enhanced system coordination [13]. Renewable-powered DC charging stations based on photovoltaic-fed DC buses have demonstrated stable voltage control during transient connection events [14]. A broader perspective on direct electrical energy storage technologies confirms the high efficiency potential of supercapacitors, while also identifying cost and integration complexity as key challenges [15]. Hybrid battery–supercapacitor architectures allow rapid short-duration energy intake followed by controlled transfer to lithium-ion batteries, thereby reducing peak stress and improving lifecycle performance [16]. Early feasibility analyses of renewable-based vehicle charging confirm the viability of wind and photovoltaic integration under specific sizing conditions [17]. Supercapacitor integration into urban lighting subsystems has been experimentally demonstrated, validating stable regulation and improved energy buffering through dedicated DC–DC conversion stages [18]. Optimization of battery-based photovoltaic charging stations using predictive and heuristic algorithms further improves operational scheduling and lifecycle management [19]. Finally, supercapacitor-based power units for event-driven systems provide practical experience with burst-power delivery and storage-interface design patterns relevant for distributed pulsed-energy applications [20]. The existing literature confirms the technical feasibility of high-power supercapacitor buffering, renewable integration, and intelligent charging coordination.

Despite extensive research on EV charging infrastructure, renewable integration, and supercapacitor-based energy storage, several limitations remain evident in the current body of work. First, existing studies primarily investigate centralized fast-charging stations [6], wireless charging systems [2, 3], or renewable-powered charging hubs with battery storage [14, 19]. While these approaches improve efficiency and user convenience, they typically rely on dedicated high-power grid connections or substantial stationary storage systems. The distributed reuse of existing urban infrastructure as charging nodes remains insufficiently explored. Second, although supercapacitor-based buffering for ultra-fast charging has been experimentally validated in public transport scenarios [6] and analyzed for urban charging nodes [12], these implementations are designed as standalone charging stations rather than as embedded micro-energy modules integrated into existing public assets. Similarly, supercapacitor integration into lighting systems has been demonstrated for energy buffering and regulation purposes [18], but not in the context of high-power EV charging support. Third, macro-level infrastructure studies indicate significant grid reinforcement requirements under increasing EV penetration [9, 10]. However, there is limited investigation of architectures that explicitly decouple instantaneous charging power from grid power at a highly distributed, pole-level scale using direct electrical storage technologies [15]. Hybrid battery–supercapacitor approaches focus primarily on vehicle-side integration [16], whereas distributed off-board supercapacitor buffering within low-power feeder networks has not been systematically addressed. The systematic embedding of supercapacitor-based ultra-fast pulsed charging functionality directly into public lighting poles as distributed urban energy nodes remains insufficiently explored. This research gap motivates the present study.

2 Distributed Supercapacitor-Based Charging Architecture for Lighting Pole

The objective of the proposed architecture is to transform public street lighting poles into distributed micromobility charging nodes by integrating compact supercapacitor-based energy storage units directly into the pole structure. Rather than constructing centralized charging stations, the approach leverages the already deployed lighting infrastructure as a spatially dense electrical backbone.

The practical amount of supercapacitor-based energy storage that can be integrated into a standard street lighting pole is primarily constrained by internal volume and allowable mass. To assess feasibility, a simplified geometric model of the pole is considered. A typical urban steel lighting pole can be approximated as a hollow cylinder with an internal diameter D and usable internal height h. Assuming representative values:

$$D \approx 150\,\text{mm} = 0.15\,\text{m}$$

$$h \approx 1.5\,\text{m}$$

the maximum theoretical internal volume is:

$$V_{\text{pole}} = \pi \left(\frac{D}{2}\right)^2 h \tag{1}$$

$$V_{\text{pole}} = \pi \left(\frac{0.15}{2}\right)^2 \cdot 1.5 \approx 0.0265\,\text{m}^3 \approx 26.5\,\text{l} \tag{2}$$

In practice, not all of this volume can be used for energy storage, since space is required for structural reinforcement, cable routing, connectors, thermal management, and protection devices. Nevertheless, this value provides an upper physical limit. Current commercial supercapacitor modules, including packaging and interconnection hardware, typically achieve effective volumetric energy densities in the approximate range:

$$\rho_{E,SC} \approx 5 - 40\,\text{Wh/l} \tag{3}$$

depending on whether classical EDLC or hybrid/pseudocapacitor technology is used. The maximum achievable energy inside the pole can therefore be estimated as:

$$E_{\max} = V_{\text{pole}} \cdot \rho_{E,SC} \tag{4}$$

For the lower bound:

$$E_{\text{low}} = 26.5 \cdot 5 \approx 132.5\,\text{Wh} \tag{5}$$

For the optimistic upper bound:

$$E_{\text{high}} = 26.5 \cdot 40 \approx 1060\,\text{Wh} \tag{6}$$

Thus, under current technological assumptions, the realistically achievable supercapacitor storage capacity inside a standard pole envelope is on the order of:

$$E_{SC,\text{pole}} \approx 0.1 - 1\,\text{kWh} \tag{7}$$

A similar estimation can be performed using gravimetric energy density. With representative values:

$$\rho_{m,SC} \approx 5 - 40\,\text{Wh/kg} \tag{8}$$

the mass required for a given storage capacity E is:

$$m = \frac{E}{\rho_{m,SC}20} \tag{9}$$

For a 0.5 kWh storage system:

$$m_{0.5kWh} = \frac{500}{20} \approx 25\,\text{kg} \tag{10}$$

For a 1 kWh system:

$$m_{1kWh} = \frac{1000}{20} \approx 50\,\text{kg} \tag{11}$$

Based on the volumetric and mass constraints discussed above, a realistic supercapacitor storage capacity that can be directly integrated into a standard lighting pole is expected to lie in the upper half of the theoretical range, typically between 0.5–1 kWh. Rather than aiming at full vehicle charging, this capacity defines the system as a distributed micro-buffer designed for short, high-power energy transfer events.

Each pole would therefore contain a supercapacitor-based energy storage unit within this range. The storage would be gradually charged through controlled low-power intake from the distribution grid, preferably during low-tariff periods. In addition, the architecture allows integration of surplus photovoltaic energy through a virtual battery scheme, small locally mounted photovoltaic panels, and energy savings achieved by adaptive dimming of the lighting system during low-demand nighttime hours. All energy sources contribute to the same local buffer, which remains electrically decoupled from instantaneous charging demand. The stored energy is intended to support short opportunity charging sessions for vehicles parked along the street. With a storage capacity of 0.5–1 kWh, the system can deliver short-duration pulses in the range of approximately 5–15 kW for typical session durations, depending on discharge time. For example, a 0.8 kWh energy packet delivered over 5 min corresponds to an average charging power of:

$$P = \frac{0.8}{5/60} \approx 9.6\,\text{kW} \tag{12}$$

If delivered over 2–3 min, the instantaneous power level may reach 15–25 kW, depending on converter capability and allowable voltage window. However, practical converter ratings for pole-integrated systems are expected to remain in the 5–10 kW range. Such charging sessions are not intended to replenish the full traction battery, but to provide incremental range extension during routine urban stops, such as short shopping visits, service stops, taxi waiting periods, or ride-sharing standby. The concept therefore targets urban opportunity charging rather than conventional fast charging. The objective is to provide frequent, distributed micro-energy injections that reduce range anxiety and increase flexibility of daily vehicle operation without imposing high transient loads on the distribution grid. By storing energy locally and releasing it in short pulses, the architecture separates continuous low-power energy intake from short high-power output. This temporal decoupling reduces feeder peak stress and avoids the need for heavy grid reinforcement. Supercapacitors are selected as the storage technology because they tolerate high charge/discharge rates, support a very high number of cycles, operate reliably across wide temperature ranges, and present significantly lower fire risk compared to lithium-ion batteries. These characteristics make them particularly suitable for outdoor, high-frequency urban charging applications integrated into public infrastructure.

Figure 1 illustrates the conceptual architecture of the proposed supercapacitor-integrated streetlight charging node. Each public lighting pole is extended with a local energy storage unit based on supercapacitors, power conversion stages (AC/DC and DC/DC), and a controlled EV charging interface. The storage unit is charged from multiple coordinated energy sources, including off-peak grid supply, local photovoltaic generation, virtual battery surplus, and energy saved through lighting dimming. The stored energy is then delivered to electric vehicles in short-duration charging sessions,

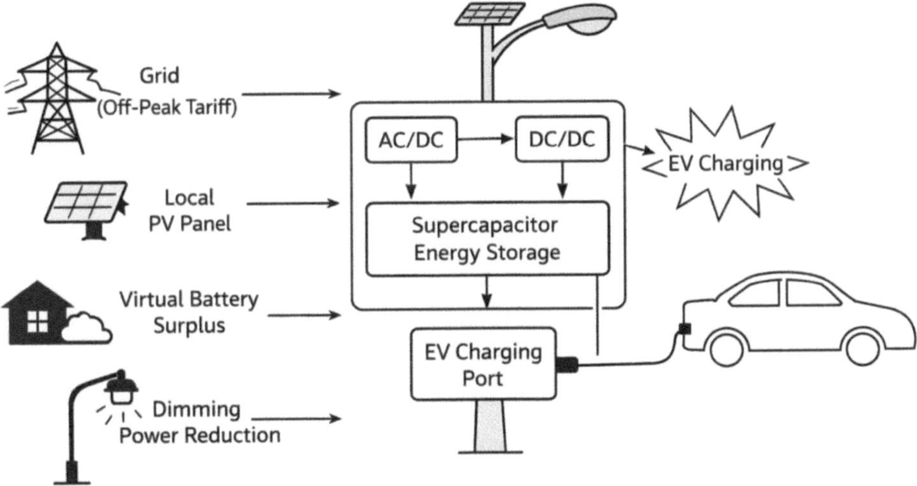

Fig. 1. Conceptual diagram of the distributed supercapacitor-integrated streetlight charging node

enabling opportunity charging during on-street parking. The architecture separates continuous low-power energy intake from short high-power output, thereby reducing stress on the distribution network while maintaining user-level charging performance.

To relate the available supercapacitor storage to a meaningful user benefit, the delivered energy can be expressed in terms of additional driving range. For typical urban operation, the specific energy consumption of modern battery electric vehicles lies in the range:

$$15 - 20 \, \text{kWh}/100 \, \text{km}. \tag{13}$$

This corresponds to an energy demand per kilometer of

$$e_{\text{low}} = \frac{15}{100} = 0.15 \, \text{kWh/km}, \tag{14}$$

$$e_{\text{high}} = \frac{20}{100} = 0.20 \, \text{kWh/km}. \tag{15}$$

If a single lighting pole provides a supercapacitor-based energy buffer of

$$E_{\text{SC}} = 0.5 \, \text{kWh}, \tag{16}$$

the achievable additional driving range Δd is approximately

$$\Delta d = \frac{E_{\text{SC}}}{e}. \tag{17}$$

For the conservative (higher-consumption) and optimistic (lower-consumption) cases:

$$\Delta d_{0.5,\text{high}} = \frac{0.5}{0.20} = 2.5 \, \text{km}, \tag{18}$$

$$\Delta d_{0.5,\text{low}} = \frac{0.5}{0.15} \approx 3.3\,\text{km}. \tag{19}$$

Similarly, for a storage capacity of

$$E_{SC} = 1.0\,\text{kWh}, \tag{20}$$

the incremental range becomes

$$\Delta d_{1.0,\text{high}} = \frac{1.0}{0.20} = 5.0\,\text{km}, \tag{21}$$

$$\Delta d_{1.0,\text{low}} = \frac{1.0}{0.15} \approx 6.7\,\text{km}. \tag{22}$$

These results indicate that a realistically pole-integrated supercapacitor storage unit in the range of 0.5–1 kWh can extend the vehicle's range by approximately 2.5–7 km per short charging stop, depending on vehicle efficiency and driving conditions. Though this is far below a full battery recharge, it is sufficient to cover typical "last-mile" distances, bridge the gap to the next planned charging opportunity, or provide operational flexibility for urban fleets such as taxis, shared vehicles, and delivery vans. While the incremental range extension for passenger electric vehicles is moderate, the same pole-integrated supercapacitor storage can have a substantially larger impact on light urban mobility devices such as electric scooters and electric bicycles.

Typical electric scooters consume approximately $0.8 - 1.5$ kWh/100 km or $0.008 - 0.015$ kWh/km what means:

For a 0.5 kWh energy packet:

$$\Delta d_{\text{scooter}} = \frac{0.5}{0.015} \approx 33\,\text{km} \tag{23}$$

For 1 kWh:

$$\Delta d_{\text{scooter}} = \frac{1.0}{0.015} \approx 67\,\text{km} \tag{24}$$

This corresponds to a full recharge for many shared urban scooters, whose typical battery capacities range between 0.4–0.8 kWh.

Typical electric bicycle (E-Bike) consumes approximately $1 - 2$ kWh/100 km or $0.01 - 0.02$ kWh/km what means:

For a 0.5 kWh energy packet:

$$\Delta d_{\text{e-bike}} = \frac{0.5}{0.02} = 25\,\text{km} \tag{25}$$

For 1 kWh:

$$\Delta d_{\text{e-bike}} = \frac{1.0}{0.02} = 50\,\text{km} \tag{26}$$

This again corresponds to a full recharge for many standard e-bikes, whose typical battery capacities range between 0.4–0.7 kWh. The consumption comparison indicates that the relative impact of a pole-integrated supercapacitor storage unit increases significantly as vehicle-specific energy demand decreases. While the available storage capacity represents only a partial energy supplement for passenger electric vehicles, it becomes fully sufficient for light electric mobility devices. In particular, e-bikes and electric scooters can be completely or near-completely recharged within a single energy transfer event.

3 Energy Storage Dimensioning

The dimensioning of the supercapacitor storage unit is driven by the requirement to deliver short-duration high-power charging pulses while maintaining a limited continuous grid draw. The storage must therefore be sized according to the energy content of a single opportunity charging session rather than long-term daily energy balancing.

Let the target energy delivered during a curbside opportunity charging session be

$$E_{session} \tag{27}$$

For a high-end configuration near the upper storage bound, a representative session energy can be assumed as

$$E_{session} = 0.8\,\text{kWh} \tag{28}$$

Assuming a charging duration

$$T_{session} = 5min = \frac{1}{12}\,\text{h} \tag{29}$$

the required average charging power at the vehicle interface is

$$P_{pulse} = \frac{E_{session}}{T_{session}} \tag{30}$$

$$P_{pulse} = \frac{0.8}{1/12} \approx 9{,}6\,\text{kW} \tag{31}$$

This power level defines the instantaneous output capability of the storage-converter system.

The energy stored in a supercapacitor bank is given by:

$$E_{SC} = \frac{1}{2}C_{eq}V_{SC}^2 \tag{32}$$

where:

- C_{eq} is the equivalent capacitance of the bank,
- V_{SC} is the operating voltage.

Since supercapacitors operate over a voltage range, the usable energy between maximum and minimum operating voltage is:

$$E_{usable} = \frac{1}{2} C_{eq}(V_{max}^2 - V_{min}^2) \tag{33}$$

then the required equivalent capacitance becomes:

$$C_{eq} = \frac{2E_{usable}}{V_{max}^2 - V_{min}^2} \tag{34}$$

This relationship provides the primary design equation for storage sizing.
Let the maximum allowed continuous grid power per pole be

$$P_{grid,lim} \tag{35}$$

The minimum recharge time required to refill the storage after one session is approximately:

$$T_{recharge} = \frac{E_{session}}{P_{grid,lim} \cdot \eta_{ch}} \tag{36}$$

where η_{ch} is the charging efficiency.
For example, with:

$$P_{grid,lim} \approx 2\,\text{kW} \tag{37}$$

$$E_{session} = 0.8\,\text{kWh} \tag{38}$$

and assuming $\eta_{ch} \approx 0.95$,

$$T_{recharge} \approx \frac{0.8}{2 \cdot 0.95} \approx 0.42\,\text{h} \approx 25min \tag{39}$$

This illustrates the grid replenishes the storage over approximately half hour at a feeder-friendly power level.

Beyond energy capacity, the supercapacitor bank must support the required discharge current. The instantaneous power delivered is:

$$P_{pulse} = V_{SC} \cdot I_{SC} \tag{40}$$

Thus, the maximum discharge current at minimum voltage is:

$$I_{SC,max} = \frac{P_{pulse}}{V_{min}} \tag{41}$$

This condition defines conductor sizing, internal resistance constraints, and thermal management requirements.

4 Electrical Interface and Integration into Public Lighting Circuits

The integration of supercapacitor-based energy storage into public lighting poles requires a carefully designed electrical architecture that remains compatible with existing low-voltage lighting circuits while ensuring safe user interaction and grid-compliant operation. In most urban environments, lighting poles are supplied from 230 V AC low-voltage radial feeders that were originally dimensioned for luminaire loads in the range of 50–200 W per pole. Therefore, the proposed system is designed to operate within conservative continuous intake limits, typically in the range of 0.5–2 kW per pole, without requiring major feeder reinforcement.

The internal architecture of the charging node consists of four main subsystems: AC grid interface, supercapacitor storage stack, bidirectional DC/DC power conversion stage, and user charging interface. The grid interface includes an AC/DC rectifier stage with power factor correction to ensure compliance with low-voltage harmonic and power quality requirements. When local photovoltaic panels are installed on the pole, a dedicated DC/DC converter with Maximum Power Point Tracking (MPPT) is integrated to optimize energy harvesting. The MPPT stage operates independently of the grid rectifier and feeds the same DC link used for supercapacitor charging. Energy storage is implemented using a high-voltage supercapacitor stack composed of individual 2.7 V cells connected in series. To achieve a practical DC link voltage compatible with medium-power DC charging (for example 120–200 V DC), approximately 45–75 supercapacitor cells are required in series configuration:

$$N = \frac{V_{DC}}{V_{cell}} = \frac{120 - 200}{2.7} \approx 45 - 75 \tag{42}$$

Each cell must be equipped with passive or active voltage balancing circuitry to prevent overvoltage during charging. Assuming a target usable storage energy of 0.5–1.0 kWh and a DC link voltage window between $V_{max} = 200V$ and $V_{min} = 120V$, the required equivalent capacitance lies within technically achievable ranges for commercially available modules (35). The stack is enclosed in an IP-rated compartment located in the lower section of the pole, with integrated thermal conduction to the metallic pole body for passive heat dissipation. The bidirectional DC/DC converter regulates both charging of the supercapacitor from the grid and discharge toward the vehicle. During grid charging mode, current is limited according to the predefined continuous intake power $P_{grid,lim}$. During discharge mode, the converter provides controlled constant-power output in the 3–8 kW range depending on session duration and state of charge. Current limiting and fast electronic protection are mandatory due to the low internal resistance of supercapacitors and their ability to deliver very high short-circuit currents. For example, at 5 kW discharge and 120 V minimum voltage, the peak current is approximately 42 A (43). Copper conductors with cross-sections in the range of 10–16 mm2 are sufficient for short internal connections under these current levels, considering temperature rise and installation method. Grid-side AC wiring follows standard lighting circuit conductor dimensions, typically 2.5–6 mm2 depending on feeder rating. The external charging connector is designed primarily for micromobility platforms. Depending on the deployment scenario, this may consist of a weather-protected DC output port with configurable voltage levels (e.g., 48 V, 60 V, or 72 V DC for scooters and e-bikes) or a standardized low-power DC interface. For enhanced flexibility, the high-voltage DC link can feed an isolated DC/DC output stage that adapts voltage to the connected vehicle. Residual current protection, DC isolation monitoring, and overcurrent protection are integrated into the charging interface to ensure user safety.

User interaction is intentionally simplified to minimize cost and vandalism risk. A basic LED-based status indicator is mounted on the pole at accessible height. A green LED indicates that the storage is sufficiently charged and the pole is ready for a full charging session. A yellow LED indicates partial charge availability, meaning that a reduced energy session is possible. A red LED indicates insufficient stored energy and temporary unavailability. This minimal graphical interface reduces maintenance complexity while still providing clear operational feedback. Control logic is implemented on an embedded control board based on an industrial microcontroller or low-power single-board system. The controller supervises supercapacitor voltage balancing, temperature monitoring, grid intake current limitation, charging session management, and communication with supervisory systems if network connectivity is available. Optional connectivity through LTE or LoRaWAN enables remote monitoring, firmware updates, and coordinated feeder-level load management. From a protection standpoint, the system includes AC-side circuit breakers, DC fusing between converter and storage stack, surge protection devices due to lightning exposure, and thermal sensors integrated into the supercapacitor module. Although supercapacitors do not exhibit thermal runaway behavior characteristic of lithium-ion batteries, their high short-circuit current capability necessitates robust electronic current limiting and fault detection mechanisms.

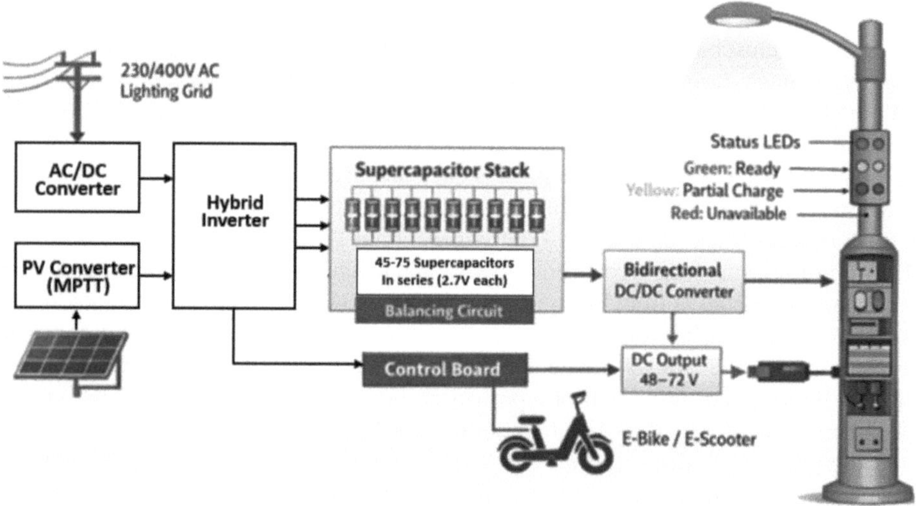

Fig. 2. Schematic diagram of the proposed system

Figure 2 illustrates the architecture of proposed system. It combines controlled grid energy intake, optional photovoltaic harvesting, high-voltage supercapacitor storage, and bidirectional power conversion within a single public lighting pole. The system operates as a localized energy buffer, enabling gradual energy accumulation at feeder-compatible power levels and short-duration charging delivery to connected micromobility devices. The schematic highlights the electrical interface, control electronics, and simplified user interaction implemented through LED-based status indication.

4.1 Thermal Feasibility and ESR Loss Estimate

To obtain a first-order estimate of thermal stress in the supercapacitor stack, the conduction loss during a charging pulse can be approximated by

$$P_{\text{loss}} = I_{\text{SC}}^2 R_{\text{ESR}} \tag{43}$$

where I_{SC} is the stack current and R_{ESR} is the equivalent series resistance of the series-connected supercapacitors. For a representative peak current of $I_{\text{SC}} \approx 42A$ (cf. (43)) and a realistic stack resistance on the order of $R_{\text{ESR}} \approx 20\,m\Omega$, the instantaneous loss is

$$P_{\text{loss}} \approx 42^2 \cdot 0.02 \approx 35\,\text{W} \tag{44}$$

For a 5-min charging pulse, the corresponding energy dissipated as heat is

$$E_{\text{loss}} = P_{\text{loss}} \cdot T_{\text{pulse}} = 35W \cdot \frac{5}{60}h \approx 2.9\,\text{Wh} \tag{45}$$

which is small compared to the delivered energy packet of $0.4 - 0.8\,\text{kWh}$. Given the low duty cycle of charging events and the thermal coupling of the module to the metallic pole structure, this preliminary estimate indicates that stack heating remains manageable. A detailed thermal model including ambient conditions, enclosure geometry, and converter losses is left for future work.

4.2 Economic Feasibility

In addition to technical feasibility, the practical deployment of distributed supercapacitor-integrated charging nodes depends on their economic viability. This section provides a first-order estimate of capital costs, operational considerations, and indicative cost per delivered energy. The total cost of a single pole-integrated charging unit is primarily determined by three components: the supercapacitor storage module, power electronics, and integration into the existing lighting infrastructure. Based on current market estimates, system-level supercapacitor modules exhibit costs in the range of approximately 500–2000 € per kWh, depending on technology, packaging, and production scale. For a storage capacity of 0.5–1.0 kWh, this corresponds to a cost of approximately 250–2000 €. It should be noted that small discrete supercapacitor cells exhibit significantly higher cost per unit energy due to their low individual energy capacity, often reaching tens of € per Wh. However, practical implementations rely on modular architecture, where the effective cost per kWh is substantially reduced. The power conversion stage, including AC/DC rectification, DC/DC conversion, and control electronics, is estimated to add approximately 500–1000 € per unit. Mechanical integration, protection systems, and installation costs are expected to contribute an additional 500–1000 €. Consequently, the total capital expenditure per pole can be estimated in the range of approximately 1500–4000 €, depending on system configuration and scale of deployment. Although the cost per kWh is higher compared to lithium-ion batteries, the significantly longer cycle life and high power capability of supercapacitors can lead to competitive cost per delivered energy over the system lifetime.

To estimate the effective cost of delivered energy, a simplified operational scenario can be considered. Assuming an average usable storage capacity of 0.8 kWh per pole and 50 charging cycles per day, the system would deliver approximately 40 kWh per day. Over a 10-year operational period, this corresponds to a total energy throughput of approximately 146 MWh per pole. Under these assumptions, the amortized capital cost corresponds to an indicative cost of approximately 0.05–0.15 € per kWh, excluding electricity purchase costs, maintenance, and communication infrastructure. While this simplified estimate does not account for all operational variables, it indicates that the proposed system can achieve competitive cost levels, particularly in high-utilization urban environments. It should be noted that the economic performance is highly sensitive to utilization rate. Low usage scenarios may lead to significantly higher effective costs per kWh, whereas dense urban deployments with frequent charging events can substantially improve cost efficiency. Additional revenue streams, such as integration with smart city services, advertising, or fleet-based charging contracts, may further improve the economic viability of the system. A more detailed techno-economic analysis including sensitivity to energy prices, maintenance costs, and deployment scale is considered as future work.

4.3 Practical Deployment Challenges

While the proposed system is technically feasible, its practical deployment in real urban environments introduces several important challenges that need to be considered. The system must be designed for reliable outdoor operation. All components integrated into the lighting pole, including supercapacitors and power electronics, are exposed to varying environmental conditions such as humidity, temperature changes, dust, and mechanical stress. Therefore, adequate enclosure design and protection are required to ensure long-term stability. Thermal behavior is another relevant aspect. Although supercapacitors are safer than conventional batteries, repeated high-power charging and converter losses can generate heat. In most cases, passive cooling through the metal structure of the pole may be sufficient, but this depends on usage intensity and ambient conditions. Since the infrastructure is publicly accessible, protection against vandalism and misuse is also important. The charging interface and enclosure must be mechanically robust and resistant to tampering. This includes proper connector design, fault detection, and safe shutdown mechanisms. From a system perspective, large-scale deployment requires consideration of grid interaction. Even though each pole operates with limited continuous power, the combined effect of many units may influence local distribution networks. Coordinated operation and load management strategies may therefore be necessary. User interaction in real deployment scenarios may also require additional functionality beyond simple status indication. Practical systems are likely to include user identification, billing mechanisms, or integration with mobility services, which introduces requirements for communication and basic cybersecurity. Maintenance and lifecycle aspects should be taken into account as well. While supercapacitors provide long operational lifetime, other components such as converters, connectors, and protection devices may require periodic inspection or replacement. A modular design approach can simplify maintenance and improve system availability.

The proposed system is primarily intended for light urban mobility devices such as electric scooters and electric bicycles, where the available energy per charging event is sufficient for full or near-full battery recharge. These devices typically require less than 1 kWh of energy, which aligns well with the storage capacity achievable within a single lighting pole. In contrast, the system is not designed to replace conventional charging infrastructure for passenger electric vehicles. It provides incremental energy support in the form of short charging sessions that extend driving range. This makes the concept particularly suitable for urban environments, where vehicles are frequently parked for short periods. A typical usage scenario can be described as follows. A user parks an electric scooter or e-bike near a lighting pole and connects it to the charging interface. The system delivers a short charging session using energy previously stored in the supercapacitor unit. After the session, the storage is gradually recharged from the grid at a limited power level, without introducing high peak demand. In the case of passenger electric vehicles, the system can provide a small but useful range extension during short stops, such as parking near shops, service areas, or urban pickup points. Although the delivered energy is limited, repeated short charging opportunities distributed throughout the city can improve overall operational flexibility.

5   Conclusion

This paper investigated the feasibility of integrating supercapacitor-based energy storage directly into public street lighting infrastructure to enable distributed opportunity charging in urban environments. Supercapacitors were selected due to their high cycle life, high power capability, wide operating temperature range, and improved safety characteristics compared to conventional lithium-ion batteries. These properties make them well suited for outdoor, high-frequency, infrastructure-integrated applications. The analytical feasibility assessment indicates that, under realistic volumetric and mass constraints, a storage capacity up to approximately 1.0 kWh can be mechanically integrated into a standard lighting pole using current supercapacitor technology. Although such capacity does not enable full charging of passenger electric vehicles, it provides meaningful incremental range extension during short urban stops. More importantly, the same storage capacity is fully sufficient for micromobility platforms such as electric scooters and e-bikes, where it enables complete or near-complete recharging within a single session. This highlights the particular suitability of the proposed architecture for mixed urban mobility ecosystems. From a power systems perspective, the key contribution of the architecture lies in the temporal decoupling of energy intake and energy delivery. Energy is accumulated gradually under limited grid power and subsequently released in short high-power pulses. This approach significantly reduces peak demand at the feeder level and avoids the need for extensive grid reinforcement, while maintaining high spatial density of charging points. The results show that distributed supercapacitor-integrated lighting poles represent a technically feasible and grid-friendly approach to supporting incremental electrification of urban mobility, particularly in dense environments where infrastructure scalability is critical.

References

1. Narayanaswamy, H.K., Venkataswamy, S.B., Ramesh, A.B., Patil, K.S.: Optimizing and securing electric vehicle charging infrastructure for resilient energy systems using AI and quantum key empowered in smart grids. Int. J. Syst. Assur. Eng. Manage. **17**(3), 759–778 (2026). https://doi.org/10.1007/s13198-025-02994-z
2. Nguyen, D.M., Kishk, M.A., Alouini, M.-S.: Dynamic charging as a complementary approach in modern EV charging infrastructure. Sci. Rep. **14**, 5785 (2024). https://doi.org/10.1038/s41598-024-55863-3
3. Grabherr, P., Würz, T., Lämmle, C.: Standardized inductive charging to integrate autonomous driving fleets into the energy infrastructure. In: Heintzel, A. (ed.) Antriebe und Energiesysteme von morgen 2024, ATZLive24 2024 Proceedings. Springer Vieweg, Wiesbaden (2025). https://doi.org/10.1007/978-3-658-47675-5_7
4. Rao, B.K.K.: Application of power converters in EV charging infrastructure. In: Giri, A.K., Singh, M. (eds.) Electric Vehicle Charging Infrastructures and its Challenges. Springer, Singapore (2025). https://doi.org/10.1007/978-981-96-0361-9_12
5. Kowsalya, M., Elango, S., Karthigayini, R.: Integrated renewable energy-powered wireless charging system with smart battery management for IoT-based electric vehicles. Electr. Eng. **108**, 53 (2026). https://doi.org/10.1007/s00202-025-03381-4
6. Ortenzi, F., Pasquali, M., Prosini, P.P., Lidozzi, A., Di Benedetto, M.: Design and validation of ultra-fast charging infrastructures based on supercapacitors for urban public transportation applications. Energies **12**, 2348 (2019). https://doi.org/10.3390/en12122348
7. Munir, B., Dyo, V.: On the impact of mobility on battery-less RF energy harvesting system performance. Sensors **18**, 3597 (2018). https://doi.org/10.3390/s18113597
8. Omran, A.E.-F.A., Fahmy, F.H., Nafeh, A.E.-S.A., Yousef, H.K.M.: Experimental implementation of a stand-alone photovoltaic smart traffic light system with MPPT and battery charge management. Sustainability **18**, 1959 (2026). https://doi.org/10.3390/su18041959
9. Plesovskikh, A.E., Kolyan, N.S., Gordeev, R.V., Pyzhev, A.I.: Infrastructure barriers to the electrification of vehicle fleets in Russian cities. World Electr. Veh. J. **17**, 51 (2026). https://doi.org/10.3390/wevj17010051
10. Tang, C., Liu, H., Song, G.: Designing heterogeneous electric vehicle charging networks with endogenous service duration. World Electr. Veh. J. **17**, 46 (2026). https://doi.org/10.3390/wevj17010046
11. Pal, S., Gupta, S.K., Shah, N.L., Tiwari, P.N., Soni, A.: Electric vehicle charging infrastructure and DC–DC converter control towards sustainable transportation. In: International Conference on Computational, Communication and Information Technology (ICCCIT 2025), pp. 793–796. IEEE, Indore (2025). https://doi.org/10.1109/ICCCIT62592.2025.10927937
12. Busacca, A., Campagna, N., Castiglia, V., Miceli, R.: Supercapacitor-based shuttle bus characterization for urban charging infrastructure. In: 10th International Conference on Renewable Energy Research and Application (ICRERA 2021), pp. 270–275. IEEE, Istanbul (2021). https://doi.org/10.1109/ICRERA52334.2021.9598678
13. Li, Z., Lin, D., Li, Y., Jiang, G., Sun, Z., Jiang, S.: Design of intelligent charging system for new energy vehicles and research on supercapacitor control scheme. In: 6th International Conference on Energy, Power and Grid (ICEPG 2024), pp. 1503–1507. IEEE, Guangzhou (2024). https://doi.org/10.1109/ICEPG63230.2024.10775807

14. Shivankar, S.B., Mounica, M., Rajpathak, B.: Design and control of DC fast charging stations for electric vehicles powered by photovoltaic energy. In: IEEE 4th International Conference on Sustainable Energy and Future Electric Transportation (SEFET 2024), pp. 1–6. IEEE, Hyderabad (2024). https://doi.org/10.1109/SEFET61574.2024.10718227

15. Boya, M., Tekaya, K., Spaeth, U., Schmuelling, B.: Exploring the methods and future directions of direct electrical energy storage systems: a systematic review. In: International Conference on Clean Electrical Power (ICCEP 2025), pp. 930–937. IEEE, Villasimius (2025). https://doi.org/10.1109/ICCEP65222.2025.11143769

16. Shanmugapriya, P., Bengeri, P.M., Dhanya, K., Dakshina, R., Abinaya, V.: Hybridization of supercapacitor and battery for fast charging of electric vehicles. In: International Conference on Power, Energy, Control and Transmission Systems (ICPECTS 2022), pp. 1–5. IEEE, Chennai (2022). https://doi.org/10.1109/ICPECTS56089.2022.10047266

17. Li, X., Lopes, L.A.C., Williamson, S.S.: On the suitability of plug-in hybrid electric vehicle (PHEV) charging infrastructures based on wind and solar energy. In: IEEE Power & Energy Society General Meeting 2009, pp. 1–8. IEEE, Calgary (2009). https://doi.org/10.1109/PES.2009.5275171

18. Canilang, H.M.O., Lim, W.: Street lighting with supercapacitor energy storage using a four-switch buck-boost DC–DC converter. In: IEEE Canadian Conference on Electrical and Computer Engineering (CCECE 2025), pp. 780–781. IEEE, Vancouver (2025). https://doi.org/10.1109/CCECE64018.2025.11364390

19. Fatnani, M., Naware, D., Mitra, A.: Design of solar PV based EV charging station with optimized battery energy storage system. In: IEEE First International Conference on Smart Technologies for Power, Energy and Control (STPEC 2020), pp. 1–5. IEEE, Nagpur (2020). https://doi.org/10.1109/STPEC49749.2020.9297719

20. Kochláň, M., Ševčík, P.: Supercapacitor power unit for an event-driven wireless sensor node. In: Federated Conference on Computer Science and Information Systems (FedCSIS 2012), pp. 791–796. IEEE, Wroclaw (2012)

From Fragmentation to Federation
Implementing a Single-Window Municipal Data Request and Delivery Pipeline

Leendert W. M. Wienhofen[(✉)], Audun Vennesland,
and Soudabeh Khodambashi

Trondheim kommune, Trondheim Digital, Postboks 2300 Torgarden 7004 Trondheim,
Norway
{leendert.wienhofen,audun.vennesland,
soudabeh.khodambashi}@trondheim.kommune.no
https://www.trondheim.kommune.no/

Abstract. Municipalities are increasingly expected to function as data-driven organizations while simultaneously providing access to data for research, innovation, and the creation of public value. Despite having large volumes of potentially high-value data, municipalities face significant barriers to data sharing due to legal fragmentation, vendor lock-in, and limited organizational capacity. This position paper presents the MUNDAT use case from the EU-funded DataPACT project, in which Trondheim Municipality, together with technology providers, explores how a federated "single-window" data request and delivery pipeline can address these challenges. Today, municipal data requests are often handled ad-hoc and are labor-intensive, leading to inconsistent compliance assessments, high resource consumption, and increased legal risk. MUNDAT reframes the challenge not as a lack of data, but as a lack of an efficient infrastructure between municipal operations and regulatory requirements. The paper examines two contrasting data sharing cases: HR sick leave data, where legal and ethical constraints dominate, and infrastructure IoT data, where vendor lock-in, security, and critical infrastructure concerns prevail. By combining automated legal assessment, policy enforcement, and technical data pipelines, the proposed single-window approach aims to provide a lawful, scalable, and reusable data sharing infrastructure, while supporting consistent, transparent, and auditable compliance with applicable legal and ethical requirements.

Keywords: Data federation · Data governance · Data sharing · GDPR compliance · Public sector · Single-window access

1 Introduction

1.1 Problem Definition

Municipalities are increasingly mandated to operate as data-driven entities, in addition to delivering data for research and other purposes, yet they face a

K. Kirchner et al. (Eds.): I4CS 2026, CCIS 3007, pp. 298–308, 2026.
https://doi.org/10.1007/978-3-032-27096-2_16

paradox: while they possess vast amounts of data valuable for research and innovation, the barriers to sharing this data are often insurmountable due to legal fragmentation and vendor lock-in. This position paper presents the MUNDAT (short for municipal data) use case, a collaborative initiative between Trondheim kommune (TK)—acting as the use case provider and problem owner—and a consortium of technology partners within the DataPACT project, a project that has received funding from the European Union's Horizon Europe research and innovation program under grant agreement No 101189771.

Currently, requests for data are often made on a non-coordinated ad-hoc basis and are sent directly to municipal employees. Municipal data sharing is not primarily a data availability problem, but a governance and workflow fragmentation problem. So, one of the goals of the project is creating a federated single-window architecture as a scalable solution for data requests to ensure that data can always be delivered in a manner that is compliant with current laws and regulations, as well as in an easy-to-use format. Compliance evaluations as well as delivery are typically manual, inconsistent, and resource-intensive. In general, there are very few employees that are well-versed in both legislation and technology, which is the main reason why such a "single window" can help alleviate some of the issues at hand. We would like to point out that this claim is generally valid, except for the GDPR Subject Access Request (SAR), which allows individuals to ask if we are processing their personal data and to receive a copy of that data, along with supplementary information about its usage. The SAR process is handled in a structured manner by our archive department.

Since Norway is not a member of the European Union, not all EU acts, directives, and regulations are directly applicable in Norway. Legislation relevant for data sharing, gathering, re-use, AI, and so on, such as the Data Act [4], Data Governance Act [5], AI Act [6] and the High Value Datasets Implementing Regulation (HVD) [7] are currently not valid in Norway. All are being adjusted to fit within the Norwegian legal framework, however, such adjustments can often take years to complete. In order to be prepared for upcoming changes, we already now aim to implement measures to ease compliance once the legislation is in place and valid for Norway. Trondheim Kommune is legally obligated to deliver over 200 distinct services to its citizens, ranging from healthcare and education to urban planning and water management. Many of these services generate massive volumes of data that are highly sought after by external actors (academia, industry) and internal departments.

This paper contributes a federated architectural perspective on municipal data sharing, grounded in a real-world use case and focused on operationalizing compliance, governance, and technical interoperability. In the following sections, we describe the MUNDAT case in more detail and show how we aim to solve the issues mentioned in this introduction by applying technology from the DataPACT project.

2   The MUNDAT Case

The DataPACT project has multiple use cases, MUNDAT is the one pertaining to TK. The project also has many partners that serve as tool providers and over the course of the three-year project, tools contribute to solving the issues in the use cases. Tools consist of data pipelining, legal checking, agreement negotiation, and so on. Many tools are applicable to be used on the two distinct datasets (described in Subsect. 2.2). As a use case provider, TK defines the requirements, provides the raw data "sandbox," and validates the results against real-world legal obligations. TK's role is to articulate the friction points—specifically the struggle to legally clear data for sharing or technically extract it from monolithic systems. The Technology Providers, on the other hand, deploy the DataPACT Toolboxes.

2.1   Technology Enablers

The technology partners provide, among others, the PipelineR tool for visual pipeline design, AssessR for legal/ethical compliance, and PolicyR for managing consent and contracts. The problem is therefore framed not as a lack of data or technology, but as a lack of connective tissue—technologies that together can help bridge TK's operational reality with the rigid requirements of EU data regulation. Examples of technology that we intend to use are [1–3].

2.2   The Data

To demonstrate the complexity of solving the Single Window concept (described in Sect. 3), TK brings into the project sick leave data as well as IoT data. These cases illustrate that "data access problems" are not monolithic; they vary drastically based on availability, legality, and perceived utility.

Case A: Human-Centric Data (Job Rotation, Sick Leave, Work Environment Surveys).

- The Data: A rich historical dataset (2022–2024) containing registrations regarding municipal employee movements, sick leave data as well as results from work environment surveys.
- Perceived Usefulness: High value for academic research in social sciences, economics, and organizational psychology.
- The Problem (Legality): The barrier here is not technical availability; the data exists in accessible internal databases. The barrier is strictly legal and ethical. Because the data contains personally identifiable and sensitive information, it triggers strict GDPR compliance requirements. The "Single Window" must essentially act as a privacy firewall—automatically enforcing strict use policies (NDAs), anonymization pipelines, and consent management before the data can be released.

Case B: Infrastructure Data (Water and Wastewater Sensors)

- The Data: Time-series data from sensors deployed in sand traps, inland waters and water management facilities. Among others: sand level, water level, water flow, septic sensors.
- Perceived Usefulness: High value for industrial innovation, specifically predictive maintenance and IoT development.
- The Problem (Availability and Security):
  - Technical Availability: Unlike the HR data, data are often locked in by third-party vendors. Vendors are frequently unwilling or technically unable to provide raw data via APIs, creating a "lock-in" effect.
  - Legal/Security: Even if extracted, this data could pose a critical infrastructure risk. Deductive disclosure (combining datasets) could reveal the exact location of vulnerable infrastructure, raising security concerns.
  - The Solution Requirement: Here, the technology partners must provide tools that not only leverage the Data Act to enforce data portability from vendors but also automatically obfuscate location data to render it safe for public sharing.

TK intends to use the findings and tools of the DataPACT project to be applied to other data sources and scenarios to streamline the process surrounding the obtaining and delivering of data both internally and externally.

3 The Single Window Concept

As mentioned above, the as-is situation is that requests for data are generally handled rather ad-hoc. A federated single-window municipal data request and delivery pipeline is how we intend to solve the whole data flow. However, this requires that legal, technical and organizational challenges need to be addressed. Figure 1 describes the to-be scenario where we have designed an overall workflow, as depicted in the BPMN [8] diagram.

The process is initiated by someone in need of data. A data catalog, consisting of metadata, open data, example data (in case the actual data cannot be shared) is envisioned to be built incrementally. By providing this openly to everyone, data requestees can take a look first and with the understanding they gain, be able to submit a good data request. One of the current problems is that for example students request something, find out that it does not quite work out and need more details, submit a new request triggering manual work, etc.

Currently, we do not have any of the "bricks" needed to enable this functionality. Some of the elements will be provided by DataPACT partners, others will be developed by TK. In the following sections, we show images that correspond to the steps in Fig. 1, and for each of the steps we give a rationale of the technology choices we make.

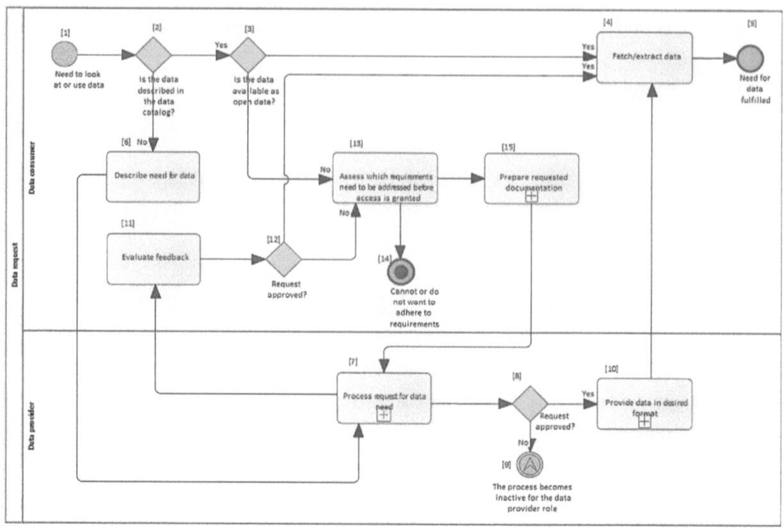

Fig. 1. High level BPMN diagram

3.1 Describing Municipal Datasets

To be able to efficiently match data sharing requests with available municipal datasets, rich and well-defined metadata descriptions are needed. All datasets will be annotated according to the MUNDAT-ONTO ontology developed by the municipality. We use this definition "An explicit specification of a conceptualization" for the concept ontology [9]. The MUNDAT-ONTO ontology reuses other ontologies and vocabularies defined in the DCAT-AP-NO application profile [10], an implementation of the W3C DCAT standard [11]. These annotations include data access specifications, available formats, temporality, thematic descriptions and data quality metrics that will support retrievability as well as clear definitions of the scope and contents of datasets shared. Internally the MUNDAT-ONTO ontology will be integrated into a larger ontology network, which effectively establishes the schematics and logic of the municipality's data fabric. This data fabric acts as a semantic layer conceptually residing on top of all datasets stored in Trondheim kommune's data management platform offering a wide range of reasoning opportunities.

3.2 Compliance Lineage

Datasets made available in the data catalog are annotated with metadata defined according to the MUNDAT-COMP-ONTO, also developed by the municipality. In practice, this ontology extends the MUNDAT-ONTO ontology by introducing concepts and properties that allow more fine-grained definitions of compliance status and compliance lineage associated with data shared externally and internally.

During external data sharing these metadata annotations enable data consumers to quickly assess the compliance status, and if relevant, the chain of compliance activities associated with offered datasets (lineage). Providing such compliance information can reassure data consumers that the data are safe to reuse and in general strengthen trust in data sharing. Internally, the compliance ontology supports the municipality in maintaining an inventory of their data compliance activities, and when required, efficiently respond to audits by the national data protection authority, using simple SPARQL queries. The MUNDAT-COMP-ONTO is extensible, so as to support future compliance requirements, e.g., specifying compliance details (e.g., risk classification, explainability, accuracy and robustness, etc.) related to AI applications developed by the municipality.

3.3   Mock-Up User Interface

We have used the AI tool Stitch [12] to create a mock-up user interface based on the descriptions above and iterate through the various screens. We found that these mock screens helped communicate our wishes for the "to be scenario" to the partners in the consortium. Please note that all data examples, review outcomes and so on in the images described in the conceptual workflow are generated by AI and only serve the purpose of explaining what the interface and its functionality might look like. The actual contents will be based on the actual data catalog once it is in place (Fig. 2, 3 4, 5, 6, 7 and 8).

3.4   Conceptual Workflow

The first screen is the search interface for the data catalog, which caters to steps 1, 2, 3, 4 and 5 (depicted between brackets in Fig. 1).

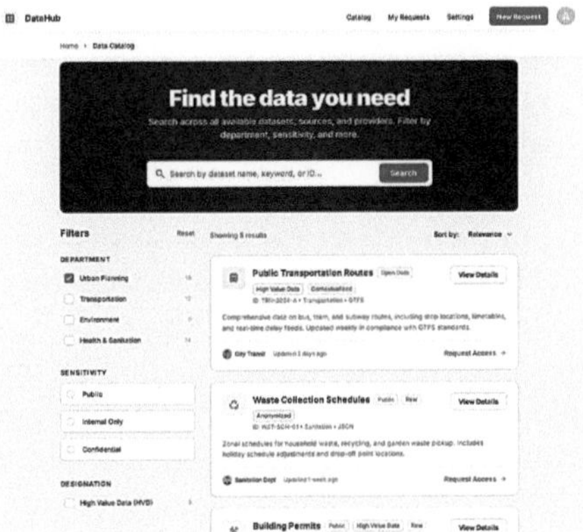

Fig. 2. Search interface

In the case that data are not available, a user can create a request for obtaining data (step 6 in Fig. 1). Depending on the context of the request, different rules may apply, hence the need to specify what the data are intended to be used for.

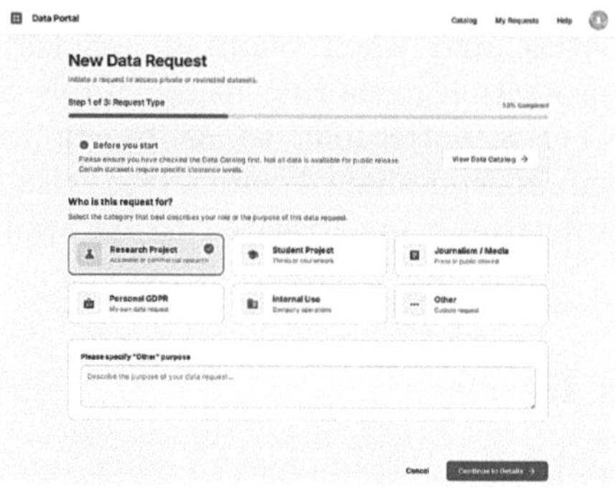

Fig. 3. Initiate data request

We also require the user to specify a short description about the availability of the data (to help ensure that the user indeed has made an effort to look for available data first) and purpose for the request. Then the type of data as well as the timeframe, and in which format the user wishes to receive the data. DataPACT provides tools to assess supporting documents, which may for example be an approval from a local ethics committee. When the request is complete, it will be assessed by various DataPACT tools and depending on the outcome, additional documentation can be requested. Figure 5 is an interpretation of the interface for the processing of the request, which caters to step 7 (in Fig. 1).

By using DataPACT tools to automate certain assessments, we reduce the burden on human resources. However, while AI assists with the evaluation, the final decision is always made by a human. In order to keep track of the requests, we wish to provide a dashboard showing the queue of requests and some statistics regarding the characteristics of the requests as well as a response time (see Fig. 6).

Once the request has been evaluated, feedback is given to the requester. In the same style as the admin overview, we wish to provide a similar overview to the users (see Fig. 7) so that it is easy to review the status of multiple requests at a glance. This caters to step 11 and 13 in Fig. 1.

In some cases the requester needs to provide documentation before a request can be granted. Examples of additional documentation can be a data use agreement, or an approval from the regional ethics committee. Figure 8 caters to step 15 in Fig. 1.

Once all documentation has been approved, either with or without the additional steps, the data can be provided in the requested format. We will also add the data to our data catalog, so that it will be built incrementally and over time it should form a more or less complete overview of the data that the

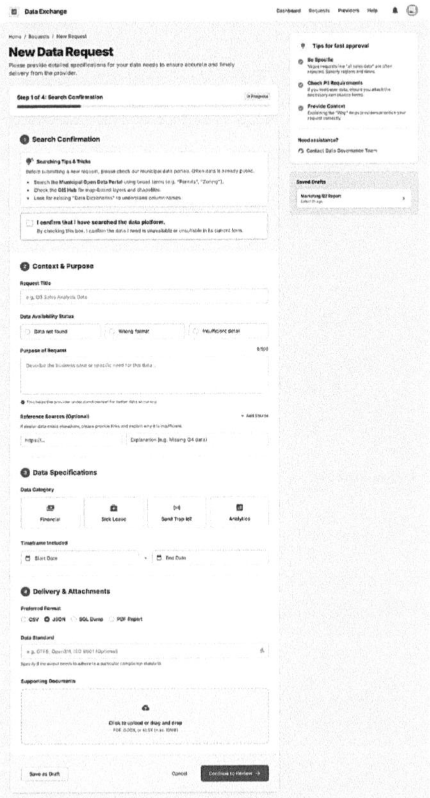

Fig. 4. Initiate data request step 2

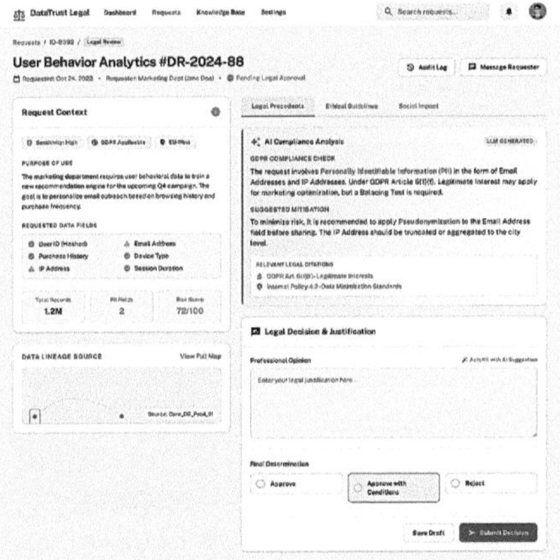

Fig. 5. Assessment outcome

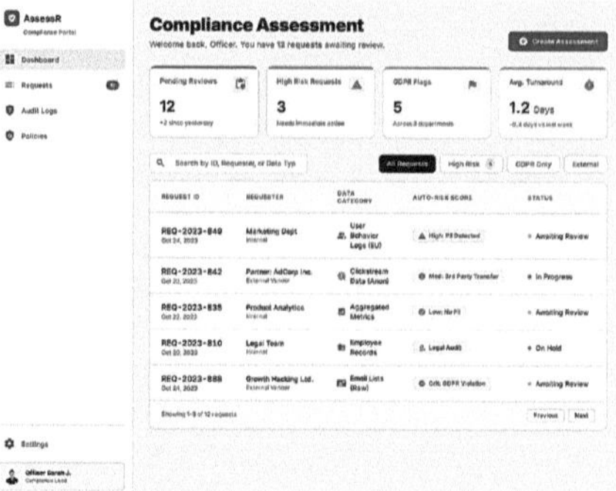

Fig. 6. Admin overview

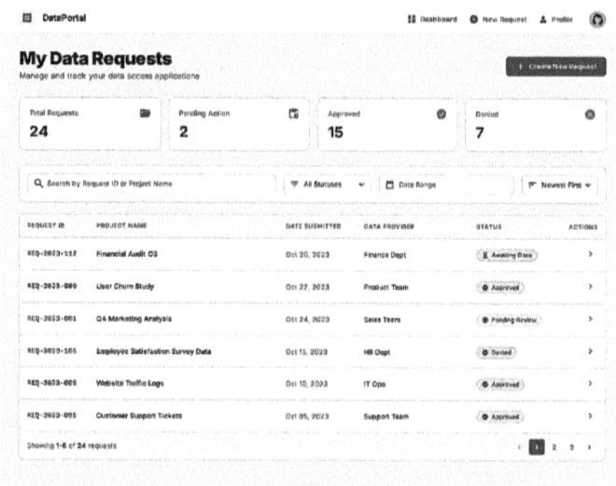

Fig. 7. End-user data request status overview

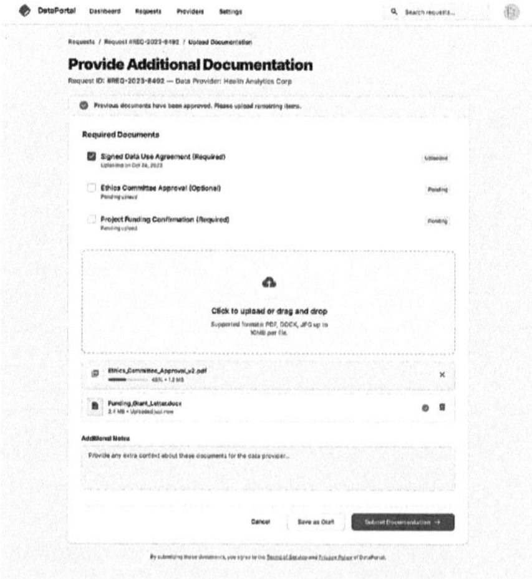

Fig. 8. Need for additional documentation

municipality holds. We wish to provide as much data as possible as open data, though datasets that include personally identifiable information or data that is of sensitive nature, will of course not be available openly. We do however create metadata as well as a sample with synthetic data and populate the data catalog with that.

Our data catalog will be based on Google Cloud Platform (GCP) and we provide role-based access to the data. Depending on your role, you either see more or less of the details pertaining to the stored data. We use the medallion architecture [13] as a data design pattern, ensuring that we can use the data on different levels of maturity and abstraction.

4 Discussion and Further Work

This position paper has articulated three main contributions. First, it conceptualizes municipal data sharing as a problem of fragmented legal–technical workflows rather than data availability, and motivates a federated single-window model as a response. Second, it presents the MUNDAT use case from Trondheim Municipality, using two contrasting datasets to illustrate how legal, ethical, technical, and security constraints differ substantially across municipal domains. Third, it outlines an integrated design approach that combines data cataloging, compliance lineage, automated assessment, and policy-driven delivery pipelines, thereby positioning municipalities as accountable data stewards aligned with emerging European data regulation. Ultimately, the single-window approach reframes municipal data sharing from an exception-driven activity into a governed, repeatable capability—an essential prerequisite for municipalities seeking to operate as trustworthy data stewards in the European data ecosystem.

Further work will focus on developing a detailed architecture showing all components and interactions and thereafter implement and evaluate the single-window pipeline in operational settings. Key evaluation criteria include reductions in processing time for data requests, increased consistency of compliance decisions, perceived reduction of legal risk among municipal staff, and the reusability of data pipelines across datasets.

While the proposed single-window architecture addresses technical and legal fragmentation, organizational and cultural barriers remain significant. Municipal data sharing practices are often deeply embedded in departmental routines and informal networks, relying on individual expertise rather than institutionalized processes. Introducing a federated single-window therefore requires not only technical integration, but also changes in roles, responsibilities, and decision-making authority. In particular, clarifying ownership of compliance decisions and establishing trust in partially automated assessments will be essential for long-term sustainability and adoption.

Acknowledgments. DataPACT is a project that has received funding from the European Union's Horizon Europe research and innovation programme under grant agreement No 101189771.

References

1. Thomas, A., Nikolov, N., Pultier, A., Roman, D., Elvesæter, B., Soylu, A.: SIM-PIPE DryRunner: an approach for testing container-based big data pipelines and generating simulation data. In: 2022 IEEE 46th Annual Computers, Software, and Applications Conference (COMPSAC), pp. 1159–1164. IEEE (2022)

2. Videsjorden, A.N., et al.: Positioning LLM-enabled agents as legal compliance aides for data pipelines. In: Hogan, A., Satoh, K., Dağ, H., Turhan, AY., Roman, D., Soylu, A. (eds) Rules and Reasoning. RuleML+RR 2025. Lecture Notes in Computer Science, vol 16144. Springer, Cham (2026). https://doi.org/10.1007/978-3-032-08887-114

3. Roman, D., Konstantinidis, G., Palmonari, M., Musidlowska, M., Prodan, R.: DataPACT: compliance by design of data/ai operations and pipelines. In: Selected Papers of the 3rd International Workshop on Hybrid Artificial Intelligence and Enterprise Modelling for Intelligent Information Systems (HybridAIMS 2025) and the 1st Workshop on Compliance in the Era of Artificial Intelligence (CAI 2025) co-located with the 37th International Conference on Advanced Information Systems Engineering (CAiSE 2025), pp.38–46. CEUR-WS (2025)

4. Regulation (EU) 2023/2854 of the European Parliament and of the Council of 13 December 2023 on harmonized rules on fair access to and use of data and amending Regulation (EU) 2017/2394 and Directive (EU) 2020/1828 (Data Act) (Text with EEA relevance). https://eur-lex.europa.eu/eli/reg/2023/2854. Accessed 20 Feb 2026

5. Regulation (EU) 2022/868 of the European Parliament and of the Council of 30 May 2022 on European data governance and amending Regulation (EU) 2018/1724 (Data Governance Act) (Text with EEA relevance). https://eur-lex.europa.eu/legal-content/EN/TXT/?uri=CELEX:32022R0868. Accessed 20 Feb 2026

6. Regulation (EU) 2024/1689 of the European Parliament and of the Council of 13 June 2024 laying down harmonized rules on artificial intelligence and amending Regulations (EC) No 300/2008, (EU) No 167/2013, (EU) No 168/2013, (EU) 2018/858, (EU) 2018/1139 and (EU) 2019/2144 and Directives 2014/90/EU, (EU) 2016/797 and (EU) 2020/1828 (Artificial Intelligence Act) (Text with EEA relevance). https://eur-lex.europa.eu/eli/reg/2024/1689/oj/eng. Accessed 20 Feb 2026

7. Commission Implementing Regulation (EU) 2023/138 of 21 December 2022 laying down a list of specific high-value datasets and the arrangements for their publication and re-use (Text with EEA relevance). https://eur-lex.europa.eu/eli/regimpl/2023/138/oj. Accessed 20 Feb 2026

8. Business Process Model and Notation, BPMN 2.0.2. https://www.omg.org/spec/BPMN. Accessed 20 Feb 2026

9. Thomas, G.R.: A translation approach to portable ontology specifications. Knowl. Acquisition 5(2), 199–220 (1993)

10. Norwegian standard for description of datasets, data services and data catalogs, DCAT-AP-NO. https://data.norge.no/specification/dcat-ap-no. Accessed 20 Feb 2026

11. Data Catalog Vocabulary (DCAT) - Version 3, W3C Recommendation 22 August 2024. https://www.w3.org/TR/vocab-dcat/. Accessed 20 Feb 2026

12. Google Stitch landing page. https://stitch.withgoogle.com/. Accessed 20 Feb 2026

13. Medallion Architecture. https://www.databricks.com/glossary/medallion-architecture. Accessed 20 Feb 2026

Technology-Supported Living and Aging in Place in a Smart Neighborhood: A Multi-level Qualitative Analysis of Success Factors and Barriers

Sabina Hölzer[(✉)], Lucie Schmidt, Wesley Preßler, and Christian Erfurth

University of Applied Sciences Jena, Jena, Germany
{Sabrina.hoelzer,Lucie.schmidt,Wesley.pressler,
Christian.erfurth}@eah-jena.de

Abstract. Population aging and the growing desire for independence in later life increase pressure on health and social care systems and heighten the need for socio-technical solutions that enable healthy living and aging in place. While Ambient Assisted Living (AAL), smart-home technologies, and digital health services are widely discussed as promising approaches, empirical evidence remains largely confined to pilot settings and often reflects only a single stakeholder perspective. Addressing this gap, this paper examines the implementation of socio-technical solutions in an inhabited smart neighborhood. It investigates (RQ1) which success factors and barriers different stakeholder groups identify regarding implementation of socio-technical solutions in a smart neighborhood and (RQ2) how do these success factors and barriers differ across stakeholder groups. Data from semi-structured interviews, focus groups and document analysis were examined using thematic analysis. Results reveal a clear cross-level asymmetry. Macro-level actors emphasize innovation, transferability, and system transformation. Micro-level actors engage pragmatically, prioritizing usability, perceived usefulness, and privacy. Meso-level actors perform the translation work between these domains. Facilitation, spatial infrastructures, and on-site support prove more decisive for stabilizing use than technological sophistication alone. Success factors at one level frequently coexist with barriers at another. By conceptualizing the smart neighborhood as a socio-technical system shaped by cross-level tensions, the study challenges technology-centric narratives of digital aging and highlights the central role of meso-level alignment in bridging strategic ambition and lived experience.

Keywords: Ambient assisted living · Community management · Healthy aging in place · Implementation barriers and success factors · Micro-meso-macro analysis · Smart neighborhood · Socio-technical systems · Telehealth room · Telemedicine

---

Sabrina Hölzer and Lucie Schmidt—Shared co-first authorship

1 Introduction

Population aging, accompanied by rising multimorbidity, is placing increasing pressure on health and social care systems. Beyond service capacity, this pressure concerns how care arrangements can preserve autonomy, participation, and quality of life in later years. Demographic projections highlight the scale of this shift: the World Health Organization estimates that the population aged 60 and above will reach 2.1 billion by 2050 [1]. In response, healthy aging has become a central policy objective. The WHO defines it as "the process of developing and maintaining the functional ability that enables wellbeing in older age," emphasizing mobility, social connectedness, and independence [2]. A closely related concept is aging in place, commonly understood as remaining in one's own home and familiar community for as long as possible [3].

At the neighborhood level, this environment becomes particularly salient. Aging in place depends on how housing infrastructures, local services, mobility arrangements, and community support structures are coordinated. Digital health solutions and smart-home technologies such as Ambient Assisted Living (AAL) systems and telemedicine services are therefore increasingly positioned as potential enablers of independence and care access [4]. However, when embedded in inhabited neighborhood settings, implementation extends beyond deploying a technological artifact and unfolds across interconnected layers of a socio-technical system. In such contexts, technological initiatives become intertwined with housing infrastructures, governance arrangements, regulatory conditions, and everyday residential life.

Accordingly, success or failure cannot be attributed solely to technical functionality or individual acceptance. Outcomes depend on how actors at different system levels interpret, coordinate, and align expectations and responsibilities over time. Yet, empirical insight into how success factors and barriers are distributed across macro, meso, and micro levels in inhabited smart neighborhoods remains limited particularly for neighborhood-based digital health solutions such as shared telemedicine rooms or other place-based access points embedded in residential settings.

To address this gap, this paper examines the implementation of socio-technical solutions designed to support healthy living and aging in place in an inhabited smart neighborhood equipped with smart-home technologies and a shared telemedicine facility. Conceptualizing the neighborhood as a multi-level socio-technical system, the study analyses how success factors and barriers are identified by different stakeholder groups and how they vary across macro, meso, and micro levels.

The study is guided by two research questions:

- RQ1: What success factors and barriers do different stakeholder groups identify regarding the implementation of socio-technical solutions in smart neighborhoods to support healthy living and aging in place, as illustrated by a telemedicine room and smart-home solutions?
- RQ2: How do these success factors and barriers differ across stakeholder groups?

The contribution of this paper is threefold. *First*, it provides empirical evidence from an inhabited smart neighborhood, extending the evidence base beyond laboratory studies and short-term pilots. *Second*, it offers a structured multi-level analysis of implementation dynamics within a socio-technical system. *Third*, it derives implications for the responsible design and governance of digital innovations in smart neighborhoods.

The remainder of the paper is structured as follows. Section 2 reviews related work. Section 3 outlines the study context and methodology. Section 4 presents the findings. Section 5 discusses implications. Section 6 concludes with limitations and directions for future research.

2 State of the Art

Technology-supported aging in residential contexts has primarily been examined along three complementary lines: *first*, in-home smart home/AAL and smart home health technologies; *second*, telemedicine as a mode of care delivery; and *third*, implementation-oriented research that explains how technologies become sustained or fail to become sustained in routine practice.

Prior AAL research has also highlighted that technology-supported aging is shaped not only by technical functionality and service provision but also by psychological and social dimensions such as autonomy, safety, privacy, trust, digital competence, and social participation. Earlier work on AAL context modeling already suggested that assisted living systems rely on the integration of multiple context layers rather than isolated device data alone. This perspective is relevant here because it draws attention to the interdependence of technical, spatial, organizational, and user-related conditions in lived smart-neighborhood environments [5]. In the in-home domain, smart home/AAL solutions are repeatedly associated with benefits such as perceived safety, support for self-management, and reduced burden on caregivers; these benefits, however, are frequently constrained by persistent barriers, most notably usability and learnability challenges, technical unreliability, interoperability limitations, and cost-related access constraints [6].

These constraints are reinforced by adoption-focused syntheses indicating that uptake among older adults depends on digital competencies, attitudes, and social support, while organizational and governance conditions are often only partially captured in predominantly user-centered work [7]. Such conditions also include privacy and autonomy demands: perceived safety can coexist with concerns about control, transparency, and appropriate data use in smart-home surveillance [8], and privacy barriers in health monitoring vary by context and role rather than constituting a single uniform obstacle [9].

In parallel, telemedicine has moved beyond pandemic-era substitution toward more routinized service provision; this routinization shifts attention from feasibility to sustainability requirements, making governance, financing, integration into care pathways, and data/IT security decisive implementation conditions [10]. These conditions become particularly salient in regulated settings; in Germany, for example, video consultations are tied to concrete compliance requirements such as certified providers and defined data protection and information security standards [11]. Such requirements intersect with equity concerns: beyond individual characteristics, neighborhood-level broadband availability is associated with telehealth use among older adults, pointing to place-based access inequalities that shape who can practically benefit from digital care [12].

Against this backdrop, neighborhood-based access points such as health kiosks or shared telemedicine rooms are proposed as low-threshold infrastructures for people with limited devices, connectivity, or digital skills; this potential, however, depends on service-level integration. Specifically, kiosk research highlights that usability evaluation and training concepts are often underreported despite being critical for real-world deployment, alongside the need for on-site support and workflow integration [13]. This integration challenge aligns with living-lab evidence, which positions real-world co-creation as valuable for contextual fit but simultaneously resource-intensive and vulnerable to role ambiguity and sustainability constraints [14, 15]. Implementation frameworks make these observations analytically actionable by conceptualizing non-adoption and limited sustainability as outcomes of multi-domain and practice-based work rather than "technology alone": NASSS (Non-adoption, Abandonment, Scale-up, Spread, and Sustainability) foregrounds interacting domains that shape scale-up and sustainability [16], while Normalization Process Theory (NPT) specifies the work through which practices become normalized in everyday settings [17].

Taken together, the literature provides robust evidence on benefits and barriers of smart home/AAL and telemedicine and offers strong explanatory lenses for implementation. What remains comparatively under-evidenced are inhabited smart-neighborhood settings that combine in-home AAL with neighborhood-embedded access points, where spatial infrastructure, operational support, and governance must be aligned across system levels over time [10, 13, 16].

3   Study Context and Methodology

3.1   Study Context

This study is situated in an inhabited smart neighborhood in Jena (Germany)[1] (Fig. 1) that forms part of the city administration's Smart City strategy [18–20]. As part of this municipal strategy, the neighborhood was developed as a residential environment in which digital and socio-technical solutions related to housing, everyday living, and health services were implemented within a broader framework of urban digital transformation.

In this paper, a *smart neighborhood* refers to a residential setting in which digital services and technology-enabled housing infrastructures are coordinated across local actors and everyday residential life. The neighborhood combines apartment buildings with shared community spaces and locally embedded support structures aimed at facilitating independent living and social participation. The Smart Quarter in Jena, Germany, is a small smart neighborhood consisting of three residential complexes with around 200 apartments and approximately 240 apartments, including families, seniors, and students. Since around 2021, residents have moved in gradually as the development progressed through three construction phases. The quarter combines built-in smart-home features (e.g., heating and shutter control via wall-mounted tablets) with a community manager who provides on-site support and a range of third-party smart services such as carsharing, energy monitoring, parcel services, and smart laundry (see Fig. 1).

---

[1] https://www.smartes-quartier.de/

The study focuses on socio-technical elements designed to support healthy living and aging in place. These include a neighborhood-based telemedicine facility, and smart-home–oriented infrastructure components integrated into housing units and building-level systems (see Fig. 2). A central component is a dedicated telemedicine room that serves as a place-based access point for digital health services. It provides a private setting for video consultations and digitally mediated interactions with health care providers. Beyond serving residents, the telemedicine room was intended to inform the development of neighborhood-based digital health configurations within the broader Smart City strategy [21]. In addition, the neighborhood incorporates smart-home features aligned with AAL approaches. In this study, these components are conceptualized not as isolated technological artifacts but as elements of a socio-technical system, as their practical relevance depends on integration into everyday routines, support structures, and organizational embedding within the neighborhood [22, 23].

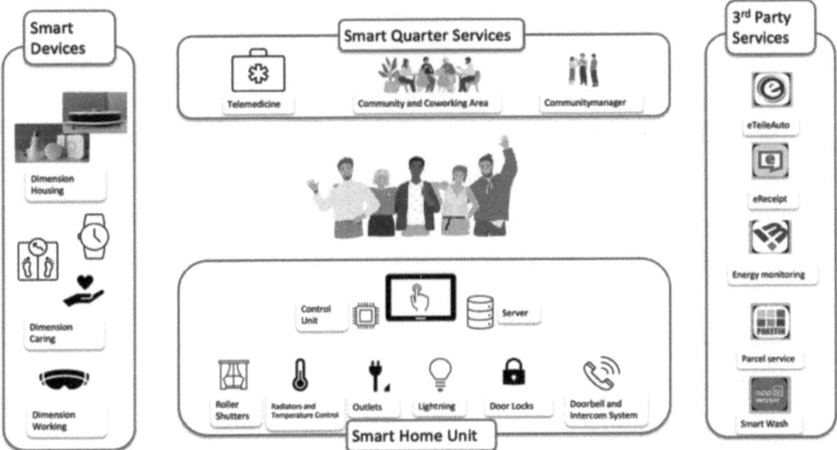

Fig. 1. Overview of the smart quarter living environment [24]

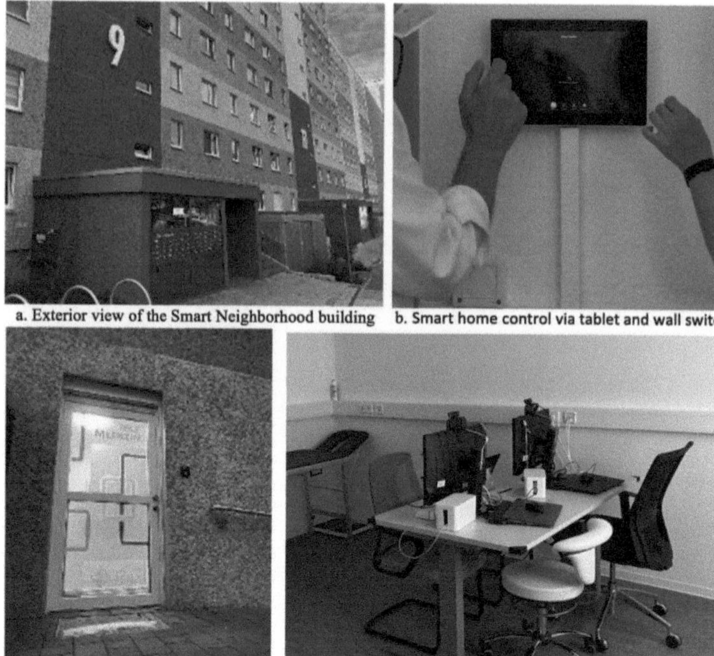

a. Exterior view of the Smart Neighborhood building　b. Smart home control via tablet and wall switch

c. Exterior view of the telehealth room　d. Initial pilot setup of the telehealth room (2025)

Fig. 2. Smart neighborhood Jena-Lobeda (Photograph by the authors)

3.2 Research Design

This study adopts a qualitative single-case study design to examine the implementation of socio-technical solutions within a real-world smart neighborhood. The single-case approach is appropriate because it allows for an in-depth investigation of complex implementation processes within a bounded and context-rich setting in which multiple actors and system levels interact. Rather than aiming for statistical generalization, the study seeks analytical generalization by examining cross-level dynamics within one integrated socio-technical system.

The case under study is the smart neighborhood itself, which is used as a living lab. As a living lab, the neighborhood constitutes an inhabited experimental environment in which digital and socio-technical solutions are introduced, tested, and iteratively adapted under real-life conditions. Unlike controlled pilot settings, this living lab embeds innovation processes within ongoing residential life and existing institutional arrangements, thereby enabling the observation of implementation dynamics as they unfold in practice.

Within this context, digital solutions - including smart-home infrastructures and a neighborhood-based telemedicine room - were implemented and further developed over time. The study therefore focuses on implementation in practice rather than on technological functionality alone. It examines how these solutions are introduced, organized, and sustained within a real-world neighborhood setting shaped by institutional arrangements and everyday use.

3.3 Data Collection and Analysis

Qualitative data were collected between 2022 and 2025 from multiple sources to capture implementation dynamics across socio-technical levels. The primary dataset consists of semi-structured interviews conducted as part of a structured maturity assessment at two implementation stages (pre and post). In total, 13 interviews were conducted in the pre phase and 7 in the post phase, covering strategic orientations (macro), operational coordination (meso), and everyday use experiences (micro). Participants were purposively recruited based on their role in planning, operating, or using the neighborhood's digital solutions. Micro-level participants were primarily residents, while meso- and macro-level participants included housing management representatives, municipal actors, and stakeholders associated with the Smart City initiative. A subset of participants took part at both time points, enabling a within-participant perspective on how perceptions and practices shifted as implementation progressed; in addition, the two-stage design allows phase-sensitive comparison across the broader stakeholder sample.

Interviews followed a semi-structured guide tailored to each stakeholder group while maintaining a shared core across groups. Core topics included: (1) participants' role and involvement in the Smart Quarter; (2) experiences with smart-home features and digital health services (including the neighborhood-based telemedicine room); (3) perceived benefits and drawbacks (e.g., usefulness, usability, privacy); (4) support structures and responsibilities (including the role of community management); (5) barriers and enabling conditions for adoption and sustained use (e.g., interoperability, reliability, access, costs, regulation); and (6) expectations regarding scaling, transferability, and long-term operation. Probing questions explored concrete incidents of success and breakdowns, as well as perceived differences between strategic intentions and everyday practice. The interviews were conducted in German, lasted around 45–60 min, were conducted in person and transcribed verbatim. To contextualize participants' responses, we monitored initiatives and events that could plausibly shape perceptions. No major disruptive events occurred during the interview period. However, a tenant festival was held in the community building during which the telemedicine room was introduced to residents and visitors. Participants were asked whether and how this event influenced their awareness, expectations, or evaluations of the services; any explicit references to the festival were coded and considered during interpretation to account for potential framing effects.

To complement the interviews, participatory requirement elicitation sessions were conducted for the telemedicine room during pre and mid-implementation (pre resident workshop: n = 8, August 2023; mid multi-stakeholder focus group: n = 6, February 2024). These sessions lasted around 3 h, involved project leaders, a technology provider, physicians, researchers, and residents, and served to surface coordination needs and boundary conditions specific to place-based telehealth delivery.

In addition, project-related documents (e.g., internal reports, meeting notes, concept papers, emails, and public materials) were reviewed to reconstruct planning rationales, contextualize decision-making, and support triangulation.

Data were analyzed using reflexive thematic analysis following Braun & Clarke [25]. Coding was carried out iteratively by three researchers, moving from initial open coding to refined thematic categories. Analytical rigor was supported through regular team discussions and memoing to challenge interpretations and consolidate theme definitions.

After theme development, a micro/meso/macro lens was applied as an organizing framework to attribute where themes were predominantly articulated and to enable cross-level comparison. Where a theme spanned multiple levels, it was coded as cross-level and discussed until agreement on the predominant level(s) was reached. Constant comparison across data sources was used to identify convergent and divergent patterns and to trace tensions between strategic intentions, organizational arrangements, and lived experiences. Quotations were translated into English by the authors.

An overview of the data sources, collection phases, and sample sizes is provided in Table 1.

Table 1. Overview of data collection

Data Source	Phase	n	Content
Maturity assessment interviews	Pre, Post	13, 7	Semi-structured interviews across system levels
Telehealth workshop / focus group	Pre, Mid	8, 6	Participatory requirement elicitation
Document analysis	Ongoing	-	Meeting notes, internal reports, emails, concept papers

4   Results

4.1   Overall Success Factors and Barriers

This section presents the empirical findings of the study. In line with the analytical framework, the results are structured across three socio-technical levels: macro, meso, and micro. This organization reflects how enabling conditions and constraints were articulated by different stakeholder groups and how they emerged within the socio-technical system.

For the purposes of this analysis, the *macro level* refers to governing and steering actors shaping the strategic direction of the initiative, including political decision-makers and representatives of municipal utilities and housing organizations. The *meso level* comprises mediating and coordinating actors responsible for operational implementation, particularly community management and associated facilitation structures. The *micro level* captures residents' lived experiences with smart-home technologies and neighborhood-based digital health services.

Across these levels, differentiated patterns of success factors and barriers become visible. To maintain a clear distinction between empirical reporting and interpretive synthesis, findings are first presented descriptively. Cross-level implications are addressed in the discussion section.

Due to the limited number of actors in some stakeholder groups and to ensure anonymity, socio-demographic information is reported only in aggregated form where relevant.

Table 2 provides a consolidated overview of the identified success factors. The table summarizes analytically derived themes and assigns them to the level(s) at which they were predominantly articulated. Application domains distinguish between health-related (H), living-related (L), or combined (H + L) contexts. Theme labels represent analytic descriptors grounded in participants' accounts.

Table 2. Overview success factors

ID	Theme	Application Domain	Level		
			Macro	Meso	Micro
SF-01	Shared Vision & Societal Value Orientation (Non-solutionism)	H + L	x		
SF-02	Targeted (Additional) Political Funding as Innovation Enabler	H	x		
SF-03	Strategic Scalability Orientation (Blueprint Logic)	H + L	x	x	
SF-04	Health Strategy Alignment: Aging in Place & Prevention Orientation	H	x		
SF-05	Built-in Spatial Provisioning for Services	H + L	x		
SF-06	Institutional Anchor: Organization	H + L	x		
SF-07	Living Lab / Pilot Logic (Iterative Adaptation & Learning)	H + L	x		
SF-08	Core-Competency Focus & Partner Ecosystem	H + L	x		
SF-09	Socio-technical Facilitation Roles (Community Management, Community Health Nurse)	H + L	x	x	x
SF-10	Structured Participation & Analog Encounter Formats	H + L		x	x
SF-11	Low-threshold Smart Home Design (Simplicity & Redundancy)	L		x	
SF-12	Location & Accessibility Supporting Everyday Autonomy	H + L			x

(continued)

Table 2. (*continued*)

ID	Theme	Application Domain	Level		
			Macro	Meso	Micro
SF-13	Perceived Autonomy & Comfort Gains through In-home Smart Functions	L			x
SF-14	Socially Equitable Access to High-quality Housing & Technology	L		x	x
SF-15	Neighborhood-based Convenience Services as Life-Logistics Support	L			x
SF-16	Perceived Usefulness of Digital Health Services	H			x
SF-17	High-density Care Setting as Safe Testbed for Redundancy & Process Learning	H	x		

Across success factors, macro-level enabling conditions emphasize strategic orientation, institutional ownership, funding structures, and experimental learning environments. Meso-level enabling conditions center on facilitation, coordination, and accessibility-oriented system design. Micro-level success factors predominantly relate to perceived everyday value, convenience, autonomy, and usefulness.

Table 3 summarizes the identified barriers. Similar to Table 2, themes are assigned to the level(s) at which they were articulated and categorized by application domain (H, L, H + L).

Table 3. Overview barriers

ID	Theme	Application Domain	Level		
			Macro	Meso	Micro
BF-01	Funding and Funding-Related Frameworks	H	x		
BF-02	Sustainable Financing Models	H + L	x		
BF-04, BF-15	Regulatory Frameworks	H + L	x	x	
BF-05, BF-12, BF-21, BF-23, BF-24	Structural and Spatial Implementation Constraints	H	x	x	x
BF-06, BF-11	Personnel Structures	H + L	x	x	

(*continued*)

Table 3. (*continued*)

ID	Theme	Application Domain	Level		
			Macro	Meso	Micro
BF-07	Interest in Health-Related Services	H	x		
BF-08	Lack of Needs and Market Analysis at Project Outset	H + L	x		
BF-09, BF-16, BF-26	Heterogeneity of residents' digital competencies	H + L	x	x	x
BF-10, BF-27	Age- and Language-Related Barriers to the Use of Digital Solutions	L		x	x
BF-13, BF-14, BF-20, BF-22, BF-29, BF-31	Technical Implementation Constraints	H + L		x	x
BF-17	Limited Identification with the Smart Neighborhood	L			x
BF-18	Privacy and Data Protection Concerns	H + L			x
BF-19, BF-25	Perceived Benefits versus Expectations	H + L			x
BF-28	Lack of Complementary Social Infrastructure	L			x
BF-30	Insufficient Communication	H			x

Across barriers, macro-level constraints are primarily shaped by funding logics, regulatory conditions, and strategic planning decisions. Meso-level barriers emerge at the interface of organizational capacity, spatial configuration, and technical implementation. Micro-level barriers relate to everyday usability, understanding, perceived relevance, autonomy, and trust.

4.2 The Macro Level: The Vision of "Future Healthy Living"

Macro Level Success Factors: Success factors (Strategic–Institutional Context). Macro-level stakeholders linked implementation success to a strategic–institutional context in which a long-term vision, enabling resources, and clear ownership created the conditions for neighborhood-based services to be piloted and potentially transferred beyond the initial setting. An overarching, needs-driven **vision (SF-01)** framed the smart neighborhood as *"more than housing"* integrating domains such as health, logistics, shopping, equipment, and energy supply, while explicitly prioritizing resident needs over technology push: *"It's not about what ideas we have, but what people want."* (SF-01). **Additional funding (SF-02)** was described as political/municipal support for the telemedicine room beyond the core project, providing a protected budget for experimentation that would not have been feasible under baseline financing (SF-02; document/context notes). **A deliberate transfer and scaling orientation (SF-03)** positioned telemedicine as a transferable service model rather than a building-bound feature, described as a *"product"* intended to extend into the wider district and potentially rural regions, and as an approach whose successful elements should be brought into the broader housing stock and shared with other cities and housing organisations: *"The things that work well... we want to bring [them] into the existing stock... and also share our experience and knowledge with other cities and housing organizations... this should not remain a secret"* (SF-03). **A health and aging-in-place rationale supported by partnerships (SF-04)** linked telemedicine and related services to enabling residents to remain longer in their familiar home environment *"...the telemedicine room... as an option so that people can stay longer in their home environment"* (SF-04), while emphasising collaboration with multiple health partners (e.g., AOK, DRK) to explore additional health-promotion options (SF-04). Early provision of **dedicated spaces (SF-05)** referred to the fact that key spaces (telemedicine room, community space, community-management office) were planned and available from the outset, although documentation indicates partial misfit with later workflow and compliance requirements and limited feasibility of major structural adaptations (SF-05; document/context notes). **Clear institutional ownership through anchor organisations (SF-06)** highlighted housing organisations and municipal utilities as actors expected to assume responsibility and oversight, supported by a housing-related rationale of stabilising tenancies and avoiding turnover-related process costs: *"...you need someone... to take it on... I see that more with housing or utilities"* (SF-06). **A pilot/real-world lab (SF-07)** characterised implementation as iterative and changeable rather than bound to a rigid plan, valuing learning through *"trying things out"* in practice: *"...we are completely free... not bound by a rigid corset"* (SF-07). **Role boundaries and collaboration (SF-08)** emphasised that telemedicine delivery could not be provided by housing actors alone, requiring external health partners, while positioning the organisations' mandate in operating infrastructure and service processes (including operation and billing): *"We can't do this alone... we can't build a medical department... we depend on partners"* or *"...our core business is operating infrastructure and service processes..."* (SF-08). **Facilitation roles (SF-09)** described community management (and, in planning, community health nursing/medical assistance) as core implementation infrastructure, providing repeated on-site explanation, locally tailored documentation, hands-on support in residents' apartments where needed, and coordination of practical access procedures: *"It is completely clear to us that people may not be able to handle this at the beginning... That's why we installed a community manager... and if a tenant comes for the fourth time because they didn't understand it, she will explain it the fourth time"* (SF-09/ document/context notes). Finally, **Location as a learning and testing condition (SF-17)** was framed less as a response to unmet healthcare provision and more as a favourable site for testing processes, learning, and maintaining redundancies due to proximity to the university hospital: *"Opposite the university hospital we surely need little additional healthcare... but it's the best place to learn processes, try things out, and have redundancies"* (SF-17).

Macro Level Barriers.   Macro-level barriers primarily concern structural conditions that delimit what can be implemented and sustained over time, particularly funding logics, regulatory frameworks, early planning decisions, and institutional dependencies. **Funding and funding-related frameworks** (BF-01) created tension between Smart City requirements especially open-source expectations aimed at transferability and healthcare-specific constraints where certified platforms and regulated infrastructures are mandatory. This conflict was described as complicating procurement and reducing flexibility: *"Within the Smart City framework, the approach is that we are only allowed to use open-source products... [but] within healthcare... certified platforms... are mandatory."* (BF-01). Closely related, **Sustainable financing models** (BF-02) were identified as missing for long-term operation, maintenance, and support. While pilot implementation was considered feasible within project-based funding schemes, participants questioned the financial viability of scaling or transferring services beyond the specific neighborhood setting. This concern applied to both health-related services and living-related support structures: *"It is not financially viable at scale. I want to say that very clearly: We cannot make this work. Apart from that, we now have a high-rise building where, in the end, I don't know, maybe 500 people live. That is more than in some villages around Jena."* (BF-02). Beyond financing, **Regulatory frameworks** (BF-04, BF-15) were repeatedly described as constraining operationalization through unresolved issues around liability, reimbursement, data protection, hygiene, and formal medical-service requirements. These uncertainties limited the translation of general interest into legally secure, routinized use cases and kept collaborations with healthcare partners at an exploratory stage: *"To this day, there is still no concrete use case, even though we have been discussing these issues with the hospital for three or four years. [...] Everyone finds it very interesting. But when you try to break it down into a concrete use case, you reach the point where you say: yes, this is now difficult in terms of care, we cannot guarantee that. The technical systems are still under development, and we cannot simply roll them out like this."* (BF-04). In addition, **Lack of needs and market analysis** at project outset (BF-08) was reported as constraining later adaptation because solutions were introduced without systematic knowledge of residents' needs, socio-demographic characteristics, or everyday practices: *"I think a market analysis and a needs assessment should have been carried out beforehand, to really look at what people actually want and who the people living there are. [...] I believe no one really asked residents what kinds of smart technologies they would like to have in their apartments."* (BF-08). Finally, **Personnel structures** (BF-06, BF-11) were described as a vulnerability where momentum depended on individual actors and implicit knowledge rather than institutionalized responsibilities, limiting continuity: *"There was a lot of implicit knowledge, many informal agreements, and the momentum came from individual actors who had a vision and brought the project team along with them."* (BF-06).

Taken together, these structural barriers show how funding, regulation, early planning, and institutional dependencies set the feasibility boundaries for technology-supported healthy living, within which meso-level coordination and micro-level routinization must subsequently be achieved.

4.3 The Meso Level: Translating Vision into Workable Routines

Meso Level Success Factors.   At the meso level, implementation success was attributed to organizational coordination and socio-technical service work that translates strategic ambitions into workable routines, complemented by structured encounter formats and inclusive design decisions. **Shared responsibility spanning housing quality, accessibility, and local service provision (SF-03)** positioned aging in place not as a purely medical objective but as a neighborhood responsibility spanning housing quality, accessibility, and local services; "*self-determined aging is not only about health, but also about housing quality, accessibility…*" (SF-03). In the same logic, housing-provider objectives were described as stabilizing tenancies and avoiding transitions into institutional care: "*We don't want that… We want tenants to identify with us and say: I like living here.*" (SF-03). **Socio-technical facilitation and on-site support (SF-09)** was described as central because telemedicine was seen as not yet functioning autonomously and therefore requiring translation into concrete steps for residents. Support was emphasized particularly during move-in phases and when residents encountered difficulties: "*It is completely clear to us that people may not be able to handle this at the beginning… that was partly our task, especially at the beginning or when someone moves in… it is important for residents that they know someone is there.*" (SF-09). Facilitation included repeated explanations, neighborhood-specific documentation, and hands-on assistance, while also extending to community-building work around shared spaces that "must be accompanied" to function as intended (SF-09). **Structured encounter formats and analogue touchpoints (SF-10)** complemented this facilitation by creating low-threshold opportunities for information exchange and trust-building (e.g., tenants' festival, workshops combined with social activities), which field notes described as positively received and helpful for making services such as telemedicine tangible (SF-10; field notes). Within the smart-home domain, **deliberate design choices and redundancy in interaction modes (SF-11)** was described as a deliberate strategy to lower entry barriers by keeping configurations relatively simple and offering alternative control routes beyond tablets: "*We tried to keep it relatively simple… so that a lighter access is possible.*" (SF-11). Finally, **access expansion through high-quality in-home equipment in subsidized housing (SF-14)** was framed as enabling socio-economically diverse residents - including lower-income groups and those receiving state support - to access smart functions and equipment standards that are often associated with higher-income contexts (SF-14).

Taken together, these meso-level success factors show how facilitation, encounter infrastructures, and inclusive design operate as translation mechanisms that stabilize everyday use under real-world conditions.

Meso Level Barriers.   A recurring barrier concerns **Heterogeneity of residents' digital competencies (BF-09, BF-16, BF-26)**. Interviewees described substantial differences in residents' familiarity with and confidence in digital technologies, which complicated standardised onboarding and created ongoing demand for individualised support particularly for shared services such as the telemedicine room: *"There was a lot of fear about using the space [telemedicine room] and the technology; people could not really imagine it."* (BF-09). At the same time, differences were also reported across age groups, with younger residents described as exploring digital technologies more independently: *"From what I observed, especially among younger people - many students and so on - there were fewer questions. I think they manage quite well. They explore it [smart home devices] and understand it fairly quickly…"* (BF-09). In everyday smart-home use, this heterogeneity becomes harder to compensate because technologies are embedded in private living spaces and often lack non-digital alternatives; reliance on support for routine activities (e.g., heating control) was described as uncomfortable and potentially undermining residents' sense of independence. One interviewee explained: *"Many older residents are simply overwhelmed by the technologies that they are required to use, as there are no alternatives available… While community management is intended to compensate for these challenges to some extent, relying on such support does not necessarily feel positive for residents"*. Needing assistance in order to manage everyday activities in their own homes such as adjusting the heating was described as uncomfortable and undermining residents' sense of independence (BF-09). A second barrier relates to **Organizational and personnel-related conditions (BF-06, BF-11)**. Implementation was described as relying on a small number of key individuals (e.g., community management, project coordination) who held implicit knowledge and drove coordination. Interviewees reported that high turnover and limited capacities reduced continuity of support and that personnel-intensive facilitation models were costly and therefore difficult to scale or transfer: *"We do not have a community manager in the other residential areas. That also has to do with costs."* (BF-11). **Spatial conditions** formed a further barrier through **Structural and spatial implementation constraints (BF-05, BF-12, BF-21, BF-23, BF-24)**. Interviewees described scarce or unsuitable communal space as limiting social and health-related initiatives: *"We have very little communal space. It is all municipal property, basically a large parking lot. It does not really lend itself to doing much there."* (BF-12). These constraints became particularly operational in the telemedicine facility, where regulatory and workflow requirements implied spatial configurations that exceeded initial planning assumptions (e.g., hygiene procedures, treatment processes, accessibility) and thereby narrowed implementation options: *"This experimental field turns out to be a very tough challenge, because the regulatory aspects involved - right down to hygiene requirements - are particularly demanding in such a space."* (BF-05). Technical limitations were reported as **Technical implementation constraints (BF-13, BF-14, BF-20, BF-22, BF-29, BF-31)**. Predefined configurations and fixed installations reduced flexibility over time, while long planning and construction cycles were seen as misaligned with rapid technological development: *"When you finally reach the point… the tablet is mounted on the wall, it is already outdated."* (BF-14). Beyond obsolescence, interviewees noted that predefined system logics shaped everyday practices in ways that could be experienced as autonomy-restricting (e.g., when residents perceived the system as dictating heating behaviour): *"People sometimes feel that their autonomy is being restricted, for example when they have the impression that the system dictates how they should heat their apartment."* (BF-13). Finally, **Regulatory frameworks**

(BF-15) manifested at the meso level as day-to-day operational uncertainty, affecting compliance procedures, responsibility allocation, and the transition from pilot testing to routine operation. Interviewees described the need to navigate complex requirements (e.g., hygiene, treatment processes, data protection, accessibility) before telemedicine could be stabilised as a routine service: *"It is a difficult topic, because you run into many obstacles, for example regarding treatment processes. You first must familiarize yourself with all these requirements. For instance, the patient cannot disinfect the space themselves, and then questions arise such as whether the room meets accessibility standards, whether the doors are wide enough, and so on."* (BF-15).

Taken together, these meso-level barriers show how digital-competency heterogeneity, staffing dependencies, spatial constraints, technical lock-ins, and operationalised regulatory demands shape whether neighborhood-based digital health and smart-living services can be coordinated, made accessible, and routinised in practice.

4.4 The Micro Level: Everyday Meaning and Routinised Use

Micro Level Success Factors. At the micro level, residents described benefits that were immediately tangible in everyday life, spanning social support, neighborhood accessibility, in-home convenience, and expected usefulness of telemedicine. Readily available **community management** as an everyday point of contact **(SF-09)** was repeatedly framed as reassuring because a known person was directly accessible in the building, providing continuity for questions about services and technologies: the community manager was described as *"our first contact person"* who is *"always in the building"* (SF-09). **Analogue encounter formats (SF-10)** were valued as part of neighborhood life, with residents referring to spontaneous encounters in shared spaces: *"Down at the sports field, we sometimes meet with other residents."* (SF-10). In addition, residents emphasised the **location and accessibility (SF-12)** as an enabling condition for aging in place, especially when mobility is constrained or when driving may no longer be possible. One resident highlighted disability-related accessibility needs and the value of nearby public transport: *"I am severely disabled... where we are located, it couldn't be better... all of a sudden I have two stops."* (SF-12). Within the home, **in-home smart functions** as convenient and future-oriented **(SF-13)** were described as offering practical control and comfort (e.g., lights, sockets, heating, programmed features), and were framed as a forward-looking housing standard: *"It's enormous what you offer here... I actually think, this should be the future."* (SF-13). Residents also expressed **a socially equitable access (SF-14)**, describing the combination of housing quality and technology provision as equitable relative to income and as enabling access to standards often associated with higher-income contexts (SF-14; field notes). Beyond housing and technology, residents highlighted **neighborhood-based convenience services** for daily logistics **(SF-15)** as reducing time pressure and administrative burden, for example through parcel services and low-threshold booking of shared spaces: *"You can just book online... super easy, and I like that a lot."* (SF-15). Finally, **expected usefulness of digital health services (telemedicine) (SF-16)** was articulated in strongly pragmatic terms, focused on reducing effort and complexity of routine care coordination: when asked whether telemedicine would make daily life easier, one resident replied, *"Oh my God. Yes."* (SF-16).

Taken together, these micro-level success factors show how support structures, accessibility, everyday convenience, and anticipated health-service benefits translate "smartness" into perceived quality of life in residents' lived experience.

Micro Level Barriers.   At the micro level, barriers became visible in how residents interpreted, trusted, and routinised digital services and smart-living functions in everyday life. A first barrier concerned **Limited knowledge and understanding of digital health concepts (BF-16)**. Several residents could not clearly describe what telemedicine entails or how it would be used, which contributed to hesitant engagement: *"Well, I think you can somehow get in contact directly with a doctor or something like that."* (BF-16). Relatedly, **Heterogeneity of residents' digital competencies (BF-26)** shaped whether technologies could be used at all; some residents described feeling overwhelmed and therefore using functions selectively or not at all: *"The technology is there. But I cannot operate it."* (BF-26).

Everyday interaction was further constrained by **Usability and technical reliability issues (BF-20, BF-22)**, including non-intuitive interfaces and system logics that did not match residents' routines. One resident described the heating system as misaligned with their expectations and experienced it as producing a predefined pattern rather than individual control: *"It does not work the way we imagine it… you end up with a predefined heating pattern."* (BF-20). In addition, **Technical malfunctions disrupting daily life (BF-29)** were reported as practical breakdowns with immediate consequences, for example when basic infrastructure such as the doorbell failed: *"The technology, for example the doorbell, often does not work…"* (BF-29). Beyond functionality, residents also articulated **Perceived restrictions of autonomy (BF-13)** in relation to predefined configurations, describing a sense of reduced self-determination when the system appeared to dictate how to behave (e.g., how to heat). Residents described feeling constrained by system configurations: *"a bit restricted in their self-determination because they have the feeling that they are being told how to heat."* (BF-13).

Trust-related barriers appeared through **Privacy and data protection concerns (BF-18)**, particularly in the telemedicine context where residents associated use with processing sensitive personal data: *"I would have concerns about that. These are very personal and sensitive data."* (BF-18). Value-related barriers emerged as **Perceived benefits versus expectations (BF-25)**, when residents questioned whether neighborhood-based services provided added value compared to already available alternatives: *"Why would I need that if my doctor already offers video consultations?"* (BF-25). Beyond service value, some residents expressed **Limited identification with the smart neighborhood (BF-17)**, stating that technology was not central to their housing choice: *"I did not move here because of the technology."* (BF-17).

Finally, everyday uptake was undermined by **Insufficient communication (BF-30)**, which reduced awareness of what services existed or were planned: *"I do not know what is planned."* (BF-30). This communication gap also fuelled scepticism about the smartness claim, reflected in practical uncertainty (e.g., booking procedures) and critical evaluations of whether the neighborhood could be considered *"smart"* in lived practice (BF-31).

Taken together, these micro-level barriers show how understanding, competence, usability, autonomy, trust, perceived value, identification, and communication filter macro ambitions and meso arrangements into actual everyday engagement.

5 Discussion

This study examined (RQ1) which success factors and barriers different stakeholder groups identify in implementing socio-technical solutions for healthy living and aging in place in an inhabited smart neighborhood and (RQ2) how these factors vary across different stakeholders. Overall, the findings show that success criteria are level-specific and that alignment between macro ambitions and micro-level routines is non-automatic, relying on meso-level translation work. The discussion interprets these insights through implementation lenses (5.1), highlights cross-level tensions and boundary conditions (5.2), and derives implications including a meso-first proposition (5.3).

5.1 Cross-Level Interpretation

Building on the overall findings, two cross-level patterns stand out. *First*, success and failure are not defined uniformly across the system but follow level-specific evaluative logics: macro-level perspectives foreground strategic direction, institutional positioning, and transferability; micro-level perspectives highlight everyday fit, autonomy, usability, and lived experience; and meso-level perspectives focus on whether socio-technical arrangements can be operationalized and stabilized through coordination, facilitation, and service delivery. This configuration aligns with socio-technical adoption accounts that conceptualize digital health implementation as a multi-level alignment problem rather than a purely technical deployment or an individual acceptance issue [26]. *Second*, cross-level alignment does not occur automatically. Macro-level vision and transfer ambition do not translate into routinised use at the micro level unless they are converted into concrete workflows, accessible entry points, and resident-relevant use scenarios. Implementation therefore emerges as an ongoing process of cross-level negotiation rather than linear diffusion.

Interpreted through implementation lenses, these findings underscore a core transition challenge: pilot feasibility does not equal sustainability. The empirical material reflects a dynamic widely described in telemedicine and digital health research: protected project funding and pilot arrangements can enable experimentation and rapid progress, while long-term embedding often stalls when financing models, reimbursement pathways, liability allocations, and governance responsibilities remain unresolved [4, 10, 27]. This pattern is captured by NASSS, which conceptualizes non-adoption, abandonment, scale-up, spread, and limited sustainability as outcomes of interacting determinants across domains beyond the technology itself, including organizational capacity and wider system conditions [16]. In the present case, macro-level aspirations to scale or transfer neighborhood-based services coexisted with operational fragility where procedural, regulatory, and resourcing issues had to be stabilized for routine practice illustrating how strategic intent and technical availability alone do not secure sustainable implementation.

A second interpretative insight concerns the meso level as the primary site of translation and normalization. Across the data, technologies became functional not primarily through device availability but through continuous facilitation work that translated strategic ambitions into everyday practice. Here, translation work refers to activities such as repeated explanation and communication, onboarding, troubleshooting, coordination of access procedures, and trust-building in the neighborhood setting. This observation resonates with Normalization Process Theory (NPT), which conceptualizes sustained embedding as dependent on coherence (shared understanding of what the intervention is and why it matters), cognitive participation (commitment), collective action (operational enactment), and reflexive monitoring (ongoing appraisal and adjustment) [17]. In the smart neighborhood, facilitation roles performed precisely this normalization work by reducing information asymmetries, lowering thresholds for engagement, and stabilizing routines around access and support. At the same time, the material suggests vulnerability through dependence on a limited number of highly motivated individuals, consistent with evidence that champions can accelerate implementation while also introducing risk if roles and resources are not institutionally anchored [28].

Taken together, these interpretations indicate that implementation success in inhabited smart neighborhoods hinges on the capacity to sustain meso-level translation work over time: macro-level direction can create legitimacy and resources, and micro-level engagement ultimately determines meaning and routinization, but the meso layer operationalizes ambitions, mediates frictions, and maintains coherence across heterogeneous stakeholders and residents [16, 17, 26].

5.2 Cross-Level Tensions and Boundary Conditions

The cross-level analysis shows that enabling conditions do not automatically reinforce one another. Instead, success factors at one level can be neutralized or amplified by tensions at adjacent levels, producing fragile trajectories even when single components appear "in place". A *first tension* concerns scalability ambitions versus operational viability. Macro-level narratives emphasized transferability and the potential to scale neighborhood-based services beyond the pilot setting, yet scaling would require replicating the labor-intensive facilitation work that residents and frontline actors described as essential for everyday use. This mismatch echoes a central implementation dilemma: sustainability depends on organizational capacity and ongoing service work, not only on the availability of technical artifacts [16]. Telemedicine policy and synthesis work similarly stresses that mainstreaming beyond pilots hinges on durable financing, governance, and integration into routine care pathways conditions that are frequently unresolved when projects shift from protected innovation settings to regular operations [4, 10, 27]. In this sense, "scale" becomes less a question of replicating a room or device configuration and more a question of replicating a socio-organizational service model.

A *second tension* concerns artifact-centered funding logics versus the underfunding of social infrastructure. Project schemes often prioritize deliverables that are legible as technology outputs (e.g., platforms, devices, open-source components), while the empirical material indicates that everyday functionality depends heavily on relational and organizational work: onboarding, repeated explanation, troubleshooting, communication, and coordination of access procedures. This discrepancy is consequential because it structurally under-resources precisely the meso-level capacities that enable coherence and routinization. The tension is particularly visible in digital health contexts where regulatory, quality, and liability requirements cannot be "engineered away" but require continuous operational support and clearly allocated responsibilities [10, 16]. From this perspective, success factors such as political funding or living-lab experimentation can inadvertently produce fragility when they finance pilots but fail to institutionalize the ongoing service roles that make neighborhood-based solutions workable over time.

A *third tension* relates to built-environment lock-in versus evolving compliance and workflow requirements. Neighborhood-based digital health infrastructures are spatially and technically embedded in the built environment and therefore shaped by long planning horizons. At the same time, compliance standards, procedural requirements, and operational workflows may become clearer only during implementation. For regulated telemedicine provision, concrete requirements such as certified providers, data protection, information security, and procedural standards define feasibility boundaries and can necessitate adjustments in workflows and spatial arrangements [11]. Where architectural and technical decisions are made early, later adaptation can become costly or constrained, creating lock-in effects that undermine flexibility. This dynamic aligns with NASSS accounts of how wider system conditions and organizational constraints interact with technology and service design to shape sustainability outcomes [16]. It also suggests that infrastructure-heavy innovation requires earlier coupling between spatial design, compliance considerations, and end-to-end service workflows than is typically assumed in pilot logics.

Beyond these three structural tensions, the findings point to cross-cutting conditions that amplify or moderate implementation outcomes. First, place-based digital inequalities shape who can access and benefit from digital care; evidence linking neighborhood broadband availability to telehealth use among older adults underscores that adoption cannot be treated as purely individual choice when local infrastructure conditions differ [12]. Second, privacy and autonomy operate as both experiential and governance constraints: smart-home surveillance research shows persistent concerns about control and appropriate data use [8], and health-monitoring work highlights that privacy barriers are context- and role-dependent rather than uniform [9]. More broadly, these findings point to psychologically relevant dimensions that are well established in AAL research, including autonomy, trust, perceived usefulness, privacy sensitivity, and digital competence. While the present study does not measure these constructs in a standardized way, it shows how they become consequential within socio-technical implementation processes and are shaped by meso-level communication, support, and operational arrangements. In home-based technologies, these concerns intersect with the broader set of barriers reported in smart home health technology syntheses, including usability, reliability, and interoperability constraints that directly shape everyday trust and willingness to routinize use [6]. Third, co-creation and living-lab formats can mitigate misfit by enabling iterative learning, yet living-lab research also highlights resource intensity and sustainability risks, particularly when facilitation roles and responsibilities remain ambiguous or project-bound [14, 15].

Taken together, these tensions and boundary conditions clarify why alignment across macro ambitions, meso service arrangements, and micro everyday practices must be actively maintained: implementation success depends less on isolated enabling factors than on sustained cross-level coordination of governance, resourcing, and everyday usability in lived neighborhood contexts [10, 16].

5.3 Implications and a Meso-First Proposition

The findings suggest that socio-technical innovation in inhabited smart neighborhoods should be designed and governed for cross-level translation rather than mere deployment. *First*, the meso layer needs to be planned and resourced as core infrastructure: facilitation work—onboarding, repeated explanation, troubleshooting, coordination of access procedures, and trust-building—was constitutive for routinization and therefore requires role clarity, staffing, and durable financing beyond pilot periods. *Second*, implementation should be anchored in resident-relevant use cases and coherent access pathways. Abstract labels do not translate into routines unless services are rendered concrete through a small set of everyday scenarios and transparent guidance; in NPT terms, coherence is a prerequisite for normalization and sustained embedding [7]. *Third*, neighborhood-based digital health infrastructures should be specified through end-to-end workflows and compliance requirements early enough to avoid lock-in, because sustainability depends on aligning technology with organizational capacity and system conditions rather than treating the artifact as the main unit of replication [1]. *Fourth*, privacy and autonomy should be operationalized as service and governance requirements through transparent procedures and role-based access, thereby strengthening trust and routinization. Synthesizing these implications, we formulate a meso-first proposition: in inhabited smart neighborhoods, alignment between macro ambitions and micro-level routines is non-automatic and is stabilized through meso-level translation work that converts strategic direction into workable practices and channels everyday experience into organizational learning [1, 7]. Figure 3 visualizes this proposition by positioning the meso layer as the primary translation site between macro actors and residents within a contextual frame.

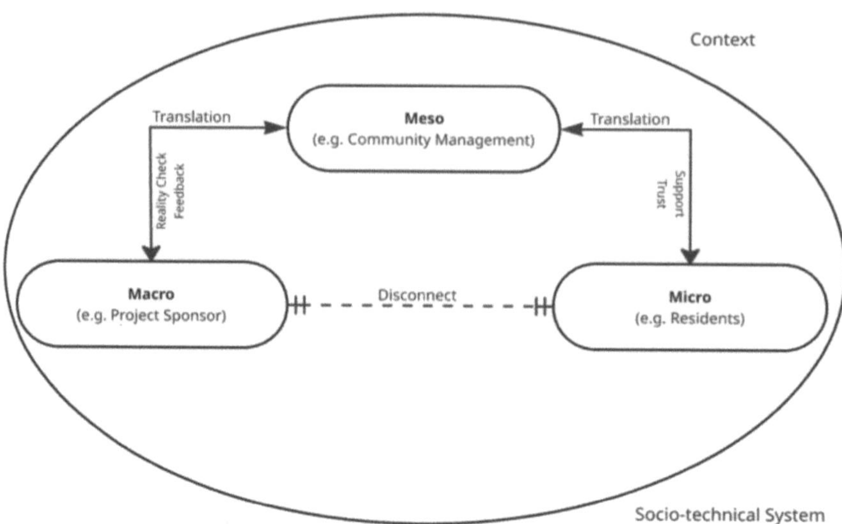

Fig. 3. Meso first approach

Here, *meso-first* denotes an implementation logic in which the meso layer is treated as the primary leverage point because it performs the translation work that converts macro ambitions into workable routines and channels micro-level experience into organizational learning. It frames sustained adoption as a service- and practice-based achievement rather than an artifact-centered rollout.

6   Conclusion and Future Research

This study set out to examine (RQ1) which success factors and barriers different stakeholder groups identify in the implementation of socio-technical solutions for healthy living and aging in place in an inhabited smart neighborhood, and (RQ2) how do these success factors and barriers differ across stakeholder groups.

The findings show that enabling conditions and barriers are unevenly distributed across levels and do not automatically reinforce one another. Macro-level actors emphasize vision, scalability, and structural conditions; micro-level actors evaluate everyday usability, relevance, and autonomy implications; and meso-level actors perform the critical translation work that connects strategic ambition with lived practice.

Across levels, the decisive enabling condition was not the technological infrastructure itself but the emergent meso-level structure: a form of social infrastructure shaped by facilitation, coordination, and trust-building. Implementation stability depended on the continuous translation between macro-level vision and micro-level experience. Based on these insights, the study proposes a Meso-First Approach, conceptualizing digital transformation in inhabited environments as a process of cross-level alignment rather than technological rollout.

The study is limited by its single-case focus and by the dynamic nature of implementation processes. Some barriers identified at the time of analysis such as limited awareness, coherence gaps, or incomplete routinization may shift as services stabilize, whereas structural constraints related to financing, regulation, and spatial lock-in may persist. In addition, the study did not triangulate qualitative insights with longitudinal usage data or outcome measures.

Future research should therefore combine qualitative and quantitative approaches to track routinization processes over time and assess how usage patterns evolve across implementation phases. Comparative studies across multiple neighborhoods with different governance and financing configurations could further clarify which structural conditions support sustainable embedding. Real-world living lab research should continue to examine how socio-technical translation mechanisms operate under varying contextual conditions. Finally, the proposed Meso-First Approach should be empirically tested and refined in other smart neighborhood and aging-in-place contexts to assess its transferability and explanatory power.

Acknowledgments. This study was part of the project Multi-Generation Smart Community (mGeSCo). The project was funded by the Carl Zeiss Foundation.

Disclosure of Interests. The authors have no competing interests to declare that are relevant to the content of this article.

References

1. World Health Organization: Ageing and health (2026). https://www.who.int/news-room/fact-sheets/detail/ageing-and-health?
2. World Health Organization: Healthy ageing and functional ability (2020). https://www.who.int/news-room/questions-and-answers/item/healthy-ageing-and-functional-ability?
3. National Institute on Aging: Aging in Place: Growing Older at Home (2026). https://www.nia.nih.gov/health/aging-place/aging-place-growing-older-home?
4. Kruse, C.S., Williams, K., Bohls, J., Shamsi, W.: Telemedicine and health policy: a systematic review. Health Policy Technol. **10**, 209–229 (2021). https://doi.org/10.1016/j.hlpt.2020.10.006
5. Wojciechowski, M.: End user context modeling in ambient assisted living. Int. J. Adv. Pervasive Ubiquitous Comput. **1**, 61–80 (2009). https://doi.org/10.4018/japuc.2009090804
6. Tian, Y.J.A., Felber, N.A., Pageau, F., Schwab, D.R., Wangmo, T.: Benefits and barriers associated with the use of smart home health technologies in the care of older persons: a systematic review. BMC Geriatr. **24**, 152 (2024). https://doi.org/10.1186/s12877-024-04702-1
7. Schroeder, T., Dodds, L., Georgiou, A., Gewald, H., Siette, J.: Older adults and new technology: mapping review of the factors associated with older adults' intention to adopt digital technologies. JMIR aging **6**, e44564 (2023). https://doi.org/10.2196/44564
8. Percy Campbell, J., Buchan, J., Chu, C.H., Bianchi, A., Hoey, J., Khan, S.S.: User perception of smart home surveillance among adults aged 50 years and older: scoping review. JMIR Mhealth Uhealth **12**, e48526 (2024). https://doi.org/10.2196/48526
9. Sun, L., Yang, B., Kindt, E., Chu, J.: Privacy barriers in health monitoring: scoping review. JMIR Nurs. **7**, e53592 (2024). https://doi.org/10.2196/53592

10. Keelara, R., Sutherland, E., Almyranti, M.: Leading practices for the future of telemedicine: Implementing telemedicine post-pandemic. OECD Publishing, Paris (2025)
11. Kassenärztliche Bundesvereinigung (KBV): Videosprechstunde (2026). https://www.kbv.de/praxis/digitalisierung/anwendungen/videosprechstunde?utm_source=chatgpt.com
12. Okoye, S.M., Mulcahy, J.F., Fabius, C.D., Burgdorf, J.G., Wolff, J.L.: Neighborhood broadband and use of telehealth among older adults: cross-sectional study of national survey data linked with census data. J. Med. Internet Res. **23**, e26242 (2021). https://doi.org/10.2196/26242
13. Maramba, I.D., Jones, R., Austin, D., Edwards, K., Meinert, E., Chatterjee, A.: The role of health kiosks: scoping review. JMIR Med. Inform. **10**, e26511 (2022). https://doi.org/10.2196/26511
14. Hossain, M., Leminen, S., Westerlund, M.: A systematic review of living lab literature. J. Clean. Prod. **213**, 976–988 (2019). https://doi.org/10.1016/j.jclepro.2018.12.257
15. Russo-Spena, T., Salvatore, C., Fairfield, B., Giordano, A., de Simone, S., Illario, M.: Living labs in digital health: a collaborative ecosystem approach for continuum of care. Front. Public Health **13**, 1728904 (2025). https://doi.org/10.3389/fpubh.2025.1728904
16. Greenhalgh, T., et al.: Beyond adoption: a new framework for theorizing and evaluating nonadoption, abandonment, and challenges to the scale-up, spread, and sustainability of health and care technologies. J. Med. Internet Res. **19**, e367 (2017). https://doi.org/10.2196/jmir.8775
17. May, C.R., et al.: Development of a theory of implementation and integration: normalization process theory. Implementation Sci. IS **4**, 29 (2009). https://doi.org/10.1186/1748-5908-4-29
18. Stadtverwaltung Jena: SMARTCITY JENA (2022). https://smartcity.jena.de/smart-city/startseite
19. Stadtverwaltung Jena: Smart City Strategie der Stadt Jena (2023). https://smartcity.jena.de/smart-city-projekt/projektbeschreibung
20. Stadtwerke Jena: Smart City: Modern services for a vibrant city (2026). https://www.stadtwerke-jena.de/en/nachhaltigkeit/smart-city.html
21. Stadtwerke Jena Gruppe: Telemedizin für alle: Raum in Jena-Lobeda jetzt stadtweit zugänglich, vol
22. Opielka, M., Erfurth, C.: Soziale Digitalisierung. Perspektiven zu den Schnittstellen von Technik und Gesellschaft. Springer VS, Wiesbaden, Heidelberg (2025)
23. Stadtwerke Jena Gruppe: Smartes Quartier (2026). https://www.smartes-quartier.de/#quartier
24. Hölzer, S., Honner, L., Preßler, W., Schulz, A., Erfurth, C.: Towards designing a user-centered local community platform to foster social cohesion in a multi-generational smart community. In: Krieger, U.R., Eichler, G., Erfurth, C., Fahrnberger, G. (eds.) Innovations for Community Services. Communications in Computer and Information Science, vol. 1876, pp. 277–291. Springer, Cham (2023). https://doi.org/10.1007/978-3-031-40852-6_15
25. Braun, V., Clarke, V.: Using thematic analysis in psychology. Qual. Res. Psychol. **3**, 77–101 (2006). https://doi.org/10.1191/1478088706qp063oa
26. Rauner, Y., Stummer, H.: The socio-technical adoption and diffusion of digital health innovations: the development of the STAD-HC model based on telemedicine in Germany. Digital Bus. **5**, 100135 (2025). https://doi.org/10.1016/j.digbus.2025.100135
27. Scott Kruse, C., Karem, P., Shifflett, K., Vegi, L., Ravi, K., Brooks, M.: Evaluating barriers to adopting telemedicine worldwide: a systematic review. J. Telemed. Telecare **24**, 4–12 (2018). https://doi.org/10.1177/1357633X16674087
28. Pettersen, S., Eide, H., Berg, A.: The role of champions in the implementation of technology in healthcare services: a systematic mixed studies review. BMC Health Serv. Res. **24**, 456 (2024). https://doi.org/10.1186/s12913-024-10867-7

Distributed Systems

A Web Platform for Multi-Sensor Monitoring and Analysis of Large-Area Glass Surfaces

Peter Šarafín[✉], Michal Hodoň, Lukáš Formanek, and Matúš Formanek

Department of Technical Cybernetics, University of Žilina, Žilina, Slovakia
`peter.sarafin@fri.uniza.sk`

Abstract. Monitoring large-area glass elements (e.g., window panes and facade panels) benefits from distributed sensing and reproducible post-processing workflows. This paper presents a prototype platform that integrates ESP32-based sensor nodes, an HTTP ingestion service, a time series database, and a web application for interactive exploration of heterogeneous measurements collected on a spatial sensor grid. The system supports time-stamped ingestion of mixed sensor modalities with different sampling periods, including both slow environmental variables (e.g., temperature, humidity, illuminance) and faster structural-response signals (e.g., strain, displacement, acceleration-derived metrics). The user interface provides synchronized time series views, spatial heatmaps, time-window selection, configurable filtering, and dataset export with processing provenance. The platform is validated using simulated signals and demonstrated on glass dynamic property measurements acquired from a grid-mounted sensor setup.

Keywords: Glass dynamics · Sensor grids · Structural health monitoring · Time series database · Visualization

1 Introduction

Large-area glass structures are increasingly used in architectural and industrial contexts where mechanical excitation, thermal gradients, and boundary conditions influence performance and safety. Experimental characterization of glass dynamic properties often relies on sensor grids installed directly on the pane to capture spatially distributed responses such as vibration and temperature. In laboratory settings, recurring measurement campaigns often require the same core steps: data acquisition, centralized storage, visualization, and post-processing [1,2].

To reduce repeated engineering effort and standardize these workflows, a platform was developed for the acquisition of heterogeneous sensor signals from distributed embedded nodes, the storage of time-stamped measurements in a centralized database, and web-based visualization and analysis for both real-time monitoring and historical review. The platform was motivated and initially validated on a glass dynamics measurement task in which temperature

K. Kirchner et al. (Eds.): I4CS 2026, CCIS 3007, pp. 335–345, 2026.
https://doi.org/10.1007/978-3-032-27096-2_18

and acceleration sensors were installed on a grid across the glass surface, with measurements stored in a database for subsequent analysis.

In contrast to experiment-specific scripts or dashboards, the approach emphasizes a uniform data model and reusable visualization workflows that remain stable as sensor modalities and sampling regimes change. Although the proposed system is motivated by structural monitoring, the main contribution of this paper is not a new damage-detection, synchronization, or anomaly-detection algorithm. Instead, the paper focuses on the design of a reusable monitoring and analysis platform for laboratory-scale experiments on large-area glass surfaces and on prototype-level validation under simulated and real measurement scenarios.

1.1 Contributions

This paper makes the following contributions:

- An end-to-end architecture for multi-sensor monitoring of large-area glass surfaces using ESP32-based nodes, HTTP ingestion, time series storage, and an interactive web application.
- A uniform data and visualization workflow that supports heterogeneous sensor types, mixed sampling intervals, spatial indexing on a sensor grid, preprocessing, and reproducible export.
- A prototype-level validation on synthetic and real glass-monitoring scenarios, together with a comparative positioning of the proposed platform with respect to generic dashboards, custom tools, and representative SHM visualization approaches.

2 Background, Related Work, and System Requirements

Structural health monitoring (SHM) systems commonly rely on distributed sensing to capture quantities such as vibration, strain, temperature, and acoustic emissions [3]. The practical value of such systems depends not only on sensing hardware but also on correct timestamp handling, synchronization, data integrity, and efficient storage and querying of time-stamped measurements. For this reason, time series databases are frequently used in monitoring applications because they support windowed queries, aggregation, and downsampling of timestamped measurements [4].

Generic IoT and dashboard stacks offer robust ingestion, storage, and plotting capabilities, but they are usually not organized around experiment-oriented workflows for spatially arranged sensor grids. Conversely, SHM-oriented visualization solutions often emphasize asset-scale monitoring, digital twins, or BIM integration, which can be useful in infrastructure-scale deployments but are often heavier than needed for laboratory experiments on a single instrumented glass element. Custom scripts remain flexible, but they are often difficult to reuse across repeated experiments, sensor modalities, and users.

Based on these observations and the motivating glass dynamics use case, the platform was designed to ingest heterogeneous sensor signals while preserving timestamped measurements and their temporal ordering. It was also designed to support mixed sampling periods, real-time and retrospective exploration, spatial visualization on a sensor grid, configurable preprocessing, and reproducible export. In addition, the implementation emphasizes reliability under repeated submissions, responsiveness for interactive queries, and maintainability through separation of sensing, ingestion, storage, and visualization components.

2.1   Comparison with Existing Monitoring and Visualization Platforms

Table 1 summarizes the positioning of the proposed platform with respect to representative classes of alternative solutions.

Table 1. Comparison of representative monitoring and visualization approaches with the proposed platform. Entries denote direct support (Yes), partial or indirect support (Partial), or no explicit support (No).

Approach	Real-time view	Heterog. sensors	Grid heatmaps	Filtering in UI	Export provenance	Glass/lab focus
Generic dashboard stack	Yes	Yes	No	No	Partial	No
Generic IoT platform	Yes	Yes	No	No	No	No
SHM/BIM visualization tools	Yes	Yes	Partial	No	Partial	No
Custom experiment scripts	Partial	Partial	Partial	Partial	No	Yes
Proposed platform	Yes	Yes	Yes	Yes	Yes	Yes

The comparison does not imply that the proposed system is universally superior to these alternatives. Rather, it highlights that the platform is deliberately optimized for a narrower use case: reproducible experimental monitoring and analysis of spatially distributed measurements on glass surfaces. In this respect, the main differentiators are spatial indexing on a sensor grid, synchronized exploration of mixed-rate data, configurable preprocessing, and export with processing provenance.

3   Overall Architecture and Implementation Choices

Figure 1 summarizes the platform. Embedded sensor nodes transmit timestamped measurements to an HTTP-based ingestion API. The backend stores data in a time series database and exposes query endpoints for visualization and analysis. The web application provides interactive views, filtering, and export.

A time series database was selected to optimize the storage and retrieval of timestamped signals. ESP32-based nodes were used as sensor endpoints due to

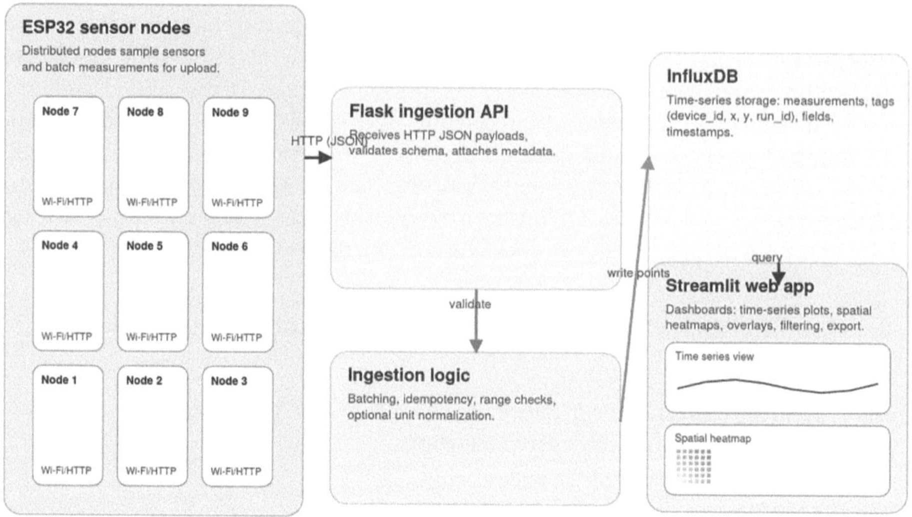

Fig. 1. Platform architecture: ESP32 sensor nodes transmit measurements to a Flask-based ingestion API, which writes to InfluxDB. A Streamlit web app queries and visualizes time series data and spatial heatmaps.

their integrated wireless connectivity and suitability for distributed sensing [5]. Each node may host one or more sensors and is assigned a unique identifier used by the ingestion interface. A representative embedded sensing node is shown in Fig. 2.

The ingestion layer was implemented as a REST-style API using Flask, which validates incoming payloads, associates them with device and sensor metadata, and writes them to InfluxDB [6–8]. The web application was implemented in Streamlit to support rapid development of interactive dashboards, including time-range selection, overlay plots, spatial heatmaps, filtering, and export [9]. This separation of sensing, ingestion, storage, and visualization keeps the architecture lightweight while allowing incremental extension to additional sensor types and experiments.

4   Data Model and Ingestion Workflow

To avoid experiment-specific data pipelines, the platform uses a uniform time series representation with explicit metadata describing sensor type, units, location, and quality indicators. This allows heterogeneous scalar measurements to be handled through a common query and visualization workflow while preserving modality-specific semantics through metadata.

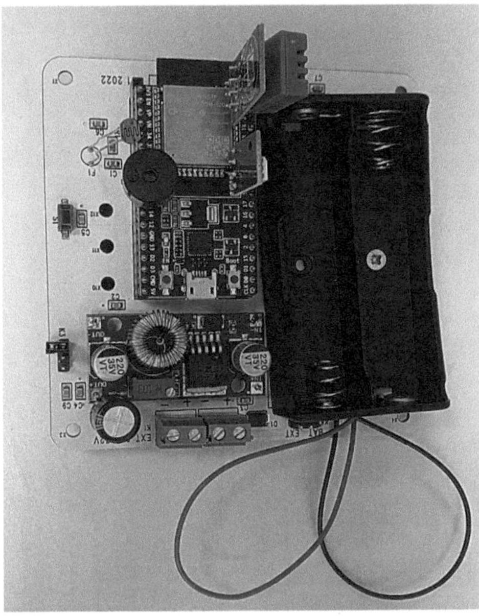

Fig. 2. Embedded sensing node

4.1   Measurement Representation

Each recorded sample is associated with a timestamp, a device identifier, a monitored object identifier, a sensor identifier, one or more measured values, a declared unit, and optional quality flags. For scalar modalities, the value reduces to a single numeric field; for vector-valued measurements such as multi-axis acceleration, multiple numeric fields can be stored under the same timestamp and tag set. This common structure allows different sensor types to be processed uniformly while still preserving relevant contextual metadata.

The same representation is intended to support both slow environmental variables and faster structural-response signals without requiring separate storage schemas. In practice, differences between modalities are handled through metadata and processing defaults rather than through different database structures. This makes it possible to apply common operations—such as time-window selection, plotting, spatial mapping, filtering, and export—across heterogeneous measurements while still preserving units, sensor identity, spatial context, and optional quality information needed for interpretation.

4.2   Series Organization in the Time Series Database

Measurements are organized in the time series database by sensor type, while indexed tags store the device identifier, monitored object, sensor identifier, spatial position, and optional experiment or session identifier. Numeric fields store the measured value and, when needed, raw or quality-related values. This organization enables generic plotting and heatmap components across heterogeneous scalar modalities while preserving modality-specific processing defaults such as aggregation or filtering. The use of a run or session identifier also allows repeated experimental campaigns to be separated without changing the underlying schema.

4.3 Validation, Idempotency, and Reliability

Because laboratory deployments often involve intermittent connectivity and repeated submissions, the ingestion pipeline performs schema validation, range checks, idempotent writes, partial acceptance with per-sample error reporting, and batched transmission to reduce overhead. These mechanisms support repeated experimental runs and mixed sampling periods without requiring modality-specific ingestion logic.

In practical terms, the ingestion interface accepts batched payloads containing device identifiers, optional run identifiers, timestamped samples, sensor type information, spatial coordinates, values, units, and optional quality indicators. This keeps the API general enough for heterogeneous measurements while preserving the information required for later filtering, spatial visualization, and export.

5 Visualization and Analysis Workflows

The visualization layer is designed to reduce the time between data acquisition and interpretation in laboratory experiments [10–12]. The workflow is intentionally modality-agnostic: users select a run, choose a time window and sensor subset, inspect the data through temporal or spatial views, optionally apply preprocessing, and export selected windows for offline analysis. A representative configuration view of this workflow is shown in Fig. 3.

5.1 Temporal and Spatial Views

The web application supports per-channel plots, multi-sensor comparison, aggregated feature views, and spatial heatmaps derived from grid coordinates. Time series views help identify missing data, saturation, drift, and excitation-related changes, while heatmaps help localize spatial gradients or abnormal behavior across the pane. A representative time series view is shown in Fig. 4. Because scalar modalities differ in sampling rate and noise characteristics, the interface uses modality-aware defaults such as smoothing or decimation when appropriate.

In addition to direct inspection of raw samples, the platform supports aggregated feature views such as mean, median, range, peak-to-peak values, RMS, and variance. These summaries reduce visual clutter, support rapid screening of large datasets, and help identify time intervals or sensor locations requiring deeper inspection. In grid-mounted experiments, such aggregated values are especially useful for spatial comparison across repeated runs.

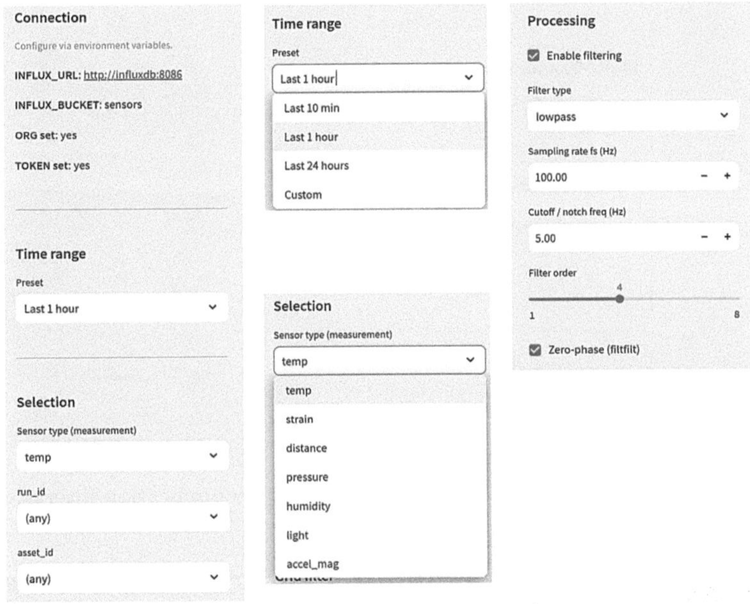

Fig. 3. View setup applicable across the platform

5.2   Cross-Modal Exploration and Preprocessing

Mixed-modality experiments benefit from comparing variables measured at different rates. The platform therefore supports cross-modal overlays on a shared time axis using nearest-neighbor alignment or optional resampling to a common grid. Filtering is provided as an optional preprocessing step and includes low-pass, high-pass, band-pass, and band-stop filtering. Filter parameters are user-selectable, and modality-aware presets help reduce misuse [13, 14].

5.3   Export and Reproducibility

The platform supports export of selected windows and sensor subsets to common formats such as CSV. Exported datasets include timestamps, values, sensor identifiers, spatial coordinates, units, and processing provenance. Capturing provenance is important for reproducibility in iterative laboratory workflows and supports consistent reporting across repeated experiments.

This export functionality is intended to complement, rather than replace, downstream domain-specific analysis. In practice, it allows users to perform interactive selection and preprocessing in the web interface while preserving a documented path from stored measurements to exported datasets used for later reporting or offline analysis.

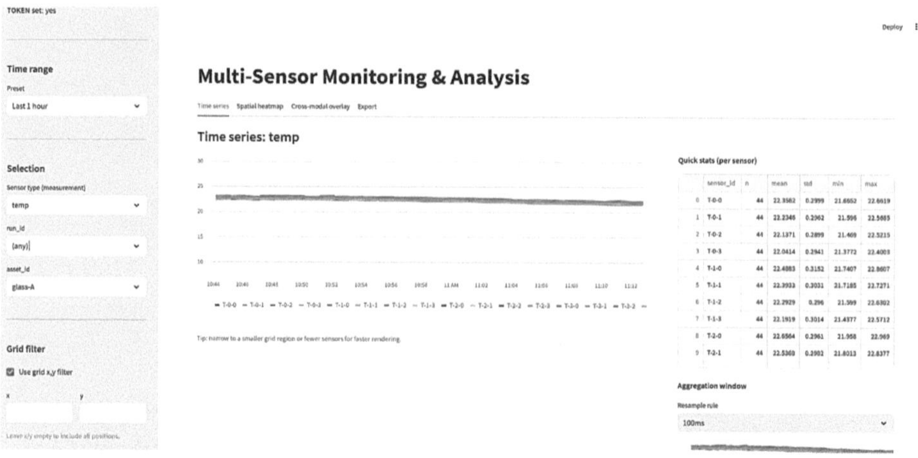

Fig. 4. Time series plot accessible from the web application interface

6   Case Study: Glass Dynamic Property Measurements

6.1   Experimental Context and Validation

In the motivating experiment, temperature and acceleration sensors were installed on a grid distributed across a glass pane [15], as illustrated in Fig. 5. Measurements were collected during excitations intended to probe dynamic behavior and were stored with timestamps for subsequent visualization, filtering, correlation analysis, and export.

The demonstrated workflows support temperature-compensation inspection, spatial response mapping, and event-focused analysis. In the tested runs, selected time windows made it possible to distinguish excitation-related changes in acceleration-derived response, compare their magnitude across grid positions, and relate these differences to sensor placement on the pane. Synchronized inspection of temperature and dynamic-response signals also provided a practical basis for distinguishing changes associated with excitation events, slower environmental drift, or sensor-specific behavior.

Spatial response mapping is particularly relevant in this context because grid-mounted sensing makes it possible to compare response patterns across different parts of the pane rather than only along a single measurement channel. In the same way, synchronized overlays of environmental and structural-response variables help distinguish whether observed variation is more likely linked to transient excitation, slower contextual change, or local sensor behavior.

Before integrating physical sensors, end-to-end ingestion and visualization were also validated using synthetic signals, including temperature ramps with additive noise, damped sinusoids or multi-tone accelerations, and irregular sampling patterns. These tests helped assess database schema consistency, API behavior, mixed-rate handling, filtering correctness, and the practical operation of the visualization workflow independently of sensor hardware constraints. They

Fig. 5. Sensor placement on the glass window pane

also provided a controlled way to verify that known signal features remained visible after ingestion, alignment, and preprocessing.

The current evidence should be interpreted as prototype-level validation rather than as a full quantitative benchmark. It confirms functional feasibility on simulated and real measurement scenarios, but it does not yet provide a systematic characterization of throughput limits, latency distributions, synchronization accuracy, scalability, or fault tolerance. A more comprehensive benchmark remains future work.

7   Discussion

The proposed work is primarily a systems and workflow contribution rather than a new synchronization, anomaly-detection, or structural-identification method. Its main value lies in providing a reusable and experimentally validated foundation for experiment-oriented monitoring and analysis of large-area glass measurements.

7.1   Practical Value

By unifying ingestion, storage, visualization, filtering, and export, the platform reduces repeated setup effort across experiments and supports more consistent handling of heterogeneous sensor data. This is especially useful in laboratory environments, where repeated measurement campaigns often require comparable processing steps but may differ in sensor configuration, run duration, or selected analysis windows.

7.2   Limitations

The current prototype focuses on visualization and exploratory analysis. Important topics for production-grade deployment remain open, including stronger security, improved time synchronization and drift correction, scalable deployment, and automated anomaly detection. The system should therefore be interpreted as a laboratory-scale research prototype rather than as a complete methodological solution to synchronization, drift correction, or anomaly detection.

8   Conclusion and Future Work

A web-based platform for multi-sensor monitoring and analysis of large-area glass surfaces was presented. The system combines distributed ESP32-based sensing, HTTP ingestion, time series storage, and an interactive web application for synchronized visualization, spatial heatmaps, preprocessing, and export. Its main contribution is a reusable end-to-end workflow for heterogeneous sensor data organized on a spatial grid, together with prototype-level validation on simulated and real glass-monitoring scenarios.

The platform was also positioned with respect to representative alternative approaches, highlighting its focus on reproducible laboratory workflows rather than on generic dashboards or advanced SHM inference methods. A key practical outcome of the design is that different scalar modalities and repeated experimental campaigns can be supported without redesigning the storage or visualization pipeline.

Future work includes stronger security, improved time synchronization and drift correction, automated feature extraction, and more comprehensive quantitative evaluation. These directions are important if the platform is to evolve from a laboratory-scale research prototype toward a broader monitoring and analysis framework.

References

1. Farrar, C.R., Worden, K.: An introduction to structural health monitoring. Phil. Trans. R. Soc. A **365**(1851), 303–315 (2007). https://doi.org/10.1098/rsta.2006.1928
2. Worden, K., Cross, E.J.: Structural health monitoring: from structures to systems-of-systems. IFAC-PapersOnLine **48**(21), 214–219 (2015). https://doi.org/10.1016/j.ifacol.2015.09.497
3. Mardanshahi, A., et al.: Sensing techniques for structural health monitoring: a state-of-the-art review on performance criteria and new-generation technologies. Sensors **25**(5), 1424 (2025). https://doi.org/10.3390/s25051424
4. Grzesik, P., Mrozek, D.: Comparative analysis of time series databases in the context of edge computing for low power sensor networks. In: Krzhizhanovskaya, V.V., Computational Science, pp. 371–383, vol. 12141. Springer, Cham (2020). https://doi.org/10.1007/978-3-030-50426-7_28

5. Espressif Systems: ESP32 Series Datasheet. https://www.espressif.com/sites/default/files/documentation/esp32_datasheet_en.pdf. Accessed 17 Feb 2026
6. InfluxData: InfluxData Documentation Portal. https://docs.influxdata.com/. Accessed 17 Feb 2026
7. InfluxData: Time Series Database Explained. https://www.influxdata.com/time-series-database/. Accessed 17 Feb 2026
8. Pallets Projects: Flask Documentation. https://flask.palletsprojects.com/en/stable/. Accessed 17 Feb 2026
9. Streamlit: Streamlit Documentation. https://docs.streamlit.io/. Accessed 17 Feb 2026
10. Vignali, L., et al.: Interactive visualization tools for managing the monitoring system of the piazza del duomo UNESCO site in Pisa. Heritage **8**(1), 5 (2024). https://doi.org/10.3390/heritage8010005
11. Valdivia, F.L.P., et al.: Guidance for interactive visual analysis in multivariate time series preprocessing. Sensors **25**(18), 5617 (2025). https://doi.org/10.3390/s25185617
12. Deng, L., et al.: Visualization and monitoring information management of bridge structure health and safety early warning based on BIM. J. Civ. Eng. Manag. **28**(4), 427–438 (2022). https://doi.org/10.1080/13467581.2020.1869013
13. Widmann, A., Schröger, E.: Digital filter design for electrophysiological data–a practical approach. J. Neurosci. Methods **250**, 34–46 (2015). https://doi.org/10.1016/j.jneumeth.2014.08.002
14. SciPy Contributors: `scipy.signal.filtfilt` Documentation. https://docs.scipy.org/doc/scipy/reference/generated/scipy.signal.filtfilt.html. Accessed 17 Feb 2026
15. Vandi, L., et al.: Structural health monitoring for prefabricated building envelope under stress tests. Appl. Sci. **14**(8), 3260 (2024). https://doi.org/10.3390/app14083260

Distributed Cluster-Based Scheme for Priority-Aware Management of Road Intersections

Ramzi Boutahala[(✉)], Cyril Rabat, and Hacène Fouchal

Lab-I*, Université de Reims Champagne Ardenne, Reims, France
{ramzi.boutahala,cyril.rabat,hacene.fouchal}@univ-reims.fr

Abstract. Cooperative Intelligent Transport Systems (C-ITS) provide the communication framework supporting Cooperative and Connected Automated Mobility (CCAM) via standardized Vehicle-to-Everything (V2X) message exchanges. Complex traffic environments require real-time coordination among vehicles to ensure safety, fairness, and smooth traffic flow, particularly in the absence of centralized control or fixed roadside infrastructure such as traffic lights or Roadside Units (RSUs). This paper proposes a **Cluster-based Priority-Aware (CPA)** coordination mechanism for intersection management. In the proposed scheme, vehicles approaching an intersection form a temporary cluster, within which a *Cluster Head (CH)* is dynamically elected to compute and broadcast a priority-based crossing schedule.

Keywords: Cooperative and Connected Automated Mobility (CCAM) · Distributed coordination · Intersection management

1 Introduction

According to the European Telecommunications Standards Institute (ETSI), C-ITS communications rely on a layered protocol architecture, in which Cooperative Awareness Messages (CAMs) constitute the fundamental message type. CAMs are periodic broadcasts (typically 1 – 10 Hz) that allow vehicles to share dynamic status information—such as position, speed, and heading—with nearby nodes. Despite these capabilities, one of the most critical challenges that remains insufficiently addressed in C-ITS is the management of *road intersections*. Conventional intersection management still relies heavily on centralized or infrastructure-assisted control schemes. Conversely, fully decentralized perception-based solutions eliminate communication dependencies but often result in overly conservative and inefficient behaviors, as vehicles act based on limited situational awareness. In this paper, we propose a **Cluster-based Priority-Aware (CPA)** coordination mechanism for intersection management. In the proposed scheme, vehicles approaching an intersection form a temporary cluster, within which a *Cluster Head (CH)* is dynamically elected to compute

K. Kirchner et al. (Eds.): I4CS 2026, CCIS 3007, pp. 346–356, 2026.
https://doi.org/10.1007/978-3-032-27096-2_19

and broadcast a priority-based crossing schedule. The CPA approach determines dynamic priorities based on each vehicle's spent time within the intersection zone and potential route conflicts computed by the elected CH. This distributed mechanism enables fair, efficient, and low-latency coordination without the need for fixed infrastructure or centralized control.

2   Related Work

Efficient management of unsignalized intersections approaches can be grouped into three main categories: *centralized and infrastructure-assisted schemes*, *sensor-based decentralized strategies*, and *V2V cooperative mechanisms*. Our work falls in the last category, combining clustering and V2V scheduling for fully distributed coordination.

2.1   Centralized and Infrastructure-Assisted Approaches

Centralized solutions rely on RSUs or Mobile Edge Computing (MEC) servers for coordination. The work in [2] proposes optimal scheduling models for signal-free intersections using metaheuristic and linear programming optimization, respectively. Although such approaches achieve near-optimal coordination, their computational cost increases non-linearly with traffic density, making real-time application difficult.

A more advanced example is the Digital Twin-based framework in [1], where a hybrid reinforcement learning (RL) system leverages bird's-eye-view (BEV) perception to coordinate vehicles. Despite its safety advantages, this approach imposes heavy infrastructure and maintenance costs, with the RSU remaining a single point of failure.

2.2   Decentralized Sensor-Based Approaches

Sensor-based approaches, such as the Communication-free Distributed Control Algorithm (CfDCA) proposed in [3], rely solely on onboard sensors for collision-free navigation. Vehicles infer priorities from local perception without explicit V2V communication. This guarantees robustness to communication loss but leads to conservative behavior and reduced throughput, as vehicles must assume worst-case conditions.

2.3   Decentralized V2V Cooperative Strategies

V2V-based methods use direct communication to improve coordination efficiency.

Virtual Traffic Lights (VTL). VTL systems elect a temporary leader vehicle to emulate a traffic light, as proposed in [4, 12]. Although simple, they face fairness issues and vulnerability to leader failure [13]. Enhanced models, such as the quantum-annealing-based VTL in [5], reformulate the scheduling problem as QUBO for cloud-based optimization, reintroducing centralization and latency.

Consensus and Negotiation-Based Protocols. Consensus-driven systems, like the distributed Raft-inspired coordination in [6], use multi-round voting to agree on crossing order. Similarly, auction-based [7] establishes fair schedules through negotiation or graph optimization. These solutions introduce high decision latency and degrade under dense traffic.

Clustering in VANETs. Clustering has been widely applied for VANET topology control and resource allocation. The works in [8] employs CHs for collaborative caching and vehicular cloud formation, while [14] introduces collision-aware clustering to reduce redundant cooperative perception data. These studies demonstrate the robustness of clustering but do not address safety-critical scheduling or intersection control.

2.4   AI and Learning-Based Coordination

Deep Reinforcement Learning (DRL) and Genetic Algorithms (GA) have been used to optimize signal control or lane assignment [9,11]. The CoLMDriver system [10] represents a novel paradigm using Large Language Models (LLMs) for vehicle negotiation. While promising for high-level planning, such models are unsuitable for low-latency, deterministic decision-making due to their stochastic and computationally expensive inference.

2.5   Research Gap and Motivation

Centralized approaches offer accuracy but are costly; perception-based ones are safe but inefficient; and existing V2V strategies face fairness or delay issues. Clustering techniques in VANETs, though mature, have not been used for tactical intersection scheduling. Our contribution addresses this gap by integrating V2V clustering and priority-based scheduling. The elected CH serves as a temporary, distributed scheduler, using extended CAMs to compute and broadcast dynamic crossing priorities. This design combines the stability of clustering with the responsiveness of cooperative V2V control, enabling efficient, infrastructure-free intersection management.

3   Cluster-Based Priority-Aware (CPA)

This section presents the operational mechanism of the proposed CPA protocol, designed to manage vehicle crossing priorities through distributed and cooperative coordination at unsignalized intersections. Unlike centralized schemes relying on roadside infrastructure (RSUs) or traffic lights, CPA operates solely through vehicle-to-vehicle (V2V) communication, ensuring scalability and robustness in dynamic traffic scenarios.

Table 1. Extended CAM Fields for CPA Protocol

Field	Description
toEdge	Identifier of the intended exit road segment
timeInZone	Accumulated spent time within the intersection zone
priorityList	Encoded list of vehicle priorities (broadcast by CH only)

3.1 Overview of the CPA Mechanism

The main idea behind CPA is to enable vehicles approaching an intersection to exchange essential situational information—such as their current approach, destination road, and the time spent within the intersection—using extended Cooperative Awareness Messages (CAMs). As summarized in Table 1, these additional fields are embedded within the *optional container* of the standard CAM message structure, ensuring backward compatibility while allowing richer vehicular context sharing.

Based on the received CAMs, vehicles dynamically form a temporary *cluster* representing all nodes currently approaching the intersection. Within this cluster, a CH is elected according to proximity and unique vehicle identifiers. The CH serves as a distributed and trusted controller that locally coordinates intersection access in real time. Specifically, the CH computes a *priority-based virtual traffic light* schedule that ranks vehicles according to two main criteria: (i) their cumulative waiting time within the intersection's approach zone, and (ii) the presence of potential route conflicts between their intended trajectories.

3.2 CAM Message Extension for Cooperative Awareness

To support the distributed coordination required by the CPA protocol, we introduce a lightweight extension to the ETSI CAM standard. Specifically, additional information fields are embedded within the *optional container* of the CAM message, enabling vehicles to exchange contextual and decision-level data.

We extend the CAM payload to include optional parameters that are transmitted only once when required, for instance, during the intersection coordination phase. These fields are inserted into the Basic Container extension of the CAM, as shown in Table 1. This design preserves full interoperability with existing ITS-G5 communication stacks while enabling cooperative awareness among vehicles approaching the same intersection. Consequently, vehicles can collaboratively build a shared understanding of intersection dynamics, which enables the subsequent cluster head election and priority-based control mechanisms.

3.3 Cluster Head Election and Maintenance

The selection of the Cluster Head (CH) is driven by both proximity and identity to ensure fairness and stability. Let (x_v, y_v) denote the current position of vehicle

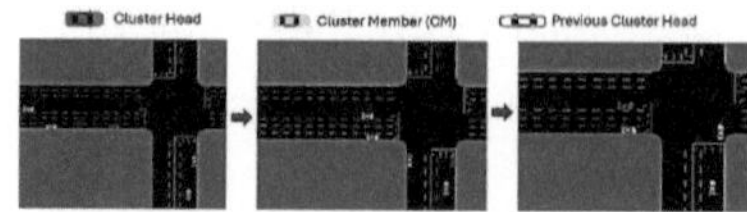

Fig. 1. Cluster head selection and update mechanism

Algorithm 1. Cluster head election and maintenance procedure

1: **Input:** Active vehicle set V, intersection center (x_c, y_c), zone radius R_z
2: **Output:** Current Cluster Head CH
3: **for all** vehicle $v_i \in V$ **do**
4:     Compute $d_i = \sqrt{(x_i - x_c)^2 + (y_i - y_c)^2}$ {Distance to intersection center}
5:     **if** $d_i < R_z$ **and** v_i is on entry lane **then**
6:         Mark v_i as `active`
7:     **else**
8:         Remove v_i from active set
9:     **end if**
10: **end for**
11: **for all** entry lanes L_j **do**
12:     Select candidate $C_j = \arg\min_{v_i \in L_j} d_i$
13: **end for**
14: $CH_{\text{new}} = \arg\min_{C_j} \text{ID}(C_j)$ {Smallest ID among lane leaders}
15: **if** CH_{current} is inactive **or** $CH_{\text{current}} \notin V$ **then**
16:     $CH_{\text{current}} \leftarrow CH_{\text{new}}$ {Reassign new Cluster Head}
17:     Reset local priority lists and broadcast CH status
18: **end if**
19: **return** CH_{current}

---

v and (x_c, y_c) the coordinates of the intersection center. The Euclidean distance between the vehicle and the intersection center is computed as:

$$d_v = \sqrt{(x_v - x_c)^2 + (y_v - y_c)^2}. \tag{1}$$

Each vehicle periodically evaluates its own distance d_v and broadcasts it within CAMs. The election rule is as follows:

- For each approach lane, the vehicle with the smallest d_v (i.e., closest to the intersection) is nominated as a *candidate leader*.
- Among all candidate leaders, the vehicle with the smallest unique identifier (ID) is elected as the Cluster Head.

Algorithm 1 summarizes this distributed election process. The elected CH assumes the role of a local coordinator. This maintenance mechanism is triggered automatically, as illustrated in Fig. 1, whenever the current CH disappears (e.g., exits the intersection or becomes inactive). Upon re-election, the new CH immediately resets the active priority list and recomputes a new one to maintain consistent coordination. This ensures a seamless and fault-tolerant cluster leadership transfer, eliminating the need for explicit signaling or infrastructure support.

Algorithm 2. Priority list computation by the cluster head

1: Collect set V of active vehicles within the intersection zone
2: **for all** $v_i \in V$ **do**
3:     Compute $T_{v_i}(t)$ using the spent-time model
4: **end for**
5: Select one leading vehicle per incoming lane
6: Sort leaders in descending order of $T_{v_i}(t)$
7: Initialize priority rank $r = 1$
8: **for all** vehicles in sorted order **do**
9:     **if** v_i has no route conflict with any higher-ranked vehicle **then**
10:         Assign same rank r (non-conflicting group)
11:     **else**
12:         Increment r and assign new rank
13:     **end if**
14: **end for**
15: Encode and Insert priority list into CAM
16: Broadcast extended CAM once to all neighboring vehicles

3.4   Priority Computation and Coordination

After the CH has been elected, it periodically computes a *priority list* for all vehicles approaching the intersection. The computation relies on two complementary criteria:

1. **Spent time in the intersection zone:** vehicles that have spent longer within the intersection's communication zone are given higher priority;
2. **Route conflict avoidance:** vehicles whose paths do not geometrically intersect with higher-priority vehicles may share the same crossing window.

Each vehicle v maintains its accumulated spent time $T_{\text{accum}}(v)$ and the timestamp of its last entry into the zone, $t_{\text{enter}}(v)$. The CH estimates the current spent time as:

$$T_v(t) = T_{\text{accum}}(v) + \begin{cases} t - t_{\text{enter}}(v), & \text{if } d_v < R_z, \\ 0, & \text{otherwise,} \end{cases} \tag{2}$$

where d_v denotes the Euclidean distance of vehicle v from the intersection center and R_z is the radius of the intersection's zone of influence.

The CH first identifies the leading vehicle on each incoming lane (the one closest to the center), computes $T_v(t)$ for each, and sorts them in descending order of $T_v(t)$. Then, it refines this ranking by analyzing route conflicts: if two vehicles v_i and v_j have non-conflicting trajectories, they can be assigned the same effective priority group and allowed to cross simultaneously.

Algorithm 2 summarizes the CH's computation process.

This mechanism ensures that the CH generates a fair and collision-free crossing schedule based on vehicles' *spent time within the intersection zone* rather than static arrival order. The resulting priority list is serialized and embedded within the CAM optional field, enabling all vehicles to synchronize their local decision logic.

Algorithm 3. Local control decision for each vehicle

1: Retrieve latest priority list L from received CAM.
2: Determine own rank r_v and route $\mathcal{R}_v$.
3: **if** $r_v = 1$ **then**
4:     Proceed immediately and mark as released.
5: **else**
6:     Identify leader vehicle v_1 and check if released.
7:     **if** v_1 released **and** no active higher-priority vehicle conflicts with $\mathcal{R}_v$ **then**
8:         Proceed and mark as released.
9:     **else**
10:         Remain stopped until next update.
11:     **end if**
12: **end if**

3.5   Local Control Decision

After receiving the extended CAM containing the computed priority list from the CH, each vehicle executes a local control policy to decide whether it can safely proceed through the intersection or must remain stopped. The vehicles locally interpret and apply the CH's transmitted schedule. Each vehicle identifies its assigned rank r_v and the current leader vehicle v_1 (rank $= 1$). The local control rules are defined as follows:

- If $r_v = 1$, the vehicle belongs to the leader group and can immediately proceed.
- If $r_v > 1$, the vehicle must verify that:
    1. the leader vehicle v_1 has already been released (i.e., has started crossing), and
    2. none of the higher-priority vehicles ($r_u < r_v$) still active in the intersection have conflicting routes with its own.
- If both conditions are satisfied, the vehicle proceeds; otherwise, it remains at a full stop until a new CAM update is received or stopped vehicles are released.

4   Performance Evaluation

To evaluate the proposed approach in a simulation environment that closely reflects real-world conditions, we used several complementary simulators and frameworks. First, we employed the OMNeT++ network simulator, which is developed as a set of independent modules that can be combined to form complex systems. OMNeT++ is designed to model communication systems, networks, multiprocessors, and other distributed systems. It is implemented in the C++ programming language and uses the Network Description Language (NED) to define network topologies. The simulator operates based on discrete-event scheduling rather than continuous-time simulation. We also used

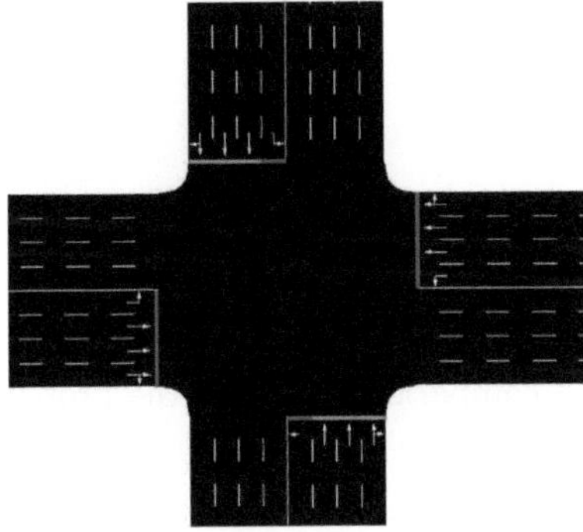

Fig. 2. Four-way intersection scenario used for the CPA evaluation

the Artery framework, which provides support for V2X communications and extends OMNeT++ with modular and event-driven capabilities. Each simulated vehicle was equipped with the full ETSI C-ITS protocol stack, including the security mechanisms. Message exchanges were performed through the IEEE 802.11p physical layer provided by the VEINS framework, while the network and security layers were implemented using the Vanetza framework.

Traffic mobility was simulated using SUMO, which generates realistic vehicle movements and traffic flows. Artery was coupled with SUMO to achieve real-time synchronization between mobility and communication. To assess the efficiency of the proposed CPA scheme, we simulated several vehicle flows at a four-way intersection composed of two perpendicular roads. Each road contains four lanes per direction, and vehicles approaching the intersection may perform one of three possible maneuvers: turning left, going straight, or turning right, as illustrated in Fig. 2. For benchmarking, the same traffic scenarios and mobility conditions were also tested under a conventional fixed-time traffic light control strategy. The traffic signal operated on an eight-phase static cycle that alternated green, yellow, and red lights for each direction. Each green phase lasted 66 s, followed by a 6 s yellow transition, and then a red phase to stop conflicting traffic streams. The same vehicle flows and arrival rates were used for both control schemes to enable a fair and consistent performance comparison.

The performance results demonstrate that the proposed CPA protocol significantly improves the overall efficiency of intersection management compared to the conventional fixed-time traffic light baseline. The evaluation considers multiple performance metrics, including average delay, average travel time, average speed, and CO_2 emissions. As shown in Fig. 3, the CPA approach significantly reduces the average travel time compared to the baseline traffic light control. Vehicles coordinated through the cluster-head mechanism maintain smoother trajectories and experience fewer stops, resulting in shorter overall traversal durations across the intersection.

Similarly, Fig. 4 shows that the total average travel time under CPA is reduced from 103 s to 79.1 s, with a noticeable decrease in waiting time com-

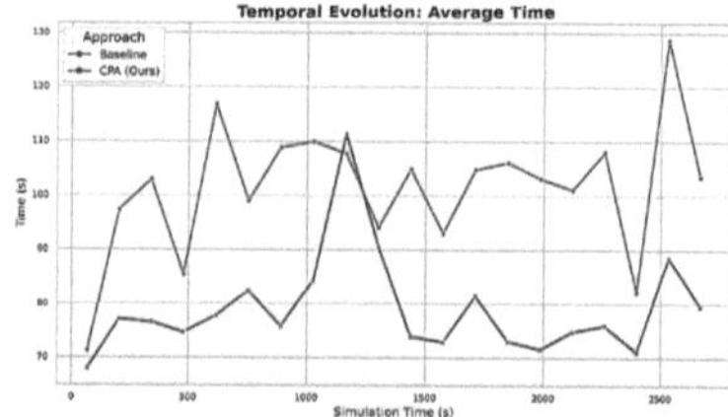

Fig. 3. Average travel time comparison between the proposed CPA and the baseline traffic light approach

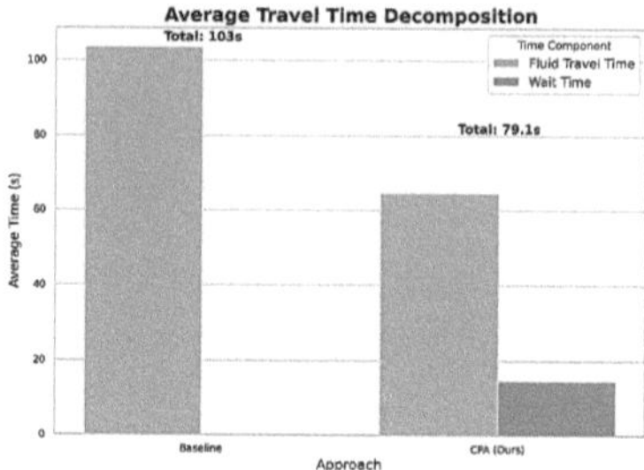

Fig. 4. Temporal evolution of average travel time across all vehicles under both control strategies

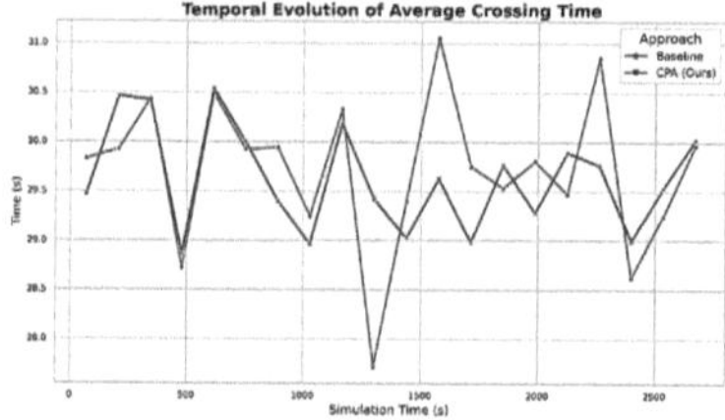

Fig. 5. Temporal evolution of average crossing time over the simulation period for CPA and baseline approaches

ponents. This improvement highlights the ability of the CPA protocol to maintain a continuous vehicle flow without the rigid timing constraints of traditional traffic lights. The temporal evolution results in Fig. 5 indicate that the average crossing time remains more stable and consistently lower with CPA throughout the simulation period. This stability reflects the protocol's capacity to adapt dynamically to variable traffic densities and vehicle arrival patterns.

As shown in Table 2, the proposed CPA approach achieves a higher average vehicle speed of 11.9 m/s compared to 10.4 m/s for the baseline traffic light control. This improvement indicates that CPA enhances intersection throughput and maintains smoother vehicle movement by reducing unnecessary stops and delays. Finally, regarding environmental impact, Fig. 6 reveals a clear reduction in average CO_2 emissions when using the CPA scheme. This improvement is

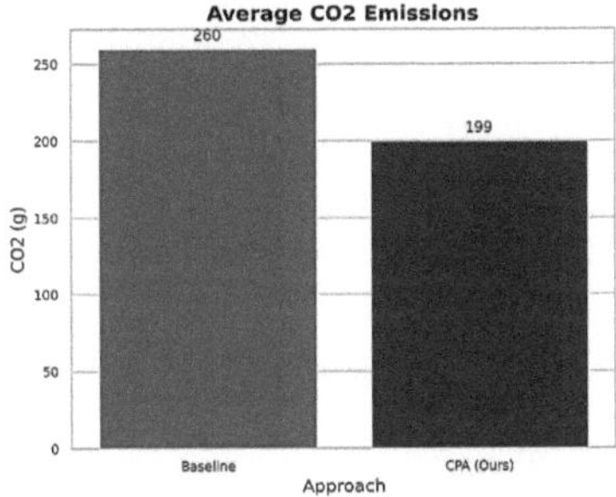

Fig. 6. Temporal average CO_2 emissions during the simulation for CPA and baseline systems

Table 2. Comparison of average vehicle speed between CPA and baseline approach

Approach	Average Speed (m/s)
CPA (Proposed)	11.9
Baseline (Traffic Light)	10.4

attributed to the smoother traffic flow and the reduction in stop-and-go behavior, which typically causes higher fuel consumption in traditional signalized intersections. Overall, these results demonstrate that the CPA framework effectively balances safety, fairness, and traffic fluidity in a fully distributed V2V coordination environment. By replacing static signal timing with dynamic, cluster-based decision-making, the CPA approach achieves superior performance in terms of both traffic efficiency and environmental sustainability.

5 Conclusions

This paper presented the **Cluster-based Priority-Aware (CPA)** protocol, a distributed mechanism for managing vehicle crossings at unsignalized intersections through V2V communication. Unlike infrastructure-dependent systems, the CPA protocol enables vehicles approaching an intersection to form a temporary cluster and elect a *Cluster Head (CH)* responsible for coordinating access in real time. The CH determines and disseminates a priority-based schedule according to each vehicle's spent time in the intersection zone and potential route conflicts, ensuring both fairness and safety. Simulation results demonstrated that the proposed CPA scheme significantly outperforms conventional fixed-time traffic light control. Specifically, CPA reduces average travel time and waiting delay while increasing average vehicle speed and lowering CO_2 emissions. These improvements confirm the effectiveness of decentralized coordination enabled by cooperative V2V communication. Future work will extend the CPA mechanism to manage multiple adjacent intersections, developing a more robust priority computation algorithm, and supporting mixed traffic scenarios involving both connected and non-connected vehicles. In addition, novel adaptive learning techniques will further optimize scheduling decisions under varying traffic conditions.

References

1. Li, Y., et al.: A digital twin-based cooperative driving system for unsignalized intersections, arXiv preprint arXiv:2509.15099 (2025)
2. Wang, H., et al.: An optimal scheduling model for connected automated vehicles at an unsignalized intersection. Algorithms **18**(4), 194 (2025)
3. Singh, A., et al.: Communication-free Distributed Control Algorithm (CFDCA) for Managing Autonomous Vehicles at Signal-free Intersections. University of Sydney, TransportLab (2025)
4. Hagenauer, F., et al.: Advanced Leader Election for Virtual Traffic Lights, In: Proceeding IEEE Vehicular Networking Conference (VNC), pp. 1–8 (2014)
5. Khan, S., Majumder, R.: A quantum annealing-enhanced virtual traffic light (VTL) system for roadway intersections, arXiv preprint arXiv:2412.18776 (2024)
6. Lee, H., Yoon, J., et al.: A distributed consensus algorithm for prioritizing autonomous vehicle passing at unsignalized intersections under mixed traffic, arXiv preprint arXiv:2507.03486 (2025)
7. Xu, Z., et al.: Collection auctions-based autonomous intersection management considering users' preferences. Systems **11**(5), 573 (2023)
8. Tokunaga, H., Tang, S.: Efficient V2V communications by clustering-based collaborative caching. Electronics **13**(5), 883 (2024)
9. Shen, J., et al.: Optimizing Urban Intersection Management In Mixed Traffic Using Deep Reinforcement Learning And Genetic Algorithms, IEEE Access (2025)
10. Liu, C., et al.: CoLMDriver: LLM-based negotiation benefits cooperative autonomous driving, In: Proceeding IEEE/CVF International Conference on Computer Vision (ICCV) (2025)
11. Guo, J., et al.: CoTV: cooperative control for traffic light signals and connected autonomous vehicles using deep reinforcement learning. IEEE Trans. Intell. Transp. Syst. **24**(10), 10501–10512 (2023)
12. Tonguz, O.K., et al.: Virtual Traffic Lights System Design and Implementation, ResearchGate (2018)
13. Neudecker, T., et al.: Analysis of failures in virtual traffic light systems. IEEE Trans. Intell. Transp. Syst. **20**(3), 1123–1134 (2019)
14. Cheng, X., et al.: Collision-aware clustering for redundancy reduction in cooperative perception. IEEE Trans. Veh. Technol. **74**(5), 6789–6801 (2025)

Data Catalogs in Data Mesh and Data Space Implementations

Attila Papp[(✉)] [iD] and Udo Bub [iD]

Faculty of Informatics, Eötvös Lóránd University (ELTE),
Pázmány Péter sétány 1/C, Budapest 1117, Hungary
{attila.papp,udobub}@inf.elte.hu

Abstract. Data mesh and data spaces are emergent paradigms for scalable data sharing within and across organizations. Despite different motivations and trust assumptions, both rely on data catalogs to provide visibility and discovery of data products. This paper studies data catalogs as a convergence point between the two paradigms. First, we analyze data access and usage policy placement by distinguishing policy source of truth, policy binding, and policy enforcement. We show that in data meshes, catalogs can serve as a single source of truth for policy bindings and enable governance automation through workflow-driven or reconciliation-based approaches integrated with enterprise platforms, whereas in data spaces, catalogs primarily support discovery and contract initiation, with enforcement remaining boundary- and contract-driven at participant connectors. Second, we examine the feasibility of modeling catalogs as knowledge graphs to represent relational metadata, improve discovery, enable semantic interoperability, and support context-aware classification with conservative propagation along lineage. The results clarify how catalogs, policies, and enforcement components align in each paradigm and provide a basis for future design science guidelines for data-sharing system design.

Keywords: Data architecture · Data catalog · Data governance · Data management · Data mesh · Data sovereignty · Data space · Knowledge graph

1 Introduction

Organizations aspire to embrace data-driven decision-making more and more, yet they continue to face friction when scaling data sharing beyond isolated teams and systems. Within enterprises, centralized data platforms can become bottlenecks as many domains compete for shared engineering capacity and governance decisions. Across organizational boundaries, data exchange is further constrained by trust, compliance, and the need to preserve sovereignty over how data is used. These pressures have contributed to two emergent socio-technical paradigms for data sharing: data mesh for intra-organizational data sharing and data spaces for inter-organizational exchange [1,2].

© The Author(s), under exclusive license to Springer Nature Switzerland AG 2026
K. Kirchner et al. (Eds.): I4CS 2026, CCIS 3007, pp. 357–366, 2026.
https://doi.org/10.1007/978-3-032-27096-2_20

Although data mesh and data spaces originate from different problem settings, both emphasize decentralization, data products, interoperability, and governance. This commonality points to possible convergence, yet their implementations differ in important ways, especially regarding how discovery and governance are operationalized. A central enabling capability in both solutions is the data catalog. In a data mesh, catalogs support self-service discovery of data products across domains and are often integrated with enterprise governance workflows and platform enforcement. In data spaces, catalogs support the discovery of externally consumable offerings across participants, generally through the publication of self-descriptions, while enforcement remains under participant control through boundary components such as connectors [2,3]. Despite this shared reliance on cataloging, gaps in the literature remain on how catalogs relate to policy placement, governance automation, and richer semantic representations.

This paper studies the role of data catalogs as a convergence point between data mesh and data space implementations. We focus on two questions. First, we analyze where access policies should reside and how catalogs support governance execution and automation across paradigms. Second, we examine the feasibility and value of representing catalogs as knowledge graphs to improve discovery, enable semantic interoperability, and support automated classification.

2   Scientific Methodology

In this paper, we extend our earlier work on convergence potential and situate the results within a wider research program aimed at developing scientifically grounded yet practically useful guidelines for designing data-sharing systems, ultimately resulting in design science artefacts as described by [4]. As an intermediate step toward these guidelines, we focus on identifying and analyzing architectural patterns, understood as reusable design elements together with their benefits and application contexts [4].

Our research follows the Design Science Research (DSR) approach, as outlined by Hevner et al. [5] Offermann et al. propose a DSR process model that we apply for artifact development, structuring the work into Problem Identification, Artifact Design, and Artifact Evaluation [6]. For the Problem Identification phase, we build on a comprehensive literature review and expert interviews previously reported by Papp et al. [3,7]. We distill these findings as the starting point for the present paper and extend them with thoughts on data catalog patterns to support a subsequent, more comprehensive design. Based on the former results, we formulate the following research questions:

- **RQ1:** How should data access and usage policies be placed in data mesh and data space implementations (source of truth, binding, enforcement), and what role do data catalogs play in governance execution and automation?

– **RQ2:** To what extent can data catalogs be modeled as knowledge graphs in data mesh and data space settings, and how can such graph-based catalogs support discovery, semantic interoperability, and automated data classification?

3 Background

A key convergence point between data mesh and data spaces is the data catalog: in both paradigms, it provides a unified view of available data assets, yet its scope, architectural placement, and governance role differ because the underlying motivations differ [3]. Data meshes typically operate within a single enterprise, in which identity, tooling, and platform strategy can be standardized. Data spaces operate across organizational boundaries, where participants are sovereign and heterogeneous, and interoperability and trust are established through ecosystem agreements and shared governance structures. Consequently, both solutions aim for discoverability and reuse, but they achieve this goal through different catalog objects, federation strategies, and enforcement methods [1,2].

Purpose and Catalog Objects. In a data mesh, the catalog primarily enables self-service discovery and consumption across domains, supporting the 'data as a product' principle through self-describing entries that are intended to be directly consumable [8]. In data spaces, the catalog enables discovery across legal, organizational, and technical boundaries, often without shared identity providers or a shared platform, also containing data products [9]. The catalog therefore focuses on publishing externally consumable offerings, typically as participant-provided self-descriptions of connectors, datasets, and services [2]. In both cases, the catalog may also reference data sharing agreements or contract-related artifacts.

Architecture and Governance Execution. Data mesh catalogs are commonly implemented as a shared mesh capability even when data products are domain-owned. They are often integrated with governance workflows and platform enforcement, surfacing ownership, lineage, quality signals, classifications, and access rules, and supporting federated computational governance where global standards are defined centrally and executed locally through automation [10]. In contrast, data space catalogs are typically federated: each participant exposes a catalog endpoint, and one or more aggregators or brokers may provide a unified search view, or connectors may query each other directly. Governance is ecosystem-level and rulebook-driven, with enforcement primarily executed at the provider level: offers are published with usage constraints, agreements are negotiated via connector protocols, and the provider connector acts as the enforcement point during access or transfer [2].

Metadata Authority, Contracts, and Risks. Although catalogs are often treated as the enterprise representation of analytics metadata in a data mesh, they are not the strict single source of truth. Instead, the authoritative source is typically the data product definition and its data contract, commonly stored in version control and synchronized into the catalog through automation [11]. In data spaces, catalogs are also not a strict single source of truth because multiple catalogs are able to coexist; the authoritative source remains the participant's published self-description and the enforcement capabilities of its connector. Both impose risks: data mesh catalogs can fallback into passive inventories curated by central teams, undermining decentralization, while data space catalogs risk fragmentation and inconsistency across registries and semantic models, not to mention synchronization and caching challenges in federated discovery. Both risks can be reduced through automation, clear definitions of done, and rulebooks that specify publication, interoperability, and synchronization requirements [12].

Overall, catalogs are a convergence point: they provide visibility across data products in both solutions. However, their governance roles differ: data mesh catalogs are integrated into enterprise governance loops and permission rollout workflows, whereas data space catalogs primarily support discovery and contract initiation, with enforcement distributed across participant boundaries via connectors [3].

4 How Governance Is Executed

The first research question of this paper is: in both data mesh and data space implementations in which should access and usage policies reside, and what is the role of catalogs in executing governance? In order to answer this question we distinguish three complementary layers of policy placement: (i) a policy *source of truth* where policies are authored, versioned, and reviewed; (ii) a policy *binding* layer where policies are linked to cataloged assets and contextual metadata (e.g., classifications, purposes, jurisdictions); and (iii) a policy *enforcement* layer where access decisions and obligations are applied at runtime. This separation is necessary because catalogs do not contain the data itself, only metadata about the data. The data mesh paradigm distinguishes local and global governance [1], in this case we focus on local governance, namely managing data access through policies, data sharing agreements. The difference between local and global governance is explored in our previous paper [7].

4.1 Policy Placement

In data meshes, policies are authored and managed within enterprise governance processes and implemented through data platform control mechanisms (e.g. row or column level filters). Apart from potentially storing policies [13], the catalog plays a binding and orchestration role: it links policies to data products and their interfaces and may drive access workflows. Governance execution often follows enterprise identity and access management patterns, enabling granular row- or column-level access control. A consumer requests access to a data product, the request is approved by a data domain steward or responsible party, and then permissions are deployed. Catalogs in this setting may orchestrate workflows that either push permissions into the target system or record policy decisions that downstream systems pull and enforce [3]. As a result, policy enforcement in data meshes tends to be integrated with a shared platform, while policy definitions remain aligned with federated computational governance, where standards are global but execution is local to domains [1]. Policies can also be treated as code and embedded directly into the data product quantum. A data product encapsulates code, data, metadata, and potentially access policies. For example, policies regarding usage rules can be attached to specific output ports of a data product [14].

In data spaces, policy placement must respect participant sovereignty and heterogeneous technology stacks. Governance is primarily executed through the Dataspace Governance Authority (DSGA), a manual decision-making role responsible for establishing, managing, and enforcing the technical policies and business rules of the dataspace. This governance is realized through a multi-level framework that includes operational rules, semantic models, and transparent accountability systems to define participant obligations and the repercussions for failing to meet them. Execution relies on a combination of manual supervision, such as manual contract drafting and dispute resolution, and automated technical mechanisms, in which machine-readable policies and claims protocols enable the automated verification of participant identities and rights [2]. Consequently, policy enforcement is boundary- and contract-driven rather than centrally provisioned: offers are published with associated usage constraints, consumers discover offers through catalog services, and then negotiate an agreement with the provider through their respective connectors. The provider connector acts as a policy enforcement point by verifying identity and agreement state, issuing access tokens or establishing data-plane sessions, and enforcing constraints during access or transfer. In this model, catalogs support discovery and initiation, while enforcement remains under the provider's control at each participant boundary [2] (Fig. 1).

4.2   Governance Automation

The separation of policy authoring, binding; and enforcement enables automation in both paradigms but still different automation mechanisms exist. In data mesh, automation is commonly driven by enterprise workflows and platform APIs: catalog events (new access request) can trigger approval workflows, policy creation, approval, and permission rollouts. Two automation strategies appear in practice: *push-based* automation (events), where catalog workflows deploy permissions into the target system; and *pull-based* automation (syncing to a desired state), where catalogs store policy decisions and platform enforcement layers periodically reconcile and apply them [15]. The former provides instant rollout of the policies, while the latter improves decoupling and provides an easier restore process in case of a disaster recovery.

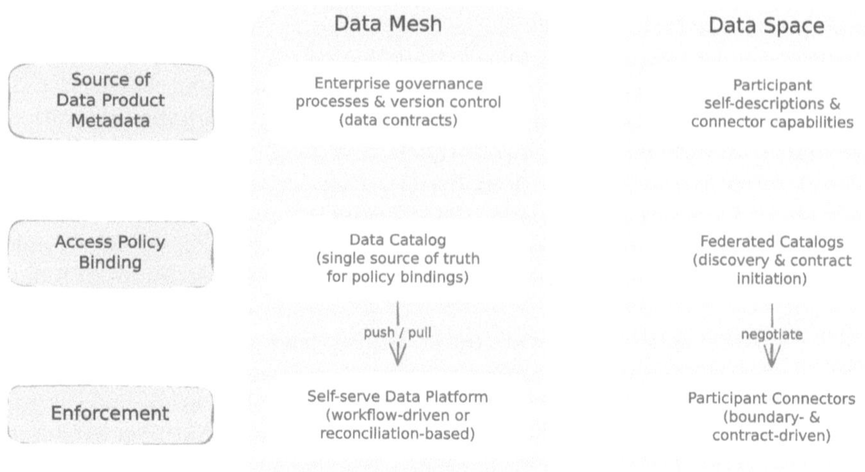

Fig. 1. Policy placement layers in data mesh and data space implementations

In data spaces, automation focuses on scalable trust establishment and contract execution across organizations. Machine-readable policies and claims can support automated verification of participant identities and rights, while connectors operationalize negotiated terms and enforce obligations at runtime. The automation scope is therefore centered on contract lifecycle steps (publication of offers, negotiation, agreement state management) and policy checks at the boundary, rather than on centrally orchestrated permission rollout. This distinction reveals a key difference between mesh and space implementations: enterprise meshes automate governance primarily by integrating catalogs with a shared identity and a platform control plane, whereas data spaces automate governance by standardizing control-plane protocols for discovery and negotiation and by embedding enforcement into participant-controlled boundary components [2,16].

4.3 Summary

Across both approaches, data catalogs are well-suited to store the access policies and the binding layer between policies and assets. They also serve as automation triggers in response to user requests, but they are not the enforcement mechanism because they contain only metadata. In a data mesh, the catalog may be close to enforcement, e.g., a logically decentralized data mesh may be implemented through a solution like Databricks, which also contains a catalog, but is still considered logically a separate component. In a data space, the catalog is also separated from enforcement, as participants must retain sovereignty, and enforcement occurs through connectors.

Therefore, in a data mesh, we suggest that a data catalog can serve as the single source of truth for access policies and their bindings, and that, through workflows, they can trigger the actual policy enforcement layer residing in the self-serve data platform. In data spaces, since multiple data catalogs may coexist in an ecosystem, they may not be the single source of truth for policies, but can contain them and their bindings, and, similarly to data meshes, policy enforcement is applied elsewhere, namely at the connector level.

5   Data Catalogs as Knowledge Graphs

Data catalogs are relational inventories of datasets and metadata records and the core problem they address is also relational: data products reference owners, domains, concepts, systems, schemas, output ports, transformations, quality assertions, consumers, and policies. This motivates representing catalog metadata as a *knowledge graph* (KG), where nodes capture entities (e.g., data products, fields, services, people, controls) and edges capture explicit semantics (e.g., `producedBy`, `ownedBy`, `derivedFrom`, `classifiedAs`, `governedBy`). In this view, the catalog becomes a queryable and extensible graph of metadata that supports discovery, reasoning, and governance automation.

5.1   Building Common Understanding

A data catalog represented as a Knowledge Graph (Enterprise Knowledge Graph) can connect domains within an organization, providing a common understanding of data products and their relationships [10]. A KG-backed catalog consists of three layers: (i) an ontology or metamodel that defines entity types and relations (data product, data contract, output port, column, term, policy); (ii) an instance graph populated by ingestion from technical systems and manual stewardship; and (iii) services for querying and indexing the graph. The metamodel may be aligned with enterprise vocabulary (e.g., a business glossary) and external vocabularies when interoperability is required. Compared to flat metadata stores, the KG approach makes relationships first-class and enables traversals that match how practitioners search for data in reality, for example: "show all data products derived from source X that contain PII and are consumed by team Y".

For inter-organizational data spaces (such as the European public procurement data space), KGs based on standard ontologies (e.g., OWL, ePO) enable different organizations to map their local data formats to a shared semantic layer, facilitating automated integration and interoperability [17].

5.2 Knowledge Graphs for Classification and Semantic Enrichment

Knowledge graphs can improve data classification in two complementary ways.

Context-Aware Classification. Classification decisions can leverage graph context beyond the content of a single table. For example, a column name may be ambiguous in isolation, but becomes clear when linked to a glossary term, an upstream system, or a domain concept. KG context, therefore, reduces false positives and supports explainability by showing which relations triggered a classification.

Propagation and Inheritance. Once classifications are attached to nodes (fields, datasets, products), they can be propagated along lineage edges according to explicit rules. A conservative strategy marks downstream assets as at least as sensitive as upstream inputs unless transformations prove otherwise. This creates consistent 'classification closure' across pipelines and supports automated governance responses such as approval requirements or retention constraints. Propagation rules can be domain-specific and encoded as policies over the graph, enabling local refinement while remaining compatible with global governance standards.

5.3 Limitations

While scientifically promising, widespread commercial adoption of KGs in off-the-shelf data catalog tools is still limited compared to simpler tagging systems [18].

6 Conclusion

This paper analyzed data catalogs as a convergence point between data mesh and data space implementations. We showed that, while both solutions rely on catalogs to provide a unified view of available data products, their governance roles differ. To address policy placement, we distinguished three layers: policy source of truth, policy binding, and policy enforcement. In data meshes, catalogs can serve as a single source of truth for access policy bindings and automate governance via push-based workflows or pull-based reconciliation into platform control mechanisms. In data spaces, catalogs support discovery and contract initiation, whilst policy enforcement remains boundary- and contract-driven and is executed at participant connectors under ecosystem governance structures.

We further argued that catalogs can be modeled as knowledge graphs to represent the inherently relational nature of metadata, enabling richer discovery, common understanding, and context-aware classification. Knowledge graphs can also support conservative propagation of classifications along lineage and improve the explainability of governance decisions.

This paper extends our prior work in two specific directions. In [7], we provided a broad comparative analysis of data mesh and data space paradigms with a focus on governance structures, while [3] identified reusable architectural patterns across both paradigms. The present paper goes beyond these earlier results by introducing a layered analysis of policy placement (source of truth, binding, and enforcement), examining concrete governance automation strategies (push-based and pull-based), and exploring the feasibility of modeling data catalogs as knowledge graphs for improved discovery, semantic interoperability, and classification propagation, none of which were addressed in the preceding publications.

Overall, the results clarify how catalogs, policies, and enforcement components align in each paradigm and provide a basis for future work toward design science guidelines and artifacts for data-sharing system design.

References

1. Dehghani, Z.: Data mesh principles and logical architecture. https://martinfowler.com/articles/data-mesh-principles.html. Accessed 17/02/2026
2. ISO/IEC. ISO/IEC DIS 20151: Information technology — Cloud computing and distributed platforms — Dataspace concepts and characteristics. In: International Organization for Standardization (ISO) and International Electrotechnical Commission (IEC), Draft International Standard (DIS), ISO/IEC DIS 20151. (2026)
3. Papp, A., Bub, U.: Architectural patterns for data mesh and data space implementations. In: 28th International Conference on Enterprise Information Systems (ICEIS). SCITEPRESS (2026)
4. Offermann, P., Blom, S., Schönherr, M., Bub, U.: Artifact Types in Information Systems Design Science – A Literature Review. Proc. Intern. Conf, DESRIST, St. Gallen (2010)
5. Hevner A. R., March S. T., Park J., Ram S. Design science in information systems research. MIS Quarterly, 75–105 (2004)
6. Offermann, P., Levina, O., Schönherr, M., Bub, U.: Outline of a Design Science Research Process. Proc. Intern. Conf, DESRIST, Malvern, PA (2009)
7. Papp, A., Bub, U., Lähteenoja, V., Kuikkaniemi, K., Turpeinen, M., Jokela, S.: Data mesh and data space: a comparative analysis with a focus on governance. In: International Conference on Innovations for Community Services. Springer, Cham (2025)
8. Dehghani, Z.: Data mesh: delivering data-driven value at scale. O'Reilly Media (2022)
9. Kuikkaniemi K., Guggenberger T.: Data products in mesh and space. DSSC. https://dssc.eu/space/News/blog/108199969/Data+Products+in+Mesh+and+Space. Accessed 21/01/2026
10. Karkošková, S.: Data mesh: guiding principles and patterns, and data catalog architectural concept. In: 2024 10th International Conference on Control, Decision and Information Technologies (CoDIT). IEEE (2024)
11. Wasser, J., Kumara, I., Monsieur, G., Van Den Heuvel, W. J., Tamburri, D.A.: Data contracts in data mesh: a systematic gray literature review. In: International Symposium on Business Modeling and Software Design. Springer Cham (2025)

12. Morejón, A., Berenguer, A., Espona, L. D., Tomás, D., Mazón, J.N.: Exploring content-based catalogs for enhanced discovery services in data spaces (2025)
13. Gudepu, B.K., Jaladi, D.S., Gellago, O.: How data catalogs are transforming enterprise data governance: a systematic literature review. Metascience 1(1), 249–264 (2023)
14. Dolhopolov, A., Castelltort, A., Laurent, A.: Implementing federated governance in data mesh architecture. Future Internet 16(4), 115 (2024)
15. Wider, A., Verma, S., Akhtar, A.: Decentralized data governance as part of a data mesh platform: concepts and approaches. In: 2023 IEEE International Conference on Web Services (ICWS). IEEE (2023)
16. Hutterer, A., Krumay, B.: Scopes of Governance in Data Spaces. In: Australasian Conference on Information Systems 2024, Canberra (2024)
17. Guasch, C., Lodi, G., Van Dooren, S.: Semantic knowledge graphs for distributed data spaces: the public procurement pilot experience. In: International Semantic Web Conference. Springer International Publishing, Cham (2022)
18. Kropshofer, J., et al.: A Survey on the Functionalities of Data Catalog Tools. IEEE Access (2025)

Author Index

FSC
www.fsc.org
MIX
Papier aus verantwortungsvollen Quellen
Paper from responsible sources
FSC® C105338